IMAGES
OF SHAKESPEARE

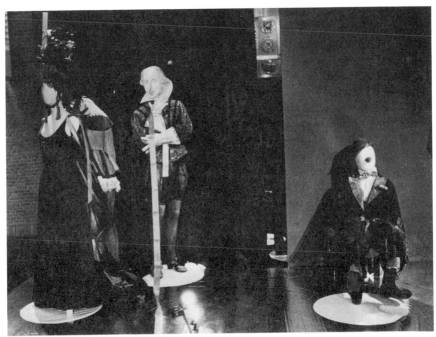

Royal Shakespeare Company exhibition, designed by Brian Glover, held at the Technical University during the 1986 Congress. *(Photo courtesy of Ingeborg Lommatzsch.)*

Images
of Shakespeare

Proceedings of the Third Congress
of the International Shakespeare Association, 1986

Edited by
Werner Habicht
D. J. Palmer   Roger Pringle

DELAWARE
Newark
University of Delaware Press
London and Toronto: Associated University Presses

Associated University Presses
440 Forsgate Drive
Cranbury, NJ 08512

Associated University Presses
25 Sicilian Avenue
London WC1A 2QH, England

Associated University Presses
P.O. Box 488, Port Credit
Mississauga, Ontario
Canada L5G 4M2

The paper used in this publication meets the requirements
of the American National Standard for Permanence of Paper
for Printed Library Materials Z39.48-1984.

Library of Congress Cataloging-in-Publication Data

International Shakespeare Association. Congress
    (3rd : 1986 : Berlin, Germany)
    Images of Shakespeare.

    Includes bibliographies.
    1. Shakespeare, William, 1564–1616—Criticism
and interpretation—Congresses. I. Habicht, Werner.
II. Palmer, D. J. (David John), 1935– .
III. Pringle, Roger, 1944– . IV. Title.
PR2889.I57 1988   822.3′3   87-30223
ISBN 0-87413-329-7 (alk. paper)

Printed in the United States of America

Contents

Introduction

In April 1986, in the islanded, divided, and walled city of Berlin there was reason to remember the words of Günter Eich:

> Denke daran, dass nach des grossen Zerstörungen
> Jedermann beweisen wird, dass er unschuldig war.

> (Think of this, that after the great cataclysms
> Everyone will prove himself innocent.)

And to recall that it is a very young and naive Lord in *All's Well* who says to the Duke of Florence:

> Holy seems the quarrel
> Upon your Grace's part; black and fearful
> On the opposer.

Shakespeareans, one hopes, go about on tiptoe to hold cataclysms at arm's length and to cultivate a critical spirit incompatible with the virulent self-righteousness that so often threatens to destroy what remains of our civilization. It is good to report that the several hundred scholars and enthusiasts who formed and re-formed themselves into groups large and small in the halls and corridors of the Technical University composed themselves into an auspicious international community, and I have no doubt that Nathaniel would have found their reasons witty without affectation, learned without opinion, and strange without heresy.

Only a selection of papers could be included in this volume, and not all are directly related to the premeditated theme. It is apt, however, that the great looking glass used in the Royal Shakespeare Company's versions of *Measure for Measure* and *As You Like It*, and displayed in the University, should be taken by the editors as an emblem of the Congress topic—the images of Shakespeare. For in that glass we see the world as it is and as it might be, we see Shakespeare and we see ourselves. Yet even without the topic and topos we might discover since the last Congress a continuing and advancing recognition of the evanescent and occasional nature of theatrical art, and of the dependence of our understanding upon the perspectives afforded by our cultural conditions. Where Dover Wilson and W. W. Greg hoped with magnifying glass and induction to solve the problems and establish a text, we are now alert to the inescapable energies and confusions of the playhouse behind the printed page. Where Hardin Craig and Jasper Sisson hoped to put themselves into a position from which they could describe a definitive performance, we now know that every play is rich in a variety of performance potentials and that our texts often fossilize inconsistent performances from the past. In the histories of Shakespearean theater, criticism, and biography, we know not only that there are changes from generation to generation, but also that our understanding of those changes is itself inconstant, depending on our responses to the signs and significance of the past. There are rewards in the new approaches and in the redirected old ones. But there are hazards too. It would be a profound mistake to lose touch with those harmonies and symmetries of art and ideology that were specifically cultivated in the Renaissance, and we would mutilate our responses if we were to treat Shakespeare's plays as mere epiphenomenal manifestations of economic structures to which we attribute historical ascendancy. Some may think that we are less in need of refined theories and new methodologies than of a fresh current of perceptions, but it is hoped that readers of this volume will find it goes some way to meet all three needs.

The Congress was a festive as well as an academic occasion, and the city proved generous in its hospitalities, from an opening ceremony with the music and songs of Coperario, Morley, and Lawes in the great Hall, to a reception from the Senate of Berlin in the newly reconstructed Reichstag. Beyond the wicked and courteous wall many made their way through crannies and chinks to a performance of A Midsummer Night's Dream at the Deutsches Theater (during which, a Chinese colleague told me, none dared to laugh), or to an austere but moving version of Troilus and Cressida, in which young and innocent lovers seemed trapped at once in a veterans' futile war and in the aging traditions of Brecht's Berliner Ensemble and its delightful theater.

In the West there was no Shakespeare on the regular stage, but, in a most magnanimous response to Congress interest, the Deutsche Oper put on Verdi's Macbeth and Otello, and Nicolai's Merry Wives, a feat unlikely to be matched in Congresses to come. An enterprising range of peripheral events contributed by groups from the Hochschule der Künste, the Technical University English Drama Group, and the Schiller-Theater, went some way toward atoning for the absence of the professional companies.

There were formal and informal tours of the city, with much time profitably wasted drinking coffee either in the Kurfürstendamm or in the art-nouveau cafés still to be found in eastern side-streets. It may be that some participants are still there, for there was a great reluctance to leave on the last day.

The occasion owed its comprehensive success to a great range of sponsors, organizers, and contributors, most of whom are listed in the Congress

Program. For hospitalities we owe our thanks to the Herr Regierende Bürgermeister of Berlin, to the Berlin Senate, to the Technische Universität, and to the Freie Universität. The British Council sponsored the delightful Royal Shakespeare Company's exhibition of properties and costumes organized by Brian Glover, together with an exhibition of English Shakespeare publications, and the presence on two occasions of John Barton, who spoke informally about Shakespeare's poetry, the director, and the actor.

For its academic success the organizing committee is deeply indebted to the Congress convenor, Professor Werner Habicht of the Deutsche Shakespeare–Gesellschaft West, and to the Berlin committee under the chairmanship of Professor Kuno Schuhmann. The Shakespeare Association of America's seminar program was ordered and assimilated into the Congress proceedings by the resourceful and indefatigable Professor Ann Jennalie Cook. Professor Robert Weimann of the Deutsche Shakespeare Gesellschaft did much to ensure the fullest possible movement of playgoers and scholars between the east and the west. Finally, as the Congress Mercury, Roger Pringle, could testify, the convivial demeanor of all participants ensured that a tradition was maintained and that the auguries for the 1991 event must be good.

J. Philip Brockbank
Congress Chairman

Acknowledgments

This volume of proceedings represents the range and variety of lectures and seminar papers given to the third Congress of the International Shakespeare Association held in Berlin in April 1986. We wish we could have included more of the extensive program, but publication space has its limits. We are most grateful to the contributors and to the University of Delaware Press for their help and cooperation. We also warmly appreciate the generosity of the Deutsche Shakespeare–Gesellschaft West in providing a grant toward the costs of publishing this volume.

All quotations from Shakespeare's plays are taken from G. Blakemore Evans, ed., *The Riverside Shakespeare* (Boston: Houghton Mifflin, 1974).

Werner Habicht
D. J. Palmer
Roger Pringle

Contributors

Klaus Bartenschlager, University of Munich
Selma Jeanne Cohen, New York, N.Y.
John Doebler, Arizona State University
Juliet Dusinberre, Girton College, Cambridge University
Jay L. Halio, University of Delaware
Maik Hamburger, Deutsches Theater, Berlin
E. A. J. Honigmann, University of Newcastle-upon-Tyne
Wilhelm Hortmann, University of Duisburg
John Dixon Hunt, University of East Anglia
Russell Jackson, Shakespeare Institute, University of Birmingham
Tetsuo Kishi, Kyoto University
Jill L. Levenson, Trinity College, University of Toronto
Kathleen E. McLuskie, Eliot College, University of Kent
J.-M. Maguin, University Paul Valéry, Montpellier
Barbara Arnett Melchiori, University of Rome "La Sapienza"
Giorgio Melchiori, University of Rome "La Sapienza"
Adrian Noble, Royal Shakespeare Company
Martin Procházka, Czechoslovakian Academy of Sciences, Prague
S. Schoenbaum, University of Maryland, College Park
Ann Pasternak Slater, St. Anne's College, Oxford
Ann Thompson, University of Liverpool
John O. Thompson, University of Liverpool
Steven Urkowitz, City College of New York
S. Viswanathan, University of Hyderabad
Herbert S. Weil, Jr., University of Manitoba
Stanley Wells, Oxford University Press
Peter Wenzel, University of Bochum
Marilyn L. Williamson, Wayne State University
Robert F. Willson, Jr., University of Missouri, Kansas City
David P. Young, Oberlin College

IMAGES
OF SHAKESPEARE

Artists' Images of Shakespeare

by S. SCHOENBAUM

Let Shakespeare's Head begin my offering; not Shakespeare's head itself, with a lower-case initial *h,* but—in this Congress devoted to images of Shakespeare—with a portrait of the poet created almost three centuries ago and recovered only recently; in fact, in the past twenty-five years.[1] That image is called, simply, Shakespeare's Head. The icon to which I refer, like most others of the subject, cannot by any stretch of the imagination be deemed an artistic masterwork. Yet—also like other artists' images of Shakespeare—it commands interest, some of it associational, and therefore may (I reckon) be a fitting starting point.[2]

The likeness, more than vaguely familiar even to those who have not seen it before, or who have never wandered into the National Portrait Gallery in Trafalgar Square, is yet paradoxically novel. Surely this is a version of the Chandos portrait that hangs there. The white collar, with the drawstrings hanging down, is more or less familiar. So too the narrow border, a carefully painted golden rim, in effect a simulated frame, for there is a circling oval, often indistinct in reproductions, in the Chandos painting. The faintest of self-amused smiles, however, playing upon the lips of Shakespeare's Head is a differing touch. And that earring makes us do a double take. Glistening from the left ear at the National Portrait Gallery, it has been transferred to the right, in which direction the sitter now faces: this is the other side of Shakespeare's Head.

The bold dark brushwork of the portrait may impress us as vigorously unfastidious, expressive less of a poet's sensibility than of masculine assertion; but its force registers. Although not now on public display, it has lately become a ubiquitous presence. Shakespeare's Head adorned the cover of the Festival brochure setting forth last season's theater schedule at the other Stratford in Ontario and the souvenir programs for individual productions offered there that summer. Now it peers at us quizzically from dust-jackets of the three substantial volumes comprising *William Shakespeare: His World, His Work, His Influence,* assembled by John F. Andrews and recently published by Charles Scribner's Sons. Neither in the programs nor on the dust-jackets is the source identified.

Painted on an oval mahogany panel, Shakespeare's Head is fully one-and-one-half times life-size (37 by 31½ inches): too big for mantelpiece display or for the walls of most dwellings. It was, however, never meant to be shown indoors. In the ring around the circumference, nail holes are evident at three-inch intervals. The back has the remains of some nails with a surrounding lead residue and also the markings left by two parallel supporting braces, with stout iron hooks still in place. This was originally a signboard. Whose? Such placards were once plentiful all over England, advertising the whereabouts of taverns, inns, shops, and the like. Almost every town in the country boasting a theater had its own Shakespeare Head sign. In Victorian times at least eight Shakespeare Head taverns in London still opened their doors to thirsty passers-by and locals. The present Shakespeare Head surfaced in 1962, and its discoverer, Jacques Villekoop of the London firm of E. P. Goldschmidt (mainly specializing in illustrated books), speculated that this was a signpost for the publisher and bookseller Jacob Tonson (1656–1736) and his nephew of the same name.

It is an appealing and not inherently implausible conjecture. "Gentleman-usher to the Muses" was the Restoration playwright William Wycherley's phrase for Tonson. Another of this stationer's authors, John Dryden, is reported to have less ceremoniously remarked, "Tell the dog that he who wrote this can write more." In print, in *Faction Displayed* (1705), Dryden was no more flattering in his references to one

> With leering look, bull-faced, and freckled fair;
> With two left legs, with Judas-coloured hair,
> And frowsy pores, that taint the ambient air.

Yet in time—and with prosperity—the elder Tonson mellowed. The great, dukes and the like, played host to him, and he in turn reciprocated with gifts of cider. Even Dryden warmed to him. Tonson became secretary of the Kit-Cat Club when it was founded and died a wealthy octogenarian.

In 1709 he published Nicholas Rowe's *Works of Mr. William Shakespear* in six volumes, thus making the national poet available in modernized spelling to a new generation of readers, with all the plays divided into acts and scenes; this coming after the Apostolic Succession of seventeenth-century Folio editions. Of Tonson, Rowe in 1714 wrote admiringly:

> Thou, Jacob Tonson, were, to my conceiving,
> The cheerfullest, best, honest fellow living.

His edition boasted not one but two engraved renderings of the Chandos portrait. The same figures reappeared in successive editions of Rowe's *Shakespear* published by Tonson, and also in the latter's 1733 *Shakespeare* prepared by Lewis Theobald. Thus, Tonson used Chandos constantly; Shakespeare's Head had become a sort of house trademark for his shop

Figure 1. Shakespeare's Head signboard. *(Courtesy of the Folger Shakespeare Library, Washington, D.C.)*

opposite Catherine Street in the Strand. The placard, buffeted by the London wind, was gazed upon by the wits and witlings who stepped by. The wits included the most notable worthies of Restoration and eighteenth-century letters: Otway, Congreve, Addison, and Steele, Gay, Swift, and Pope—all knew the sign of Shakespeare's Head, as did many others, the foremost being Samuel Johnson, engaged upon his own great edition of Shakespeare.

This came at a time when signs, engagingly decorative in the old views of London, were increasingly regarded by many inhabitants as nuisances. When storms shook them they were noisy, sometimes dangerous—in 1716 a sign fell in Bridewell Lane, killing four pedestrians. As the eighteenth century wore on, signboards were more and more restricted. Some neighborhoods ordered them off the streets, and in 1770 they were banished altogether by law, except outside inns. When marketed, they went for a song; signboard artists applied their talents to coaches.

If as a work of art judged by the highest standards Shakespeare's Head leaves much to be desired, what can we expect of a mere signboard? Not much, until we recall the astonishing artifact depicting the interior of the shop, on the Pont Notre-Dame in Paris, owned by Edme-François Gersaint (1694–1750), a dealer in paintings and bric-a-brac, and the intimate of Antoine Watteau. Dying of consumption, Watteau late in 1720 painted it in eight mornings for his friend; the next summer he died in Gersaint's arms. Known simply as *The Shopsign* (*L'Enseigne,* or *L'Enseigne de Gersaint),* the painting originally was exhibited under the shop's canopy. Eventually it would find a place in the collection of Frederick the Great. Some time ago—just when we do not know—the painting was cut vertically in two; in the nineteenth century the two parts were separately framed. Today you can see *The Shopsign* in the Schloss Charlottenburg, in the Salon of the Empress, in Berlin.

It is Watteau's last oil, a wonderfully poignant farewell to his art and life. In *L'Enseigne,* paintings and mirrors cover the room. Three gallants are looking at a mirror that a salesgirl holds out to them: they are more interested in themselves than in the objets d'art. Packing is going on for clearance. A workman in shirtsleeves is putting a portrait in a case; another employee is unhooking a mirror; a porter contemplates the scene; while a dog (taken from Rubens's *Crowning of Marie de Medici* and *Charms of Life,* the latter now in the Wallace Collection) searches for fleas. Yet the poignance is only implied: the painting itself celebrates the art. Personally I prefer it to either of Watteau's embarkations for Cythera, enchanting as these are. The anonymous journeyman who painted Shakespeare's Head at around the same time that the Frenchman was putting the finishing touches to his final masterpiece was no Watteau. But then, who was?

Purchased by the Hydes for their magnificent collection at Four Oaks Farm in New Jersey, Shakespeare's Head was donated by Mrs. Hyde, the

Figure 2. *The Shopsign* by **Antoine Watteau.** *(Courtesy of Schloss Charlottenburg, Berlin.)*

present Viscountess Eccles, to the Folger Shakespeare Library in 1975. For a time, beginning on the Birthday in 1976, it hung in the Great Hall of the Folger until the library was shut down for renovation two years later. Now, covered with a protective plastic sheet, it languishes, hidden from view except for the curious inquirer, in a sub-basement of that great repository. Yet Shakespeare's Head, in one or other of its manifestations, is known to many who remain unacquainted with its history. The classified ad pages of the current London telephone directory reveal that Shakespeare-head public houses are not entirely of the past: I find entries for three Shakespeare's Head houses. An establishment called not Shakespeare's Head but the Shakespeare (in Notting Hill Gate?) is described by John Self, the protagonist of Martin Amis's novel *Money: A Suicide Note* (1984): "Above the entrance to the saloon bar is a picture of Shakespeare that I remember from schooldays, when I frowned over *Timon of Athens* and *The Merchant of Venice*. Haven't they got a better one? Did he really look like that all the time? You'd have thought that by now his publicity people would have come up with something a little more attractive. The beaked and bum-fluffed upper lip, the oafish swelling of the jawline, and the granny's rockpool eyes. And that rug? Isn't it a killer?" (Penguin ed., p. 145). Clearly the saloon bar picture is not a derivative of the Hyde portrait.

And what of the painting to which that anonymous signpainter offered homage by making his copy? Like Shakespearean biography, which has occupied me happily for so many years, the Chandos portrait has had a strange eventful history and has become itself the stuff of legend. This picture has the merit, as we shall see, of laying legitimate claim to having been executed in the subject's lifetime. In the eighteenth century the compulsive antiquary William Oldys ("he was so particular in his habits," according to one memorialist, "that he could not smoke his pipe with ease till his chair was fixed close to a particular crack in the floor"), this Oldys gathered materials for a comprehensive life of Shakespeare. "His notes were written on slips of paper," it was recalled, "which he afterwards classified and reposited in small bags suspended about his room." This method did not ensure efficiency; no biography was forthcoming. Fortunately, however, Oldys also annotated his copy of Gerard Langbaine's *Account of the English Dramatick Poets* (1691), now in the British Library (c.28.g.1.). "They say," Oldys writes of the portrait, that "old Cornelius Jansen" was the artist, then adds: "Others say, that it was done by Richard Burbage, the player." It has sometimes been averred that Cornelius Janssen van Keulan had not set foot in England until 1618, in which case he could not, of course, have painted Shakespeare from life. But Janssen was in fact born in London, of Netherlandish parents, in 1593, as the baptismal register of the Dutch Church at Austin Friars records. If Janssen's work lacks weight and solidity, it is not deficient in sensitivity, and he excels in painting elaborate lace collars. His first dated portrait goes back to 1617. The next year Milton, then a child of ten, sat for the Janssen portrait that now hangs at the Morgan. Amateur art historian that I am, the Chandos portrait does not look to me like a Janssen; nor does the purported Janssen portrait of Shakespeare at Folger much look like the poet. Burbage was indeed a talented amateur of the brush, but if the painting that now hangs at Dulwich College is, as generally supposed, a self-portrait, he was hardly equipped for something of the order of the Chandos.

A more reliable source of documentary testimony about the portrait is to be found in George Vertue's notebook, also in the British Library. A talented artist, Vertue (1684–1756) is perhaps best known to Shake-speareans for his sketches of the frontage and plan of New Place. He was also an enthusiast of the Chandos portrait, which is the inspiration for his recently recovered profile miniature, in private hands, that appears on the cover of my *Compact Documentary Life*. Vertue, who came on the scene before Oldys, had sought out the then-owner of the portrait, Robert Keck, a barrister who later the same year died in his early thirties while touring the Continent. The sad event occasioned an anonymous "Poem on the Death of Robert Keck, Esq.; Of the Inner-Temple, Who died at Paris, Sept. 16, 1719, by a Friend who accompany'd to Dover in his Way to France; and return'd thither to meet his Corpse, when brought over to be Buried in the Temple-Church in London" (1720). The memorialist alludes to Keck's prized possession, mentioning (in a footnote) that the barrister had a print

Figure 3. The Chandos portrait of William Shakespeare. *(Courtesy of The National Portrait Gallery, London.)*

taken from the "painted original" at his own expense, and that he had purchased the painting "with a great deal of Money and preserved with no less Care." From him Vertue learned that Thomas Betterton, the most notable actor of the Restoration stage, had several times told Keck

> that the picture of Shakespear he had, was painted by John Taylor a Player, who acted for Shakespear and this John Taylor in his will left it to Sir William Davenant and at the death of Sir William Davenant Mr. Betterton bought it, and at his death Mr. Keck bought it, in whose possession it now is. . . .[3]

The painting, then, had (according to Betterton) been painted by someone named John Taylor, as reported by Davenant before his death in 1668. No John Taylor is known to have acted with Shakespeare's company, although the King's Men did have a Joseph Taylor who became a member after Burbage's death in 1619. This Taylor however died intestate, and so could not have bequeathed the portrait to Davenant.

He has, however, succeeded in throwing scholars off the track, for a John Taylor *was* a leading member of the worshipful Company of Painter-Stainers. For the year 1631–32 this Taylor served as renter, or lower warden, of the company and was represented in the customary group portrait—a genre of which the most celebrated exemplar is Rembrandt's painting of the Syndics of the Draper's Guild—which has survived and hangs to this day in the Company's Court Room in Little Trinity Lane in London. Our acquaintance Janssen is reputedly the artist. The Renter Warden is seated to the left at the table bearing an inkstand and book; he holds in his hand "a little holy picture" (is it of St. Luke, the patron saint of painters, or—more likely—of St. Catherine of Alexandria?). Taylor cuts a handsome middle-aged figure with his pointed beard and encircling ruff. For 1635–36 he was upper warden, and for 1643–44 occupied the exalted post of master warden. In 1639–40 he paid the substantial fine of £7 rather than serve once again as upper warden. During the course of a long career Taylor presented at least five apprentices of the company for their freedom. His arms were among those embellishing the windows of Painter-Stainers Hall before the Great Fire of 1666 forever destroyed old London.

In my *Shakespeare's Lives,* published some fifteen years ago, I noted that an artist named John Taylor flourished in the seventeenth century and that Edmund Malone had mentioned seeing one of his portraits, dated 1655, at Oxford. If he was the Chandos artist, he would have had a remarkably long career. But Malone is wrong about the date: our John Taylor died in June 1651 and was laid to rest at the parish church of Saint Bride in Fleet Street. In my chapter on Shakespeare portraits for *William Shakespeare: Records and Images* (1982), I unaccountably overlooked mentioning John Taylor the artist. Now, in an excellent article demonstrating—if any demonstration were needed—that this vein for research has not been exhausted, Mary

Edmond has redirected attention to him and at the same time enhanced understanding of Taylor's career.[4] It remains now for other instances of his handiwork to be tracked down.

Betterton died indigent and without a will, and according to an oft-repeated report the Chandos portrait came into the possession of Mrs. Barry, arguably the first truly great actress of the English stage; one whose Desdemona rivaled that of Mrs. Siddons. "In the Art of exciting pity," Colley Cibber—himself no mean thespian—said of her in his *Apology*, "she had a Power beyond all the Actresses I have yet seen, or what your Imagination can conceive." Mrs. Barry, it was said, sold the picture to Keck for forty guineas. She excited more than pity; that most mischievous of eighteenth-century Shakespeare commentators, George Steevens, cognisant of Mrs. Barry's propensities, conjectured without gallantry that "somewhat more animated than canvas might have been included, though not specified, in a bargain with an actress of acknowledged gallantry." But the legend that Mrs. Barry owned the Chandos portrait between the death of Betterton in 1710 and her own demise three years later is no more than that, as Miss Edmond has demonstrated. For Keck clearly indicated to Vertue that he had purchased the portrait at Betterton's death. Unsurprisingly, in her own will Mrs. Barry mentions no pictures.

The portrait then passed into the hands of a Mr. Nicholls of Minchenden House, Southgate, who had married the Keck heiress. When his only daughter became the bride of the Marquis of Caernarvon, afterwards duke of Chandos—Handel's patron and the friend of Pope—the picture became the property of that noble family. For this reason it is called the Chandos portrait. In time it devolved to the duke of Buckingham, who had wed Lady Anne Elizabeth Brydges, Chandos's daughter. At a sale of Buckingham's pictures in 1848, the portrait was purchased by the earl of Ellesmere, by whose name it is also sometimes known. In March 1856 he presented it to the National Portrait Gallery as its first acquisition, and thus founded the collection; the Chandos was to have the first place in the Gallery's registers. Today it is displayed above a caption describing the painting as "the only picture which has any real claim to be a portrait of Shakespeare from life."

The mystique of the Chandos portait has long since been established. Distinguished original artists—Sir Godfrey Kneller, Sir Joshua Reynolds, the sculptor Louis François Roubiliac—as well as lesser portraitists and engravers, bestirred themselves to make copies. Some made copies of copies. Unconcerned about strict fidelity to the original, they reversed the head, altered the expression, and changed the costume. Kneller, Lubeck expatriate and court painter to a succession of English monarchs, made the first recorded copy, which he presented to the age's leading poet, John Dryden. It hung in the latter's study, a source of inspiration, not least for his own verse offering to Kneller in the *Fourteenth Epistle* of 1694:

Shakespear thy Gift, I place before my sight;
With awe, I ask his Blessing e're I write;
With Reverence look on his Majestick Face;
Proud to be less; but of his Godlike Race.
His soul inspires me, while thy Praise I write.

The copy that inspired Dryden passed into the collection of the Earl Fitzwilliam at Wentworth Castle and is owned by the present earl.

A handsome large eighteenth-century copy of the Kneller graces the Folger Library. In 1779 Edward Capell presented *his* treasured version of the Kneller copy to his beloved Trinity College. Of the far-flung tribe of Chandos—the inheritors of fulfilled renown—a favorite icon of my own, probably of early to mid-nineteenth-century origin, testifies to the transmutation wrought by Romanticism. Only fairly recently come to light, it is a gold cravat pin with a tiny miniature watercolor of Shakespeare, a mere two centimeters long, and painted on ivory. A few details, most notably the collar, betray its lineage. The copious expanse of forehead is familiar enough from other representations, but the wonderfully soulful eyes constitute a new touch. This Shakespeare—younger than the Chandos—might indeed have been a poet and playwright of genius. The privately owned portrait was reproduced for the first time in my *William Shakespeare: Records and Images* and only very recently appeared in color (also a first) on the dust jacket of Stanley Wells's plain-text edition of the Sonnets for the Oxford Shakespeare.

Persuaded that the Chandos portrait represented an authentic likeness of Shakespeare, Malone secured permission for a copy to be made at Chandos House in August 1783 by his acquaintance Ozias Humphry, a leading portrait artist of the day, especially noted for his miniatures and his work in crayon. In a letter to Humphry (17 August), Malone expressed his gratitude, at the same time mildly regretting that too much white showed in one of the eyes, making the subject appear to squint. Such qualms were passing; Malone treasured Humphry's crayon and noted on the back, "The original having been painted by a very ordinary hand, having been at some subsequent period painted over, and being now in a state of decay, this copy, which is a very faithful one, is, in my opinion, invaluable." The Humphry copy, a crayon, is now part of the Folger collection (Art Inv. 323).

Time has indeed not been kind to the Chandos. The painting has been rubbed and restored. Overpainting—as modern infrared photography reveals—has compromised, if only slightly, the perpendicularity of the original imposing expanse of forehead. But the portrait, if now in far from mint condition, remains on public view, and we have the Humphry crayon to convey an impression of how it looked two centuries ago. The swarthy physiognomy, no less than the "wanton lips," has stirred xenophobic anxieties. Some have discerned an Italianate look. "It is hard to believe," writes M. H. Spielmann, who devoted much of a long lifetime to the study of

Figure 4. Crayon copy of the Chandos portrait by Ozias Humphry. *(Courtesy of the Folger Shakespeare Library, Washington, D.C.)*

Shakespeare portraiture, "that this dark face, of distinctly Italian type, represents one of the pure English Shakespeare stock of the Midlands." Maybe the painting represents Shakespeare made up to play Shylock. Of course we do not know whether Shakespeare the actor ever performed as Shylock. But that gold earring, a mere detail of portraiture, most arrests notice; more than the grayish eyes or brown moustache, pointed beard or wanton lips. In the first or second decade of the seventeenth century, from which the portrait dates, such an earring was by no means an extraordinary accessory to masculine attire. Long since out of style, the earring is once again part of the sartorial landscape. Witness the media sensation made by Gary Taylor last November with a manuscript poem ascribed to Shakespeare: *Time* magazine included in its coverage a photograph of Mr. Taylor wearing his earring alongside the Chandos sitter with *his* earring.

Never mind now whether the manuscript poem is indeed by Shakespeare. Is the Chandos a portrait of Shakespeare? After all, the first written notice of a Shakespeare connection (in the Vertue notebook) occurs more than a century after the sitter—whoever he was—sat for the artist, whoever *he* was. Report traces the pedigree back to the time of Davenant, who quite likely was not yet born when the portrait was executed. A poet and dramatist of ability if not of genius, Davenant fancied himself as belonging to the tribe of Will, claiming that he was Shakespeare's godson or, when in his cups (which was frequent), the poet's natural son. In his "Brief Life" of Davenant, Aubrey takes note of the claim: "Now, Sir William would when he was pleasant over a glass of wine with his most intimate friends, e.g. Samuel Butler &c. say, that it seemed to him that he writ with the very spirit that Shakespeare, and seemed contented enough to be thought his son: he would tell them the story . . . in which way his mother had a very light report, whereby she was called a whore." However that may be, Davenant, who became a self-appointed custodian of the Shakespeare mythos, is clearly not an impeccable spokesman when it comes to establishing a lineage for the portrait. The actual particulars of the Chandos face are not inconsistent with those of the two authentic likenesses, to which I shall next be turning; no small point. The case for Chandos is a possible one, maybe even likely, but a case which, as things now stand, must in the last resort be reckoned as not proven.

Now for the two authenticated likenesses. The engraving signed by Martin Droeshout, which appears on the title page (not, as sometimes stated by those who should know better, the frontispiece) of the First Folio published seven years after the dramatist's death, may not implausibly be reckoned the most hackneyed icon in the English literary tradition. Droeshout belonged to the third generation of an Anglo-Netherlandish dynasty of artist-craftsmen that worshipped with the Janssens and other members of their small community of Protestant refugees in the Dutch Reformed Church at Austin Friars. Born in 1601, Martin was only fifteen when

Figure 5. Engraving of William Shakespeare by Martin Droeshout. *(Courtesy of the Folger Shakespeare Library, Washington, D.C.)*

Shakespeare died in Stratford retirement, so it is unlikely that the engraver ever knew personally the poet here depicted as a youngish man, although his costume, that of a well-to-do gentleman, belongs to 1610 or thereabouts, when he was—for the time—well advanced in years. Very likely the engraver transferred an image from some already existing painting or limning: that is, a portrait consisting of an outline drawing with perhaps delicate flat washes of color.

Evidently the likeness was found acceptable to the compilers of the Folio edition, John Heminges and Henry Condell, who knew Shakespeare well as a friend and colleague from the King's Men days, and who dedicated their expensive volume to those noble brethren, the earls of Pembroke and Montgomery, who also knew Shakespeare well, for, as the dedicatory epistle avouches, they had shown the author much favor when he lived. Besides, the Folio's first preliminary leaf boasts a short commendatory poem by Ben Jonson. "This figure, that thou here seest put," Ben writes,

> It was for gentle Shakespeare cut;
> Wherein the graver had a strife
> With Nature, to outdo the life.

The undifferentiated encomium does not make it clear, however, that Jonson had actually beheld the likeness he chose to commend, for such brief bread-and-butter verses were (as Spielmann notes) "manufactured to order, often without the plate being seen by the versifier." Still, like Everest, it is there, an ungainly head too big for the torso, a mouth wandering to the right, locks which fail to balance on the two sides; sans neck, and with two right shoulders. (Or is it left?) Clearly the young Droeshout was no master, and would never become one, although in time he would do better with General Fairfax and Dr. Donne as his subjects.

Yet the engraving has not wanted admirers. "To me," James Boaden, the first student of the Shakespeare portraits, confessed in 1824, "this portrait exhibits an aspect of calm benevolence and tender thought; great comprehension, and a kind of mixt feeling, as when melancholy yields to the suggestions of fancy." And in our own time Dr. Rowse—poet, historian, and contemnor of second-raters—has had his raptures over Droeshout: "What a powerful impression it gives: that searching look of the eyes understanding everything, what a forehead, what a brain!" Of course, in an age that knew no CAT-scans, the engraver cannot really be faulted for failing to depict the poet's brain.

Whatever the merits (or lack of same) of the Droeshout engraving, it presents problems by reason of the fact that its destiny has become intertwined with that of another image of Shakespeare, the Flower portrait, which hangs in the Royal Shakespeare Theatre Gallery at Stratford. Measuring only 23⅓ by 17¼ inches and painted in oil on an ancient worm-eaten panel of English oak, the Flower uncannily resembles the Droeshout

Figure 6. The Flower portrait of William Shakespeare. *(Courtesy of The Royal Shakespeare Theatre, Stratford-upon-Avon.)*

engraving. The artist's inscription, "Willm̄ Shakespeare 1609," in the upper left-hand corner, is now all but invisible in reproductions. Is this image the original of the Folio portrait, perhaps the work of young Martin's uncle, also named Martin, and old enough to be married in 1603? Maybe a family connection led to that important commission being given to the young and inexperienced engraver. But that of course is the merest speculation. Or is the Flower portrait, far from being Droeshout's model or a version of a lost original from which both it and the engraving derive, a fake (to put it bluntly) concocted to capitalize on the notoriety that would attach to a portrait from life of the national poet? A question to be asked.

The cursive script of the inscription has stirred dark suspicions, since 1609 is considered too early for cursive writing in England. But similarly idiosyncratic inscriptions (for the hand is not exclusively cursive but mixed) have been found on British paintings going back to the 1560s. A more telling cause for misgiving is the reported presence of bitumen—a brown or black mixture of tarlike hydrocarbons derived from petroleum—creating the corrugation in some dark areas of the portrait, especially the hair: bitumen was not used in painting until the late eighteenth century. Then, too, the portrait's pedigree is disappointingly meager, traceable as it is only to around 1840, when a connoisseur from Peckham Rye, H. C. Clements, purchased it from "an obscure dealer" (these dealers are always obscure). Like many another such relic, it was alleged "to have originally belonged to a descendant of Shakespeare's family." On the back of the box housing his acquisition, Clements pasted a note averring that "the picture was publicly exhibited in London nearly seventy years ago, and many thousands went to see it"; but none of these curiosity seekers left any known record of the occasion. In 1892 Edgar Flower of the prominent Stratford brewing family bought the painting from Clements's executor, and three years later Mrs. Flower donated it to the Memorial Gallery, which the family had established and generously endowed. That gallery in turn became the present Royal Shakespeare Theatre Gallery.

In his recent *The Image of the Poet,* David Piper points out, as evidence that the painting derives from the engraving, that it is not reversed, as is customary when the print has precedence. But such image-reversal does not invariably obtain. Mr. Piper believes that the painting, whatever its date, was intended to deceive, but the Flower portrait has lately found eloquent new champions in Paul Bertram and Frank Cossa, whose substantial essay on the subject has just been published in *Shakespeare Quarterly.*[5] I must confess to having been chided for making this image the frontispiece to my *Documentary Life,* and, some years later, even for expressing regret (in a preface) that I was unable to check a proof copy of the reproduction against the original prior to the publication of my *Records and Images,* the gallery then being closed for renovation. Why bother? After all, I had done my checking the first time around. But would that I had been able to view the painting a second time, for its appearance has undergone radical transformation. Scientific X-ray examination conducted at the Courtauld Institute in London had previously revealed, beneath the surface, another—considerably earlier—Netherlandish or central Italian painting showing the Madonna and Child, the latter reaching for a cross held by Saint John. Now, restoration conducted for the Stratford gallery under the auspices of the Ashmolean Museum has given the familiar icon a surreal dual identity: a half-length portrait of Shakespeare hob-nobs with a slightly more than half-length religious grouping. Thus, the artifacts that engage the biographer have their own biographies. The Flower portrait, I now believe, probably *is* a phony: that bitumen. I have no quarrel, though, with Professors Bertram and Cossa's characterization of it as "this still mystery-ridden painting." We still have our work cut out for us.

For convenience I would include the sculptor among the artists of my title, and, Droeshout excepted, the only other unquestionable image of Shakespeare is the bust or, to be more precise, half-length sculpture—in Holy Trinity Church at Stratford—fashioned by Gheerart Janssen the younger, a member of the clan of Anglo-Dutch tomb-makers with premises situated not far from the Globe playhouse on Bankside. Their most elaborate monument was the freestanding Southampton tomb at Titchfield, including a recumbent effigy of the second earl, the father of Shakespeare's patron. Another instance of their handiwork—and possibly the inspiration for the Shakespeare commission—was the effigy, recumbent also, of John Combe, old ten-in-the-hundred, in Stratford Church, close by to the Shakespeare memorial. This funerary sculpture was already in place when the dramatist died. Certainly the Shakespeare monument existed when the First Folio issued from the press, for Leonard Digges, whose mother had married Shakespeare's friend Thomas Russell, alludes to it in his verses addressed "To the Memory of the deceased Author Master W. Shakespeare" in the volume's preliminaries. "When that stone is rent," Digges proclaims in a familiar topos,

> And time dissolves thy Stratford monument,
> Here we alive shall view thee still. This book,
> When brass and marble fade, shall make thee look
> Fresh to all ages. . . .

Gheerart's likeness presumably satisfied the surviving members of the dramatist's family, who presumably footed the not-inconsiderable bill for the monument: the widow, the two daughters, and the sons-in-law. Most likely Dr. John Hall, the eminent Stratford physician who married Susanna, commissioned it. Combe, the wealthiest townsman, had made a testamentary bequest of £60 for *his* tomb.

There he stands in a sleeveless gown over a tunic. With bobbed locks, upturned moustaches, and Van Dyke beard, the sprucely barbered poet-

Figure 7. The Flower portrait of William Shakespeare after restoration. *(Courtesy of The Royal Shakespeare Theatre, Stratford-upon-Avon.)*

orator, plump of cheek and more advanced in years than the Shakespeare of the Droeshout engraving, holds a quill pen in one hand and rests the other on a quire of paper as he recites the verses he is in the act of composing. It is a stereotypical pose: witness the figure of the Elizabethan chronicler and antiquary John Stow bespoke by his widow for Saint Andrew Undershaft Church in the city, and chiseled by Nicholas Janssen, who belonged to the same numerous tribe of stonemasons. In its original state a painted object, like many of its class, the Shakespeare bust has undergone vicissitudes, and more than once been reedified. In the eighteenth century the great Malone performed (as he thought) a public service by having it whitewashed to conform with his neoclassical canons of taste, and for his pains earned a few years later an irate epigram in the Stratford *Visitors' Book:*

> Stranger to whom this monument is shown,
> Invoke the poet's curse upon Malone;
> Whose meddling zeal his barbarous taste betrays,
> And daubs his tombstone, as he mars his plays.

Then, a young gentleman, "just emerged from Oxford," extricated Shakespeare's stone pen from his fingers, and let it fall, shattering into bits, on the church pavement; these days Shakespeare holds a replaceable (is it plastic?) quill. His complexion has inevitably darkened. So too the eyes; but his hair remains auburn. In October 1973 nocturnal vandals removed the bust from its niche by chipping out part of the plinth. When I visited Holy Trinity shortly afterward to examine the sculpture, it presented a forlorn aspect away from its natural habitat, but had suffered only minimal damage.

How does this image, which in its anatomical specifics is at least compatible with those of the only other authenticated likeness, impress us? Reactions vary. To Washington Irving, visiting Holy Trinity in 1815, "the aspect is cheerful and serene," with clear indications of the sociable disposition with which Shakespeare's contemporaries credited him. But C. M. Ingleby, who had won celebrity for his remorseless indictment of J. Payne Collier for forgery in *A Complete View of the Shakespeare Controversy* (1861), found the ensemble of the face awkward. "What a painful stare, with its goggle eyes and gaping mouth!" This image was to Ingleby suggestive of "a man crunching a sour apple." For Dover Wilson this was the archetypal "self-satisfied pork butcher." Wilson preferred the young man with "large expressive eyes" of the Grafton portrait, which in 1932 he proceeded to use as the frontispiece to *The Essential Shakespeare.* But the only thing going for this image is that the sitter was twenty-four in the Armada year, when (according to the inscription) the oil was painted on its oak panel. The bust in the monument in Stratford Church indeed testifies less to poetic sensibility than to the worldly success of a local boy who through the endeavors

Figure 8. Half-length sculpture of William Shakespeare by Gheerart Janssen.
(Courtesy of the Folger Shakespeare Library, Washington, D.C.)

of his art won (as the cliché holds) fame and fortune and went on to buy the second biggest house in Stratford. It presents an image of Shakespeare with which we must reckon, and one which I myself found peculiarly moving—no doubt in large measure because of its manifold associations—when I first gazed upon it in the summer of the quatercentenary year. The occasion inspired me to undertake *Shakespeare's Lives,* and for that reason I chose this image of the great and memorable dead as my frontispiece.

This is not a fit occasion to discuss the naked cherubic infant Shakespeare of two George Romney paintings—*Shakespeare Nursed by Comedy and Tragedy* (the latter reportedly modelled on Lady Hamilton) and *The Infant Shakespeare Attended by Nature and the Passions*—or the Kesselstadt Death Mask, procured in the 1840s from a broker's rag shop in Mainz and revealing that none but Shakespeare looked thus in the repose of death; none (in the words of one observer) "bore so grandly stamped on his high brow and serene features the promise of an immortality not of this earth alone." Such images belong to the Shakespeare-Mythos and furnish matter for another discourse.

Notes

1. The subject of this paper represents for me a journey down already-traveled paths, as I trust will be self-evident from the pages that follow. I have resisted the temptation to strive after variation for its own sake, but I have, where possible, corrected previous pronouncements, and incorporated information not hitherto available to me. One of my principal exhibits this time, Shakespeare's Head, I have not discussed before. In quoting from older sources I have expanded abbreviations and modernized punctuation.

2. See the excellent short article by Mary C. Hyde, "Shakespeare's Head," *Shakespeare Quarterly* 16 (1965): 139–43.

3. *Vertue Note Books,* i (Oxford: Walpole Society, 1930), xviii, 56.

4. "The Chandos Portrait: A Suggested Painter," *The Burlington Magazine* 124 (1982): 146–49.

5. " 'Willm Shakespeare 1604': The Flower Portrait Revisited," *Shakespeare Quarterly* 37 (1986): 83–96.

"There Is a World Elsewhere": William Shakespeare, Businessman

by E. A. J. HONIGMANN

After almost four hundred years, our image of William Shakespeare is that of a preeminent dramatist and poet. How did he see himself? In his final account of himself, "I, William Shakespeare, of Stratford upon Avon in the county of Warwick, gentleman," did not wholly ignore his theatrical career (he left bequests to "my fellows John Hemminges, Richard Burbage and Henry Condell"), but he was preoccupied with other things—"all my barns, stables, orchards, gardens, lands, tenements and hereditaments," "my sword," "all my plate," and complicated financial arrangements. While he saw himself as a "gentleman," a life-long involvement in the competitive worlds of property and finance is also clearly visible in his will.

Important recent discoveries about John Shakespeare help to show that we have probably misjudged the extent of his son's business interests. John, Stratford's bailiff in 1568 (or, as we might say, Stratford's mayor), was a glover and whittawer by profession, yet we now know that he also bought and sold wool on a large scale. (Nicholas Rowe mentioned in the first life of William Shakespeare, 1709, that Shakespeare's father was "a considerable dealer in wool," and for many years this was thought a mistake on his part). In addition, John Shakespeare could have had an interest in the meat trade (according to John Aubrey, William's "father was a butcher"), an obvious sideline for anyone connected, as he was, with farm produce and leather goods. More significantly for our purposes, John Shakespeare was also taken to law for money-lending at an illegally high rate: allegedly he charged 20 percent on loans of £100 and £80, two very large sums, the equivalent of around £100,000 and £80,000 today.[1]

John Shakespeare, like many a man of his time, engaged in any business ventures that came his way, including money-lending. Even if Rowe had not assured us that William joined his father's business for a while, before turning to the theater, we would certainly expect John's eldest son to be familiar with his father's business and, as heir presumptive, to keep in touch with it. There are signs, however, that William, like his father, by no means restricted himself to a single trade or occupation, and that, among other things, he actively engaged in money-lending over a period of years, perhaps as his father's partner. First, there is the only surviving letter addressed to William—which, despite its friendliness, is really a business letter and assumes that the dramatist will procure £30 for Richard Quiney *at a price*. "You shall neither lose credit nor money by me . . . I will hold my time and content your friend, and if we bargain farther you shall be the paymaster yourself." Quiney's father saw this as a transaction in which Shakespeare was not merely a disinterested intermediary. "If you bargain with Mr. Shakespeare," he wrote, "bring your money home if you may." And Abraham Sturley, hearing that "our countryman Mr. William Shakespeare would procure us money," added, "which I shall like of as I shall hear when, and where, and how; and I pray let not go that occasion, if it may sort to any indifferent conditions." Hard conditions were a distinct possibility, and Shakespeare was involved in the bargaining. The Quiney correspondence suggests that William Shakespeare, like his father and many others at this time, took part in money-lending, and was not expected to offer easy terms to his "loving friends."

Here let me note an unusual feature of Shakespeare's will, which shows that "loving friends" in the poet's own family might still require each other to pay interest for moneys not received. When he disposed of his worldly goods, the first item was "Item, I give and bequeath unto my daughter Judith one hundred and fifty pounds of lawful English money, to be paid unto her in manner and form following; that is to say, one hundred pounds in discharge of her marriage portion within one year after my decease, with consideration after the rate of two shillings in the pound for so long time as the same shall be unpaid unto her after my decease." Second, "I give and bequeath unto my said daughter Judith one hundred and fifty pounds more, if she or any issue of her body be living at the end of three years next ensuing the day of the date of this my will, during which time my executors to pay her consideration from my decease according to the rate aforesaid." I have seen other wills in which a failure to pay is penalized in some way, but a charge of 10 percent is not usually spelled out like this, and the 10 percent interest on the blocked £150, to be paid after three years, is even more exceptional. Since John Hall and his wife, Susanna, were named as executors, Shakespeare in effect ordered one daughter to pay interest to the other—again, an unusual procedure, though perhaps not too surprising if the testator happens to have a sideline as a businesslike money-lender.

We know, again, that William Shakespeare went to law on at least two occasions to recover debts. One was for six pounds plus twenty-four shillings damages, the other for twenty bushels of malt and a loan of two shillings. At least one and possibly both of these debts arose from money-lending. Shakespeare's persistence in pursuing bad debts, said Professor Schoenbaum, "may strike moderns as heartless, but the course Shakespeare followed was normal in an age without credit cards, overdrafts, or collecting agencies."[2] I might add that if Shakespeare was in business as a moneylender, like his father, it would be all the more necessary to insist on repayment; if it were thought in Stratford that William was a soft touch, many other debtors might have been tempted to abscond.

Next, consider an intriguing lawsuit of the year 1600, and a third action for debt. John Clayton, a yeoman of Willington, Bedfordshire, was sued by "William Shackspeare" for the sum of £7, which he had borrowed in 1592. There is no ground for supposing that the dramatist "had enough spare cash" to lend this sum at this early date, said E. K. Chambers, and Leslie Hotson discovered a William Shakespeare who lived eight miles from John Clayton in Bedfordshire and thought that this man must therefore have been the money-lender.[3] That remains a possibility. Yet we know that John and William Shakespeare took part in money-lending before and after 1592; and we now know much more than Chambers did about John Shakespeare and can accept that he was indeed a man "of good wealth" in 1596, worth £500, as the heralds noted when granting him his coat of arms—so there are good reasons for not following Chambers and Hotson too hastily. The money was borrowed in Cheapside, London, on 22 May 1592, and Lord Strange's men (widely thought to have been Shakespeare's company at this time) performed on this very day for Henslowe, probably at the Rose, and also acted *Harry the Sixth* on 19 and 25 May. William Shakespeare was not a common name in London in 1592; there is no evidence that the Bedfordshire Shakespeare was in London in May 1592, whereas Stratford's William Shakespeare probably was, and he and his father were involved in money-lending.

The Clayton suit still awaits further investigation. In the meantime one may say that the mere possibility that William Shakespeare, the dramatist, could have followed his father in the money-lending business as early as 1592 gives piquancy to Robert Greene's attack, in September 1592, on an actor who, "with his tiger's heart wrapped in a player's hide . . . is in his own conceit the only Shake-scene in a country." Why did Greene choose that particular line from *Henry VI*? The crucial charge is that Shakespeare has a "tiger's heart"; after this, Greene throws in a cryptic reference to usury and then concludes with the fable of the grasshopper and the ant, converting the traditional hero of the fable into a villain—a "greedy miser" thirsting for "gain," whose "thrift is theft," whose "weal works others woe." What was the point of this rewriting of Aesop? Some years ago I suggested that Greene here resorted to the language of the antiusury tracts; the discovery that John Shakespeare was accused of exacting an illegally high rate of interest confirms me in the belief that Greene wished to hint that the tiger's heart belonged to a usurer.

Having identified John Shakespeare as a glover, wool-dealer, money-lender, property-owner, and possibly butcher, we must ask what happened to all of these business interests when he died in 1601. His eldest son, one of the Lord Chamberlain's men, lived chiefly in London and is thought to have continued there until around 1608, the year of *Coriolanus.* John's widow, Mary Arden, died in 1608, and that suggests the possibility that, like other widows at this time, she took charge of her dead husband's business interests, and that it was her illness or death that forced William Shakespeare to return to Stratford for a while and to stay on to grapple with the complexities of the Stratford estate. Since John Shakespeare still attempted, in 1599, to collect twenty-one pounds that John Walford had owed him for thirty-one years, it is conceivable that William's decision to go to law in Stratford in August 1608 to collect six pounds from John Addenbrooke, referred back to a loan also made long before by John Shakespeare, and/or that Mary Arden (who was buried on 9 September 1608) had been her son's business manager in Stratford since 1601. What is certain is that there were very extensive business interests in Stratford that needed attention in 1608.

At the very same time, as it happens, important business decisions had to be taken in London as well. Also in August 1608, Richard Burbage arranged a new syndicate of "house-keepers" for the Blackfriars Theater—including William Shakespeare, who was only forty-four years old, and pledged himself to pay his share of the rent for twenty-one years. It looks as if Shakespeare intended to tidy his affairs in Stratford and then to resume his career in London. This is confirmed by Thomas Greene's statement, in 1609, that he thought he might be allowed another year as tenant of New Place. At any rate the first of the "last plays," *Pericles,* was not written by a semiretired and languid dramatist who had lost interest in the theater and wished to live out his life in rural seclusion; on the contrary, the signs are that it belonged to a particularly busy period of Shakespeare's career, when he accepted new responsibilities in London but also had to take hold of the reins in Stratford, and was detained there against his will. The purchase of the Blackfriars Gate-House in 1613 has been called "an investment pure and simple," on the assumption that Shakespeare, who described himself as a Stratford man in the conveyance, was now living in retirement at New Place.[4] Yet having no fixed address in London, Shakespeare would inevitably call himself a Stratford man, whether retired or not; and, since this was a period of accelerating theatrical activity for him, when he wrote or partly wrote *Henry VIII, The Two Noble Kinsmen,* and the lost *Cardenio,* I see the purchase of the Gate-House, so conveniently close to the Blackfriars Theater, as another sign that Shakespeare, aged forty-nine, intended to continue his career in the theater.

That career, of course, had been his principal "business" from 1590 or, as some would say, from the 1580s. It gave him three incomes—as "sharer," as "house-keeper," and as dramatist. We may assume that as a sharer and house-keeper he earned a reasonable living. What, though, was the cash value of the plays? For too long there has been a tendency to assume that dramatists were all treated in much the same way, and that they enjoyed little freedom of financial maneuvre. "The dramatist," said Professor G. E. Bentley, "sold his manuscript to the acting company for which it had been prepared; after that it was no more his than the cloak that he might have sold to the actors at the same time."[5] Many dramatists, however, before the days of copyright, felt that they had an equitable right in their own work, and sometimes published their own plays in defiance of the actors, as in the case of *The White Devil.* "In publishing this tragedy," said Webster, "I do but challenge to myself that liberty which other men have ta'en before me." Dekker published some of his plays very soon after receiving payments for them, and Jonson also took the initiative in publishing his own plays. "We know for certain," said Sir Walter Greg, "that a small number of the plays performed by the Admiral's men from 1594 onwards were the personal property of Edward Alleyn and others of Martin Slaughter, for we find these men selling the books in question to the company at a later date." If actors could own and hire out plays, why not William Shakespeare? Let us keep in mind, again, that Henslowe's payments prove that around 1599 the prices paid for plays "begin to fluctuate considerably." Also, that a little later dramatists received their "benefits" on the third day, yet some insisted on the second and at least one demanded the first day.[6] A successful dramatist, I believe, would be able to dictate his own terms, and we have no reason to suppose that Shakespeare would be any less hard-headed in making a good bargain out of his plays than in his other business affairs. We simply do not know what his business arrangements were as a playwright; when so many options were open to him and his business relationship with his "fellows" was so much closer than that of other dramatists "attached" to a single company, we are not entitled to assume that his contract, if he ever had one, resembled Richard Brome's of 1635—or indeed that his business arrangements as a playwright remained the same throughout his working career.

I have suggested, so far, that apart from his threefold involvement in the theater, William Shakespeare must have been a partner or associate of his parents in their many financial enterprises—as in their bill of complaint, *Shakespeare v. Lambert,* 1588, in which they were joined by "William Shakespeare, their son." In addition, William made important purchases on his own. If one lists all of these various activities in chronological order it appears that there were major financial negotiations in almost every year from 1594—and that refers only to those that were concluded successfully. Add the unsuccessful ones (for example, *Shakespeare v. Lambert,* 1597, another attempt to recover Mary Arden's mortgaged inheritance in Wilmcote from her brother-in-law's family); add deeds or decisions that must have been made, but are now lost (for example, Susanna's marriage settlement in 1607); add other opportunities or dangers that had to be carefully considered (whether or not to oppose the Welcombe enclosures), and one wonders how the dramatist found time to go on writing plays. He clearly did not need to write, financially speaking, after the accession of

King James; perhaps his colleagues pestered him to continue—be that as it may, he also chose to continue. The need came from within.

Not so long ago it was customary to describe Shakespeare as the protégé of noble patrons—Southampton, Essex, Hunsdon, Pembroke, Montgomery, Elizabeth, James, and others. Southampton, according to Rowe, once gave Shakespeare a thousand pounds "to enable him to go through with a purchase which he heard he had a mind to."[7] I do not deny the importance of these patrons, but doubt whether Shakespeare was financially dependent on anyone after about 1596, except perhaps his own father. To get William Shakespeare into focus as a social-economic phenomenon we must place him not with the nobility but with his peers in the world of business—with Richard Burbage, sharer, house-keeper, and investor in property; with Thomas Savage, a wealthy goldsmith, friend of actors and investor in property; with Francis Langley, theater-owner, money-lender, investor in property, and codefendant with Shakespeare in a legal action of 1596; with Philip Henslowe and Edward Alleyn; with John Combe, the rich Stratford usurer who left five pounds to Shakespeare in his will; and, above all, his father, John Shakespeare. He wrote three dozen immortal plays, but he was also a close associate of businessmen, and he was also their kind of man.

His success as a businessman was not achieved by a conspicuously "gentle Shakespeare." Robert Greene may have been too angry to qualify as a reliable witness concerning the "tiger's heart," yet the Quiney correspondence proves that those who knew him well expected nothing less than hard bargaining from "Master Shakespeare," and the bequests to Judith in 1616, hedged about to protect her against her husband, prove that in financial affairs Judith's father was not to be trifled with. It would be unwise to conclude that "Shakespeare is Shylock," but we may say that the portrait of Shylock becomes even more fascinating when we learn that John Shakespeare had lent out money at a high rate of interest and that his son was directly and indirectly involved in the same unpopular trade.

In *The Merchant of Venice,* of course, there are two principal merchants—Shylock and Antonio, the one neurotic about his gold, the other loftily indifferent to the niggardly details of money-making. The two merchants of Venice resemble each other in their uncompromising sense of the rightness of their own business methods, if in nothing else; and their creator, it seems, was equally tough when he felt he had to be.

His most important business was the theater, and there were times when he spoke scathingly to his fellow-actors, when he felt he had to. That, I think, is implied in the final lines of Jonson's great elegy:

> Shine forth, thou star of poets, and with rage
> Or influence, chide or cheer the drooping stage.

Had Shakespeare never addressed his colleagues severely, Jonson's final image of him would have been strangely inappropriate. We know that he did. "O, it offends me to the soul to hear a robustious periwig-pated fellow tear a passion to tatters. . . ."

To conclude this "short paper," the man accused in 1592 of having a "tiger's heart" developed skills that made him, among other things, a highly successful businessman—an absolute Johannes factotum. I am sure, but cannot prove, that he would have been an excellent congress chairman—he knew how to deal with clowns who suffer from the pitiful ambition to speak "more than is set down for them." What diversity and efficiency! But perhaps the manipulative skills of a businessman and a dramatist are not really so very different. Shakespeare is not the only dramatist known to us who became that shameful thing, a very rich man.

Notes

1. See E. A. J. Honigmann, *Shakespeare: The "Lost Years"* (Manchester: Manchester University Press, 1985), 118, and *Shakespeare in the Public Records,* ed. David Thomas (London: Her Majesty's Stationery Office, 1985), 1ff.

2. S. Schoenbaum, *William Shakespeare: A Documentary Life* (Oxford: Oxford University Press, 1975), 184.

3. E. K. Chambers, *William Shakespeare: A Study of Facts and Problems,* 2 vols. (Oxford: Oxford University Press, 1930), 1:62; Leslie Hotson, *Shakespeare's Sonnets Dated and Other Essays* (London: Rupert Hart-Davis, 1949), 229ff.

4. Schoenbaum, *A Documentary Life,* 223.

5. G. E. Bentley, *The Profession of Dramatist in Shakespeare's Time 1590–1642* (Princeton: Princeton University Press, 1971), 82.

6. See *Henslowe's Diary,* ed. W. W. Greg. 2 vols. (London: A. H. Bullen, 1904, 1908), 2:119; and E. A. J. Honigmann, *The Stability of Shakespeare's Text* (London: E. Arnold, 1965), 186–7.

7. See Chambers, *William Shakespeare,* 2:266.

Shakespeare and the Paragone:
A Reading of Timon of Athens

by JOHN DIXON HUNT

It is almost fifty years since in the *Journal of the Warburg Institute* Anthony Blunt noted that the opening of *Timon of Athens* signaled Shakespeare's acknowledgment of a Renaissance commonplace, the *paragone* or comparison between the arts.[1] But we have been surprisingly slow to do anything much with his observation.[2] It is not simply a question of why Shakespeare would alert his audiences to the *paragone* at the beginning of that particular play, but why the *paragone* would concern a dramatist at all. This essay will address itself to answering the question about *Timon* and will suggest some constituents of an answer to the question of Shakespeare's larger interest in the rivalry between poetry and painting by glancing briefly at other plays, a fuller discussion of which must be reserved for other occasions.[3]

1

The title *paragone,* signifying comparison, was given by one of its nineteenth-century editors to Leonardo da Vinci's manuscript on the relationships of the liberal arts and sciences.[4] This treatise sought to exalt painting at the expense of poetry, which in Leonardo's time at the court of Milan had significantly declined since the days of Dante and Petrarch; the converse, of course, held in Shakespeare's England, when painting had not yet the scope or prestige of continental schools and was clearly inferior to poetry. I do not need to claim, even if it were possible, that Shakespeare would have known Leonardo's treatise; the debate about the rival capabilities of each art and specifically about the status of painting as a liberal art was known in England by the end of the sixteenth century. Spenser alludes to it in the proem to book 2 of *The Faerie Queene,* with characteristic emphasis upon the verbal potential for platonism ("Poets wit, that passeth Painter farre / In picturing the parts of beautie daint"). And the theme of an entertainment presented to Queen Elizabeth at Mitcham in 1598, is the contest between poet and painter.[5] But since Leonardo addressed himself most sensitively to the problems of this debate and coincidentally because his manuscript actually envisages a poet and a painter presenting examples of their art to a Renaissance patron, King Matthias of Hungary (see (pp. 67–68 and note), just as Shakespeare does at the beginning of *Timon*, a few of its ideas will serve as a springboard into my discussion.

Leonardo's determination to separate the spheres and achievements of the arts, in one or two emphases even anticipating Lessing (for example, see p. 60), was exceptional at the time. It was much more usually the coincidence or collaborative enterprise of poetry and painting that was stressed in Renaissance texts. Certainly many Renaissance creative artists including Leonardo and Shakespeare displayed a concern for the separate achievements of each of the five senses, but this is largely translated into the theme of potential harmony when their resources unite, which endorsed and sustained the sisterhood of verbal and visual arts. But Leonardo's main effort is put into arguing the superiority of the sight, a traditional claim, and of the visual arts that honor and mirror its skills. This case for the arts that "present the work of nature to our understanding with more truth and accuracy than do words or letters" ("La pittura rapresenta al senso con piu verita e certezza . . ." p. 28) is identical to a large part of the concern of anyone engaged in theater work. As dramatist and actor—let alone as an associate of someone like Burbage who was also a painter—Shakespeare had to attend to what his audiences saw. Of course, Shakespeare was by no means as complacent as Leonardo about the unproblematical nature of seeing; if the latter affirmed the exactness (p. 55), the lack of error (p. 33), the speed with which we securely grasp visual images (p. 60), and their need of no interpretation (p. 27), Shakespeare frequently questions or, rather, represents challenges to the seen: we have only to think of the ways in which the final scenes of *The Winter's Tale*, while seeming to hold up visual rather than verbal eloquence ("I like your silence") as the more authoritative, also dramatize the very limitations of seeing.[6] But equally no man of the theater could neglect the vital contribution of what audiences saw or could be made to think they saw to his larger endeavor. This must have been especially so at about the time Shakespeare wrote *Timon of Athens*, when the new theatrical possibilities of Blackfriars[7] and the related development of the masque[8] put much more emphasis than had the public theaters upon scenery and costume and upon the framed experience of the action.

Other parallels between theater and painting, in the light of Leonardo's praise of the latter's separate and superior achievements, may be noted briefly. Both share a uniqueness of performance that "cannot be reproduced indefinitely (questa non fa infiniti figlioli) as is done in the printing of books" (p. 28). Neither theater nor painting could be accomplished without what Leonardo calls manual operation ("la manuale operatione": p. 27), a language of gesture that Leonardo also allows by implication to oratory, an art closer to the actor's than the poet's.[9] And perhaps most important of all parallels was that theater partook of painting's concern to communicate inward states via outward gestures. Indeed, the Elizabethan and Jacobean theater increasingly came to unite with great sophistication two major concerns of Renaissance poetics—action and character. These two modes were actually seen as quite distinct by another champion of the radical difference between the arts, Benedetto Varchi: his *Due Lezioni* of 1549 distinguished between *istorie* that describe the visible world and *poesie* that imitate the conceptions and passions of the soul; narrative poetry was like the former and therefore was comparable with painting, but poetry that sought to reveal what lay within—concepts and passions—was like sculpture.[10] In this Varchi is close to Leonardo's praise of painting's adaptation of figures to express mental states (pp. 37, 57), made despite Leonardo's acknowledgment of the traditional literary objection that portraits could not picture the soul of a sitter (p. 50). Any claim that visual art *can* depict a person's inner state is relevant to theatrical art and to the eloquence of its gestures. So it is perhaps no accident that (as the modern Arden editor notes) the poet's praise of his rival's picture ("this comes off well") in *Timon* 1.1.29 echoes Hamlet's advice to the players ("Now this o'erdone, or come tardy off . . ."). Finally, painting may be seen to align itself with dramatic representations by the use of inscriptions—words actually written on or about portraits, which may be compared to the essential feature of theater, its glossing of outward gesture by verbal attention to inward. Interestingly, Leonardo's rare enthusiasm for literary strategies in the *Paragone* is saved for poetry's ability to represent "the words created by the human voice [which] are natural phenomena in themselves" (p. 51).

2

Let me now turn to the one Shakespeare play where these comparisons and rivalries between the arts are explicitly addressed. *Timon of Athens* opens with an encounter between a poet and a painter.[11] On this edgy scene whose problematical text is not solely to blame for its gnomic tone, I think four comments are crucial.

First, the Poet and Painter are not at first the action so much as a medium through which we view the actions of Timon's suitors, "this confluence, this great flood of visitors" (1.1.42). Their role as watchers is established before we reach the actual *paragone* debate by their discussion of the other suitors. Poet and Painter are our surrogates upon the stage as well as themselves the objects of our gaze and hearing. They teach an audience from the first, what it might otherwise of course take for granted, that its function is to watch and hear in order to judge or come to some opinions about, in this case Timon, and that only through the double focus of sight and hearing does it function fully as beholder. Both verbal and visual modes constitute theatrical action. Of course, the visual is essentially what is arranged upon the stage for us to behold rather than any painterly images, but the mere presence of a painter must signal the role of sight in the representation of Timon that is just beginning.

Furthermore, since we watch the Painter together with the Poet watching the crowds we are instantly involved in a perspectival situation to which our attention is drawn by the dialogue between Jeweller and Merchant set, so to speak, behind that of the Poet and Painter. This is a fundamental theatrical device that Shakespeare often uses,[12] and it surely derives from the wide-spread Renaissance fascination with optics and in particular with perspective.[13] Leonardo noted the relationship of painting and perspective ("prospettiva [è la] figliola della pittura," p. 31); and I would suggest that Shakespeare's frequent invocation of perspectival structures for crucial scenes is his acknowledgment of this painterly device. After all, sonnet 24 had celebrated "perspective it is best painter's art."

My second point arises from the absence of any actual painterly activity in the visual component of this scene: the Painter is not even given any opportunity to describe his own picture, for it is the Poet who speaks of it— "this comes off well and excellent,"

> How this grace
> Speaks his own standing! What a mental power
> This eye shoots forth! How big imagination
> Moves in this lip! To th' dumbness of the gesture
> One might interpret.

and finally, "It tutors nature. Artificial strife / Lives in these touches, livelier than life" (ll. 30–38). But while the Poet clearly gestures to an actual, specific image that the Painter is showing to him ("this grace . . . This eye . . . this lip"), he barely describes it; rather he moves quickly to what words might say of it, what his own art could extrapolate from the painted images ("One might interpret"). All visual descriptions in poetry ambiguously honor their own medium as much as that of the visual art they offer to represent: "Poetry," wrote Leonardo, "eloquently sings her own praises" (p. 52); Shakespeare clearly engages in that enterprise when he describes the painting in *The Rape of Lucrece*. This imbalance in Shakespeare's presentation of the painter—in his later appearance he is also unable to tell us what image he proposes—might be used to argue that it is poetry that Shakespeare wishes to promote over painting; but since seeing is of such importance to this play (as later analysis will show) it also suggests that Shakespeare maybe is elevating his own stage pictures at the expense of the Painter's.

A third crucial point is that the Painter is showing a portrait, perhaps (since it is evidently portable) a miniature; whereas what the Poet invents for his verbal representation of Timon is some allegorical scene. In other words, the Poet makes his poem from the kind of implied visual imagery where interpretation depends upon seen items with a largely precoded significance, whereas the Painter must articulate his larger ideas via the individual features of his sitter rendered lifelikely. And indeed the Painter's comment is derisive:

> A thousand moral paintings I can show
> That shall demonstrate these quick blows of Fortune's
> More pregnantly than words.
>
> [1.1.90–92]

The latent antagonisms of their very first social exchange ("Good day, sir," answered by "I am glad y' are well") suddenly surface at this point, and the rivalry of the verbal and visual artists is revealed: exactly the *paragone* that Blunt diagnosed.

A fourth point concerns the absence of Timon himself from this preliminary scene. Poet and Painter compete to represent somebody who is not on the stage nor has yet appeared so that we have nothing to compare with their endeavors, a not-infrequent Shakespearean device but one that I shall suggest dominates his later plays. Or, to put it differently, the Painter's portrait is not seen by us and therefore its skill at likeness cannot be judged at the point when Timon enters; while the Poet's utterances are directed more at Timon's situation than at his character, which is therefore only considered by implication. Yet both artists are involved in an effort of representation, as is Shakespeare himself, who similarly uses verbal and visual imagery: explicit or direct like the Painter's—the actors on stage in their roles; indirect or situational like the Poet's vision of Timon courting Lady Fortune (ll. 65–74). The delayed entrance of Timon until about line 100 serves to foreground the play's interest in competing or collaborative modes of representing character in action. It is an interest that seems to preoccupy Shakespeare at this point in his career, for even physical presence does not always guarantee a "likeness," as anyone who considers *Coriolanus* will acknowledge: for all of his visibility, what we see and what we hear do not readily represent Caius Martius in any perdurable shape.

Recently it has been suggested that the relationship of verbal and visual modes in the depiction of Timon is not that of the emblem—explicit, generalizing, and visually-verbally cooperative—but that of the impresa—riddling, individualizing, and with word independent of, even tensed against, image. By forcing us to tease some congruence out of what we see and hear of Timon, Shakespeare effectively dramatizes the impresa's mysterious utterances about a particular human being. This argument sees a parallel between the impresa portrait, an image of the sitter with enigmatic insets often containing words but without explicit connections between constituent parts, and the endeavor to present the eponymous character in *Timon of Athens*.[14] It is a rewarding notion in that it focuses upon not only a specific Elizabethan and Jacobean concern with words and images, a concern that effectively localizes the topos of the *paragone*, but also a form with which we know Shakespeare engaged. It is then a most useful insight. But what I want to do is stepside its argument by analogy and focus directly upon Shakespeare's actual realization of the *paragone*, which in its contrast between the visual and verbal actually subverts the analogic claim of *ut pictura poesis*.[15] By dramatizing the competition between visual and verbal languages—explicitly in the encounter between Poet and Painter, then implicitly (as will be argued) throughout the rest of the play—Shakespeare surreptitiously urges the claim of theater as a stage for a special liaison of the two.

Contemporary commentary upon the theater did not appear to think of the stage as a unique medium, let alone as a tilting ground between poetry and painting; at its most complimentary it treated the dramatic text as a poem and playwrights as makers. But by the 1590s the London theatrical world had a vitality and a seriousness that implied larger and different claims, claims that the following decades substantiated—most obviously in the masque work of Inigo Jones and his various literary collaborators. By the date when we assume *Timon* to have been written (after 1604; perhaps 1607–8), Shakespeare shows himself particularly attentive to the special role of theatrical art. His interest in the *paragone* stemmed from his recognition explicitly and implicitly that he was, as a dramatist, both verbal and visual artist, and that he was uniquely placed to engineer a special dialogue between them. He could explore the rivalries, the different modes of verbal and visual, counterpoise them or let them complement each other; indeed, precisely in the theater was the rivalry between poet and painter that preoccupied his nondramatic contemporaries actually capable, not of simple resolution, but of a new and richly suggestive symbiosis. The implication, thus, was that theater transcended the achievements of either poetry or painting.

3

Timon of Athens, I want to suggest, is Shakespeare's fullest and most explicit exploration of the potentialities of that vision of theater (this is, however, not the same as claiming that *Timon* is the most accomplished of the plays). Criticism of the play has focused largely upon its social and moral themes, but I would suggest that what is in question here, as with other plays like *Coriolanus* and *Antony and Cleopatra* written soon afterwards, is just as much how we reach judgments as what those judgments are. Indeed, the *how*, not the *what*, is perhaps more prominent in *Timon*. From its opening sequence, it establishes that we will be involved in viewing, hearing, and only then, upon the basis of those means—neither of which is unproblematical—judging the central, eponymous character.

In *Timon* Poet and Painter stress the role of seeing and hearing: seeing is often emphasized in the play, but the problems of translating what we see are quickly highlighted. As Cupid says to Timon at the banquet, "The five best senses / Acknowledge thee their patron" (1.2.123–24). But since both Poet and Painter are skeptical of the sense basis of each other's art—a mistrust echoed also by Apemantus, who scorns both alike—how are we to judge? Timon himself participates in an early, vital commentary upon this problem:

> The painting is almost the natural man;
> For since dishonor traffics with man's nature,
> He is but outside; these pencill'd figures are
> Even such as they give out. I like your work . . .
>
> [1.1.157–60]

Interpretations of this passage differ radically. H. J. Oliver explains it— perversely, in my view—as painting gives "man as he really is, not the man whom dishonesty makes pretend to be better than he is"; J. C. Maxwell, contrariwise, paraphrases "Painting can almost be called natural, in comparison with the deceitfulness of human nature; a painting professes to be no other than it is."[16] The difficulty of the speech is perhaps essential: we may hear a version of Oliver's message, but surely the primary meaning— Timon's—that we register is the one offered by Maxwell, namely, that painting shows only the outside and none of that within which passeth show. Timon's praise of painting's meretricious signs is, we come to learn, apt.

The play teases us and our surrogates upon the stage with the problem of reading the nature of Timon: exactly what has human nature achieved in his makeup, what kind of man is he? The word *kind,* like *see,* oscillates throughout the dialogue. Apemantus alone at first sees through Timon to diagnose something rotten in him, and we tend to attribute this to his ineluctable cynicism. But it is not always so explained in the play. Apemantus is present, he says, to observe (1.2.34). Like *see,* this is a sharply double word. "I see," signaling "I understand," betrays the fundamental assumption, like Leonardo's, that to see is to grasp. To "observe" is to watch or see, but it also implies passing judgments or observations, and accordingly seems to acknowledge the problematics of vision. The man who scorned both Poet and Painter in the preceding scene now provides an alternative vision. And what Apemantus sees, he glosses, first in his own sardonic grace before eating (1.2.62–71), then in his commentary upon the visual masque of "Ladies as Amazons, with lutes in their hands, dancing and playing," a commentary that begins with "What a sweep of vanity comes this way" (ll.132–45). He glosses (literally—etymologically—he gives a tongue to) what his eyes see. The ceremonies with which Timon entertains his guests are not, he assures them, mere outward show—"Ceremony was but devis'd at first / To set a gloss on faint deeds" (1.2.15–16); but Apemantus's gloss says otherwise. Similarly, while an audience may think they see obsequiousness, bowing, scraping, and answering Timon's beck and call, Apemantus sees it as "Serving of becks and jutting-out of bums" (1.2.231). All this is more of the perspectivism of the sort that was established in the opening scene, here linked to the verbal forms into which we translate visual experience.

To complicate matters, our viewing of Apemantus is in fact as problematical as our viewing of Timon. The stage direction that ushers Apemantus into the banquet describes him as "like himself." This authorial fossil surviving into the Folio stage direction is enormously revealing: it contrasts Apemantus visually with the dolled-up and sycophantic followers assembled at Timon's feast; he appears as himself. But then we realize that this part of the honest, straightforward man is studied, too; the role—and with it perhaps an apt costume—is adopted. And if we are using him to "observe" Timon, we are further distanced, perspectively again, from that task. This is especially so at that point in the play when Timon presents a masque (mask) to his guests and they, including Apemantus, and ourselves have to interpret it.

The masque, Timon observes, "entertain'd me with mine own device" (1.2.150). Commentators tell us that if this cannot mean that he was the author of the masque, then he must be saying that his own devising of the feast has entertained him as much as his guests.[17] But surely there is also the strong suggestion that everything the guests have seen and heard—a masque's essential features being that doubleness of visual and verbal arts and a further complicity of art and life when the masquers dance with the spectators—is Timon's device, something like a heraldic device or devise, an impresa. But this theatrical version of an impresa—doubly theatrical in that Timon presents a masque and we assist at the play in which it appears—is complicated in that we have various perspectives upon its words and images. Apemantus, Poet, Painter, and all the other suitors have each his own view (sight/interpretation) of Timon's "devise."

By the end of the first act the Steward is lamenting that Timon's words do not square with his bank accounts—"what he speaks is all in debt"—and that his master's nature is itself usurous—"He is so kind that he / Pays interest for't" (1.2.199–200). Indeed, Timon's largesse, whether it is interpreted as generosity, prodigality, or foolish waste, was as much in words heard as gifts we saw distributed. The Senator says this (2.1.26) and Timon is told so himself ("my good lord, the world is but a word; / Were it all yours to give it in a breath, / How quickly were it gone," 2.2.152–54). We have heard those lavish words, seen the luxurious spectacle, yet still we cannot assess what his nature really is—his "kind." At best, like his steward—yet another perspective—we register only a paradox that "never mind / Was to be so unwise, to be so kind" (2.2.5–6).

Always in this play there are bystanders who, like Poet and Painter earlier, must alert us to the act and action of seeing: "Do you observe this, Hostilius?" or "O, see the monstrousness of man" (3.2.62, 72) And act 3 also stresses, just when others' views of Timon begin to be crucial, the unreliability of these spectators. Timon's erstwhile friends cannot live up to their empty words: there are explicit and implicit fractures of seeing and saying—doing one thing but saying another ("say thou saw'st me not" 3.1.44). By now we should be on our guard not to see too confidently, not to see/understand the play's face values. We are always reverting literally as we watch Timon and metaphorically as we assess him to that portrait that Timon himself valued in the first scene for its ambiguous representation of the natural man, man in his kind.

The difficulty of making up one's mind about Timon[18] is highlighted and complicated by his own metamorphosis in act 3; though it is possible to "explain" this switch into misanthropy as some sort of reaction to the greedy shallowness of Athenian society, its extremeness does not—deliberately, I feel—sanction such an explanation but rather highlights the inexplicable. Attention is perhaps directed to this aspect of the volte-face by the preceding scene (3.5), usually taken as an instance of Athenian ingratitude. In it the senators judge an unspecified friend of Alcibiades solely (as far as we are concerned) on the basis of verbal accounts that they judge "too strict a paradox, / Striving to make an ugly deed look fair" with words (ll.24–25); the scene closes with Alcibiades's banishment, " 'Tis in few words, but spacious in effect" (l.96). Once again in this play is represented a viewing, a judging of someone whom we never see, followed by a judging of Alcibiades himself: in both, words and images are problematical. That scene is our introit into the central metamorphosis of Timon himself.

Timon's change is signaled at another banquet, which at its start is outwardly, visibly, like its predecessor. It is surrounded by variations on the theme of putting words to what we see happening—his friends faking excuses for themselves, devising explanations for Timon's requests for money and then seeing those explanations confirmed in his behaviour at the feast ("This is the old man still," 3.6.61); these "mouth-friends," as he calls them (l.89), or "painted . . . varnish'd friends" in the steward's phrase (4.2.36), are last seen groping among the stones he has hurled at them for a lost and apparently indistinguishable jewel and for the remnants of their outward selves—caps and gowns.

Once Timon takes himself into exile, he is again the center of fresh efforts to understand him. Perhaps because he is now isolated from any social context, we (and those on stage who, like us, seek to understand him) think this task may be easier. A series of visitors—Alcibiades, Apemantus, some banditti, the Poet and the Painter, Timon's steward, some Athenian senators, and finally a soldier—performs on stage what we, too, as audience undergo: a quest for the truth about Timon. We are frequently alerted to the perspective of others: "Is yond despis'd and ruinous man my lord?" asks the Steward (4.3.459), and his *yond* verbally enacts his middle place between us watching him and him watching Timon. Indeed, I wonder whether the puzzling textual crux of Apemantus's saying "Yonder comes a poet and a painter" (4.3.351) two hundred lines before they speak is not a verbal clue to their physical arrival on stage, watching the series of visitors trying to make Timon out. If so, it would parallel their actions on first entry into the play. Their presence upon the stage would also reiterate the problematics of seeing and hearing.

Timon is no longer the richly arrayed patron of the first half; visibly changed, as Apemantus's speech ensures that we register (4.3.202–18), he now inhabits a cave in the woods. But is this outward transformation "real"? Is it not another mask (masque)? Timon himself half-suggests that it is a role ("I am Misanthropos, and hate mankind," 4.3.), and Apemantus repeatedly insists that Timon is only acting—"Thou dost affect my manners," "putting on the cunning of a carper," and finally, "Do not assume my likeness" (ll. 199, 209, 218). The use of *likeness*, a painterly, portrait-associated term, implies that in his bafflement with understanding the new Timon Apemantus grasps at an explanation that deals solely with exteriors. Just as Timon castigated counterfeit society in his exchange with Alcibiades and the whores, so he may simply himself be counterfeiting. Timon responds to Apemantus's accusation in a way that forces the issue out into the open, yet without clarifying it;

> *Timon.* Were I like thee I'd throw away myself.
> *Apem.* Thou has cast away thyself, being like thyself, a madman so long, now a fool.
>
> [4.3.219–21]

The Poet and Painter now intervene for the second time in the play, at the high point of our and others' bafflement. They are sycophantic, time-servers, but their concern with fashioning a likeness of Timon is still prominent. The Painter claims to have nothing ready yet for Timon—he has come to see, to look again at his sitter. The Poet, however, plans to respond to the new Timon's apparent subterfuge of pretending misanthropy by "a personating of himself" (5.1.34). Ironically, at this point they are both watched by Timon, a brief switch of perspective that builds dramatically upon Timon's previous exchange with Apemantus, where each character watched the other and we were forced to read one through the mediating vision of the other. Faced with the two artists, Timon's scorn for poetry and painting is now of a piece with his outrage against society. But it tellingly undermines our residual confidence in those arts as satisfactory agents of likeness: Timon's wrath takes its cue from the Poet's affected modesty:

> I am rapt, and cannot cover
> The monstrous bulk of this ingratitude
> With any size of words.
>
> [5.1.64–66]

Timon responds with "Let it go naked, men may see't the better" (l. 67); words are simply a disguise. Similarly, he ascribes to the Painter and his visual art the skill only of counterfeiting (l. 79). He taunts them with being deceived by a knave—they "hear him cog, see him dissemble" and yet fail to grasp his knavery (ll. 95–98). But what they equally do not see—but we perhaps do—is that this very "knave" whom they hear and see is (at least by implication) Timon himself—a counterfeiter outwitting a verbal and a visual counterfeiter by his own acting that relies upon both. It is, I think, the closest the play comes to claiming for itself a skill with fiction superior to either of the two arts usually embattled in *paragone*.

The play does not end with Timon's death scene, as we might expect and as all of Shakespeare's other tragedies do. This representation of Timon, as happens often in life itself, faces us at the end only with epitaphs after the event of the unseen death itself. Yet unlike those that Aufidius utters over Coriolanus or Octavius over Cleopatra, themselves inadequate summations, Timon's epitaph is double and, in more ways than one, contradictory.

First we see a soldier (5.3) trying to find Timon's habitation by a "description"; he calls out, "Who's here? Speak, ho!" But the only reply is some written notice that is first presented to his sight:

> "Timon is dead, who hath outstretch'd his span:
> Some beast read this; there does not live a man."
>
> [5.3.3–4]

Those words he can read; others he can only see and he takes a wax impression of those. Elaborate editorial annotations at this point in the text, which seek to explain that one is obviously a notice in his language and the other in Latin that he cannot read, may be right,[19] though such an explanation would surely not intrude upon an audience at the play. But these annotations are also less than apt: one's attention is drawn here again to words and images. The waxen images taken by the soldier, which he actually calls "insculpture" (5.4.67), are interpreted by Alcibiades. The Folio stage direction says that he "reades the Epitaph," which he must hold in his hands, just as the Painter at the start of the play held a visual image in his hands.

The text that Alcibiades reads has four lines:

"Here lies a wretched corse, of wretched soul bereft;
Seek not my name: a plague consume you, wicked caitiffs left!
Here lie I, Timon, who, alive, all living men did hate;
Pass by and curse thy fill, but pass and stay not here thy gait."
[5.4.69–73]

Shakespeare may indeed have copied two epitaphs from North's Plutarch, "meaning to omit one or the other (probably the first) on revision," as the Arden editor puts it.[20] But other explanations of this apparent textual crux are more consonant with the play's vision as I have outlined it. Inasmuch as the two couplets contradict each other, that is wholly in line with the paradoxes the play has presented. Further, one defies the user of words ("Seek not my name"), just as Timon's very last speech also castigated language—"Lips, let four words go by and language end" (5.1.220); while the epithet's other couplet that Alcibiades reads out accepts verbal naming and the opportunities of cursing.

4

I am arguing then for *Timon of Athens* as a play abut seeing and hearing in the theater of Blackfriars (or Globe) and the theater of the world represented on those stages. But unlike other theatrical occasions when to see and to hear lead to judgments, this play recalls us constantly to the difficulties of matching word and image; indeed, unlike painting, even those turning pictures so loved of the Elizabethans,[21] a play is capable of offering us various perspectives in each of which word and image seem to establish their own treaty. The whole movement of the play, awkwardly tailored to readings that stress its social satire, seems much more apt when *Timon* is to be viewed as a representation of a human being whose behavior, character, and indeed whole nature are difficult to comprehend, not least because he changes so strikingly at a certain point in his life. We are shown habitual modes of inquiry and understanding—conversations between those who supposedly "know" the character; obituaries. We are also given the opportunity to assess how poetic and painterly fictions would cope with representing an adequate likeness.

But all these modes of inquiry are contained within, given performance by and in, a theatrical work. Theater, by implication, succeeds in representing Timon where poetry and painting fail, partly because it can dramatize uncertainties or ambiguities and continue to do so not once, like painting, but throughout the dramatic experience. Above all, of course, the theater can provide both verbal and visual language either simultaneously or in counterpoint. It can *stage* perspectives, and in a fashion that makes contemporary delight in anamorphic pictures seem very simplistic. For both turning pictures and such anamorphic images as those contained in Holbein's *Ambassadors* or the portrait of Edward VI in the National Portrait Gallery,

London, depend upon the viewer's having to shift his position in order to register the alternative image: he can never see both at once. But in the theater the simultaneity of double views is allowed by the combination of word and image and by the physical possibilities of an audience watching a deep stage space where rival perspectives are displayed.[22] Finally, painting, as Shakepeare himself had written, strives with "nature's workmanship" to surpass the life,[23] the stage's pictures actually incorporate life in the shape of an actor's presence: in short, the traditional *paragone* of word and image and the age-old rivalry of art and life are both resolved upon the stage.

5

This is therefore how I would explain Shakespeare's interest in the *paragone*. He is seldom explicit, rebuking our contemporary bent for theorizing, though we have to take into account also the somewhat rough-hewn state of the *Timon* text. But after highlighting this Renaissance topos, *Timon of Athens* goes on to dramatize ways in which the theater can reconcile the rival modes of word and image by setting them in a situation where their competition, though still acknowledged, can be transcended. This therefore explains why the play is, in M. C. Bradbrook's terms, an experimental reshaping of the Elizabethan "show."[24]

This discussion of Shakespeare and the *paragone* can clearly be related to the substantial recent interest in performative readings of Shakespeare's plays. Discussions by Alan Dessen, for example, or Ann Pasternak Slater[25] are concerned to establish how Elizabethan dramatic texts yield directions for performance, for how we see as well as how we hear. But I do not see this as containing the full thrust of my argument, which is concerned to explore the various forms of rivalry or collaboration by which Shakespeare manipulated words and images to achieve subtle effects. My focus upon the explicit and implicit *paragone* yields not just a critique hospitable to the verbal and visual construction of drama, to the procedures of *ut pictura poesis*, but strives for an understanding that is alert to an audience's perception of their relationship, whether hostility, rivalry, or mutual collaboration and elaboration. And this implicitly raises theater above the habitual rivalry, even gives it a special place in the exemplifications of *ut pictura poesis*.

This is not the occasion on which to extend my analysis of *Timon of Athens* into the rest of Shakespeare's oeuvre, let alone into the work of his contemporaries in poetry, painting, and drama. But it is worth lingering, by way of conclusion, upon why Shakespeare raises the issue of the *paragone* so prominently at this stage of his career. Obviously he was always fascinated by verbal and visual forms—*The Comedy of Errors* makes that clear and shows the vital involvement of these two, often opposed, modes of communication. But if I am right in my insistence on the opportunities for more subtle presentations of character in action that dramatic implementations of the *paragone* allow, then Shakespeare will inevitably be seen to invoke it increasingly as his career develops. It is highlighted explicitly in *Timon of Athens*, but is implicit also in *Coriolanus* and *Antony and Cleopatra*.[26]

I would offer four suggestions as to why the *paragone* features so much more prominently in these plays. First, in these Shakespeare seems concerned to foreground the ambiguities, the problematics of character to a greater degree than before. Second, this theme is clearly suggested and available to Shakespeare in Plutarch's sophisticated biographical material that he made his major sources for these plays: Plutarch not only narrates history through character, but he is fascinated (though not to the point of being sidetracked) with the difficulties of assessing and describing character.[27] Third, while Lomazzo had claimed that a good likeness of some great man made viewers wish to emulate his deeds, the rapid developments in English portraiture around 1600 actually highlighted the exact requirements of a likeness[28]; and incidentally the interest in a portrait's "shadows" as contributing to a lifelikeness, which increased hugely from the 1580s, echoes in the theater's absorption with actors as shadows ("Dost dialogue with thy shadow?" asks Apemantus in 2.2.51). Fourth, the development of the masque to which of course Shakespeare responded in his last plays laid greater and more self-conscious emphasis on the mutual contributions of word and image.

Shakespeare's response to these stimuli was to concentrate his and his audiences' energies on the rival potential of words and images. Definition of character preoccupies him in the figures of Timon, Coriolanus, Antony, and Cleopatra, but this is focused largely upon what words will describe or will suit and match our sight of those figures; and equally whether what can be seen is accessible to words, is adequately transcribed in its language.

Antony and Cleopatra addresses this series of theatrical challenges at its very beginning.[29] Demetrius and Philo start the play with their comments upon Antony's "view" of Cleopatra ("his goodly eyes . . .now turn . . . their view"); then as the lovers enter these bystanders' "Look," "see," "behold and see," and "tell" dramatize for the audience a perspectival situation that will be maintained throughout the play—us watching others seeing, observing, judging. It is clear that Demetrius and Philo's view of a degenerate Antony and his gipsy does not jibe with the lovers' own feelings; yet they are themselves hyperbolically concerned with the adequacy of language to describe ("tell . . . reckon'd") their own state. The play constantly juxtaposes verbal judgments of the two central figures, these rival versions being themselves predicated upon how the speakers see them: Enobarbus's famous speech offers in miniature this concern with how words and images may variously represent reality. His speech is perhaps the most prominent example of a concern with "report,"[30] spoken versions of the leading figures, which are a feature, too, of *Coriolanus* from its initial scene. Verbal judgments clash not only with each other but with our sight of them; and these sightings are themselves perspectively shaped, as we view Coriolanus from patrician or plebian or Volscian directions. Indeed, this play is a succession of scenes in which we see others, not always used to the particular context, observing and assessing Caius Martius. In the climactic scene of act 5 we must both hear ("I prate") and see ("Holds her by the hand silent") and so register these rival modes upon a stage; and Coriolanus himself actually underlines this conjunction of theatrical perspective with the *paragone* by invoking its endless extent—"The gods look down, and this unnatural scene / They laugh at" (5.3.184–85). Even the gods are an audience engaged in the slippery and ambiguous act of interpreting character in action.

Timon, I would suggest, simply highlights concerns at the center of these Roman plays. It begins crucially with the longish absence of the character whose dramatic likeness is to be attempted. This gives Poet and Painter, the traditionally and self-established purveyors of likeness, the opportunity to debate their skills before the dramatist himself begins to assume that role and in so doing pass judgment upon their kinds of achievement. We have noticed how the Painter is put down during *Timon;* our last sight of the Poet, equally, is of him being pelted off stage with gold as Timon shouts, "You are an alcumist, make gold of that" (5.1.114). At that point, Bradbrook asks, "What is Shakespeare doing there to himself?"[31] I would answer that he is relegating those who use words or images by themselves and erecting in their place the dramatist's more subtle combinations of each. It was always Shakespeare's concern to promote "the very faculties of eyes *and* ears," but in *Timon* he chooses to remind us explicitly and to show us how the drama, as Spenser had argued, was the medium "By which man's life in his likest image / Was limned forth."[32]

Notes

For comments upon earlier drafts of this essay I am grateful to Professor Philip Edwards for a most useful response at the Berlin conference, to members of the Faculty of English Renaissance research group at Oxford University, who responded to a revised version, and to Dr. Michael Leslie, who has commented most helpfully at all stages.

1. A. Blunt, "An Echo of the 'Paragone' in Shakespeare," *JWI* 2 (1938–39): 260–62.

2. See Jean Hagstrum, *The Sister Arts: The Tradition of Literary Pictorialism and English Poetry from Dryden to Gray* (Chicago: University of Chicago Press, 1958), 69–70; W. M. Merchant, "*Timon* and the Conceit of Art," *Shakespeare Quarterly* 6 (1955): 249–57; and David Bevington, *Action Is Eloquence: Shakespeare's Language of Gesture* (Cambridge: Harvard University Press, 1984), 26 and 28.

3. This essay is a preliminary excursion into a large territory, and consequently betrays its attempt to circumscribe a far too ambitious project, but one which nevertheless needs mapping in a sketchy fashion if the scope and implications of my discussion of *Timon* are to be appreciated. I have other essays in progress on the *paragone* in England, notably as it concerns

the presentation of character, and on verbal/visual disputes in early Shakespeare, in *Antony and Cleopatra*, and in the last plays.

4. See *Paragone: A Comparison of the Arts by Leonardo da Vinci*, with introduction by I. A. Richter (Oxford: Oxford University Press, 1949), on which I draw; all references in the text are to this volume. On the *paragone* see also n. 10.

5. *Queen Elizabeth's Entertainment at Mitcham*, ed. Leslie Hotson (New Haven: Yale University Press, 1953).

6. Bevington, *Action Is Eloquence*, 19–20 *et passim*, discusses Shakespeare's ambiguous stance towards visual imagery.

7. On the original stage for *Timon* see both M. C. Bradbrook, "The Comedy of Timon: A Reveling Play of the Inner Temple," *Renaissance Drama* 9 (1966): 83–103, and "Blackfriars: The Pageant of *Timon of Athens*," in *Shakespeare the Craftsman*, ed. Bradbrook (Cambridge: Cambridge University Press, 1969), 144–67, as well as E. A. J. Honigmann, *"Timon of Athens," Shakespeare Quarterly* 12 (1961): 3–20.

8. In this context I am thinking specifically of the work by D. J. Gordon on the visual/verbal rivalries and collaborations of Ben Jonson and Inigo Jones: see variously in *The Renaissance Imagination*, ed. Stephen Orgel (Berkeley and Los Angeles: University of California Press, 1975).

9. Leonardo meets the objection that poetry's "words will move a people to tears or to laughter" more readily than visual arts by arguing that it is not the poet but "another science"—that of the orator—which is responsible (p. 65).

10. See the extremely useful discussion both of this important commentator on the rivalries between the arts and of the larger Renaissance context in Leatrice Mendelsohn, *Paragoni: Benedetto Varchi's "Due Lezzioni" and Cinquecento Art Theory* (Ann Arbor: University of Michigan Press, 1982). Another important commentary upon the *paragone* is David Summers, *Michelangelo and the Language of Art* (Princeton: Princeton University Press, 1981), chap. 19. See also the work cited in n. 4 above.

11. All references are to the Riverside edition of the play by G. Blakemore Evans (1974), and are given in the text within brackets. I have taken for granted Shakespeare's authorship of the whole play, in part because other claims for part-authorship are unconvincing and in part because it is precisely my ambition to read the play as having more authority and cohesion than arguments for divided authorship (or, indeed, incompletion) are, by their very nature, willing to allow.

12. For instance, *Two Gentlemen of Verona*, 4.2, and *Troilus and Cressida*, 5.2; much of the plot of *Much Ado About Nothing* also depends upon this strategy. See also note 22 below.

13. See, primarily, Ernest B. Gilman, *The Curious Perspective: Literary and Pictorial Wit in the Seventeenth Century* (New Haven: Yale University Press, 1978), especially chaps. 4 and 5.

14. Michael Leslie, "The Dialogue between Bodies and Souls: Pictures and Poesy in the English Renaissance," *Word & Image* 1 (1985): 28–29.

15. It is this interest of Shakespeare in the rival claims of word and image that makes me somewhat skeptical of approaches to his plays via emblem and iconography that stress only parallels and not their dramatic competition: see my "*Pictura, Scriptura*, and *Theatrum*—Shakespeare and the Emblem," forthcoming in *Poetics Today*.

16. Oliver's note is on pp. 13–14 of the Arden edition (1959), Maxwell's on p. 108 of his Cambridge edition (1957).

17. See Arden editor's comment, p. 29.

18. It has been suggested to me by Barbara Everett that there is really no "problem" with reading Timon's character. To answer that characters on the stage have difficulties—even before his volte-face in act 3 the Poet and Painter among others are concerned with understanding him—is perhaps insufficient. But Shakespeare's dramatization of others' puzzlement over Timon surely foregrounds what is his major concern in later plays—the complexities of human behavior and personality and the difficulties of representing them. Furthermore, though it is awkward to invoke standard analyses of *Timon* when I am engaged in revising

them, there is a long and imposing tradition of critical puzzlement about Timon that it is part of my aim to involve in a reading of the play.

19. Such is the Arden editor's gloss, pp. 134–35.

20. Ibid.

21. See both Gilman, cited in n. 13 above, and Allan Shickman, "Turning Pictures in Shakespeare's England," *Art Bulletin* 59 (1971): 67–70. Turning pictures actually foreclose or limit options, which Shakespeare theatrical portraits do not.

22. I think the best example of this must be *Troilus and Cressida* 5.2, where the depth of stage (even the inner stage) must be used to stage Thersites watching Ulysses watching Troilus watching Cressida and Diomed: and we watch them all.

23. *Venus and Adonis,* ll. 289–94

24. Bradbrook, *Renaissance Drama,* 84 n.

25. Alan C. Dessen, *Elizabethan Stage Conventions and Modern Interpreters* (Cambridge: Cambridge University Press, 1984), and Ann Pasternak Slater, *Shakespeare the Director* (Brighton: Harvester Press, 1982).

26. In the final stages of revising this essay for publication I have come across R. M. Frye, "Relating Visual and Verbal Art in Shakespeare," *Proceedings of the Conference of College Teachers of English* 19 (1980): 11–28. Frye touches upon the relations of portrait painting and literary characterization, but to my mind indulges in subjective analogies and casual parallels rather than concentrating on how Shakespeare's theatrical practice absorbed and utilized contemporary arts and their rivalries, above all the debates about "likeness."

27. See, for example, in *Shakespeare's Plutarch,* ed. T. J. B. Spencer (Harmondsworth, Middlesex: Penguin Books, 1964), 296–97.

28. On contemporary portraiture and its relevance to the *paragone* see Claire Pace, " 'Delineated lives': Themes and Variations in 17th-Century Poems about Portraits," *Word & Image* 2 (1986): 1–17.

29. All quotations from *Antony and Cleopatra* and *Coriolanus* are from the respective Riverside editions.

30. I am grateful to Cedric Barfoot of Leiden University for making me aware of the centrality and relevance of "report" to this play of messengers, rumors, gossip.

31. Bradbrook, *Shakespeare the Craftsman,* 160.

32. *Teares of the Muses,* ll. 201–2.

Venus and Adonis: *Shakespeare's Horses*

by JOHN DOEBLER

"Thus did they celebrate the funeral of Hector, tamer of horses."

"Tamer of horses": these last words of the *Iliad* celebrate an heroic ideal that persisted from the ninth century B.C., when Homer reputedly wrote his epics, to the nineteenth century, nearly three thousand years later and only yesterday in the continuity of a culture. Shakespeare's *Venus and Adonis*, published in 1593, is a mere four hundred years old, but it is also deeply embedded in that ancient cultural ideal. The persistent importance of the horse as a topos suggests why the first readers of the poem apparently paused a little longer at the digression to the stallion and the breeding jennet, to judge from marginal notations written in early copies of the poem during the 1590s. In like manner, nineteenth- and early-twentieth-century literary criticism of the poem devoted disproportionate attention to Shakespeare's description of the stallion. Biographically concerned critics tended to find in this digression clear indication that the poet knew country ways from Stratford and was well versed in the sizing up of horseflesh. If we read Shakespeare's introduction of the horse of Adonis, however, we find that the poet is not leading him in by the reins for appraisal; rather we, the readers, are directed to view the animal as it were in a painting:

> Look when a painter would surpass the life
> In limning out a well-proportioned steed,
> His art with nature's workmanship at strife,
> As if the dead the living should exceed;
> > So did this horse excel a common one,
> > In shape, in courage, color, pace, and bone.

> Round-hoof'd, short-jointed, fetlocks shag and long,
> Broad breast, full eye, small head, and nostril wide,
> High crest, short ears, straight legs and passing strong,
> Thin mane, thick tail, broad buttock, tender hide:

> Look what a horse should have he did not lack.
> Save a proud rider on so proud a back.
>
> [Ll. 289–300]

The context for this famous passage is important for an understanding of its literary coherence. Early in the poem Adonis manages to break the wrestler's hold of Venus, her powerful and rapacious fingers locked "one in one" (l. 228). Some thirty lines later, he finally springs loose from her "twining arms" and races to his horse, only to be frustrated in turn by the digression to the breeding jennet luring the "strong-neck'd steed." Breaking the rein that ties him to a tree,

> The iron bit he crusheth 'tween his teeth,
> Controlling what he was controlled with.
>
> [Ll. 269–70]

The transition from Adonis, breaking away from the restraint of a lusting Venus, to a stallion in the full pride of youth, breaking his own restraints and pursuing a mate into the discreet cover of a wood, is the center of many reversals, including the reversal of naive male immaturity and disinclination into adult animal fulfillment and joy.

Few scholars or critics have seemed fully confident in their understanding of the relationship between this digression and the body of the poem, but nearly all of them since the New Criticism have made attempts at organic interpretation. Originally, as I have indicated, in the nineteenth and early twentieth centuries, when horses were still very much a vital part of life, the episode was regarded as a full digression, indulging in the description of magnificent horseflesh as a glorious end in itself. The next phase in twentieth-century literary criticism was to regard the horses as emblems of unrestrained and irrational passion pointing up the folly of an unchaste Venus. Among the Neoplatonic variations on this theme was a positive view of the animals as representing a natural generative contrast of procreative love, making of Venus a victim of mere lust inevitably doomed to self-defeat. This positive Neoplatonic approach often involves the authority of the *Venus genetrix* described in the fifteenth-century *Convito* of Ficino, a Venus who is also one of two acceptable forms of love illustrated in the familiar sixteenth-century painting by Titian called *The Twin Venuses* by Panofsky, and according to Panofsky erroneously titled *Sacred and Profane Love* by earlier art historians. The poem surely has Neoplatonic elements, but I would also add to the Titian the possibilities of a painting by Veronese. We know that Sidney had a lost portrait painted by Veronese when the English courtier was on tour in Italy. Topics shared with the poem, despite substantial variations, occur in one of the most highly regarded extant Veroneses. In his *Mars and Venus* (ca. 1576–84), at the Metropolitan Museum of Art, the horse is a very emphatic element (fig. 1), in contrast to

Figure 1. *Mars and Venus United by Love* by Paolo Veronese. *(Courtesy of The Metropolitan Museum of Art, New York.)*

the obscure bas-relief horse on a cistern in the Titian. In the Veronese picture, according to iconographers, Mars and Venus are ideal lovers, thus comparable to the horses in *Venus and Adonis* as an ideal of procreative love. Here in the painting, however, we find the horse, rather than Shakespeare's mythological lovers, in need of rational restraint. The powerful stallion is securely tied to a laurel tree and kept under further check by a winged putto or cupidon, using the sword of Mars. Mars, in turn, conceals the female concupiscence of Venus with a drapery and she calms his male irascibility by a gentle hand on his broad shoulder: a graceful and balanced *discordia concors*. If we were to follow Neoplatonic leads into Shakespeare's poem, this Veronese is probably one of the most comprehensive statements ever made of relevant issues shared by the poem with the visual arts. Finally, in the history of criticism, during the "cultural revolution" of the 1960s, especially in the United States, the *joie de vivre* of Shakespeare's horses was placed in contrast to Adonis's prim rejection of presumably no less than life itself, and there the full range of interpretations came to a momentary rest.

Four hundred years before this wide diversity of opinion in the last one hundred years, however, some fairly straightforward and commonplace associations with horses were firmly established in Shakespeare's own European time and place.

Characteristic of both mythography and the traditional exegesis of highly regarded texts such as Homer and Vergil was the explanation of a given image or emblem *in bono* and *in malo*. The 1505 Dürer engraving of "The Small Horse" (fig. 2) is a widely known instance of the horse *in bono,* the horse perfected in art, if not in life. Shakespeare could also have said of the Dürer: "Look when a painter would surpass the life / In limning out a well-proportioned steed." Horses as the animals bringing nature closest to perfection, further brought toward perfection by the artist, is fundamental to Western thought, surviving despite all satiric convolutions as Swift's Houyhnhnms, in the fourth and last part of *Gulliver's Travels* (1726). During his three-year stay with the Houyhnhnms, Gulliver "fell to imitate their gait and gesture . . . now grown into a habit, and my friends often tell me in a blunt way that I 'trot like a horse'; which, however, I take for a great compliment . . ." (chap. 10). Over a century before Swift, but like Swift, Sir Philip Sidney represented the horse *in bono* both comically and seriously, although in separate texts. In Sidney's "Shepherd's Song," from the *Old Arcadia,* Jove grants the animals a human ruler described as "a naked sprite" invested by Earth with "clay," by the lion with heart, and by the horse, the paragon of beauty, "with good shape." The comic treatment is in Sidney's famous exordium to his *Defence of Poetry,* where he reports the insistence on the part of Pugliano, equerry to the Emperor Maximilian II, that "the peerless beast the horse" was "the only serviceable courtier without

Figure 2. The Small Horse by Albrecht Dürer. *(Courtesy of Kupferstichkabinett, Berlin.)*

flattery, the beast of most beauty, faithfulness, courage, and much more," that Pugliano almost persuaded Sidney to wish himself a horse.

Many more literary instances can be augmented by dead-serious Renaissance treatises on everything from horsemanship to the artistic canons for the ideal horse, such as the one delineated by Dürer. Possibly familiar to Shakespeare was Gervase Markham's *Discourse of Horsemanship* (1593), the year of our poem, or Thomas Blundeville's *The Four Chiefest Offices of Horsemanship* (also published that same year). Both Markham and Blundeville share a worshipful attitude toward the animal. Back across the channel, a half-century after Dürer's "Small Horse" of 1505, Hans Sebald Beham (1500–1550) was published posthumously as *Kunst und der Büchlin Malen* (1565), a handbook for artists. In it Beham, or Behem, sets forth the ideal canons for the proportions of the human head, but no less loving is Beham's artistic scheme for "the principal lines of the horse" (fig. 3).

As readily accessible to Shakespeare as the horse *in bono* was a pervasive cultural tradition of the horse *in malo*. Most undergraduates in the world know of Plato's fable of the charioteer and the horses in the *Phaedus*. Despite the careful qualifications made by Plato about the distinctions between the two horses pulling the chariot, most students in all centuries have come away with the simple impression that the charioteer, Reason, must control the horses, Passion. Close to ten years before the publication of *Venus and Adonis*, Bocchi's emblem book, *Symbolicae quaestiones* (1574), demonstrates the concept in all its full simplicity. Symbol 117: "Prudence restrains passion" *(Semper libidini imperat prudentia)* puts the motto into a visual form of perfect clarity (fig. 4). On a more sophisticated level, the Henrik Goltzius engraving of "The Fall of Phaeton" (about 1588) is among a suite of Four Classical Falls. The literal fall of Phaeton from the Chariot of the Sun he has usurped from his father, Apollo, flings four powerful horses about the sky.

Despite the authority of even so formidable a cultural force as Plato, my own sense of the popular cultural consensus in all centuries is that, like the automobile, horses are both hated and loved, but mainly adored. Edward Topsell puts it in short compass in 1607, in his *History of Four-Footed Beasts:*

> Carnal copulation is more acceptable to horses . . . for there is no other kind (man only excepted) that is so . . . nimble in generation as is a horse or mare. [P. 300]

The episode of the horses in *Venus and Adonis* is an erotic and visual variation on the attempted seduction of Adonis by Venus. Both "man" and horses are alike in carnality; both the classical lovers and the animals are images of physical perfection inviting the attention of an artist; but the stallion and the mare do with grace and ease what Venus and Adonis make awkward and tiresome. Shakespeare has set two objectified images in comparison and contrast, plot and subplot. The official judgment may be

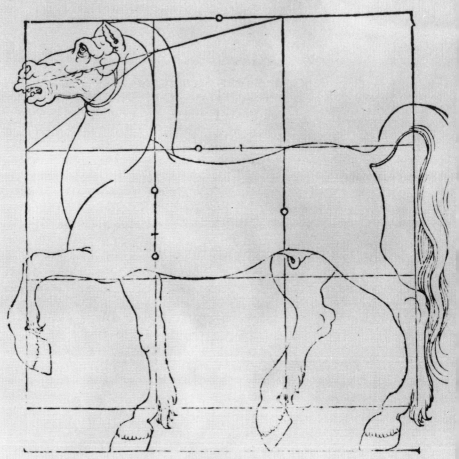

Mag auch wie die andern obgeſetzten aufge.
ſcharpfiert werden.　　　　　　　**G** ij

Figure 3. Ideal horse from Hans Sebald Beham, *Kunst und der Büchlein Malen* (1565).

SEMPER LIBIDINI IMPERAT PRVDENTIA.

Symb. CXVII.

Figure 4. Untamed horses from Achilles Bocchi, *Symbolicae quaestiones* (1574).

moral, but the artistic emphasis is more clearly visual and aesthetic. Venus and Adonis, though beautiful individually, look ridiculous together. The horses always look wonderful. Philip Sidney was almost persuaded by Pugliano to wish himself a horse; Gulliver clearly crossed that line of desire. Perhaps Shakespeare in some measure also wished man to be more like a horse, at ease with himself and in nature, freed of the necessity for coercion and even authority, beautiful in himself and in courtship. Instead, the absurdity of lust among even gods concludes in assured death for man. The life of Adonis is finest in conclusion, in an artfully conceived nature, when Shakespeare describes the metamorphosis of Adonis:

> . . . in his blood that on the ground lay spill'd,
> A purple flow'r sprung up, check'red with white,
>   Resembling well his pale cheeks and the blood
>   Which in round drops upon their whiteness stood.
>   [Ll. 1167–70]

The change is into a flower rather than a horse, but the insufficiency of man and the submerged yearning to enter into an artistically perfected nature remain the same. Veronese allows the fulfillment of this desire among the gods; Shakespeare, the temporal English dramatist, finds his aesthetic ideals among flowers and horses.

Degrees of Metaphor: King Lear

by GIORGIO MELCHIORI

The definition of *metaphor* in the *OED* is austere—the word has only one meaning:

> The figure of speech in which a name or descriptive term is transferred to some object different from, but analogous to, that to which it is properly applicable; an instance of this, a metaphorical expression.

It is a far cry from Umberto Eco's thirty-six-page entry on metaphor in the *Enciclopedia Einaudi* (1980) beginning with the words, "The most splendid, and for this very reason the most necessary and pregnant of all tropes, metaphor defies definition in any encyclopedia"; and Eco notes that a bibliography on metaphor published in 1971 recorded about three thousand entries. Surely if we take into account the more recent work in the fields of philosophy, linguistics, aesthetics, psychology, and even science that number must be considerably increased. Remaining within the field of literature we are immediately confronted with Jakobson's typology of literary forms that places at one end metaphor as the type of pure poetry and at the other metonymy as the type of pure prose.

But what we are confronted with now is neither poetry nor prose—it is drama; and the general title of this conference, "Images of Shakespeare," suggests a more precise approach to metaphor, if we consider that for a long time in the middle years of the twentieth century Shakespearean criticism focused on the study of imagery—a fruitful approach founded by Wolfgang Clemen—and imagery effectively and totally englobed the very concept of metaphor.

There is no question, though, that Shakespeare was familiar with the good old Aristotelian term of metaphor in the acceptation offered in the rhetorical treatises current in his time. Thomas Wilson in his *Arte of Rhetorique* (1553) said that "a metaphor is an alteration of a woorde from the proper and naturall meanynge, to that which is not proper, and yet agreeth thereunto, by some lykenes that appeareth to be in it." In *The Garden of Eloquence* (1577) Henry Peacham gave it prominence as the first of the "tropes of words" (as contrasted with those of sentences) and devoted several pages to a classification of metaphors according to what he called the "places" they are taken from or translated into. Less enthusiastically George Puttenham in *The Arte of Englishe Poesie* (1589) called it "the figure of transport," classing it with "the figures which we call sensable, because they alter and affect the minde by alterations of sence in single words." The rare and always ironical uses of the word in Shakespeare's plays bear witness to his awareness of such definitions. Here is the first meeting of Sir Andrew Aguecheek with Maria (*Twelfth Night*, 1.3.64–79):

> *Sir And.* Fair lady, do you think you have fools in hand?
> *Mar.* Sir, I have not you by th' hand.
> *Sir And.* Marry, but you shall have—and here's my hand.
> *Mar.* Now, sir, thought is free. I pray you bring your hand to th' butt'ry-bar, and let it drink.
> *Sir. And.* Wherefore, sweetheart? What's your metaphor?
> *Mar.* It's dry, sir.
> *Sir And.* Why, I think so. I am not such an ass but I can keep my hand dry. But what's your jest?
> *Mar.* A dry jest, sir.
> *Sir And.* Are you full of them?
> *Mar.* Ay, sir, I have them at my fingers' ends. Marry, now I let go your hand, I am barren.
>
> *(Exit)*

The only other occurrence of the word is in *All's Well That Ends Well*, when in the last act a disgruntled Parolles reaches the court of Rossillion (5.2.2–14) and addresses the clown, Master Lavatch:

> I have ere now, sir, been better known to you, when I have held familiarity with fresher clothes; but I am now, sir, muddied in Fortune's mood, and smell somewhat strong of her strong displeasure.
> *Clo.* Truly, Fortune's displeasure is but sluttish if it smell so strongly as thou speak'st of. I will henceforth eat no fish of Fortune's butt'ring. Prithee allow the wind.
> *Par.* Nay, you need not to stop your nose, sir; I spake but by a metaphor.
> *Clo.* Indeed, sir, if your metaphor stink, I will stop my nose, or against any man's metaphor. Prithee get thee further.

Maria's and Parolles's metaphors are translated into puns, and the insistence on buttery and buttering suggests a peculiar connection in Shakespeare's mind between the idea of metaphor and that of food and drink. This is confirmed by Touchstone, the court fool turned clown, when he wants to discourage William, the country bumpkin, from wooing Audrey (*As You Like It*, 5.1.35–46):

> *Touch.* You do love this maid?
> *Will.* I do, [sir].

> *Touch.* Give me your hand. Art thou learned?
> *Will.* No, sir.
> *Touch.* Then learn this of me: to have, is to have. For it is a figure in
> rhetoric that drink, being pour'd out of a cup into a glass, by
> filling the one doth empty the other. For all your writers do
> consent that *ipse* is he: now, you are not *ipse,* for I am he.
> *Will.* Which he, sir?
> *Touch.* He, sir, that must marry this woman.

The figure in rhetoric that Touchstone has in mind is metaphor, always
described as transport or translation, the wresting, according to Puttenham, of a word "from this owne right signification, to another not so
naturall, but yet of some affinitie or conveniencie with it," like wine poured
from a cup into a glass.

"Glasses, glasses is the only drinking," Falstaff had exclaimed (*2H4,*
2.1.143) in order to convince the Hostess to procure him money by pawn-
ing her plate. The newly produced glass drinking vessels were much
cheaper than pewter tankards or silver goblets. Metaphor is seen as a way
of transferring the same content from a richer to a poorer container, a
degradation, a cheapening. And the other rhetorical figures fare no better
in the plays. When Iago plays the fool to Desdemona in order to beguile
her anxiety for the delay in Othello's arrival in Cyprus, she comments (*Oth.,*
2.1.138–39): "These are old fond paradoxes to make fools laugh i' th'
alehouse."

Should we conclude from these quotations that Shakespeare's view of
rhetorical figures—apart from metaphor and paradox, hyperbole and
other "quirks of blazoning pens" receive no kinder treatment—is that they
are no more than signs of the drunkenness of language? The very reference to "old fond paradoxes" in *Othello* (a tragedy, not a comedy) should
warn us against accepting such hasty dismissal of rhetoric. In fact, as I have
tried to point out elsewhere, the structure itself of *Othello* is based on that
discredited figure—the old but by no means fond paradox that black is fair
and fair is foul, transposed onto the moral plane.

What I am suggesting is that, side by side with the humorous discredit
cast upon the pedantic rules of rhetoric set down by grammarians to
beautify speech, there is in Shakespeare the apprehension and practice of a
very different sort of rhetoric, as the art—not the artifice—of ordering
discourse for the purpose of producing consensus—consensus in the sympathy for Othello and Desdemona as well as in the repulsion (antipathy) for
Iago or Richard III. When Cleopatra tells Dolabella that Antony's

> face was as the heav'ns, and therein stuck
> A sun and moon, which kept their course, and lighted
> The little O, th' earth.
> . . . .
> His legs bestrid the ocean, his rear'd arm

Crested the world,
. . . .
                    realms and islands were
As plates dropp'd from his pocket
                                    (*Ant.*, 5.2.79–83, 91–92)

she is of course making an utterly unrestrained use of the figure of
hyperbole. But it would be wrong to accuse her of being a "hyperbolical
fiend"—the formula used by the clown in the habit of Sir Topas to exorcise
Malvolio driven to near insanity (*Twelfth Night*, 4.2.25). Cleopatra is simply
using the language that we had learned from the very beginning of the
tragedy, hearing about "The triple pillar of the world transform'd/Into a
strumpet's fool" (*Ant.*, 1.1.12–13). Hyperbole is the structural principle of
the tragedy of *Antony and Cleopatra,* it gives it a new dimension, well beyond
that of the private tragedy of mature love and even beyond the public
tragedy of the conflict of two civilizations and two worlds. The hyperbolical
framework of the play lifts it onto the realm of the absolute, where private
passions (love and hate) and public passions (cultural and power conflicts)
live in themselves and for themselves, in a sort of complete purity: "I am
fire and air; my other elements / I give to baser life" (*Ant.*, 5.2.289–90) is the
crowning hyperbole.

In other words, I believe that Shakespeare had discovered the power of
rhetorical figures as controlling factors in the structure of tragedy, able to
communicate a meaning beyond the meaning, so that each of his great
tragedies is shaped as an infinite extension of a basic figure. I have already
mentioned paradox for *Othello,* but before going any further in the definition of the leading tropes, let me state that this realization came to him only
when he reached full maturity as a dramatist. An example from *Romeo and
Juliet* can perhaps suggest how it came about. In the first scene Romeo is
raving in the conventional language of courtly love poetry about Rosaline
(*Rom.*, 1.1.176–82):

> O brawling love! O loving hate!
> O anything, of nothing first create!
> O heavy lightness, serious vanity,
> Misshapen chaos of well-seeming forms,
> Feather of lead, bright smoke, cold fire, sick health!
> Still-waking sleep, that is not what it is!
> This love feel I, that feel no love in this.

An impressive sequence of oxymora, providing a perfect example of rhetorical *ornatus,* the embellishment of speech. Then, in act 3, Juliet learns
that Romeo has killed her cousin Tybalt, and we know her reaction (3.2.73–
79):

> O serpent heart, hid with a flow'ring face!
> Did ever dragon keep so fair a cave?
> Beautiful tyrant! fiend angelical!

> Dove-feather'd raven! wolvish ravening lamb!
> Despised substance of divinest show!
> Just opposite to what thou justly seem'st,
> A damned saint, an honorable villain!

The two speeches appear exactly symmetrical, following identical rhetorical patterns, the triumph of the figure of oxymoron. But something very important has happened between the two: the author had discovered the true nature and function of oxymoron—not just a pleasing and surprising poetic ornament, but the most effective way of expressing a condition of extreme, passionate, insoluble, inner contradiction. I have used four adjectives to qualify the noun *contradiction.* This excess, I discover, was but an attempt to extend the semantic range of that word, to get to its essence, to give it an extra dimension. As in the case of hyperbole in respect to the whole tragedy of *Antony and Cleopatra,* here, in this single speech of Juliet, oxymoron is the means by which we are transported beyond the world of private or public passions into the absolute, where the notion of conflict is at its purest. No wonder that after this discovery oxymoron became the rhetorical framework for the most dialectical of Shakespeare's tragedies, *Hamlet.*

But it is not with *Hamlet* I want to deal now, or with the dominance of antithesis in *Macbeth* (it is only natural that the first three great tragedies should privilege figures of contrast, drama being the representation of conflict). I must go back to the theme of this section of the conference: "Shakespeare's metaphors." Shakespeare, from the moment the Chamberlain's Men in 1599 had decided to call their newly built playhouse the Globe, was reminded daily of the most splendid and pregnant of rhetorical tropes: that name—and one would like to think that Shakespeare himself was responsible for its choice—was in fact the most ambitious and triumphant of all metaphors for a man of the theater. The motto of the Globe, *Totus mundus agit histrionem,* could be freely rendered as "the theater is a metaphor for the world": this is what the statement "all the world plays the actor" amounts to. I shall not attempt to point out the nearly obsessive recurrence in Shakespeare's plays of the time-honored metaphor of the world as stage, most pedantically elaborated by Jaques in his famous speech in *As You Like It* (2.7.139ff.). Frequently the metaphor is implicit, acting directly on the mind, as Puttenham says of "the figures that we call sensable," by vivid visual presentations of what is in fact an abstract concept. The metaphoric function of the theater is implicit in the very beginning of one of the first plays presented in the new Globe in 1599, *Henry V,* when the prologue refers to the physical aspect of the playhouse, right in front of the eyes of the audience at the moment (prol. 11–14):

> Can this cockpit hold
> The vasty fields of France? Or may we cram
> Within this wooden O the very casques
> That did affright the air at Agincourt?

It is easy to see the transition from the metaphor of the "wooden O" for the new Globe—the theater as world—to Cleopatra's hyperbole I mentioned before, the face of Antony lighting "this little O, the earth." The prologue of *Henry V* expresses in the next few lines Shakespeare's conception of the real function of metaphor: comparing the collective O represented by actors and audience with a cipher, a "crooked figure," he says (17–18):

> let us, ciphers to this great accompt,
> On your imaginary forces work.

The appeal of the rhetorical figure is in its capacity to liberate in the audience their imaginary forces—that is, the ability to create vivid visual images. As Peacham said (sig.Bii*v*) defining metaphor, "First, we translate a word from the sences of the body to the thinges in the mind . . . when by any word which is proper to the sences, we signify something belonging to the mind, which translation is very vsuall & common, but chiefly from the sight which is the most principall and perfect sence."

The metaphor of the theater as world and of the world as theater finds its most powerful and explicit realization in *King Lear* (4.6.182–83):

> When we are born, we cry that we are come
> To this great stage of fools.

This is indeed the synthesis of the whole play of *Lear* in its outer and inner structure. *Lear* is Shakespeare's supreme tribute to the power of metaphor, and it is appropriate that the whole play should be deliberately constructed on that particular metaphor, and that we should be continually reminded throughout that the old legend of the king and his three daughters is to be understood not in its literary pseudo-historical sense as an ancient chronicle, but as projected into another dimension: a cosmic dimension. What is involved is much more than Lear's humanity, his personal drama, more even than humanity's condition on earth—it is a questioning of the order of nature itself. It is acknowledged that nature is the key word of the play, a word explored in all its meanings, as divine order, as social order, as unrestrained instinct, as mental derangement. It is through this exploration that the basic metaphor of the theater as world acquires the wider significance of the theater as a universe presenting a number of different levels of apprehension, so that the all-englobing central metaphor generates a number of other more specific and circumscribed metaphors.

In his recent book *Shakespeare's Universe of Discourse*, which explores the rhetorical structures of the comedies, Keir Elam observes that Shakespeare's poetics, in its pursuit of structural and rhetorical complexities, is governed by the spirit of what he calls baroque and I would rather define as mannerism. He goes on to state that "the pleasures of Shakespeare's eminently self-interrogating dramatic art are in this respect the same pleasures derived from the mirroring games of the visual and other art forms of the period," and refers to André Gide's notion derived from heraldry of the *mise en abîme*, when elements of the outer structure are placed within the central blazon of a coat of arms. I suggest that this is exactly the governing structural principle of *Lear*, taking the metaphor that we have been talking about as the outer structure. *Lear* is constructed as what used to be called a Chinese box—now one prefers Russian doll—of metaphors. By unscrewing the outer shell of the *matrioshka*, the theater-world metaphor, what is revealed is another englobing metaphor—the central storm, which stands for disorder not only in nature but more, in Lear's mind and, still more, in the social order. So when Gloucester, not yet blinded and therefore still conforming to the established values, is faced by the mad king with the request to share the offered shelter with poor Tom a' Bedlam—"I will keep still with my philosopher"—he delegates the solution of this unprecedented breach in etiquette to a menial, by ordering Kent, a mere servant, "Take him you on" (*Lr.*, 3.4.172–79). The disorder in nature and that in Lear's mind have disordered the social hierarchy in the eyes of a man who does not see that an earl (Kent) and the son of another earl (Edgar) are indeed fit company for a monarch.

The mention of Gloucester and Edgar leads to the next metaphorical layer. While most comedies are articulated into main plot and subplot—frequently the second reflecting the first at a different social level—*Lear* is the only tragedy in which Shakespeare has deliberately interwoven the historical events of Lear's reign with a parallel plot taken from the romance tradition. The structural function of the story of Gloucester and his two sons, out of *Arcadia*, is to provide a powerful visual representation of a further metaphorical construction: Gloucester's physical blindness, as we all know, is the counterpart—or shall I say, the retribution—of Lear's inability to see behind appearances, so that the blinding of Lear himself in Edward Bond's remake of the tragedy comes as a shock but hardly as a surprise. From Kent's "See better, Lear," in the first scene (1.1.158), to Gloucester's "I stumbled when I saw" (4.1.19), sight and blindness imagery represents the most extensive metaphorical field in the whole play. The one character who sees clearly is of course the Fool. With the Fool we come to the core of *Lear*, to the central blazon that picks up the essential elements from the outer structure—"we are come to this great stage of *fools*." The Fool is the projection in scenic terms of Lear's madness, which turns out to be, as in Erasmus's *Moriae Encomium* (The Praise of Folly), the supreme wisdom. The Fool is not only a metaphor for that wisdom: he is metaphor personified, the prosopopoeia of metaphor, the figure of a figure. This is the final *mise en abîme* of metaphor, where *en abîme* has, beyond its heraldic meaning, its original significance: going in depth, reaching the heart of the matter. By exploiting all possible degrees of a rhetorical figure, *Lear* reaches the ultimate goal of all art, the meaning beyond meaning.

The Syntax of Metaphor in Cymbeline

by ANN THOMPSON and JOHN O. THOMPSON

We have just completed a book called *Shakespeare, Meaning and Metaphor* in which we look at what happens when the findings of a number of recent discussions of metaphor in the fields of linguistics and philosophy are brought to bear on Shakespearean examples.[1] Something that surprised us when we were working on that project was the comparative neglect of Christine Brooke-Rose's book, *A Grammar of Metaphor*.[2] Because this was published in 1958 it was too early for inclusion in our study, which concentrates on work done in the last decade, but we decided that it would be valuable at some point to return to her text and try to use its categories and analytical method.

We were especially interested in the insistence, built into Brooke-Rose's project from the start, on the syntactic *variety* of metaphor—that is, on the number of different syntactic forms into which metaphorical meanings can be cast. A feature of nonliterary treatments of metaphor of the kind we consider in our book is their tendency (understandably, given the complexity of the problems metaphor raises) to discuss examples of maximal syntactic simplicity, such as "Man is a wolf" or "My love is a rose"—the later albeit sometimes daringly expanded to Burns's simile with reiterated "red." Against this, Brooke-Rose reminds us of all the other important possibilities.

She categorizes metaphors according to the kinds of words involved (nouns, verbs, and other parts of speech) and the grammatical links between them. This results in eight basic categories, each of which has a number of subdivisions.[3] Although she sees noun metaphors as the most significant and most complex type (five of her eight categories are types of noun metaphor), it is notable that she finds the straightforward copula link (as in "Man is a wolf") to be comparatively rare in poetic texts, apparently because it is too obvious, too categorical, or even didactic (p. 105).

To exemplify the various syntactic possibilities, Brooke-Rose presents examples drawn from fifteen British poets (ranging chronologically from Chaucer to Dylan Thomas) among whom Shakespeare naturally figures. Determining which poets are especially drawn to, and judging which poets

80

are especially good at, particular syntactic possibilities, becomes a central focus of Brooke-Rose's concern.

Writing well before the recent explosion of serious interest in metaphor, Brooke-Rose in surveying her predecessors found herself arguing for a linguistic approach to the problem as opposed to "the philosophical approach, which concerns itself with idea-content" (p. 3). One of her justifications for what she is doing is that idea-content approaches have tended to be mutually incompatible as well as being in one way or another unsuited to the discussion of what is specific to the literary imagination. On the other hand,

> Whatever the mental process involved in calling one thing by another name, the poet must use nouns, verbs, adverbs, adjectives and prepositions. . . . [T]here should be a way of cutting right across [idea-content] categories by considering the syntactic groups on which metaphor must, willy-nilly, be based. [Pp. 15–16]

Interesting poets will be resourceful in their varied employment of these syntactic patterns for metaphoric ends yet the patterns themselves will be ordinary enough, characteristic of nonmetaphoric as well as of metaphoric language, parts of everyday language. It is the metaphoric content that makes students of metaphor interested in these constructions.

But what if the poet is doing striking and unusual things with the syntax itself, independently of or at least over and above the creation and elaboration of metaphors? This is not an issue Brooke-Rose addresses directly, though it emerges in her acknowledgment of the extraordinary degree of syntactic complexity and syntactic experiment in Shakespeare, especially in his original and daring use of verbal metaphors (see pp. 234, 296). And if this is a feature of *Antony and Cleopatra,* the source of her examples, how much more significant is it in the late plays, whose syntactic complexities have have been widely recognized?

To explore the resources and limitations of Brooke-Rose's typology of metaphorical syntax in a context in which syntax itself becomes one of the principle means of "heightening" diction, we have chosen to look very closely at three passages from *Cymbeline.* Each happens to be spoken by Iachimo in the presence of Imogen, and to involve reference to eyes and sight, but these facts will not be central to our discussion. What we will be most concerned with will be the microlevel grammatical elaborateness, difficulty, perhaps finally indeterminacy, of the passages, and how their figurative aspects interact with their nonstandard syntax.

(I)   What are men mad? Hath Nature giuen them eyes
               To see this vaulted Arch, and the rich Crop
               Of Sea and Land, which can distinguish 'twixt
               The firie Orbes aboue, and the twinn'd Stones
               Vpon the number'd Beach, and can we not

Partition make with Spectacles so pretious
Twixt faire, and foule?

[F, 628–34][4]

What, are men mad? Hath nature given them eyes
To see this vaulted arch and the rich crop
Of sea and land, which can distinguish 'twixt
The fiery orbs above, and the twinn'd stones
Upon the number'd beach, and can we not
Partition make with spectacles so precious
'Twixt fair and foul?

[1.6.32–38][5]

There are four chief syntactic puzzles in this passage:

1. How is it that the pronoun shifts from "them" (l. 628) to "we" (l. 632)? This shift accompanies a movement with respect to agenthood within the sentence. At the outset, the agent, and grammatical subject, is nature, personified. Human beings are recipients of nature's gift. Next it is the gift itself, the eyes, that become agents and do the distinguishing. Finally, it is "we" human beings who are the agents and grammatical subjects: it is we who "partition make."

2. The most natural way of reading the clause in which "'twixt" appears is, "[eyes] which can distinguish the fiery orbs above from the twinned stones upon the numbered beach." Editors have firmly insisted, however, that what the eyes are doing is distinguishing one fiery orb from another and one stone from another. It is hard to make the syntax do this, just as it would be hard to hear "Jack can distinguish between the stars and the pebbles" as meaning "Jack can distinguish star from star and pebble from pebble."[6]

3. The participial adjectives "twinn'd" and "number'd" are not transparently meaningful, especially not the latter. Their apparent morphological similarity needs to be discounted in interpretation as "twinn'd" turns out to mean "as alike in twins" while "number'd" turns out to mean "able to be numbered."[7]

4. "Spectacles" causes difficulty. If it means "eyes" (or "organs of vision" characterized as "precious"), the syntax is fairly straightforward; "Can we not with our eyes distinguish ["make partition"] between fair and foul?" The problem with this is that the metonymy whereby an aid to sight is used to stand for the eye itself seems deviant. If on the other hand "spectacles" are things to be looked *at* (including precious things such as Imogen), we gain an easier sense for the word at the expense of a more difficult syntax. In order to make this reading acceptable, "with" must have the syntactic

fluidity of "given," whereas in Shakespeare's actual sentence, "with" is hard to detach from the strong gravitational field of the preceding "make" ("Partition make"—how? Make *with* spectacles. . . .) And it is very hard to understand how the spectacles themselves can be the instrument we use to make distinctions between fair and foul spectacles. So, if "spectacles" are to mean "things to look at," "with" *must* be understood as having the force of "given" and as being detached from "make." Punctuation—representing, of course, intonation and pause phenomena in the language as spoken on stage—can just about be deployed so as to support such a reading:

> and can we not
> Partition make, with spectacles so precious,
> 'Twixt fair and foul?

Then the problem becomes the nonpreciousness of the most recently mentioned spectacles, the pebbles on the beach. But the deixis of "so precious" *could*—as uttered on stage with some gestural accompaniment—be directed toward Imogen herself as though, in purely verbal terms, we were to understand the phrase as meaning "with spectacles as precious as you, Imogen, are."

With this outline of the passage's syntactic difficulties in mind, let us turn to the grammar of its metaphors. What strikes one, at first sight, is that there is not a great deal to say.

"This vaulted arch" is, in Christine Brooke-Rose's terms, a Simple Replacement metaphor: "the proper term [i.e., "sky"] is not mentioned and so must be guessed; we either have to know the code or the code must be broken" (p. 26). If "sky" *had* been mentioned earlier, we would have what she calls a Pointing Formula, which "consists in speaking of one thing, and later pointing to it with a replacing name" (p. 69). Arguably, a gesture by Iachimo upwards (especially in a roofless theater) would have the same overall effect as an actual mention of "sky"; without such a gesture, the interpretation of the "vaulted" arch as metaphorical must depend on the auditors either "knowing the code" instantly (that is, they must be familiar with the metaphorical applications of these terms to the sky)[8] or working back from "sea and land" to the likelihood that Iachimo has in mind a broader entity than a literal arch.

"Crop of sea and land" is more interesting. It is an example of Brooke-Rose's Genitive Link, and in fact illustrates rather well a distinction she makes within that category between "the three-term formula" and "the two-term formula." In the three-term formula, we hear "the x of the y" but understand "the z of the y": this is "essentially a replacing relationship, and has this in common with Simple Replacement, that the metaphor has to be fairly self-evident" (p. 150). The appropriate question to ask about "crop of sea and land" would then be, "What is to be understood by 'crop'?" The answer to this question was not self-evident to Warburton, Coleridge, and Collier, who preferred to read "cope":[9] the "rich cope of sea and land" is the covering of sea and land, namely the sky again (so the phrase would be in apposition with "this vaulted arch"). Those who prefer to read "crop" need to come up with a relevant (and self-evident) entity that "crop of sea and land" could express. Or do they? Brooke-Rose describes the two-term formula—"of in its least logical and most ambiguous usage"—as involving the interpretation of "the x of y" to mean virtually "$x = y$" ("the fire of love," for example, means virtually the same as "the fire which is love"). On this reading the "crop" would simply *be* the sea and land. In what sense are they a crop? Vaughan paraphrases "the rich harvest which the eye gathers in, consisting of sea and land."[10] This gives the eyes another action to perform, that of harvesting. A three-term formula reading would be only slightly different, involving, presumably, taking everything that can be seen on or in the sea or land *as* a "crop," deliberately grown and valuable, as grain or hay is. The implied harvester of this more plural crop is still, however, the eyes.

And that is the sum total for metaphor proper, apart from the utterly straightforward personification of nature and, just possibly, a metaphorical as well as a metonymic element in the "spectacles = eyes" equation, if one does take spectacles to be eyes here. The latter would be another example of Pointing Formula, with the pointing back to eyes being done by the phrase "so pretious."

Yet the overall effect of these lines is more metaphorical than such an enumeration would suggest. In fact, the small-scale metaphorical effects that a Brooke-Rose-level count picks up are here subordinated to a larger overlapping of semantic fields that only the sentence as a whole gives us access to.

The broad metaphor that underlies Iachimo's speech might be characterized, in a Lakoff-and-Johnson manner, as JUDGING IS SEEING.[11] The first half of the elaborate rhetorical question advances the unchallengeable proposition that men can see; by the second half this is taken to imply that (*unless* they are mad) they must be able to judge. To make this argument feel valid, the donor conceptual field[12] of sight is characterized in ways that already highlight, as proto-judgmental, the perception of *distinctions*.

Is it overly ingenious to find in the syntactic elaboration and misdirection a way of slowing the hearer down, postponing (perhaps indefinitely) the moment in which the judgmental quality of sight becomes perfectly clear? The work the hearer has to do in "solving" the arch and crop metaphor then becomes just part of a wider cognitive labor: sky, sea, and land (and *their* "crops"?), stars and stones are each presented with a little heightening (a little "difficulty"), and their relationships not only with one another but with the eyes (as harvesters, as distinguishing " 'twixt") are also kept non-transparent. In keeping with the spirit of this puzzle-quality it hardly matters just which "solutions" to the more puzzling verbal moments one ends up favoring; for instance, the metonymic-metaphoric reading of "spectacles" and the literal one with the difficult syntax each reiterate a different element already presented in the overall configuration previously built up (either eyes or—as implicit next term in the things-seen series— Imogen). Of course, the configuration is sufficiently determinate overall to eliminate any number of nonpertinent readings, such as taking "partition" to be a physical object or "arch" to be a literal one.

(II)   the Flame o'th'Taper
              Bowes toward her, and would vnder-peepe her lids.
              To see th'inclosed Lights, now Canopied
              Vnder these windowes, White and Azure lac'd
              With Blew of Heauens owne tinct.

                                                    [F, 926–30]

                          The flame o'th' taper
              Bows toward her, and would under-peep her lids,
              To see th' enclosed lights, now canopied
              Under these windows, white and azure lac'd
              With blue of heaven's own tinct.

                                                    [2.2.19–23]

Reversing our order of exposition, let us look first at the metaphors in the passage, before considering syntactic difficulties as such.

1. Personification of the flame is effected by the verb metaphors "bows" and "would under-peep" along the lines sketched by Brooke-Rose in her chapter "The Verb" (see especially p. 212). Whether "To see" is part of the same set will need to be discussed below.

2. "Lights" ("enclosed") is a Simple Replacement metaphor, where "lights" are to be understood as "eyes."

3. "Windows" is an example of a Pointing Formula, namely the Demonstrative, since "these" sends us back to an earlier noun—presumably "lids."

4. "Canopied" would also be classed by Brooke-Rose as a Pointing Formula, in this case Parallelism: "canopied" is parallel to the (literal) "enclosed."

5. While Brooke-Rose wants to make a firm distinction between simile and metaphor (see, for example, p. 14), the unnaturalness of that distinction could be argued for on the basis of such cases as "blue of heaven's own tinct," which can be simile, hyperbole, or metaphor, depending on the precise relationship one takes to obtain between the blue of veins (or eyes? see below) and the blue of the sky.

Word-by-word, then, it does not seem difficult to make the metaphoric substitutions required, or to assign each case to an appropriate Brooke-Rose pigeonhole. However, the syntax of the passage raises two difficulties that such an exercise in classification fails to highlight.

Let us look first at the last three lines of the passage. The problem here is the apparent awkwardness and repetitiveness of "white and azure laced with blue. . . ." Something is being described, it would seem, as white and blue laced with blue. What is that something, and how exactly are white, azure, and blue distributed in it?

In many ways the most straightforward answer is to say that it is "these windows" that are white and blue, and that "these windows" are Imogen's eyelids. On the latter point, while Nosworthy, the Arden editor, is not strictly correct in saying that "windows" regularly means "eyelids" rather than "eyes" elsewhere in Shakespeare,[13] the preposition "under" does seem to fix the meaning of "windows" fairly firmly (though "canopied" might reopen this question; see below). But do we want *all* of "white and azure laced With blue of heaven's own tinct" to refer to the eyelid? Malone thought not, arguing that "the poet would not have given so particular a description" of eyelids; he wanted the "windows" (= eyelids) to be white and azure, but the "lights" (= the eyes themselves) to be sky-blue.[14] A comma after "azure" will help such a reading along, but the problem with it is the greater appropriateness of "laced" to a network of veins than to the pupil-iris picture.

Capell, on the other hand, while similarly skeptical about the expression's referring simply to eyelids, moved in another direction: "there is much more propriety in applying these words to all the visible parts of the lady, pronouncing them rapturously. . . ."[15] Such a reading would virtually need a period after "windows"; curiously, given its failure to be adopted by any other editor, it is consonant with a passage later in the play, where Shakespeare again uses "azure" in a similar context when Arviragus promises the supposedly dead Imogen

> thou shalt not lacke
> The flower that's like thy face. Pale-Primrose, nor
> The azur'd Harebell, like thy Veines;
> [F, 2530–32, Riverside 4.2.220–22)]

Here the veins in question are clearly not confined to the eyelid. However, the editorial consensus has been that the words succeeding "windows" all refer to Imogen's eyelids. Can they be saved from redundancy? J. C. Maxwell's solution in The New Shakespeare is syntactically elegant: he reads "white and azure-laced With blue of heaven's own tinct"; now it is the blue of the azure-lacing that is heavenly.[16] A different solution was proposed by Hudson, who asks us to see "laced with blue" in apposition to "white and azure," both phrases modifying "windows" independently (and reiteratively). Finally, we should mention a bravura attempt to save the passage for realism by Knight, who held that "white and azure" is an exact description of the *general* tint of "the eyelid of an extremely fair young woman," and that it is this overall coloration that is "laced with blue," i.e., "marked with the deeper blue of the larger veins."[17]

Clearly the syntax allows for a number of readings. But each of the readings discussed so far is compatible with the word-order as we have it. For an example of an interpretation that is prepared to move beyond any syntactic construal we can think of, one can go to Nosworthy's Arden note. After stating that the "windows" are the eyelids and the "lights" are the eyes, he writes:

> "Lights" canopied with heaven's blue suggests a secondary strand of cosmic imagery, the lights in Imogen's eyes, though now enclosed yet resembling the sun in the firmament.[18]

And he adduces a passage from *Hamlet* in which "canopy" does mean firmament (2.2.229–301). Earlier he has written

> The complete image is, I think, of windows with shutters closed and curtains drawn ("canopied")—not a very exact analogy for eyelid and eye, but one which effectively conveys the *deepness* of Imogen's sleep.

The "inexactness" here is a question of what the canopy is: we have two tenor terms (eyelid, eye) but three vehicle terms (window, canopy, light). Whatever solution one finds for this puzzle, however,[19] the whole of this "complete image" needs to be jettisoned by Nosworthy when it comes to his "secondary strand." Suddenly the canopy is the sky and Imogen's lights are the sun. No longer are the eyes canopied *under* anything, if they are to be canopied *with* blue of heaven's own tinct. This "secondary strand" can be brought into being by effectively omitting line 929, or at least suspending it:

> To see th' inclosed Lights, now Canopied—
> Under these windowes, White and Azure lac'd—
> With Blew of Heaven's owne tinct.

One difficulty with this is that "now" obstinately reminds us that Imogen's eyes are currently *not* visible as suns in the blue sky. Anyway, how would they look if they were? *What* is blue? If the eyes, then we have blue on blue. Or is it that looking at her eyes covered by the *exterior* blue of the eyelids is, supposing you were in there "under-peeping," like looking at something bright against the *interior* surface, which is the dome of the sky? An impossible point-of-view shot, indeed, and an example of how proponents of "imagery" sometimes come up with the most impossible-to-image sort of examples. In this case, arguments from the metaphorical structure of the lines and from their syntax join to leave the "cosmic imagery" looking difficult to justify.[20]

The other major syntactic difficulty in the passage revolves around the Folio punctuation, whereby a period after "lids" implies a new sentence beginning with "To see." Virtually all editors have omitted this period (usually changing it to a comma) to allow the sense to run on. Thus emended, the "flame o'th' taper" remains the subject of the sentence: it not only "Bows toward her" but "would under-peep her lids To see th' enclosed lights." (If this reading is intended we would not normally expect any punctuation at all between "lids" and "To," but despite general agreement that run-on lines are very frequent in late Shakespearean verse, only one modern editor leaves the end of the line unpunctuated.)

But is it true that F's period is syntactically impossible or unacceptable? It could be retained if we suppose that Iachimo has stopped talking about the taper and is moved by Imogen's beauty to a more general exclamation that could be paraphrased "Oh that I might see . . ." or "How wonderful it would be to see th' enclosed lights!" Such a reading could be supported by the generally exclamatory and syntactically elliptical nature of the speech as a whole, as exemplified by the lines before our passage:

> *Cytherea,*
> How brauely thou becom'st thy Bed; fresh Lilly,
> And whiter than the Sheetes: that I might touch,
> But kisse, one kisse.
>
> [F, 921–24]

> Cytherea,
> How bravely thou becom'st thy bed! fresh lily,
> And whiter than the sheets! That I might touch!
> But kiss, one kiss!
>
> [2.2.14–17]

How does puzzling over these constructions enrich our grasp of the functioning of the passage's metaphors? It is surprising how little it matters whether it is the flame or Iachimo who would "see th' enclosed lights"— surprising at least until we remember that the personified flame is a stand-in for Iachimo anyway: the obvious reason for the speaker to ascribe this desire to see to the flame figuratively is that he desires to see literally. Difficulty with just what is blue and white in the eye-vein-skin realm seems more worrying, once the different possibilities are laid out; before that point, the possible construals of the lines—and perhaps some impossible ones—might each individually "work," in the sense of being consonant with the expression of the sleeping Imogen's beauty. After losing our "syntactic innocence" by confronting the range of readings and the difficulties with each, one may be left feeling that the effect of the indeterminacy is to allow the mind to range through the potential of the relevant semantic fields without that evocative process being granted a secure concluding (and conclusive) outcome. Herein may lie the passage's greatest power. The syntactic resources that a Brooke-Rose analysis would pinpoint are among the straightforward, stable components of the passage's grammar; more of the metaphors' potential for evocation is released by a different sort of syntactic play, on (or over) the border of grammatical deviance.

(III)   Had I this cheeke
        To bathe my lips vpon: this hand, whose touch,
        (Whose euery touch) would force the Feelers soule
        To th' oath of loyalty. This object, which
        Takes prisoner the wild motion of mine eye,
        Fiering it onely heere, should I (damn'd then)
        Slauuer with lippes as common as the stayres
        That mount the Capitoll: Ioyne gripes, with hands
        Made hard with hourely falshood (falshood as
        With labour:) then by peeping in an eye
        Base and illustrious as the smoakie light
        That's fed with stinking Tallow: it were fit
        That all the plagues of Hell should at one time
        Encounter such reuolt.
                                                        [F, 711–24]

                                        Had I this cheek,
        To bathe my lips upon; this hand, whose touch
        (Whose every touch) would force the feeler's soul
        To th' oath of loyalty; this object, which
        Takes prisoner the wild motion of mine eye,
        Firing it only here; should I (damn'd then)
        Slaver with lips as common as the stairs
        That mount the Capitol; join gripes with hands
        Made hard with hourly falsehood (falsehood, as
        With labor); then by-peeping in an eye
        Base and illustrious as the smoky light
        That's fed with stinking tallow: it were fit
        That all the plagues of hell should at one time
        Encounter such revolt.
                                                        [1.6.99–112]

The overall structure of the speech is elaborately conditional. Iachimo is saying "If I had this, but then did that, I would deserve to be damned." He imagines himself as Posthumus, so the "this" which he imagines possessing is Imogen and the "that" which he imagines doing (and implies Posthumus is in fact doing) is an act of sexual betrayal or infidelity. Imogen and the act of betrayal are both presented in three aspects. The underlying argument therefore involves setting out and perhaps coordinating in some way the Imogen aspects ("Had I a, b, and c . . .") and the betrayal aspects (". . . and yet did x, y, and z . . ."). This might have been done straightforwardly.

Instead, Shakespeare makes the speech harder to grasp in at least four ways:

1. The first two Imogen aspects are "cheek" and "hand" that Iachimo imagines kissing ("bathe my lips upon") and touching. These coordinate nicely with the first two betrayal aspects, unfaithful kissing ("slavering") and the more robust grip of hands so promiscuous as to have hardened. But the third aspect in each series is more problematic. In Imogen's case, "this cheek" and "this hand" are followed by "this object": what object is in question? Furness suggests "Imogen herself, with cheek and hands"; this would make the sequence odd in moving from parts to a whole. If one shifts attention to the mode of action implied on the part of Iachimo/Posthumus, "object" is clearly an object of vision: it captures the eye. And the third aspect of betrayal certainly involves vision too ("peeping," "eye"). But *how* it does exactly is hard to say because "by peeping" is a textual crux (more on this below). In both sequences, then, the third item is harder to pin down than the first two, though for different reasons.

2. The speech contains, in F, three parentheses. These are preserved in most subsequent editions, though some modern editors use dashes rather than brackets to mark off the words in question. The proliferation of parentheses in F may or may not relate to the distinctive style of the scribe, Ralph Crane;[21] it certainly seems called for by the complex and frequently clotted syntax favored by Shakespeare at this period. Many speeches in *Cymbeline* could be cited for comparison, perhaps the most obvious being the tortuous opening lines of Iachimo's confession in the final scene:

> Vpon a time, vnhappy was the clocke
> That strooke the houre; it was in Rome, accurst
> The Mansion where: 'twas at a Feast, oh would
> Our Viands had bin poyson'd (or at least
> Those which I heau'd to head:) the good Posthumus,
> (What should I say? he was too good to be
> Where ill men were, and was the best of all
> Among'st the rar'st of good ones) . . .
>   [TLN 3432–39, Riverside 5.5.153–60]

After some fifteen lines of this the king understandably gets impatient ("I stand on fire: / Come to the matter"). In the earlier scene Imogen is equally irritated by Iachimo's way of speaking, asking him to "Deliver with more openness [his] answers" and encouraging him to "discover" plainly "What both you spur and stop."[22]

These three parentheses in the speech under consideration are progressively more curious. The first, "(Whose every touch)," is simply a case of heightening by repetition. The second, "(damn'd then)," is more complex, both because it is elliptical—one might expand it to something like "I would be damned if I were to do this"—and because it is a sort of flash-forward to the still-distant end of the sentence, with its "plagues of Hell." It is so positioned as to mark the shift from the Imogen aspects to the betrayal aspects, but only after we understand that the topic has shifted to betrayal are we in a position to grasp the relevance of the parenthesis. The third, "(falsehood as With labour)", combines repetition, ellipsis, enjambement, and simile. The simile may seem strange in that labor seems so much worthier a thing than falsehood—but would it have seemed so to Shakespeare? (It was a Victorian commentator, Staunton, who suggested we should emend to "(falsehood, *not* With labour)," thus saving the work ethic from dishonor.) This is to assume of course that the ellipsis is to be read as meaning "as hardened by hourly falsehood as they might have been by labour"; it could also be taken to mean "as hardened by hourly falsehood as they also are by labour," thus suggesting that Posthumus is having an affair in Rome with a woman of low social status. On the latter reading, the parenthesis is literal, except to the degree that for falsehood to harden anything (hands as much as hearts) is, strictly speaking, metaphorical. However, the context of "joining gripes" implies that the hands could literally have become hardened by the number of times they have been clasped; this would not be metaphor but hyperbole.

3. The Imogen-aspects series is syntactically coherent, though the clause structure varies: a cheek "to bathe . . . lips upon," a hand "whose touch . . . would force . . . loyalty," an object "which takes prisoner" the eye's motion. But the betrayal-aspects series is syntactically incoherent without emendation: "should I . . . slaver" and "[should I] . . . join gripes" are fine, but there is nothing for "should I" to attach itself to in the third instance. A workable emendation was proposed by Dr. Johnson, who read "then *lie* peeping in an eye." Without any emendation one could deliver the speech as if the final "should I" clause is prepared for but then omitted by Iachimo, whether euphemistically or under the pressure of his (supposed) emotion. Modern editors, perhaps puzzlingly, have tended to prefer a middle course between these extremes that involves printing a hyphenated "by-peeping" as a nonce compound meaning something like "peeping sidelong, or clandestinely" (Nosworthy); but this, while it may be semantically attractive,[23] is no better than Collier's delirious "bo-peeping" at fending off the essential syntactic problem presented by the original. Furness is splendidly unconcerned about this: "as for rejecting a participle because it is preceded by two verbs in the subjunctive, it seems to me too late a week to demand a strict sequence in tenses from Shakespeare,—a chartered libertine in a grammar which he helped us to form."

4. How far is the figurative elaboration of the two series consonant with their coordination? Nosworthy writes, "This speech is less difficult than it appears . . . [it] presents three things—lips, hands, and sight—in a contrasted pattern." This is true, but if the basic contrast (between Imogen and

the experience of being faithful to her on the one hand, and the nameless Other Woman and the experience of betraying Imogen with her on the other) is unmistakable, the "pattern" has a number of peculiarities in detail.

Let us call the two positions involved in both parts of the conditional construction Lover and Partner. In both series the Lover is, as we have already said, Iachimo putting himself in the place of Posthumus. The Partner is first Imogen and then the Other Woman. The question can now be posed: *whose* lips, hands, and sight are in question, precisely, in the two series?

The answer is most straightforward where the hands are concerned. The Partner (Imogen) touches and the Lover is touched. By contrast in the second series, the Lover and the Partner (the Other Woman) "join gripes" mutually. Some sort of courtliness ("th' oath of loyalty") is correspondingly contrasted with "labour" and calloused hands.

Something similar happens with lips. In the first series, the Lover apparently plants his kiss on the Partner's (Imogen's) cheek. In the second series, Lover's lip and Partner's lip come together indifferently—so much so that "slavering with lips" as a whole phrase (slavering being something the Lover does with his own lips) vies with "slavering with [common] lips" (the Lover slavers but the lips he imposes this behavior on are those of the Partner). In other words, the ambiguity of "with" here leaves the lips unassigned as between Lover and Partner. This might seem an appropriate sort of confusion with which to represent promiscuity. However, a parallel semantic puzzle occurs in the "lips" clause in the first series, centered on "bathe." One normally bathes *in* some liquid. What is it to bathe something *upon* something else? Lips are moist while cheeks are dry, so how can Imogen's cheek be a bath for the Lover's lips? The phrase seems to conflate the notion of simply *placing* one's lips upon a cheek with the metaphorical sense of *luxuriating* in a pleasurable environment and the suggestion that to kiss Imogen would be to *cleanse* one's lips.

Finally, and deflatingly, there is an (unintended?) flash-forward to the idea of slavering in the second series, where cheeks (the Partner's cheeks) are being bathed in saliva.

As for eyes, not only the "by peeping" crux but another textual variant, F2's "fixing" for "firing" in line 716,[24] makes a fully detailed discussion impossible here. What we can establish is that again an initially clear demarcation bet· veen Lover and Partner in the first series (the Lover's eye is immobilized by the sight of the Partner) gives way to a scenario in which, while the Lover's eye peeps or by-peeps, it does so into the Partner's eye, and it is the latter that is derogatively characterized by means of the smoky candle metaphor.

In the midst of all this grammatical tension, the grammar of the metaphors, in Brooke-Rose's sense, is again surprisingly straightforward. One could go through the passage giving bits of the text their appropriate labels. "Takes prisoner" is a verbal metaphor with an auxiliary. "Firing" is another verbal metaphor (though "fixing" would be virtually literal), and so is "bathe." The more striking figurative moments are in fact similes: lips like stairs, an eye like a candle; Brooke-Rose banishes similes from her discussion for the unusual reason that their syntax is after all virtually uniform: "my own approach excludes comparisons on the ground that they do not present any syntactic problems" (p.14). Here, as in our example II, the similes seem effective—just as do the verbal metaphors—precisely *because* uniform: they provide the element of predictability, the anchorage for the listener or reader, which other aspects of pattern-making and pattern-breaking in the passage rest on.

In the first passage, a Brooke-Rose category, her Genitive Link, did serve as an entry-point to a syntactically problematic moment. In the second and third passages, the grammar of the metaphors, taken as specific *points* in the text, seems bland (albeit essential to the text's functioning) in comparison with the elaborate and difficult aspects of the grammar taken on the basis of a sentence or a whole speech. The necessary extension of Brooke-Rose's work thus seems to involve finding ways of describing how metaphorical moments that are not in themselves syntactically remarkable can be put into more exciting play by the more remarkable syntax that surrounds them.

We conclude with a clear example of this from our final passage. Simile, in Brooke-Rose's account, is inherently syntactically bland. A simile in which the point of comparison is made limited and explicit is, it could be argued, semantically bland as well.[25] "Lips as common as the stairs that mount the Capitol" is such a simile. Why is it, in context, not flat? Because the syntax, setting up the two series with three members in each, allows "stairs" to appear to us in the light of and in contrast to Imogen's cheek. We are led cognitively to explore the idea of "stairs" more fully than we would be incited to by the simile on its own. In particular, we may reflect that the surface of the Capitol stairs is not something it would be cleansing to kiss.

Appendix

From Christine Brooke-Rose, *A Grammar of Metaphor* (London: Secker and Warburg, 1958)

Christine Brooke-Rose defines metaphor as "any replacement of one word by another, or any identification of one thing, concept or person with any other" (pp. 23–24). She categorizes metaphors according to the kinds of words involved (nouns, verbs, and other parts of speech) and the grammatical links between them. Her eight basic categories are as follows, exemplified from *Antony and Cleopatra*, one of her fifteen key texts:

Noun Metaphors (pp. 24–25)

1. Simple Replacement. The proper term A is replaced altogether by the metaphor B, without being mentioned at all.

> *These strong Egyptian fetters* I must break.   1.1.116

> *Our Lamp* is spent, it's out.   4.15.85

2. The Pointing Formulae. The proper term A is mentioned, then replaced by the metaphor B with some demonstrative expression pointing back to the proper term (A . . . that B).

> 'tis his schoolmaster,
> An argument that he is pluck'd, when hither
> He sends *so poor a pinion of his wing*.   3.12.2–4

> Antony is dead.
> The breaking of *so great a thing* should make
> A greater crack.   5.1.13–15

3. The Copula. A direct statement that A is B. This includes weaker forms whereby A seems / is called / becomes B.

> Octavia is
> A blessed *lottery* to him.   2.2.241–42

> We cannot call her *winds* and *waters*
> sighs and tears.   1.2.147–48

4. The link with "To Make." A direct statement involving a third party: C makes A into B.

> It much would please him,
> That of his fortunes you should make a *staff*
> To lean upon.   3.13.67–69

> Make not your thoughts your *prisons*.   5.2.185

5. The Genitive. The noun metaphor is linked sometimes to its proper term, and sometimes to a third term that gives the provenance of the metaphoric term: B is part of, or derives from, or belongs to, or is found in C, from which relationship we can guess A.

The greater *cantle* of the world is lost.   3.10.6

From my cold heart let heaven engender *hail*.   3.13.159

Verb Metaphors (p. 206)

6. Verb metaphors are less explicit than noun metaphors. With the noun, A is called B, more or less clearly according to the kind of link. But the verb changes one noun into another by implication. And it does not explicitly "replace" another action.

Authority *melts* from me.   3.13.90

Now I must . . . *dodge*
And *palter* in the shifts of lowness, who
With half the bulk o'th' world *play'd* as I pleas'd.   3.11.61–64

Auxiliary Words and Phrases (p. 238)

7. Other parts of speech—adjectives, adverbs, pronouns, possessive adjectives, and prepositions—are weaker in their metaphoric use than nouns and verbs.

My salad days
When I was *green* in judgement.   1.5.73–74

Hark, the drums
Demurely wake the sleepers.   4.9.29–30

The Verb Added to the Noun (p. 265)

8. Cumulative metaphor as a whole is beyond the scope of this analysis, but some of the effects of adding a metaphoric verb to a metaphoric noun are discussed.

O, *wither'd* is the *garland* of the war.   4.15.64

and to *knit* your hearts
With an unslipping *knot,*   2.2.125–26

Notes

1. Harvester Press, Brighton, 1987.
2. London: Secker and Warburg, 1958.
3. See Appendix.

4. The First Folio of 1623 is the only authoritative text of *Cymbeline*. Through line numbers are from Charlton Hinman, ed., *The First Folio of Shakespeare: The Norton Facsimile* (New York: Paul Hamlyn, 1968).

5. We quote the modernized text here and throughout our discussion from G. Blakemore Evans, ed., *The Riverside Shakespeare* (Boston: Houghton Mifflin, 1974). Other modern editions will be cited where relevant.

6. A modern speaker might express the latter meaning by saying "Jack can distinguish *among* the stars and the pebbles," but Shakespeare never uses "distinguish" with "among" in this way.

7. For the particular use of the passive participle exemplified by this meaning of "number'd," see E. A. Abbott, *A Shakespearian Grammar*, (London: Macmillan, 1872), par. 375.

8. Shakespeare uses "vault" or "vaulty" to refer to the sky in *King John* (5.2.52), *2 Henry IV* (2.3.19), *Romeo and Juliet* (3.5.22) and *Tempest* (5.1.43). He does not use "arch" to refer to the sky elsewhere.

9. These editors and commentators are quoted by Horace Howard Furness, ed., in the Variorum *Cymbeline* (Philadelphia: Lippincott, 1913), 80.

10. Ibid.

11. See George Lakoff and Mark Johnson, *Metaphors We Live By*, (Chicago: University of Chicago Press, 1980). In this seminal work on everyday, inescapable metaphoricity, Lakoff and Johnson use this method of presenting conceptual metaphors that can underlie a wide range of verbal expressions.

12. "Donor conceptual field" and "recipient conceptual field" are the equivalents of "vehicle" and "tenor," respectively when metaphor is discussed within semantic field theory. See Eva Kittay and Adrienne Lehrer, "Semantic Fields and the Structure of Metaphor," *Studies in Language* 5 (1981): 31–63. We discuss the work of Kittay and Lehrer, as well as that of Lakoff and Johnson, in our book (see n. 1).

13. See James Nosworthy, ed., The Arden *Cymbeline*, (London: Methuen, 1955), 50. "Windows" does mean "eyelids" in *Richard III* (5.3.116) and in *Antony and Cleopatra* (5.2.316), but not in *Love's Labor's Lost* (5.2.838) or in Sonnet 24: in both the latter contexts it means "eye" or "eyes."

14. See the Variorum *Cymbeline* (as cited in n. 9), p. 116.

15. Ibid.

16. See J. C. Maxwell, ed., the New Shakespeare *Cymbeline* (Cambridge: Cambridge University Press, 1968). This reading is discussed in a note on p.156.

17. Hudson and Knight are both quoted in the Variorum *Cymbeline* (as cited in no. 9), 116–17.

18. The Arden *Cymbeline* (as cited in no. 13), 50.

19. It is tempting to introduce "eyelashes" as a third tenor term, metaphorically represented by "canopy." Lucrece's eyes are "canopied in darkness" in *The Rape of Lucrece* (398), but the "canopy" there might be simply the darkness itself rather than the eyelids or eyelashes. Eyelashes are however called "fringes" in *Pericles* (3.2.100), and lids and lashes together are called "fringed curtains" in *Tempest* (1.2.409).

20. We discuss the problems and limitations of "imagery" in chap. 5 of our book (see n. 1).

21. See editors' discussions of this possibility in the Arden, xii–xiii, the New Shakespeare, 126, and the Riverside, 1561.

22. It is arguable that Iachimo's style is appropriate both here and in the last scene: the parentheses increase the dramatic tension by both creating and frustrating expectation. This is less likely in Posthumus's equally parenthesis-strewn description of the heroic deeds of Belarius, Guiderius, and Arviragus in 5.3, though Nosworthy claims that "excitement and indignation render him incoherent" (Arden, 149). Some valuable general comments on the style of *Cymbeline* can be found in F. C. Tinkler, "*Cymbeline*," *Scrutiny* 7 (1938–39): 5–19; James Sutherland, "The Language of the Last Plays," *More Talking of Shakespeare*, ed. John Garrett

(London: Longmans, 1959), 144–58; and Roger Warren, "Theatrical Virtuosity and Poetic Complexity in *Cymbeline*," *Shakespeare Survey* 29 (1976): 41–49.

23. Or is it? "By-peeping" implies a more distant physical relationship than that already established by the earlier verbs in the series. Having kissed and held hands with his low mistress, why should the lover need to glance at her thus furtively? "Lie" would carry the sequence further to more effect.

24. Maxwell adopts F2's "fixing" in The New Shakespeare and discusses this reading in a note on pp. 150–51.

25. It has frequently been pointed out in recent discussion of simile that this figure raises the same conceptual problems as metaphor (and hence cannot serve as a good basis for "explaining" metaphor); although all similes are literally true while most metaphors are literally false, there is a comparable open-endedness to the range of similarities that both figures invite us to consider. Compare simile with any literal statement of likeness, and simile's metaphorical nature becomes apparent. However, in this case the ground of likeness is so tightly specified that the figure threatens to collapse into precisely a literal likeness statement; her lips are like stairs simply because both are much used.

Holding Forth and Holding Back: Operation Modes of the Dramatist's Imagination

by J.-M. MAGUIN

Ephemerality is an essential feature of the dramatic transaction and is perhaps even the feature that dominates all others. It has an emotional repercussion on the spectator who is inclined to melancholy after the show. Its power is even more clearly perceived in the metaphysical suggestion that the ephemeral dramatic performance is the image of our ephemeral existence. This intuition forms the axis of an extensive system of analogy in which "the whole world's a stage" and life a "poor player" whose voice will soon cease to be heard.

Like conjurors dramatists have the ability to make things vanish, to withdraw at any moment—and of course they do so ultimately—all signs destined for our proximity senses: hearing, sight, and occasionally smell, which are used as alibis of the pseudoreality presented.[1]

As a technique for vanishing, "presto!" only works if on the occasion of earlier display the performer never lost sight for one moment of the necessity of withdrawal, of reabsorption. So that, in terms of space and time, the conjuror's sleeve, the wings, and the property or costume warehouse of the theater in which subtraction and retention are worked are as important as the conjuror's tabletop or player's stage, which shape the space and time dedicated to ephemeral display.

The word *rehearsal,* when used in the dramatic sense, suggests that it is impossible to conceive of any stage of the dramatic production except as an attempt to reproduce a primitive performance whose transcendental or mythical nature is a consequence of the inevitable priority of that space-time which contains the performance in a suspended state.

To explore the relationship between the dramatic performance and its mythical original state, one has to examine how the dramatist's imagination applies itself to its task and how it differs from the spectators' imagination.

For the spectators, imagining consists primarily in responding to deliberate or accidental sensorial stimuli in order to bridge gaps in the information received by processing the data stored in their memories. These data result from the experience of earlier episodes of the performance as well as from experience of all forms of entertainment and life in general. The spectators' freedom to fantasize is not suspended but is limited by their selection of the particular dramatic fantasy. Receptivity is consented to as the ticket is purchased.

The dramatist's imagination is of another kind. Yet like the spectator, his or her freedom in that direction is limited. He or she obeys archetypal and mythical patterns proper to humanity as such or determined by the cultural environment. There are also compulsively followed channels that reflect the personal episodes and accidents that marked the individual's efforts to adapt to the environment.

Freedom to imagine is first manifested by and rooted in the accepted challenge of genesis, or, to put it negatively, the refusal of the temptation to run away from creation. This temptation coexists with the creative impulse. It may outlive the completion of the work, as demonstrated by the occasional deliberate destruction of a painting or published volumes by their artists or authors.

Beyond noting the fundamental dichotomy of creating or not creating (which cannot be equated with simple idleness or engendering nothing, but consists rather in the retention of the potential of creation), I would like to show how the imagination of the person of the theater, whether dramatist, stage director, actor, designer, and so on, is at all stages of the work and down to the minutest detail constantly solicited by the radical alternatives of a binary logic that shapes the manifestation of the imaginary world. In practice, of course, the performance tends to cover its tracks and conceals from itself and the spectator the dichotomic nature of the choices originally made.

To limit the discussion to the two senses most consistently engaged by the dramatic performance, sight and hearing, the choice is between holding forth and holding back: letting see or not, letting hear or not. Both opsis and akoustikon[2] each contain the possibility of a basic denial. Each is also an alternative to the other. It is possible to show in silence or to let hear without showing anything. It is also possible to resort to visual or aural signifiers deprived of a corresponding signified, either because generally accepted codes are avoided or because the phase considered is one of presemiotization in which the sign is not yet integrated in the codes specifically evolved in the production being considered. Last, it is obvious that opsis and akoustikon may be called upon simultaneously and in complementary fashion, as they are in everyday life to achieve communication.

Since I wish to stress the importance of denial, I must insist that concealment and muting are to be regarded as extreme modalizations of dramatic imagination. Those phases of reticence in which the project to communicate the imaginary world questions itself radically, or at least refuses one part or another of the optical or acoustic spectrum, or the total spectrum in one category, seem to me to be of considerable importance. These reticences and denials are the fields of that space-time which holds the mythical primitive performance in a state of suspension between the contradictory poles of desire and fear, of love and hatred.

It thus appears that a study of dramatic rehearsing must make room for a hypothetical object, the primitive performance. Anything aimed at our sight or hearing exists in spite of a temptation to conceal and to mute; conversely—and this may be easier to accept—the unshown and the muted result from a censoring of the opsis and akoustikon of an ideal earlier state guessed at through the rehearsing.

A series of examples taken from Shakespeare's plays will show how opsis and akoustikon serve as alternatives to each other and why one is preferred to the other. A second series of cases centered on obsessional motifs will show how the relaying of akoustikon by opsis marks the crucial episode of anguished stories told piecemeal from play to play beyond the tales that make up the plots and subplots. Muting or telling, concealing or showing weave the pattern of these anguished tales. There concealing becomes tantamount to telling, showing the equivalent of muting. Sometimes the anguish is assuaged or dispelled by the most complete form of holding forth, by the coincidence of telling and showing. These concatenations, where they appear, reveal a profile of the dramatist's imagination.

Simple Variations on Opsis and Akoustikon

Enobarbus's account of the meeting between Antony and Cleopatra (2.2.190ff) is a typical substitute of opsis by akoustikon. The technical complication and expense of a lavish production are avoided by the reported action. We are at liberty to guess whether or not the chronicler-poet is also a frustrated dramatist who is dreaming of the resources that sophisticated technology and a large budget will afford a Cecil B. De Mille.

In *Julius Caesar* (5.3.9ff) a clever compromise is reached. It consists in adding to the verbal report the noises of the battle with the alarums that punctuate the changing course of military fate. This serves as background to Titinius (12–13) and then Pindarus, who comment on the fight to Cassius, whose sight is deficient. We know that the device proves fatal to Cassius, who commits suicide after Pindarus—who has mistaken friend for foe—tells him that Titinius is captured. Cassius's poor eyesight is Shakespeare's excuse for the concealment and condemns the spectator to sharing the misinterpretation.

The themes and moods of the two episodes are quite different, naturally. Also, the intensity of the mediation by Pindarus is due to the fact that speech and reported events are contemporary, while the sounds of the battle that are not identifiable with one side or the other increase the tension and move the business beyond the scenic horizon into a limbo where the dramatist manipulates the data he finds in Plutarch, his characters, and the spectators.

Poles apart from the necessary precision of compensatory verbal imagery when opsis is denied stands the vagueness of speech complemented by opsis. In *Richard II*, the entrance of the Duke of York is thus announced:

> *Green.* Here comes the Duke of York.
> *Queen.* With signs of war about his aged neck.
>
> [2.2.73–74]

Any neck- or shoulder-piece of armor, or simply the chain symbolizing the office of regent and worn in these straits will readily mold into shape the soft verbal paste especially designed to avoid the fuss and expense of specific visual constraints.

In *Hamlet,* the last apparition of the ghost "in his habit as he lived" (3.4.135) may fit almost any costume, including the Scroogelike shirt and nightcap selected some years ago in Stratford by a director of the Royal Shakespeare Company who was probably goaded by the direction in Q1, "Enter the Ghost in his nightgown," which is of course regular gear for a nocturnal visit to one's royal wife.

Opsis for *Macbeth* holds a different challenge. The actor in the title role (then the actress playing Lady Macbeth in the sleepwalking scene) must firmly suggest that he is seeing something that *we* cannot see. This occurs in the famous dagger hallucination. One may say with almost complete confidence that the dagger was not actualized on the Elizabethan stage, although modern technology may be tempted to use a laser projection. Exactly halfway through the fifteen-line speech (2.1.33–47), Shakespeare is careful to give his actor, whose hand but lately grasped the air, something material to hold, a "true" and plainly visible dagger, declared the twin of the immaterial one: "I see thee yet, in form as palpable / As this which I now draw" (ll. 40–41). This optical precaution is important. It relieves both actor and spectator; the focus shifts from the ghostly object to the concrete prop elected as referent.

Complex Variations: The Jigsaw Puzzle of Psychodrama

Beyond these simple examples I wish to concentrate on both the variable tension that results from the mutually exclusive or complementary recourse to opsis and akoustikon and on the varying degree of concretization that characterizes the proclamation of the imaginary universe. As previously mentioned, the imbalance—as well as the balance—between opsis and akoustikon betrays deep activity in the dramatist's personal imagination; play by play a tale is told that is different from the gist of the plays that host its *disjecta membra,* and is quite impervious to observation in the systematic grouping of texts in editions of the complete works.

The tales in question are subliminal because their components are scattered parts of dramatic performance. Their meaning throws light on the working of Shakespeare's imagination but also affects ours. I have chosen three examples of psychodrama. The first may be entitled "The Tale of the Pillow," the second "The Snake's Metamorphoses," and the third "A Case of Poison." The second and third tales will be dealt with simultaneously for they appear so, an ever-nesting structure, in the plays that harbor them.

Out of twenty-one uses of the word *pillow* in Shakespeare's plays, only eight coincide with an atmosphere of peace and rest and develop the connotations usually associated with this aid to comfort. In all other uses, *pillow* is affected by more or less subtle deviations, is contaminated by manifest perversions. These occur in the earliest plays of the dramatist. In *2 Henry VI* (c. 1590–92), Cardinal Beaufort, *in articulo mortis,* confides into his pillow the evil secrets that burden his soul, a release that is naturally second best to the unforthcoming confessional help. Shakespeare, like all men, would have experienced disturbed sleep; perhaps he is dramatizing the proverbial phrase "to take counsel of one's pillow" (1573). Some fifteen years later, in *Macbeth,* the last of the great tragedies, the doctor ties this case to the general law: "infected minds / To their deaf pillows will discharge their secrets" (5.1.72–73). In confiding into his pillow Beaufort thought he was blurting out the truth to his king. In *Macbeth* no such illusion remains, for the doctor at least. The pillow is deaf.

It is in *Richard III* (c. 1591–97) that the treacherous nature of the soft and seemingly friendly object begins to emerge. It is part of a melodramatic snapshot showing the little princes sleeping in each other's arms in the Tower:

> *Tyrrel.* "O, thus," quoth Dighton, "lay the gentle babes."
> "Thus, thus," quoth Forrest, "girdling one another
> Within their alablaster innocent arms.
> Their lips were four red roses on a stalk,
> Which in their summer beauty kiss'd each other.
> A book of prayers on their pillow lay,
> Which once," quoth Forrest, "almost chang'd my mind; . . ."
> [4.3.9–15]

Will the book of prayer, cushioned as seen in so many paintings in church or castle, save the innocents? The grim answer comes next: " 'We smothered / The most replenished sweet work of Nature / That from the prime creation e'er she framd' " (ll. 17–19). An emblem of mildness, the prop of confident sleep, the support of Scripture and prayer, the pillow has turned into a weapon to smother the sleepers.

From then on it keeps turning up as a sinister and morbid metaphor. In

Titus Andronicus (1594), while Titus lends his "loving breast" to pillow his grandchild (5.3.163), the sons of Tamora who have stabbed Bassianus to death intend to use his body to prop up his wife, Lavinia, whom they are about to rape:[3]

> *Chiron.* Drag hence the husband to some secret hole,
>   And make his dead trunk pillow to our lust.
>
>   [2.3.129–30]

In *King Lear* (1605–6) the foul fiend who harrows Tom with suggestions of suicide lays "knives under [his] pillow" (3.4.53–54). In *Macbeth* (1606–7) the pillows of Duncan's grooms serve as incriminating repositories for the bloody daggers laid there by Lady Macbeth to thwart suspicion:

> *Macbeth.* Their hands and faces were all badg'd with blood;
>   So were their daggers, which unwip'd we found
>   Upon their pillows.
>
>   [2.3.102–4]

Slipped under the pillow in *King Lear,* the fatal weapon, after use, surfaces to rest on top in *Macbeth.*

In *Cymbeline* (c. 1608–11), we find a euphemized version of the situation dramatized some seventeen years earlier in *Titus Andronicus.* A Roman captain asks Imogen, disguised as a page and crying over the decapitated body of Cloten, "Who is this / Thou mak'st thy bloody pillow?" (4.2.362–63). After this the word is never used again, neither literally nor metaphorically. It fades out after the cruel and perverse deviation.

Immediately after the emergence of the murderous pillow in *Richard III* and its use as a morbid and erotic movable in *Titus Andronicus,* Shakespeare gives the impression that he is investigating his fixation, offstage so to speak, in *The Rape of Lucrece* (1593–94). Here is how Tarquin discovers his adulterous victim innocently asleep. The personified pillow is called upon to account for itself:

> Her lily hand her rosy cheek lies under,
> Coz'ning the pillow of a lawful kiss;
> Who therefore angry seems to part in sunder,
> Swelling on either side to want his bliss;
> Between whose hills her head entombed is,
>   Where like a virtuous monument she lies,
>   To be admir'd of lewd unhallowed eyes
>
>   [Ll. 386–92]

A frustrated pillow; a jealous pillow; a male and tumescent pillow, swelling to fondle and to smother; a funeral pillow carved to serve the turn of the recumbent figure on the tomb; all in all a necrophilic entity. All motivations and perversions converge in this description of Lucrece's pillow, which reverses the figure of those dead human bodies pillowing the lust or grief of the living, in *Titus Andronicus* at the beginning of Shakespeare's dramatic career, or pillowing their grief as they do toward the close in *Cymbeline.* In *The Rape of Lucrece,* which by definition does not pose the problem of optical actualization, a long and baroque conceit as detailed as a list of charges tells the whole truth. We are alerted to the source of danger. The murderous pillow of *Richard III* turns out to be a sexual maniac. The purely verbal or acoustic stage is transgressed and moves fractionally toward the realm of opsis when, in *Titus Andronicus,* Bassianus's body is dragged off-stage to serve the perversion of the murderers.

The full passage from akoustikon to opsis occurs in *Othello* (c. 1603–4), in the passage from word to action as the pillow changes into a recognizable, wielded property. Remember that Iago dissuades his master from using poison to kill Desdemona. Such is the interest of poetic justice that the Moor is advised to strangle the lady in the bed she is supposed to have defiled. Desdemona *is* strangled. But this is only a final mercy gesture: "I would not have thee linger in they pain. / So, so" (5.2.88–89). The method initially chosen was stifling (Q1: "he stifles her"; F: "Smothers her"). In his admirable analysis of the play, Victor Hugo writes in his *William Shakespeare:*

> Ponder this thing of great moment: Othello is the night. Being the night and planning to kill what weapon does he choose? Poison? a club, an axe? No, he chooses the pillow. Killing is putting to sleep. Shakespeare himself may not have realized this. The artist, almost unconsciously at times, takes the cue from the type he creates, so powerful is the type. So Desdemona, the wife of the man of Night, dies smothered by the pillow which took the first kiss, and now receives the last gasp.[4]

Beyond the principle of poetic justice perceived at first by Othello (4.1.205) or the rationale of harmony stressed by Hugo, I am struck by the continuity of the obsessional symbolic system. With regard to this, and to penetrate deeper into the subconscious, one might say that Shakespeare is unconsciously trying to grant extenuating circumstances to his protagonist by placing within his reach the object long swollen with jealousy and murderous desires. Next the figure of irony commands attention. In Shakespeare's drama the pillow only kills the innocent and the pure. The choice of the weapon exonerates the victim. Last and not least, the cushion, next of kin to the pillow, is an emblem of mercy in the tradition of the Renaissance. Falstaff, who dons one in place of a crown to impersonate King Henry IV in the tavern scene, is thus careful to emblematize Justice as a nodding figure winking at crime (*1 Henry IV,* 2.4.374). Shakespeare's own mythical imagination, which multiplies sinister associations, is discrepant from the dominant collective imagination.

In *Othello*, the pillow's murderous project indicated from the very beginning of the dramatic sequence is finally acted out in sight of the spectator. There, and there only, the word *pillow* is not uttered. When it becomes actualized as property it ranks with the unspoken and the unspeakable. Up to and including *Othello*, speech and show never once coincide. Beyond this climax, the union of the word and the property is achieved twice in *Pericles* (1606–8). Its function is also normal. Newborn Marina is laid on a pillow (3.1.67–68), which props up Pericles as he lies overcome by emotion on being reunited with his daughter (5.1.234). Although the pillow-cadaver returns in *Cymbeline*, as we saw, there it promotes pity rather than rape. The nightmare is not totally erased, but time and the wiles of imagination now grappling with the word and now with the property have somewhat eased the original threat.

In closer symbolical association with the earth and in fuller physical contact with it than all other beasts of the field, according to Genesis (3:14–15) and the diagnosis of G. Bachelard (*La terre et les rêveries du repos* [Paris: Corti, 1948], 262), the snake symbolizes in Shakespeare's works the dangers specific to sleep beyond and above the noxious pillow. Lexical variety must not detract our attention from this fact: *snake, serpent, adder,* or *worm* are used as synonyms, and all have generic value. The coma of sleep that reduces man to lying on the ground for his rest makes man most vulnerable to the attack of the serpent. Its powers are considerable. Macbeth well knows its resilience (3.2.13–15). In *A Midsummer Night's Dream* (1594–98) the Queen of the Fairies herself thinks it fit to take magical precautions against reptiles (2.2.9–12). Her exorcism is in any case powerless against Oberon, that prince of snakes who pours on her eyelids the vegetable venom obtained by Puck that leads to the grotesque misunderstandings. The snake is clearly associated with Oberon's plan, and its slough is described as large enough to dress (or bind?) a fairy. The charming bank where the wild thyme blows (2.1.249)—a favorite Shakespearean quote— owns a disturbing appendix: "And there the snake throws her enamell'd skin, / Weed wide enough to wrap a fairy in" (2.1.255–56). The selective human mind separates the propitious from the baneful and chooses to forget the snake appended to the list of wildflowers or remembers it only on account of its colorful enamel.

The association between the flower and the snake, which doubtless harks back to the primitive association between the serpent and the fruit and claims its precedence since the flower antedates the fruit, emblematizes absolute evil. The flower hides the snake. Lady Macbeth resorts to the image to persuade her husband: "look like th' innocent flower, / But be the serpent under't" (1.5.65–66). This is the key to the murder of Duncan.

To return to *A Midsummer Night's Dream* and comedy, Hermia vainly beseeches Lysander to ward off the snake that is threatening her breast

(2.2.144–56). This was a nightmare. Later on, upon meeting Demetrius, she accuses him of having murdered the sleeping Lysander and the image of the snake surfaces anew:

> And hast thou kill'd him sleeping? O brave touch!
> Could not a worm, an adder, do so much?
> An adder did it! for with doubler tongue
> Than thine, thou serpent, never adder stung.
>
> [3.2.70–73]

Another comedy, *As You Like It* (1598–1600), shifts the menace from nocturnal to diurnal sleep. It is indeed poetic justice that Oliver, who wanted to do away with his brother by setting fire to his chamber at night, should be at the mercy of a snake while asleep one day in the forest (4.3.104–10).

In *Hamlet* (1599–c. 1601) the serpent's threat to the sleeper is carried out:

> *Ghost.* 'Tis given out that, sleeping in my orchard,
>   A serpent stung me, so the whole ear of Denmark
>   Is by a forged process of my death
>   Rankly abus'd; but know, thou noble youth,
>   The serpent that did sting thy father's life
>   Now wears his crown.
>
> [1.5.35–40]

Hamlet's key to the enigma assumes the shape of the snake. A symbol cannot lie. Literal understanding may be misleading. The "whole ear of Denmark" abused by a lie is the collective replica of that individual ear into which, not long before, the poison was poured, into which it will soon be poured in earnest mockery in the play within the play. This seals Claudius's defeat. He who betrayed his brother's sleep with poison is now forced to live under the explicit auspices of the snake, which sets him up as prime target for the revenge. Claudius a king? Never. As in the fable, he is but a beast who stole the crown: a crowned serpent. His only efficient weapon, like the snake's, is poison: the poison he pours into the cup destined for Hamlet and drunk by Gertrude and that in which the tip of Laertes's foil is dipped. The poisoned foil is only an extension of the poison-fang. It is easy to understand why Hamlet is so bent on making his uncle drain the fatal cup even after running him through with his blade. This is no wanton cruelty aimed at gratifying the groundlings but the unavoidable logical consequence to the plot's etiology of danger. To kill a snake is a hazardous undertaking except if it obliges by biting itself. Hamlet forces Claudius to swallow back his own venomous excretion. Fate that drove Claudius to choose the fate of the snake to avoid suspicion could only lead to this particular type of self-destruction.

It is worth noting the various stages of the progress of venom or poison throughout the play. First there is the fable of King Hamlet's death, suspended as it were in the dramatic limbo of the action, established as its absolute past. Next comes the correction by the ghost's account at the end of act 1: it is not snake's venom but murderer's poison. Then it is the contribution of opsis to the variations of akoustikon: the sham poison poured into the ear of the Player King. This is actualization in the second degree: "they do but jest, poison in jest—no offense i' th' world" (3.2.234–35). Last poison invades the play world itself with the poisoned rapier's tip and the cup that is symbolically contaminated by the *union*.

This gradual infection is well worth pondering over, starting as it does with the rumor originating in dramatic limbo, carried over in dramatic speech, nesting next in the speech and properties of the play within, resurfacing in the speech and action of the play proper—it is a chain reaction that influences all degrees of make-believe. It is only the basic convention of drama that saves the general audience from the epidemic.

The verbal poison of lies with which Claudius metaphorically abuses Denmark returns in *Othello*. It is Iago who infects the Moor's sleep with his slander of Desdemona:

> The Moor already changes with my poison:
> Dangerous conceits are in their natures poisons,
> Which at the first are scarce found to distaste,
> But with a little act upon the blood
> Burn like the mines of sulphur
> . . . .
> Look where he comes! Not poppy, nor mandragora,
> Nor all the drowsy syrups of the world
> Shall ever medicine thee to that sweet sleep
> Which thou ow'dst yesterday.
>
> [3.3.325–29; 330–33]

Othello's pitiful avowal, ten lines later, "I slept the next night well" (l. 340), confirms the diagnosis. Symptomatically Iago's caution consists in deterring his master from using poison to kill Desdemona. A very snake himself, he must avoid the possibility of an incriminating association:

> *Othello.* Get me some poison, Iago, this night. I'll not expostulate with her, lest her body and beauty unprovide my mind again. This night, Iago.
> *Iago.* Do it not with poison; strangle her in her bed, even the bed she hath contaminated.
> *Othello.* Good, good; the justice of it pleases; very good.
>
> [4.1.204–10]

Iago has succeeded in covering his tracks efficiently. To kill Desdemona, it was sufficient for him to bite a third party.

Macbeth marks the nadir of hope. The protagonist's mind is "full of scorpions" (3.2.36) and he unsuccessfully tries to face up to the serpent of

dynastic danger coiled in Banquo. Beyond this play, the only pure tragedy—aside from *Coriolanus*—is *Antony and Cleopatra*. Through Cleopatra
Shakespeare's imagination tries a ruse where sheer might, with Macbeth,
failed. The snake is Cleopatra's personal emblem and that of her dynasty.
She, whom Antony calls "my serpent of old Nile" (1.5.25), resorts to the
snake to escape captivity in Octavius Caesar's Rome. This alliance with the
snake is for the first and the last time expressed in opsis. In Cleopatra's
speech all dangerous characteristics of the snake are glossed over or transmuted into benevolent features:

> With thy sharp teeth this knot intrinsicate
> Of life at once untie. Poor venomous fool,
> Be angry, and dispatch. O, couldst thou speak,
> That I might hear thee call great Caesar ass
> Unpolicied!
>
> [5.2.304–8]

The snake undergoes a gradual metamorphosis and loses its very name in
the mouth of she who prided herself on her cognomen of "serpent of the
Nile." Cleopatra, yearning for peace and rest, adopts in the full sense of the
term the eternal enemy of man and rest. To Charmian:

> Peace, peace!
> Dost thou not see my baby at my breast,
> That sucks the nurse asleep?
>
> [5.2.308–10]

The snake is euphemized into an infant, its bite into sucking. The fame of
the historical episode imposes the only actualization of a snake on the
Shakespearean stage and promotes the miracle: the dangerous symbol is
quite subverted.[5]

After *Antony and Cleopatra*, the euphemistic treatment of venom or poison is maintained, not through metaphor but through dramatic substitution. *Cymbeline* under the auspices of good Doctor Cornelius buries the
threat once and for all as he refuses the Queen the fatal drugs that would
allow her to reach her aim and supplies an innocuous sleeping draught in
their place. He succeeds, by the way, where Friar Laurence miserably failed
in *Romeo and Juliet*. Imogen wakes up in good time and the spectator
discovers that the man she is mourning is not her husband after all.
Henceforth, neither snake nor drugs can harm man or sleep, either in the
shape of words or in the form of props.

This survey of the possibilities offered by opsis and akoustikon supports
the analogy originally drawn between the imagination of the dramatist and
the conjuror's box of tricks. He may produce noise, music, or words from
it, or else shapes to feast our eyes. Sometimes everything is pulled out and

arranged. The option of keeping the box shut is always there. The obligation of returning everything to it ultimately is the law.

As soon as the word, or the object invested with a personal relevance, is heard or seen it stands for examination by the dramatist and the spectator. It must have been in the box prior to this. Once gone, we know full well that it has fled to the wings, no doubt modified by its latest avatar, and is waiting for its cue to appear once more.

Words and objects do not have the same status. The rapport with the physical person of the anguished subject changes as word shifts to object and object to word, or as both appear in association. While the literary critic must, in this matter, leave the last word to the psychologist, a theory tentatively may be put forward: it is possible that actualization helps exteriorize anguish more surely than fleeting words. Richard II (4.1.263) hopes to rid himself of the face responsible for his past follies by smashing the mirror that reflects an inexplicably serene image. Bolingbroke then observes that it is not the face he shattered but its shadow, which tends to prove that props have a limited use as exorcism or therapy. Theater, like a mirror, may also help to delineate, magnify, soften, and transform the shapes of one's anguish to a significant degree while the play is being written or while its performance lasts—but not for a longer term.

Opsis was too long neglected in the study of dramatic imagery. Its inclusion must prompt the critic to investigate its links with akoustikon in the changing world of performance. The dramatist's imagination is a case apart in that not only does it animate a universe in three dimensions but it has access also to every resource of all arts. These particular circumstances must be duly weighed if the imaginative process is to be comprehended, and also the fact that its fantasies antedate and survive the composition and performance of any given play. Occasionally the scattered pieces of the jigsaw puzzle may be assembled and the psychodrama appears, a play never written as such, adding its shadows to the shadows of the explicit dramatic universe. While this secret, dismembered drama is far from revealing the whole truth about the personality of the dramatist, it does tell us, in fits and starts, where it emerges, that there is more to theater than writing or acting the play.

Notes

Some of the work presented here began to emerge in *La nuit dans le théâtre de Shakespeare et de ses predecesseurs,* 2 vols. (Lille: Université de Lille III, 1980), and the theory was first argued in a paper read at the annual conference of Société Française Shakespeare in 1982, and published in 1983 in French under the title "Cacher, dire, montrer, taire: régime de l'imaginaire Shakespearien" in *Du texte à la scene: Langages du théâtre,* ed. M.-T. Jones-Davies (Paris: Jean Touzot, 1983), 111–31.

1. As opposed to the contact senses of touch and taste.

2. I coin the word *akoustikon* to designate all that is aimed at the spectator's sense of hearing. It is the aural counterpart to *opsis*, a term that has become traditional in theater criticism.

3. In a note to the New Arden edition (1953, nn. 129–30, p. 45), J. C. Maxwell refers to J. D. Ebbs (*Modern Language Notes* 66 [1951]) and points to the parallel between the project of Tamora's sons and a passage of *The Unfortunate Traveller* by Thomas Nashe (*Works,* ed. McKerrow, 2:226): "Her husbands dead bodie he made a pillow to his abhomination." But I quite fail to see the justification of Maxwell's remark that "Chiron and Demetrius do not in fact do what they here propose." This note belongs in a tradition at least as old as the original Arden edition and that consists in disregarding action offstage.

4. My translation.

5. Cleopatra's suicide had, among others, similarly struck Robert Chester, who wrote in his *Love's Martyr* (1601):

> . . . the snake that Cleopatra used,
> The Egyptian queene belov'd of Anthony,
> That with her breasts deare bloud was nourished . . .

Another Part of the Castle: Some Victorian Hamlets

by RUSSELL JACKSON

"To see *Hamlet*," wrote Max Beerbohm in 1901, "is one of our natural functions, one of our needs. How restful the play is, in its hold on us, how intimate and cosy! Nowhere, I protest, have I such a sense of home as in the Castle of Elsinore. Whenever the curtain rises on that "Room of State," I seem to recognize every brick in those low arches and squat columns, every fold in those arrases of neutral-colored serge." But Beerbohm felt that it was time for a moratorium on *Hamlet* productions, and that familiarity had dulled responses to the play: "I am too much at home in Elsinore. I seem to have stayed there so often, to have written so many letters on its note-paper. . . ."[1] A year later, confronted with Forbes-Robertson's performance as the Prince, he had to admit to some surprise—a certain renewal of the freshness that had been lost in his relationship with the play. Robertson had broken with what Beerbohm calls "the ordinary classico-romantic perform-ance." The term sums up the Victorians' Prince of Denmark in a manner that gives me courage in offering to deal with this topic in a paper as brief as this. Beerbohm explains his generalization:

> Every other Hamlet has been a mysterious and abstract figure—not a man, but an incarnation (successful or otherwise) of a human soul, or of all human souls. Mr. Robertson, realistically, shows us a man—a pleasant, high-souled young man, placed in distressing circumstances, and behav-ing just as one would expect such a person in such a case to behave.[2]

A specific point of comparison in this review is between the "traditional" way of speaking "The air bites shrewdly. It is very cold," and Robertson's. It had been usual to give it in "a hollow voice, mysteriously, ruminantly, in order that our nerves may be strung up to concert-pitch for the things impending." Robertson, according to Beerbohm, spoke it "briskly, with a peevish emphasis on the 'very'" and it became a commonplace remark passed for the sake of saying something to Marcellus and Horatio rather than any indication that Hamlet is vexed with the weather.

111

Several matters arise from this review. First, there is the existence of a "tradition" to which the writer can refer his readers with some confidence that they will understand him. It no longer makes much sense to invoke "tradition" in this kind of context. Our theaters prize innovation to a degree that would have astonished and distressed the most adventurous Victorian audiences. Although it is perhaps unwise to associate it too directly with the initiatives of a few "great men," there was a "Shakespeare Revolution"—a watershed in the history of Shakespearean interpretation in the English-speaking theater, when there was a radical change in the kind of interpretative freedom expected and exercised by actors and (when they appeared on the scene) directors. A second consideration is that in Beerbohm's review of the new Hamlet an old story is repeating itself: a new "naturalness" is supplanting an acting style now perceived as mannered. The scenario is familiar to theater historians. When Henry Irving appeared at the Lyceum as Hamlet in 1874, one experienced theatergoer wrote:

> My impulse was to go to Irving, and say, "How are you, Hamlet?" I had witnessed for the first time in my life a human being named "Hamlet." I believe in no other Hamlet—for Shakespeare's men and women are all of God's own make.[3]

Another reviewer wrote of Charles Fechter's Hamlet, in 1861, that "No character in the whole range of Shakespeare's creatures has been so thoroughly *stereotyped* on our stage as *Hamlet,* and the performance is, from the outset of the scene, a complete *novelty.*" He went on to discuss Fechter's respectful study—and selective rejection—of the traditions of the part. Older actors, appearing with Fechter, were surprised to find that he ignored the "points" by which they usually navigated their way through the play—"every actor who plays with Mr. Fechter learns to place less reliance than heretofore on the pegs and wires by which he has been governed, and speaks more naturally."[4]

A further consideration arising from Beerbohm's review of Robertson's Hamlet is that "tradition" is very much in the eye of the beholders, and it is upon such more or less expert witnesses that the historian relies for much of his or her evidence. It has to be said that a good deal of what theater historians write tells us how a performance was received, rather than offering an "objective" description of what was done and said on stage. Even performances documented with the fullest resources of promptbooks and (nowadays) videotape and sound recordings have to be approached through the study of contemporary reactions. And to this we should add that reviewers—especially in the nineteenth century, when column-inches were lavished on their reports—often consciously let their responses be colored by their critical reading, which is usually on display. For every new Hamlet of any significance in the reign of Victoria there is at least one three-column essay that, *en passant,* reminds its readers of what Goethe said about an oak tree planted in a costly jar, and what various commentators from Schlegel and Coleridge onwards have said about the various topics of the critics' debate on the play and (especially) the Prince. It seems as though Carlyle's translation of *Wilhelm Meister* had the status Proust's masterpiece enjoys with us—it was the book everyone hoped you thought they had read—and knowing citation of the *Hamlet* comments was obligatory. For the historian to perceive the performance, simple and of itself, is hardly possible, even if the status of "evidence" is reserved for the prompt-books' barest data. What we *can* usefully talk about is quite substantial, though. We can examine what the Victorians saw in their successive Hamlets, and the historian can go beyond that into the fundamental question of how these readings were produced and used in Victorian culture. In this paper I can offer only a glimpse of part of this vast body of material and draw very limited and provisional conclusions. What follows is an outline of some Victorian orthodoxies with regard to Hamlets and *Hamlet*.

The orthodoxies are not so much opinions as a set of headings under which critics and performers were expected to provide answers. It will hardly be surprising that the questions center on character, and specifically on the protagonist. Not only did Victorian performance and commentary marginalize Ophelia (as Elaine Showalter has recently described)—they marginalized almost everything and everybody else in the play.[5] The various acting versions made Claudius an unrewarding part, so that it came as a surprise when Wilson Barrett in 1884 restored the usurper's soliloquy in 3.2. and allowed an accomplished melodramatic actor to make him an attractive and plausible man. The power-politics of the play received little attention: the appearance of the army of Fortinbras in 4.4 was usually omitted, as was (until Robertson's production in 1897) the appearance of Fortinbras in the final scene. Although revivals vied with one another in "authenticity" of design, trying to achieve a compromise between the assumed period and Danish setting and the need to get Hamlet into black tights and white shirt—the historical sense was devoted to "atmosphere" rather than any investigation of Danish society. And "atmosphere" was expressive of the mood of Hamlet himself, defined by its reflection of his gloomy moods or opposing those moods by its brightness and glamor. When Beerbohm speaks of his familiarity with the rooms of Elsinore, he speaks quite literally: with very few exceptions Victorian Elsinores were much of a Saxon-pillared muchness. Some were very beautiful and impressive, and some innovations were intelligently hazarded: Wilson Barrett set the play-scene outdoors; Robertson placed the scene of Ophelia's madness in the orchard that must (at least one critic supposed) have been the site of the murder of Hamlet senior; the designs for Fechter's London production seem wilder and more impressionistic than most others of their time. With the exception of its extraordinary outdoor scenes, the silent film of Robertson's performance, for which copies were built of the interior sets the actor had inherited from Henry Irving, gives a good idea of how the palace-prison usually looked.[6] Scenic artists varied in their ingenuity and accomplishment but beyond accuracy in setting and appropriateness in mood, they were not expected to make interpretative innovations. Elsinore was a constant, and the major questions of the play were to do with Hamlet and—in so far as they affected his state of mind—the other characters.

There were two principal questions: Hamlet's madness (and the behavior that reflects or expresses it) and the reasons for his delay, which might include madness. Here, for brevity's sake, I wish to concentrate on the explanations for Hamlet's madness, which were usefully summarized by Ophelia in W. S. Gilbert's *Rosencrantz and Guildenstern:*

> . . . Opinion is divided. Some men hold
> That he's the sanest, far, of all sane men—
> Some that he's really sane, but shamming mad—
> Some that he's really mad, but shamming sane—
> Some that he will be mad, some that he *was*—
> Some that he couldn't be. But on the whole
> (As far as I can make out what they mean)
> The favourite theory's somewhat like this:
> Hamlet is idiotically sane
> With lucid intervals of lunacy.[7]

Most of the speculation about madness falls into the familiar trap of assuming that dramatic characters must reproduce known types and can be praised for faithfulness to them. Thus Dr. A. D. Kellogg, of the State Asylum at Utica, New York, assures us that "the late distinguished Dr. Brigham, than whom no man in modern times has observed the insane more carefully, asserted that he had seen all of Shakespeare's characters in the wards of the Utica Asylum, of which he was the physician in chief."[6] There were many such encounters between Shakespeare's "creatures" and the mad doctors. In his copy of Dr. John Conolly's *A Study of Hamlet* (1863), Charles Cowden Clarke jotted, "the doctor thinks every one mad—being ever among lunatics," and observed that the author "does not allow for excitement without insanity."[9] Edward Fitzgerald wrote to Fanny Kemble:

> I always said with regard to the Explanation of Hamlet's Madness or Sanity, that Shakespeare himself might not have known the truth any more than we understand the seeming discords we see in people we know best. Shakespeare intuitively imagined, and portrayed, the man without being able to give a reason—perhaps—I believe in Genius doing this.[10]

Fitzgerald here sets up a romantic theory of the author-creator against the commentators' author-diagnostician: Hamlet's madness is not yet interpreted historically as a function of the play and of its theatrical language. For present purposes, rather than try to improve on Gilbert's list of the alternatives available to Victorian readers, it seems useful to accept it and to point out that the madness theories served a definite purpose in Victorian writing on the play. Hamlet's behavior was perceived as far from uniformly princely and considerate, especially towards women, and his distraction could be used to exculpate him. It was important to save the reputation of the world's most important dramatic character.

Hamlet's shocking behavior in the graveyard, his brutal treatment of Ophelia and disrespectful and violent words and deeds in other portions of the play, especially in 3, 4, could all be explained and extenuated by reference to his madness. Dr. Conolly points out that "all this conversation [in Gertrude's closet] could not have had its peculiar character if Hamlet's mind had been calm enough to remember the respect due to his mother." In the graveyard, according to the same source, Hamlet is committing the most reprehensible improprieties—unless we allow for madness. A sane Hamlet is consequently unthinkable: "It is impossible to entertain the supposition that Shakespeare would have made so worthless a moral being the principal personage of one of his noblest compositions, and have wasted his genius to adorn such singular moral deformity."[11] Thus, to be excused, Hamlet's most energetic impulses and all his impertinence, murderousness, and revenging zeal must be passed off as manic. Conolly's study at least insists that the symptoms of Hamlet's madness should not be softened by an excessive admixture of "tenderness," but in its general tendency of excusing the hero by appealing to his mental disorder it will stand for many similar projects. The discussion moves uneasily along the borders of what is defined as permissible, in literature and in life. Hamlet's spirit clearly needs to be tamed by application of commonly accepted social assumptions (this is no way for a gentleman to speak to his mother) and Shakespeare has to be protected as a source of masterpieces (that is no way to let your hero behave if you want to remain a culture-hero yourself). What was life like for this doctor's real patients?

The question of insanity had to be solved if one of the most cherished Victorian orthodoxies about Hamlet—his essential nobility—was to be protected. It was even more important in this respect than the settling of the delay problem. If the Prince is established as blamelessly unhinged (or locked into an assumption of that role), his delaying can be accounted for by appeal to the force of circumstance. The "princely" Hamlet turns up again and again, sometimes concisely, as in Hazlitt's review of Edmund Kean ("There should be as much of the gentleman and scholar infused into the part, and as little of the actor" as is possible); sometimes fulsomely, as in a magazine article by Mary Cowden-Clarke:

> . . . Hamlet is, above all things, gentlemanly; that is, in the strict sense of the word—he is a gentle man. His essential characteristic is gentleness of soul; however the unhappy circumstances by which he is involuntarily

surrounded lead him into occasional harshnesses of demeanour, and wayward petulance.[12]

She goes on to describe how he is "uniformly courteous with his inferiors," has a habit of "submissive obedience . . . as a son," is of a "sensitive and sweet" nature, loves his father, is susceptible to the cold, abhors "Danish intemperance," and even reflects in being fat and scant of breath "the constitution of the contemplative student, the sedentary inactive man." But less indulgent readers and spectators also maintained the theme of Hamlet's princeliness. Gordon Crosse, an accomplished amateur critic, noted of Beerbohm Tree's Hamlet that he was "gentle, affectionate, condescending, vacillating and dreamy, but subject to occasional fierce outbursts of passion."[13] The same observer thought that F. R. Benson's leading characteristic as Hamlet was "a dogged brooding over one idea which sometimes gives him the appearance of sullenness." H. B. Irving began well, but lapsed: "his appearance as the curtain rose for I, ii, discovered him seated by the side of the throne, lost in melancholy abstraction; [this] struck exactly the right note, and he maintained it throughout the act." In the later acts "he failed to show the gracious charm and sweetness of the character" and his personality was really too "cold, incisive and sardonic" for the part. By contrast, Robertson (whom Crosse saw in 1908 and 1909) showed a "refined, courteous and tender nature," even in his treatment of Polonius.

> He succeeds in throwing over the part a tender melancholy which has a wonderfully softening effect on the whole play. But in this case the melancholy is made to arise from Hamlet's whole disposition and not from a consciousness of the awful circumstances in which he was placed.

In using Crosse's diaries as evidence for what a given performance looked like, the historian has to square this account with, for example, Shaw's detailed critique of the Robertson production, with its praise for "a gallant, alert Hamlet, thoughtful but not in the least sentimental."[14] The "tender melancholy" of 1908–9 may have developed from the brisker Prince of 1897, and Crosse's and Shaw's sensibilities may not agree, but the general line—or rather, the consensus as to the general question to be answered—is what interests me here. Given attractive qualities of mind (variously defined), how can the character's behavior be legitimized? It is time for a brief visit to the most private part of the castle, Gertrude's closet.

Victorian hopes for the kind of impression Hamlet might make in the interview with his mother (3.4) are summed up by an essayist writing in 1848: Hamlet's behavior combines "true filial respect and regard with honest, manly censure."[15] But there were some difficult moments to get by. Hamlet's language is rough and—in Victorian terms—highly indecent; he impulsively kills the intruder he assumes to be Claudius and subsequently treats the dead Polonius with what can be construed as rueful mockery; at the end of the scene he involves Gertrude in devious plotting against her husband. On his way to her closet, moreover, he has refrained from killing Claudius because he wishes to be sure of his damnation: grounds that might seem ignoble and irreligious. Some of these problems could be dealt with by judicious cutting of the text. The indecencies of the scene could be removed, although Irving managed to refer to "the rank sweat of an *incestuous* bed." The end of the scene was simplified by cutting the thirty lines after "Thus bad begins, and worse remains behind."

Most important, Hamlet's sorrowful rebuking of Gertrude could be made elaborately dignified and pious. Such performances as Edwin Booth's, recreated in Charles Shattuck's account, would seem laughably self-righteous to a modern audience. We learn from the contemporary description used by Shattuck that in "Heaven's face doth glow,"

> . . . there is a dainty loftiness in [Booth's] voice, a manner of delivery which lifts his denunciation to a level far above a merely vulgar view of her crime. Here is disclosed a high point in Hamlet's sensibilities.[16]

The religious dimension of the scene, congenial to the Victorians, was sometimes taken to extremes. Tree had indicated Hamlet's upward turn of thoughts before the scene by having him address "let not the soul of Nero enter this firm bosom . . ." to a statue of the Virgin. Earlier in his production the religious note was struck in Hamlet's scene with Ophelia, where a *prie-dieu* was provided for the nymph's orisons and Hamlet's tone was intended to show that he sincerely recommended a nunnery as a place of sanctuary. At the conclusion of the scene with Gertrude, Hamlet led his mother "sternly" to a *prie-dieu*, at which she knelt, "sobbing."[17]

A traditional ending for the scene had Gertrude offer to bless her son on "Once more, good night," and him refusing with "And when *you* are desirous to be blest, I'll blessing beg of you." There were a number of possible elaborations. Fechter stressed the theme of filial piety, rather than religiosity, by having Gertrude try twice to embrace Hamlet. The second time ("So, again, good night") the promptbook indicates that "Queen turns—comes to him—Hamlet holds up his father's portrait—she retires in great sorrow—to L. and exits." Another source indicates that Hamlet kissed his father's portrait at this juncture.[18] Henry Irving seems to have shown Hamlet reconciled to his mother: Alan Hughes suggests that he may even have kissed her as he raised her from her knees on "I'll blessing beg of you."[19] Booth, having rejected the blessing, relented and dropped his cheek on Gertrude's head with "Mother, good night" as the curtain fell.[20] All these late Victorian versions soften the full severity of Macready's 1840 performance:

> [Hamlet] having bid his mother sorrowful good-night, she retires to-wards the door, but on gaining it stops, bursts into tears, and retraces her

steps to take a last embrace: but Macready raises his head, and motions her to stop, clearly implying by his action and melancholy countenance, that the memory of his dead parent was a sacred thought, and would not allow him to enfold in his embrace her who *even now* held communion with his murderers.[21]

This commentary implies that Victorian theatergoers were skilled in reading the signs denoting these feelings, to them so "clearly" conveyed by Macready.

In the Victorian theater the scene would thrill with its darkness and the ghostly apparition. There is an unavoidable similarity between this episode and "dark" scenes in contemporary melodrama. Irving carried a lamp, which he set on the table as he came in and which he held up over the dead Polonius as the scene closed. Tree carried a flaming torch. One reviewer of Barrett's 1884 production observed that Gertrude enjoyed "the royal prerogative of going to bed by the light of red lamps, which lend to the royal chamber something of the aspect of a railway station in miniature."[22]

With most of the corruption imagery gone—as indeed it was customarily removed from most of the play—the scene became a clash of domestic pieties, now coupled with religion rather than sex. In the "coda" of the scene Hamlet's "traditional" response to the discovery that he has killed Polonius was sorrow—marked in criticism as well as performance: Charles Lamb tells his readers that Hamlet, "his spirits being now a little quieter . . . wept for what he had done."[23] Such an interpretation was made all the more plausible by the excision of the bitter taunts of the scenes in which Hamlet is chased, apprehended, and shipped off to England.

In Gertrude's closet, the Victorian Hamlet became a preacher. Frank Marshall told an audience at the Catholic Young Men's Association that "Never was a nobler sermon preached than is embodied in these speeches; they are instinct with the truest and purest morality that knows of no compromise with evil."[24] Madness could excuse some of the harshness that remained after the overall impression of graciousness and refinement had been established; filial piety could be emphasized in Hamlet's relations with his mother and father; the desire to have Claudius well damned could be explained away (as it had been in Hazlitt's *Characters of Shakespeare's Plays*) as a studentlike speculation rather than the expression of a real intent; the depth of his love for Ophelia and grief at another woman's betrayal could excuse Hamlet's brutality towards an innocent girl. Moreover, by modifying so much the performed signs of madness, Victorian interpretation reduced the potential effect of decisions on the insanity question. Hamlet the satirist, the shocker, and the revenger were subsumed in Hamlet the moralist. *Pietas* replaced grudge; sorrow outweighed anger. In the most intimate room in the castle the couch for luxury and damned incest had been removed, the nasty sty was cleaned out, and a *prie-dieu* has been installed.

Notes

1. Max Beerbohm, *More Theatres,* ed. Sir Rupert Hart-Davis (St. Albans, Herts.: Hart-Davis Ltd., 1969), 359–60.

2. Ibid., 486.

3. James Davidson to Charles Lamb Kenney, undated, Bram Stoker Collection, Shakespeare Centre, Stratford-upon-Avon. Kenney had written to similar effect in a review, "Mr. Irving as Hamlet," in *Belgravia.*

4. "*Hamlet* at the Princess's Theatre," *St. James's Magazine* (October 1861): 371–76.

5. Elaine Showalter, "Representing Ophelia: Women, Madness, and the Responsibilities of Feminist Criticism," in *Shakespeare and the Question of Theory,* ed. Patricia Parker and Geoffrey Hartman (London: Methuen, 1985).

6. On the 1913 film, see Robert Hamilton Ball, *Shakespeare on Silent Film: A Strange Eventful History* (London: Allen and Unwin, 1968), 188–95. For illustrations of various *Hamlet* settings from the period, see Raymond Mander and Joe Mitchenson, comps., and Herbert Marshall, ed., *Hamlet through the Ages: A Pictorial Record from 1709,* 2d. ed. (London: Rockliff, 1955).

7. W. S. Gilbert, *Rosencrantz and Guildenstern,* in *Plays by W. S. Gilbert,* ed. George Rowell (Cambridge: Cambridge University Press, 1982), 173–85; 176.

8. A. D. Kellogg, M. D., *Shakespeare's Psychological Delineations: Ophelia* (New York, 1864), 4.

9. Cowden-Clarke's copy in Birmingham Shakespeare Library: the notes quoted are on pp. 125 and 129.

10. Edward Fitzgerald, *Letters to Fanny Kemble, 1871–1883,* ed. W. A. Wright, 2d. ed. (London: Macmillan & Co., 1902), 32.

11. John Conolly, *A Study of Hamlet* (London, 1863), 157 (closet scene); 200 (graveyard).

12. Mary Cowden-Clarke, "Lawrence and Kemble's Hamlet—Shakespeare's Hamlet—the World's Hamlet," *Sharpe's London Magazine* 6 (1848): 181–84.

13. Quotations are from vols. 1, 2, and 4 of the manuscript "Shakespearean Performances Which I Have Seen," 21 vols., in Birmingham Shakespeare Library.

14. Edwin Wilson, ed., *Shaw on Shakespeare* (Harmondsworth: Penguin, 1969), 99.

15. Edward Strachey, *Shakespeare's Hamlet: An Attempt to Find the Key to a Great Moral Problem by Methodical Analysis of the Play* (London, 1848), 74.

16. Charles H. Shattuck, *The Hamlet of Edwin Booth* (Urbana: University of Illinois Press, 1969), 229: the performance is here seen through the eyes of Charles Clarke, whose description of Booth's 1870 performance is used by Shattuck.

17. Herbert Beerbohm Tree, "Hamlet—from an Actor's Prompt-Book," *Fortnightly Review,* o.s., 64 (December 1895): 863–78; 875.

18. Folger Shakespeare Library Prompt Ham. 25; see also Arthur Colby Sprague, *Shakespeare and the Actors* (Cambridge: Harvard University Press, 1944), 169–170.

19. Alan Hughes, *Henry Irving, Shakespearean* (Cambridge: Cambridge University Press, 1980), 66.

20. Shattuck, *Hamlet,* 236.

21. Alan S. Downer, *The Eminent Tragedian: William Charles Macready* (Cambridge: Harvard University Press, 1966), 247.

22. *Illustrated Sporting and Dramatic News,* 25 October 1884.

23. Thomas Hutchinson, ed., *The Works in Prose and Verse of Charles and Mary Lamb,* 2 vols. (Oxford, 1908), 2:223.

24. Frank Marshall, *A Study of Hamlet* (London, 1875), 53.

Undercurrents in Victorian Illustrations of Shakespeare

by BARBARA ARNETT MELCHIORI

Most of the attention paid to illustrations of Shakespeare has been focused on stagecraft, or, more broadly, stage history. The questions that have been raised have been "How, in such-and-such a period was this play staged?" "What kind of sets were used?" "What costumes were chosen?" and even, at times, "How was a particular scene interpreted?" When one comes to the nineteenth century, and particularly to the Victorians, I wonder if these are really the right questions to be asking. Even Moelwyn Merchant in *Shakespeare and the Artist* deals with Victorian illustrators in chapters called "From Edmund to Charles Kean" and "From Kean to Granville-Barker"; that is to say, he places the emphasis squarely on the theater. I agree, however, with his comment that, always excepting the pre-Raphaelites, and he *does* except them, "in illustrative work independent of the theatre this [the Victorian] was not a distinguished period."

It was nevertheless a highly prolific period, the most prolific there has ever been, for with the turn of the twentieth century photography took over and Shakespeare's plays have since been illustrated for the most part by photographs from productions, bringing the plays back onto the boards, where, of course, they belong. An interesting contemporary initiative is the New Cambridge Shakespeare, showing a reversal of this trend and a return to the artist as illustrator, where Walter Hodges's drawings focus on controversial points of Elizabethan staging.

Going back to the nineteenth century, I think we should never lose sight of the fact that the dominant art form in the Victorian period was the novel, and that all other art forms felt its backwash. In painting the conversation piece, where the artist sets out to tell a story, becomes increasingly popular. At the same time, with the spread of literacy, a growing number of non-theater-goers were turning their attention to Shakespeare. Many nonconformists were kept away from the theater by scruples of conscience, and this I think explains the stress placed by editors of Shakespeare giftbooks on the moral teaching to be derived therefrom. Look for example at the 1862–64 edition of *The Heroines of Shakespeare,* republished in monthly parts at 2s. each: these heroines, to quote from the preface,

> are chaste, not because they are passionless, or because they have deliber-ately weighed the propriety of two courses of conduct, and decided for the better; but because, being passionful, they are also single-eyed and true hearted, and revolt instinctively from the thought of wanton dese-cration of their spotless natures.

No explanation is offered for the inclusion in the giftbook of Cleopatra and Lady Macbeth among these paragons.

These giftbooks, often expensively got up (Paul Jerrard in 1886 printed his *Shakespearian Tableaux* in costly though today almost illegible gilt letter-ing) all followed the same pattern: a series of prints of Shakespearean heroines fronting a page of carefully selected text from the play in ques-tion. The illustrations in the earlier giftbooks, such as Heath's *Shakespeare Gallery* of 1837, are of remarkably interchangeable young ladies in only slightly modified contemporary costume, who can best be identified with a particular heroine by the name printed below. This volume was extremely popular and was reprinted, in various formats and with slight changes, throughout the century, an 1862–64 deluxe edition even adding a French translation to the English text and what are advertised as "critical essays on each of the characters." These so-called essays were simply plot-summaries and far from accurate at that. *Macbeth* ends with the words "Lady Macbeth soon after dies; and her husband becomes the victim of Malcolm, the son of Duncan, whom he had hoped to have excluded from the throne." Macduff and Fleance have disappeared.

The real problem for the Victorian illustrator was posed by Lady Mac-beth and Kate the shrew, for the usual gently smiling models were seen to be inappropriate and were replaced by a dark lady with a ferocious scowl. The same solution was adopted by illustrators of the plays themselves and these heroines continue to scowl in the drawings of A. E. Chalon, Kenny Meadows, Augustus L. Egg and A. Johnston: the expression may have been borrowed from Richard Westall's painting from the Boydell Collection of the previous century where Lady Macbeth not only scowls but extends a clenched right fist. An anonymous drawing in the 1876 edition of the *Works* shows Lady Macbeth instead wringing her hands, but still scowling. It is a far cry from Sargent's majestic painting of Ellen Terry in the role.

The problem of the moral lesson to be learned from Lady Macbeth is squarely faced by Mrs. Anna Jameson in her very popular *Shakespeare's Heroines.* This book was first published in 1832 but was frequently re-published and enlarged throughout the century, and each edition was variously embellished by numerous artists until in 1897 G. Bell & Son modernized the series by replacing the earlier steel engravings with photographs (or occasionally with photographs of paintings) based on actual productions. Mrs. Jameson writes of Lady Macbeth:

> . . . those who can feel and estimate the magnificent conception and poetical development of the character, have overlooked the grand moral lesson it conveys; they forget that the crime of Lady Macbeth terrifies us in proportion to the degree of pride, passion, and intellect we may ourselves possess. It is good to behold and to tremble at the possible result of the noblest faculties uncontrolled and perverted.

When it comes to Cleopatra Mrs. Jameson has to seek even further for her justification: "I am not here the apologist of Cleopatra's historical character, nor of such women as resemble her. . . ." But a saving grace is to be found even here: "The generous devotion of her women adds the moral charm which alone was wanting."

In Victorian novels the last chapter was devoted to "drawing the moral" and to handing out rewards and punishments. Most of the illustrators of Shakespeare were also employed as illustrators of novels and of children's books, and I feel that their approach to the plays and their choice and treatment of material for illustration was in keeping with the novel tradition and was very often similar to Mrs. Jameson's.

In the Victorian period Shakespeare-for-the-reader was extremely popular, and many major publishers issued amply illustrated copies of the complete Works that vied with the great popular encyclopedias and were often adorned with opulent bindings intended to find their place in the parlor beside the family Bible.

In a short paper I can only hope to point out some of the trends that I have noticed in looking through these illustrations. The first is a preference for narrative as opposed to dramatic passages—the artist takes over where the director in the theater is forced to leave off. To take a few examples: William Mulready's painting from Jaques's monologue on "The Seven Ages of Man" in *As You Like It* was copied in engravings reproduced in both giftbooks and Illustrated Shakespeares: the moralizing tone was exactly suited to those tastes that both novelists and illustrators were, at one and the same time, catering for and helping to form. Robert Smirke had earlier produced a set of seven paintings for the Boydell Collection on the same subject.

Illustrators also took full advantage of dreams, which allowed them to achieve effects out of reach of the play in performance, something that William Blake had already discovered in his famous "Queen Katherine's Dream." With the Victorians the dream of Clarence and Richard III are favorite subjects, as are prophecies and visions.

In this the illustrator is following Shakespeare the narrator rather than Shakespeare the dramatist, but at times the impulse to do his own thing got the better of him. We are at a considerable remove from Shakespeare in the illustration to *King Lear* in Charles Knight's 1851 edition, which shows a bear with cubs and a wolf (but no lion) with the caption

> This night, wherein the cub-drawn bear would crouch
> The lion and the belly-pinched wolf
> Keep their fur dry.

Not dissimilar to this is Gordon Browne's sketch of a group of horses plunging and rearing in illustration of Ross's narrative lines in *Macbeth*, "and Duncan's horses / Turned wild in nature, broke their stalls, flung out. . . ." In both cases Shakespeare's text seems to be simply a pretext for the animal drawing the artist wanted to make, though it could be argued that in the sketch from *Macbeth* Browne is pointing up one of the dominant themes in the imagery of the play. H. S. Marks likewise in the 1879 edition of *The Shakspere Gallery* produced a full-page steel engraving of an interior where a lady is being fitted for a new dress. The tailor's measure is about her waist, and the raison d'être of the picture is simply that one of the recruits in Falstaff's rag-tag army, Feeble, gives his trade as "A woman's tailor."

But the plays where Victorian illustrators, one and all, left the theater far

Figure 1. *The Lady's Tailor* **by H. S. Marks, from** *The Shakspere Gallery* **(1879).** *(Courtesy of the Syndics of Cambridge University Library, Cambridge.)*

behind, following the romantic tradition established by Blake, were *A Midsummer Night's Dream* and *The Tempest*. The Staunton Shakespeare, illustrated by Gilbert, has a drawing of Ariel on a bat's back, and the normally more restrained Leopold Shakespeare shows Ariel naked, with wings like a swan, slightly larger than life-size. R. Huskisson's *Tempest* shows sea, cliffs, and naked nymphs perched on a rock, while semitransparent spirits of the air fly around them. In the *Dream* Gordon Browne in the Irving Shakespeare fills his picture with disembodied nymphs, R. Huskisson shows Titania and her fairies naked except for transparent veils: a large snail is placed in the foreground of his drawing to point up the dimensions of his tiny figures. R. Dadd provides a circular picture with Puck and fairies against a sickle moon; H. J. Townsend an elegant semicircular drawing of Ariel as a naked fairy swinging in a convolvulus hammock, while Frank Howard, in the Howard Shakespeare, returns to genre painting to illustrate "And sometimes lurk I in a gossip's bowl."

One of the best known, and best, Victorian Shakespeare pictures is Millais's painting (1852), now in the Tate Gallery, of the drowned Ophelia, based on the beautiful narrative monologue in which the Queen announces her death. Other illustrators chose the same theme: in Charles Knight's *Collected Shakespeare* Ophelia is shown sitting up in a brook, not yet quite ready to drown, with a water lily and basket of flowers floating beside her. The Leopold Shakespeare shows her just slipping down into the stream, which already laps the hem of her robe—her hands are full of flowers. In a semicircular engraving from a painting by A. Hughes in *The Shakspere Gallery*, Ophelia, seated on the trunk of a willow, scatters flowers into a twilit stream while a large bat skims menacingly over the water. In the 1876 *Works Hamlet* is closed by a tailpiece of a willow aslant a brook from which a garment trails down into a stream where a basket of flowers is sinking.

I feel that the attraction felt by Victorian illustrators for the drowned Ophelia goes a step beyond that escape into a fantasy world that we see in their work on the *Tempest* and the *Dream*. They are being drawn into that undercurrent of morbid sensuality that surfaces from time to time in Victorian poetry. The closest analogy to Ophelia is Tennyson's "The Lady of Shallott" (1832, revised 1842) a seminal poem of an age with a marked streak of necrophily. The lady floating down to Camelot, "the leaves upon her falling light" to be gazed on by court and citizens, and the epitaph spoken by Launcelot who sees her for the first time only as a lovely corpse, as illustrated in Dante Gabriel Rossetti's sketch, must have been in the mind of more than one artist when drawing Ophelia.

But Tennyson is not alone. The narrator in Robert Browning's "Evelyn Hope" who monologizes for an hour beside Evelyn's corpse, meditating on "the red young mouth, and the hair's young gold," closes with the words:

> So, hush—I will give you this leaf to keep:
> See, I shut it inside the sweet cold hand!
> There, that is our secret:

Figure 2. *There Sleeps Titania* by R. Huskisson, from *The Shakspere Gallery* (1879). *(Courtesy of the Syndics of Cambridge University Library, Cambridge.)*

Figure 3. *Ariel* by H. J. Townsend, from *The Shakspere Gallery* (1879). *(Courtesy of the Syndics of Cambridge University Library, Cambridge.)*

while the narrator in "Porphyria's Lover," after hesitating to touch her when alive, sits all night with the head of the dead girl on his shoulder, and again "Gold Hair" is the story of the exhumation of the body of a young girl. Fact did its best to keep up with fiction: Elizabeth Siddal, Dante Gabriel Rossetti's wife, was exhumed seven years after burial to rescue the MS of his *Poems,* which he had placed in her coffin.

William Morris, in an early poem that has survived in fragmentary form (his daughter dates it at 1855), writes voluptuously:

> Dead is she then—behold I pass my lips
> Over her cold face, moaning like a bee . . .
> I kissed her o'er and o'er right from the boddice hem
> Up to the golden locks yea sunk my lips in them—
> I never knew till now how sweet a kiss could be.

and the poem ends with a gesture of fetishism:

> I bent down till my wet cheek touched her foot
> Took off the gold shoe. I felt a sharp pain shoot
> Through all my frame, go down to the heart's root.

Even the young Kipling published a dramatic monologue in the Morris style in his early collection *Sundry Phansies* (1882). The poem is called "Paul Vaughel" and the poet sets forth the argument in these words, "how he took to himselfe an unfortunate [i.e., prostitute], and maintained her, and how she died, and how he buried her in the Pol-lourdesse and of the evil that came on him." The description of the youth burying his dead love on the seashore with his own hands and then mourning over her has a decadent ring that is not easy to associate with the Kipling we know.

> For the plague that summer brings to our town
> Seized her and held, and threw her down.
> . . . .
> And I plucked sea poppy and wind dried heather,
> And wove them into a wreath together
> And I set the wreath on her brows as night
> Came, and shut them out of my sight.
> Then I piled the sand over face and hair
> Till I left no whit of the body bare
> For I felt in the dark lest foot or hand
> Should be uncovered by the sand.
> And I staked up gorse till my fingers bled,
> Lest the sheep should pasture over head.
> And I weighted the bushes with boulder clay,
> And I sat on the dunes and wept all day.

Minor as well as major poets were attracted by the theme, such as Thomas Woolner, who in the first number of *The Germ* (January 1850) wrote "Of my

Figure 4. *Viola and Olivia* by Walter Deverell, from *The Germ* (1850). *(Courtesy of the Syndics of Cambridge University Library, Cambridge.)*

lady in death," so it is hardly surprising to find illustrators pausing on the drowned Ophelia and paying considerable attention also to the scene where Laertes and Hamlet leap into her grave. I have no space now even to list the numerous drawings of Cordelia dead in Lear's arms, of Imogen as dead in the arms of Arviragus, of Juliet dead in the Monument, or of Desdemona strangled in bed. If I may be allowed an aside, Fanny Kemble wrote a revealing comment on *Othello* in her *Records of Later Life* (1882): "That smothering scene is most extremely horrible . . . my only feeling about acting it with Mr. Macready is dread of his personal violence." Macready must, I think, have been playing up to the rising tension he felt in an audience hypersensitive to this theme as he leaned over the bed to strangle her.

To close, I want to draw attention to another theme chosen, almost without exception, by Victorian illustrators—the moment when in *Twelfth Night* Olivia puts back her veil for Viola to gaze upon her face. I would like to suggest that the key to the fondness for this subject lies in a curious variant—in the April 1850 issue of *The Germ* it is Viola herself who raises the veil, and this illustration by Walter Deverell is accompanied by an unsigned Lesbian poem entitled "Viola and Olivia." Now the theme of sisterhood and of the relations between women is recurrent in Victorian fiction, one of the best examples being Rhoda Broughton's *Doctor Cupid* (1886), where it is linked to the vampire theme so much loved by Henry James. The unsigned poem in *The Germ* is not very good, but it is interesting to find such an early treatment by a Shakespearean illustrator and by a poet of the theme of lesbianism, which only made its way with difficulty into the novel in the 1880s and 1890s with James's *The Bostonians*, George Moore's *Drama in Muslin,* and Gissing's *The Odd Women.* The head of Viola in Deverell's drawing is modeled on Elizabeth Siddal (the woman who was subsequently exhumed): she was used as model also for Millais's "Ophelia," for which she had to lie fully clothed in a bath of water, kept warm by lamps beneath the bath. To quote from the poem accompanying Deverell's illustration of Viola and Olivia,

> We have oft been curious to know
> The after-fortunes of these lovers dear;
> Having a steady faith some deed must show
> That they were married souls—unmarried here.

In conclusion, what I have been trying to suggest is in the first place that Victorian illustrators of Shakespeare were working essentially for a novel reading public and shared a preference for narrative rather than dramatic subjects, and in the second place that the ambivalence between intensive moralizing and morbid sensuality that is to be found in the novel and the poetry of the Victorian age is reflected also in the work, whether good or bad, of Shakespearean illustrators.

Petrarchanism Come True in Romeo and Juliet

by ANN PASTERNAK SLATER

Romeo and Juliet, it is generally recognized, bears some relationship to the sonneteers' presentation of love that had become so fashionable in the 1590s. Critics and editors note the sonnets spoken by the Chorus, by Romeo and Juliet when they meet, as well as the frequent use of Petrarchan tropes, particularly in the first half of the play. The precise status of Petrarchanism is still a matter of dispute, however. For some, there is a contrast between Romeo's affectation of Petrarchanism in the early days of his love for Rosaline, and the emotional and stylistic maturity evident in his love for Juliet. For others, the language of his first love is conventional without being parodic, and the play's later lapses into the formalities of Petrarchanism are an uneasy shifting between Shakespeare's old and new styles—a development not under the author's complete control. In general, the influence of Petrarchanism is agreed to diminish after the first half of the play. It is my purpose to argue that, on the contrary, Petrarchanism is central to the entire play—that in the love of Romeo and Juliet the empty paradoxes and hyperboles of Romeo's love for Rosaline become actual fact. This actualization of Petrarchan paradoxes, furthermore, is evident on every theatrical level, from linguistic texture and narrative structure to dramatic tone and stage symbol.[1]

It is obvious enough that Shakespeare begins the play as a satire of Petrarchanism. The dated nature of Petrarch's rhetoric of love is comically identified when Capulet ponderously imitates a fifty-year-old Wyatt translation of Petrarch, to describe Juliet in tears:[2]

> How now, a conduit, girl? What, still in tears?
> Evermore show'ring? In one little body
> Thou counterfeits a bark, a sea, a wind:
> For still thy eyes, which I may call the sea,
> Do ebb and flow with tears; the bark thy body is,
> Sailing in this salt flood; the winds, thy sighs. . . .
>
> [3.5.129–34]

As Wolfgang Clemen observed, Capulet's antique literary tastes are plausibly in character.[3] But he is not alone in them. Romeo, sick at heart for Rosaline, also plagiarizes freely and feebly—a weakness his friends tease him about:

> *Mercutio.* Now is he for the numbers that Petrarch flow'd in. Laura to his lady was a kitchen wench (marry, she had a better love to berhyme her). . . .
>
> [2.4.38–41]

Romeo's affectation of Petrarchanism is most apparent when he first appears on a stage scattered with the debris of the street brawl and launches into a torrent of clichéd paradoxes:

> O me! what fray was here?
> Yet tell me not, for I have heard it all:
> Here's much to do with hate, but more with love.
> Why then, O brawling love! O loving hate!
> O anything, of nothing first create!
> O heavy lightness; serious vanity,
> Misshapen chaos of well-seeming forms,
> Feather of lead, bright smoke, cold fire, sick health,
> Still-waking sleep, that is not what it is!
> This love feel I, that feel no love in this.
> Dost thou not laugh?
>
> [1.1.173–83]

Surely Shakespeare guides audience response by prompting amused glances between Romeo's friends? It is a technique paralleled in *Richard II*, where Richard's literary effusions prompt a similar embarrassed amusement among his interlocutors.[4] Romeo's speech, though, is not just unintentionally funny. In it Shakespeare makes three distinct points. The most obvious level is his parody of the Petrarchan oxymoron—a rhetorical chestnut Sidney had roasted some five years before:

> Some lovers speak, when they their Muses entertain,
> Of hopes begot by fear, of wot not what desires,
> Of force of heavenly beams infusing hellish pain,
> Of living deaths, dear wounds, fair storms, and freezing fires. . . .
>
> [*Astrophel and Stella* 6][5]

Beyond the blunt parody, Shakespeare further condemns the empty nature of such rhetoric, expressed in the very paradoxes that characterize it: Petrarchanism is ponderously trivial ("heavy lightness"), chaotically mannered ("misshapen chaos of well-seeming forms") and, above all, a loveless expression of love ("This love feel I, that feel no love in this"). Romeo is unaware, naturally, of the parodic nature of his speech, which implicitly condemns the fictional, literary nature of his love for Rosaline—a point

Shakespeare reaffirms by giving her no stage presence.[6] She might almost be, therefore, simply a figment of his imagination (a theatrical point destroyed by the early adaptations of the play, which transferred Romeo's lines about Rosaline to Juliet).[7] Finally, Romeo is quite unaware of the speech's third and most important plane of meaning, its prophetic irony: as soon as Romeo falls genuinely in love with Juliet, his literary fantasy turns into literal reality: the beloved is a real enemy, and many of the other paradoxes follow: the lightness of love becomes a serious matter, and scenes of joy are transformed into tragedy.

The basis of the play is therefore literary-critical and Shakespeare a rigorous critic, who, in Keatsian terms, makes Romeo and Juliet prove their lovers' language on their own pulses. This opening speech grimly predicts the real paradoxes of the play's ending: the trite oxymoron, "Still-waking sleep, that is not what it is," anticipates Juliet's apparent sleep of death in the Capulets' monument, while "A choking gall, and a preserving sweet" (l. 194) prefigures the drug she takes to live faithful, and the poison Romeo takes to die.

Romeo's speech, then, proclaims the play's themes in a number of ways. It locates the fluctuating contrarieties that are to be a sustained leit-motif from now on. It also identifies the play's highly experimental fusion of antithetical modes, the comic and the tragic; "heavy lightness; serious vanity" aptly characterizes the scenes of comic melodrama at the center of the play, to which critics have had such a troubled reaction. It is not surprising, perhaps, that soon after its revival in the seventeenth century, *Romeo and Juliet* should have been played as a tragedy and a tragi-comedy on alternate nights. For in many ways it is the sophisticated obverse of the "very tragical mirth" of Pyramus and Thisbe in *A Midsummer Night's Dream*—which some have thought to be a parody of the earlier play.[8]

The play's central theme, and the staging used to express it, are both outlined in Capulet's speech over the supposed corpse of his daughter on her wedding day:

> All things that we ordained festival,
> Turn from their office to black funeral:
> Our instruments to melancholy bells,
> Our wedding cheer to a sad burial feast,
> Our solemn hymns to sullen dirges change;
> Our bridal flowers serve for a buried corse;
> And all things change them to the contrary.
>
> [4.5.84–90]

The lines are closely derived from Arthur Brooke's *Tragicall Historye of Romeus and Juliet.*[9] But Brooke makes nothing of these alternating contrarieties, beyond a rhetorically mannered passage. Shakespeare acts them out in his compressed and concretized version of the story.

"All things change them to the contrary." In linguistic terms, the play is characterized throughout (and not merely in the supposedly Petrarchan first half) by a juxtaposition of opposites, which are frequently made to partake of each other's antithetical qualities. Light links with heavy, and heavy with light: "Away from light steals home my heavy son"; "Being but heavy, I will bear the light" (1.1.137, 1.4.12). Light links with dark, and dark with light: "More light and light it grows." "More light and light, more dark and dark our woes!" (3.5. 35–36). Late night and early day are one and the same thing: "Afore me, it is so very late that we/May call it early by and by"; "Is she not down so late, or up so early?" (3.4.34–35, 3.5.66). So are up and down: "Come, Montague, for thou art early up / To see thy son and heir now early down" (5.3.208–9). In and out are juxtaposed, as well as life and death: "Then, window, let day in, and let life out." "I must be gone and live, or stay and die" (3.5.41, 11). Wedding and funeral coalesce: "If he be married, / My grave is like to be wedding-bed" (1.5.134–35). Nor are these alternations restricted to tragedy. Lady Capulet and the Nurse employ the same motif farcically, persuading Juliet to marry Paris, and "By having him, making yourself no less. *Nurse:* No less! nay, bigger" (1.3.94–95).

Moreover, of course, many of these apparently facile tropes come true. Romeo's trite original definition of love as "A choking gall, and a preserving sweet" quickly turns to accurate prophecy. Tybalt echoes the line when he recognizes Romeo at the Capulet ball—just as his sense of contradictory emotions prefigures the play's mixed modes:

> *Tybalt.* Patience perforce with willful choler meeting
> Makes my flesh tremble in their different greeting.
> I will withdraw, but this intrusion shall,
> Now seeming sweet, convert to bitt'rest gall.
>
> [1.5.89–92]

Similarly, Juliet discovers the truth of Romeo's stale paradox, "O brawling love! O loving hate!", when she realizes she has fallen in love with a Montague:

> My only love sprung from my only hate!
> Too early seen unknown, and known too late!
> Prodigious birth of love it is to me,
> That I must love a loathed enemy.
>
> [1.5.138–41]

In her outcry against Romeo, Tybalt's murderer, the mannered oppositions now accurately express her confused feelings of love and outraged family loyalty:

> *Juliet.* Beautiful tyrant! fiend angelical!
> Dove-feather'd raven! Wolvish ravening lamb!
> Despised substance of divinest show!

> Just opposite to what thou justly seem'st,
> A damned saint, an honorable villain!
>
> [3.2.75–79]

But the precise tone of the passage is ambivalent, Juliet's distress being genuine enough, though its expression verges on the parodic.[10]

Verifications of Petrarchanism are not limited to the present tense. Dramatic irony riddles the play: Romeo and Juliet, and relatively minor characters like the Friar and Tybalt, have frequent premonitions of the tragic outcome.[11] These conscious forebodings are further extended by unconscious ironies working against the characters, like the prophetic ironies contained in Romeo's first, exaggeratedly Petrarchan speech, examined above. Whenever characters indulge in outrageous literary hyperbole, the plot takes them at their word. Juliet hysterically opts for any horror rather than bigamous marriage to Paris:

> *Juliet.*   bid me lurk
> Where serpents are; chain me with roaring bears,
> Or hide me nightly in a charnel-house,
> O'ercover'd quite with dead men's rattling bones,
> With reeky shanks and yellow chapless skulls;
> Or bid me go into a new-made grave,
> And hide me with a dead man in his shroud—
> Things that, to hear them told, have made me tremble—
>
> [4.1.79–86]

Done! Shakespeare and the Friar cry out in unison. And, before she can back out, Juliet finds herself agreeing to a horror that was intended as mere fiction. It was rash of Romeo, wallowing hysterically at news of his banishment, to demand of the Friar:

> *Romeo.* Hadst thou no poison mix'd, no sharp-ground knife,
> No sudden mean of death, though ne'er so mean,
> But "banished" to kill me? "Banished"?
>
> [3.3.44–46]

Oh yes, Shakespeare has those means too, both poison and knife; their time will come. Then, again, Juliet pretends anger at Romeo's murder of Tybalt, while actually expressing her love for him. She hopes to keep him safe from the poisoner that her mother (amazingly!) suggests:

> *Juliet.* Indeed I never shall be satisfied
> With Romeo, till I behold him—dead—
> Is my poor heart, so for a kinsman vex'd.
> Madam, if you could find out but a man
> To bear a poison, I would temper it,
> That Romeo should, upon receipt thereof,
> Soon sleep in quiet.
>
> [3.5.93–99]

This is nimble. But fate is cleverer than Juliet, and her words have not only a double, but a triple sense, of which she will remain unaware until the last act, when she finds Romeo, dead of poison, sleeping in peace at last.

On the linguistic level, then, Shakespeare sustains his literary-critical theme by repeated use of apparently trite Petrarchan paradoxes and literary hyperboles that are increasingly ironically actualized. Inevitably, too, the play's plot acts this out in narrative terms. The theme that "all things change them to the contrary" is often applied to the characters' frequent changes of mind. Romeo's *volte face* from Rosaline to Juliet is the prime example—marked, as it is, by the Friar's "Holy Saint Francis, what a change is here!" (2.3.65). There is a nice comic parallel when the Nurse brazenly ditches Romeo, after his banishment, to champion Paris as a fit husband for Juliet: "O, he's a lovely gentleman! / Romeo's a dishclout to him . . ." (3.5.218–19). Juliet's earlier expostulation, "What storm is this that blows so contrary?" (3.2.64) epitomizes such alterations. It is a measure of Shakespeare's artistic control that he should have prepared the ground when first introducing the audience to Juliet and her mother:

> *Juliet.*   Madam, I am here,
>   What is your will?
> *Lady Capulet.* This is the matter. Nurse, give us leave awhile,
>   We must talk in secret. Nurse, come back again,
>   I have rememb'red me, thou s' hear our counsel.
>   [1.3.5–9]

This is not a mere linguistic change of mind. It has to be acted out, with the Nurse turning to go, going, and then turning again when she is recalled. The actors' memories of their production, preserved in the stage directions of the First Quarto,[12] show that this was not the only moment when such changes of mind were staged:

> *Romeo.* Farewell good Nurse.
>   *Nurse offers to goe in and turnes againe.*
> *Nurse.* Heere is a Ring Sir, that she bad me giue you.
>   [Q1:G2]

And again:

> *Paris.* These times of woe affoord no time to wooe,
>   Maddam farwell, commend me to your daughter.
>   *Paris offers to goe in, and Capolet calles him againe.*
> *Capulet.* Sir Paris? Ile make a desperate tender of my child . . .
>   [Q1:G2v]

Realistic theatrical moments like these sustain the play's central theme in miniature. On the broadest plane, the narrative is an equivalent succession of wavelike reversals as the lovers' fortunes rise and fall—a pattern well summarized in the Friar's final résumé: "I married them, and their stol'n marriage-day / Was Tybalt's dooms-day" (5.3.233–34). The sequence of accelerated reversals culminates in the supreme irony opening act 5, when Romeo, exiled in Mantua, enters in a happy mood—"If I may trust the flattering truth of sleep, / My dreams presage some joyful news at hand"— only to be met with Balthasar's news of Juliet's death. Dramatic tableaux vividly press home this layering of joy on disaster, most strikingly in act 4 (as Granville-Barker noted), when Juliet falls back, seemingly dead, within the curtains of her bed, while the main stage is quickly taken over by the oblivious Capulet household, happily busy with her wedding preparations.[13] Indeed, the whole play is a series of bold stage tableaux, with an overall pattern of reversal: it moves from the brawl to the ball of act 1; from the fight to the bridal night of act 3; from the wedding festival-turned-funeral of act 4, to the final tomb that (as we shall see later) holds many of the visible connotations of the wedding bed in act 5. These violent polarities of plot finally come to rest at a point where, in the Chorus's words, extremes are tempered with extreme sweet.

Dramatic mood follows the same pattern of alternating extremes, with moments of comic melodrama punctuating the play's inexorable progression towards tragedy. This persistent emotional dislocation animates Juliet's realization that, far from grieving at Tybalt's death and Romeo's banishment, she should be grateful:

> Back, foolish tears, back to your native spring,
> Your tributary drops belong to woe,
> Which you, mistaking, offer up to joy.
> My husband lives that Tybalt would have slain,
> And Tybalt's dead that would have slain my husband.
> All this is comfort; wherefore weep I then?
>
> [3.2.102–7]

The Friar repeats her dogged arguments in the next scene, when he tries to buck Romeo up:

> What, rouse thee, man! thy Juliet is alive,
> For whose dear sake thou wast but lately dead:
> There art thou happy. Tybalt would kill thee,
> But thou slewest Tybalt: there art thou happy.
> The law that threat'ned death becomes thy friend,
> And turns it to exile: there art thou happy.
> A pack of blessings light upon thy back . . .
>
> [3.3.135–41]

But there is something comically pedantic in the Friar's pedestrian accountancy, however worthy—a comic note we find again and again in the extreme vicissitudes of the central acts, and a comic note that has discomfited many serious-minded critics.[14] I have already suggested that the lovers' hysteria (at Romeo's banishment and Juliet's threatened marriage to Paris) is over the top. It is absurdly hyperbolical, and Shakespeare catches them both out for it: the alarms of the central acts are to be as nothing to the disasters of the last—which the lovers face with such courageous simplicity. The play's theme, "How all things change them to the contrary," dictates the tone—the action modulates from scenes of comic melodrama in acts 3 and 4, to the genuine, understated tragedy of the last. Mercutio's death illustrates Shakespeare's delicate balance. His pun, "Ask for me to-morrow, and you shall find me a grave man" (3.1.97–98), is yet another potent miniature instance of the play's central motif. "Heavy" / "light" is one of the play's recurrent verbal antitheses, here vividly enacted, as the gravity of Mercutio's position is lightly dismissed. For Mercutio, death *is* a joking matter—and yet his quip wins our serious respect for the first time. Mixed modes like these riddle the play's central acts. Ever more extreme in their divergent simultaneity, they culminate in the absurd mock-tragedy of the supposedly dead Juliet, so ineptly mourned by her household:

> O woe! O woeful, woeful, woeful day!
> Most lamentable day, most woeful day
> That ever, ever, I did yet behold!
> O day! O day! O day! O hateful day!
>
> [4.5.49–52]

Shakespeare exploits his staging further to press home his theme. Props emphasize the negative and positive overlay of event upon event, already noted in the play's narrative structure. For example, the brawl ending in Tybalt's death and Romeo's banishment is immediately capped by Juliet's happy soliloquy in expectation of her wedding night—and her exultant speech is broken off by the Nurse's entry, *"with cords,"* according to the (probably authorial) stage direction of the second Quarto:[15]

> *Juliet.*   O, here comes my nurse,
> *Enter Nurse with cords.*
> And she brings news; and every tongue that speaks
> But Romeo's name speaks heavenly eloquence.
> Now, nurse, what news?
>
> [3.2.31–34]

But the nurse drops the cords to burst into incoherent grieving: "Ah, well-a-day! he's dead, he's dead, he's dead!" Far from heavenly eloquence, Juliet has to listen to a confused speech, from which she can hardly make out who is dead, and why. Yet through all the ensuing anguish, the ropes lie on the stage for all the audience to see, an eloquent and silent promise of the scene's happy outcome, Romeo's ascent to Juliet's bedroom and the consummation of their marriage.

People, too, are used like props, to stress the fluctuating and uniting dualities that structure the play. On several occasions in the canon, Shakespeare calls for the apparently "anticipatory" entry of a character, playing off the words of the actor stage front against the silent entrant at the back.[16] Here, the Friar enters with his basket, to meditate on the dual potential of the herbs and weeds he is gathering. Halfway through the soliloquy Romeo also comes in, presumably by one of the doors at the back of the majority of Elizabethan stages, while the Friar, unawares, continues to speak stage front. Everything he says has implicit application to Romeo (as several critics have noted). Indeed, at the end of the speech, the Friar himself makes the link between herbs and men in general. The audience, given this graphic staging, needs little prompting to take the further step from men in general to Romeo in particular:

> *Friar Lawrence.* I must up-fill this osier cage of ours
> With baleful weeds and precious-juiced flowers.
> The earth that's nature's mother is her tomb;
> What is her burying grave, that is her womb;
> And from her womb children of divers kind
> We sucking on her natural bosom find:
>
> . . . .
>
> For nought so vile that on the earth doth live
> But to the earth some special good doth give;
> Nor aught so good but, strain'd from that fair use,
> Revolts from true birth, stumbling on abuse.
> Virtue itself turns vice, being misapplied,
> And vice sometime by action dignified.
> *Enter Romeo.*
> Within the infant rind of this weak flower
> Poison hath residence, and medicine power;
>
> . . . .
>
> Two such opposed kings encamp them still
> In man as well as herbs, grace and rude will;
> And where the worser is predominant,
> Full soon the canker death eats up that plant.
> *Romeo.* Good morrow, father!
>
> [2.3.7–12; 17–24; 27–31]

After such a pointed and extended homily, it is surprising that some critics still debate the nobility or sinfulness of Juliet's love.[17] The Friar's speech clearly directs us to the deliberate moral ambivalence in Shakespeare's presentation of both Romeo and Juliet, and further, the Friar himself. His efforts, though well intentioned, have disastrous results. Romeo's dual potential is equally exemplified. In physical terms, he is capable of love and hate, murder and procreation—the death of Tybalt and marriage to Juliet. In moral terms, an equal confusion of good and bad recurs. For instance, Romeo's virtuous patience at Tybalt's taunts seems like cowardice to his amazed friends; and his suicide, though a mortal sin, is surely dignified to tragic status. Similarly, the love of Romeo and Juliet leads to their deaths but also to the reconciliation of their families. The Friar's speech is, in fact, a warning against facile moral categorization.

Shakespeare's manipulation of the minutiae of staging is broadly devoted to two ends: to make the verbal hyperboles traditionally associated with Petrarchan love rhetoric actually come true, and, therefore, to stage convincingly a series of incompatible and unstable paradoxes.

The first of these two ends is particularly clear in the earlier half of the play. Take Shakespeare's use of masks. When Romeo first appears, he indulges, as we have already seen, in a number of trite love clichés: "Alas that love, whose view is muffled still, / Should, without eyes, see pathways to his will!" (1.1.171–72). Blind Cupid is a dog-eared trope, as everyone in Verona knows; later, when Romeo and his friends plan to gatecrash the Capulet ball incognito, Benvolio dismisses it as too dated for the maskers to dramatize:

> Romeo.   . . . shall we on without apology?
> Benvolio. The date is out of such prolixity:
>   We'll have no Cupid hoodwink'd with a scarf,
>   Bearing a Tartar's painted bow of lath,
>   Scaring the ladies like a crow-keeper . . .
>
> [1.4.2–6]

Yet the cliché comes into its own when Romeo and Juliet meet. It is clear from the Second Quarto's stage directions *("Enter Romeo . . . with five or sixe other Maskers, torchbearers"; "Enter all the guests and gentlewomen to the Maskers"),* as well as from the text, that Romeo and his friends are masked. Mercutio dons his vizor on stage ("Give me a case to put my visage in . . . Here are the beetle brows shall blush for me"—1.4.29, 32). Romeo, too, is masked at the ball. Tybalt can only recognize him as a Montague "by his voice," since he is "cover'd with an antic face" (1.5.54, 56). Juliet should probably also be masked (though this is not essential), because even the Capulets' servant doesn't recognize his own mistress when Romeo asks her identity (1.5.41). In the source, Romeo unmasks when he meets Juliet, but, *pace* Granville-Barker, there is no textual indication that Shakespeare's Romeo should do so. The lovers, faces and eyes obscured by half-masks, look like blindfold Cupid. More than that, they approve Romeo's original fatuous aphorism, falling in love precisely because they are masked and consequently blind to each other's social identity.[18] Characteristically, too, Shakespeare repeats the cliché after the event, making Romeo's frends tease him for his adoration of Rosaline: "Blind is his love and best befits the dark"; "If love be blind, love cannot hit the mark" (2.1.32–33). Their mockery, however, is no longer justified; love has hit its mark and blind Cupid found pathways to his will. Their jibe is as misplaced as the sneer,

"Now is he for the numbers Petrarch flow'd in"—a criticism also made after Romeo's love had become a reality, and Petrarch's dated numbers assumed a vivid, present truth.

Cupid is not only blind but light-footed and winged. In the bad days of Romeo's first love he is comically heavy-hearted, a point made in ponderous verbal play:

> *Mercutio.* You are a lover, borrow Cupid's wings,
>   And soar with them above a common bound.
>   *Romeo.* I am too sore enpierced with his shaft
>   To soar with his light feathers, and so bound
>   I cannot bound a pitch above dull woe.
>
> [1.4.17–21]

As soon as he has met Juliet, though, his heart lightens, and we see him leap over the Capulet's orchard wall—a leap that is most probably enacted since it is remarked by Benvolio ("He ran this way and leapt this orchard wall"—2.1.4), and later corroborated by Romeo in significant terms ("With love's light wings did I o'erperch these walls"—2.2.66). Shakespeare once again effortlessly transfers Cupid's creaking allegorical attributes to the limber living man. Even without staging, the verbal point would be forcefully made.[19]

Shakespeare's use of stage lights is a further example of his actualization of a traditional love cliché. Lovers have a natural and conventional preference for the dark—a preference obediently imitated in Romeo's early days of love-apprenticeship ("Away from light steals home my heavy son"—1.1.137). When Romeo and Juliet fall in love, though, the opposite cliché comes into operation, because the lovers lighten the darkness for one another. The proverbial "dark night is Cupid's day" is yet another amorous commonplace, like Cupid's blindfold eyes and winged feet, which Shakespeare brings to life. Caroline Spurgeon rightly drew attention to the frequency of light imagery in this play, which is used primarily by the lovers for one another.[20] But she missed both the staging of these verbal images, and their reversal.

Generally in Elizabethan and Jacobean drama, night and darkness are the traditional setting for tragedy, while dawning connotes clarity, sanity, and peace.[21] Shakespeare draws on both associations throughout his plays, with increasing subtlety, and it is noticeable that in his tragedies the major scenes take place at night. Since most plays (before the indoor theaters) were acted by daylight, in the afternoon, the dramatist's prime means of indicating darkness was by verbal description, and—ironically enough—by providing the artificial illumination of lights, tapers, and torches. In *Romeo and Juliet,* however, Shakespeare turns this exigency to good effect. He follows the erotic tradition, and reverses the tragic tradition, by making night a time of light and joy. Daylight, logically enough, then becomes the setting for tragedy. This paradoxical reversal clearly underscores the play's central motif that "all things change them to the contrary." Both language and staging emphasize this reversal, the darkness of the daylight scenes being verbally stressed, while the brightness of the night scenes is visibly realized in Shakespeare's careful provision of stage lights, which are emphatically attached to the lovers.

When Romeo meets Juliet, it is on a stage crowded with lights. "*Torch-bearers*" (Q2 SD) accompany Romeo to the Capulet's ball, where Capulet constantly fusses about the lights ("More light, you knaves . . . More light, more light! . . . More torches here!", 1.5.25, 87, 125). More than that, Shakespeare's dialogue makes it clear that Romeo should himself be a torchbearer, and that their first hushed, intimate encounter should be illuminated by the torch whose light encloses them both. As Romeo and his friends gather to gatecrash the ball, they draw attention to the lights they carry in a series of semiproverbial quips ("Come, we burn daylight, ho!" 1.4.43). Romeo makes it clear that he will not dance because he feels too low about Rosaline:

> *Romeo.* Give me a torch, I am not for this ambling;
> Being but heavy, I will bear the light.
> *Mercutio.* Nay, gentle Romeo, we must have you dance.
> Not I, believe me . . .
>
> . . . .
> A torch for me. Let wantons light of heart
> Tickle the senseless rushes with their heels.
> For I am proverb'd with a grandsire phrase,
> I'll be a candle-holder and look on:
>
> [1.4.11–14; 35–38]

But, as Tilley informs us, the full proverb runs, "A good candleholder proves a good gamester."[22] In other words, the cliché comes true once more and it is while Romeo, the sad wallflower, stands aside with his torch to watch the dancing couples, that he meets Juliet, his proper partner. As so often, Shakespeare attempts to ensure this staging by the prospective and retrospective directions of the dialogue, as well as the actual stage directions. Romeo's insistence that he will not dance is confirmed by Juliet's question as the maskers leave: "What's he that follows there, that would not dance?" (1.5.132). Logically, both halves of Romeo's determination should be acted out, and he should hold a flaming torch for his and Juliet's first, dazzled meeting.

Two other major love scenes are also, most probably, lit in the same way. When Romeo is in the Capulets' orchard, he sees Juliet appear above and exclaims, "But soft, what light through yonder window breaks?", modulating immediately into the metaphor, "It is the east, and Juliet is the sun" (2.2.2–3). It is evident from the stage directions of the First Quarto that other, even more apparently metaphorical lines, were given a literal stage enactment,[23] and it seems more probable that Juliet should indeed be carrying a light here. Such a staging is suggested, too, by the lovers' parting, toward the end of the scene:

> *Juliet.* A thousand times good night!
> *Exit.*
> *Romeo.* A thousand times the worse, to want thy light.
>
> [2.2.154–55]

A director keen to act out the implicit, and natural, indications of the text might well choose to make Juliet return (as she does, two lines later) without her light, since Romeo does not notice her for six lines, even when she whispers to call him. Cibber, in his adaptation of the play, must have been aware of the dramatic oddity of this detail, since he accommodates it by making Romeo also exit, until Juliet succeeds in calling him back.[24]

Most poignant of all, however, is Shakespeare's staging of the final scene. Night is firmly established by Paris's entry with his page, bearing a torch, which he then is told to extinguish (so intensifying the audience's sense of darkness). Note here, incidentally, yet another of those thematic changes of mind:

> *Enter Paris and his Page [with flowers and sweet water and a torch].*
> *Paris.* Give me thy torch, boy. Hence, and stand aloof.
> Yet put it out, for I would not be seen.
>
> [5.3.1–2]

Romeo in his turn enters with his page *"with a torch"* (Q1 SD), takes the unextinguished light from him ("Give me the light"—5.3.25), and dismisses him in order to break his way into the Capulets' monument on his own. He is disturbed by Paris, with whom he reluctantly fights, only identifying his victim after he has fallen, most likely by bringing up his light to him ("Let me peruse this face"—5.3.74).[25] Romeo then carries Paris into the tomb, taking the light with him. As in Brooke, it is still burning there after Romeo's death:

> *Friar.*   Tell me, good my friend,
> What torch is yond, that vainly lends his light
> To grubs and eyeless skulls? As I discern,
> It burneth in the Capels' monument.
>
> [5.3.124–27]

It burns on for Juliet's awakening—and her suicide. It is still burning inside the tomb as the citizens of Verona flock on stage to find the lovers dead.

> *Page.* This is the place, there, where the torch doth burn.
>
> [5.3.171]

Once again, Shakespeare simply turns literary paradox into literal truth. Throughout the play, the lovers opted for a night that they so lit up for one another, Romeo imagined "That birds would sing, and think it were not night" (2.2.22). When he first enters the tomb with Paris in his arms, his image might appear a beautiful hyperbole, nothing more:

> I'll bury thee in a triumphant grave.
> A grave? O no, a lanthorn, slaught'red youth;
> For here lies Juliet, and her beauty makes
> This vault a feasting presence full of light.
>
> [5.3.83–86]

But the modern stage can accomplish what Shakespeare projected and could only partially achieve—a fully darkened stage whose sole source of light is the tomb in which the lovers lie.[26]

The converse of the scenes literally and metaphorically illuminated by the lovers is of course the antithetical moments of daylight tragedy. Here the stress is linguistic, rather than actual; the dawn that ends Romeo and Juliet's wedding night is, for them, a time of darkness ("More light and light it grows"; "More light and light, more dark and dark our woes!" 3.5.36). This heavy lightness reaches its ultimate pitch in the Capulet family's outcry over Juliet's supposed corpse, on the morning of her wedding day, in which this "black" and "woeful *day*" is reiterated seventeen times in some forty lines, with obviously ludicrous effect. And the play ends on a more tempered echo of the same note, when the Prince observes:

> A glooming peace this morning with it brings,
> The sun, for sorrow, will not show his head.
>
> [5.3.305–6][22]

The function of Shakespeare's stage imagery is, then, not merely to literalize clichés, but to stage the alternation and fusion of apparently incompatible paradoxes. As the play twice stresses, night and day, late and early, are, at their extremest verge, the same thing. "Afore me, it is so very late that we / May call it early by and by." Granville-Barker is sensitive to the manifestation of this theme at certain points. The layering of happy and sad, night and day, emerges as he quotes these lines, with which Capulet closes his agreement with Paris that Juliet should marry him, and comments:

> Now comes the well-prepared effect. Hardly have the three vanished below, bustling and happy, when with
> > Wilt thou begone? It is not yet near day . . .
> Romeo and Juliet appear at the window above, clinging together, agonized in the very joy of their union, but all ignorant of this new and deadly blow which (again) *we* know is to fall on them.[28]

The central acts of the play use sound effects particularly strikingly to emphasize this lightning switchover from one mode to its opposite. Thus, in this very scene, as Romeo and Juliet cling together, the audience, listening to the birdsong so clearly demanded by the dialogue, will be unable at once to determine whether it is the nightingale or the lark, the bird of dawning, or the bird of night, whose song they hear. (Shakespeare was probably exploiting a disadvantage here—the deficiencies of the whistler in the wings.) Nor will the dialogue decide the question for them straightaway:

> *Juliet.* Wilt thou be gone? it is not yet near day.
> It was the nightingale, and not the lark,
> That pierc'd the fearful hollow of thine ear;
> . . . .
> *Romeo.* It was the lark, the herald of the morn,
> No nightingale. Look, love, what envious streaks
> Do lace the severing clouds in yonder east.
> . . . .
> *Juliet.* Yond light is not day-light . . .
>
> [3.5.1–3; 6–8; 12]

The same ambivalences and dualities of interpretation recur in the next act, as Juliet summons up her courage to drink off the sleeping potion. It is clear from the internal directions of the dialogue that Shakespeare makes provision for sound effects as she does so, for as soon as she has fallen back within the curtains of her bed, Capulet bustles in, exclaiming:

> Come, stir, stir, stir! the second cock hath crowed,
> The curfew-bell hath rung, 'tis three a' clock.
>
> [4.4.3–4]

Bells tolling, cocks crowing, are staple sound effects for night hauntings and horror.[29] The audience would have heard these sounds before Capulet's speech (since he puts them in the past tense)—that is, during Juliet's horrified fantasy of Tybalt's ghost approaching her in the Capulet tomb. At that moment they are ominous sounds—but for Capulet, they are the sounds of dawn and the marriage dawn will bring. This diametric reversal of connotations is then replayed in reverse once again, as the wedding music of Paris and his train is heard playing offstage—for the discovery of Juliet's supposed corpse. The stage direction of the second Quarto is quite clear about this:

> *Capulet.* Good [faith] tis day.
> *Play Musicke.*
> The Countie will be here with musicke straight,
> For so he said he would, I heare him neare.
> Nurse, wife, what ho, what Nurse I say?
> *Enter Nurse.*
> Go waken Juliet, go and trim her up . . .
>
> (Q2 : Kv-K2)

The reversals are precisely those later outlined by Capulet: "Our instruments to melancholy bells. . . . Our solemn hymns to sullen dirges change."
Just as Paris's wedding music should play so inappropriately for the discovery of Juliet's body, so the scene ends with yet another, now comic reversal,
as the bridegroom's moronic musicians debate the appropriateness of playing a "merry dump" to cheer themselves up, and Peter lugubriously sings:

> "When griping griefs the heart doth wound,
> And doleful dumps the mind oppress,
> Then music with her silver sound"—
>
> [4.5.126–28][30]

For act 4, scene 5, is only a mock-tragic scene of comic mourning. As the
audience knows, this black funeral is a misplaced absurdity, and C. B.
Lower is right to insist that the lamentations over Juliet's corpse should be
played as the First Quarto records, with Paris, Capulet, Lady Capulet, and
the Nurse all speaking simultaneously (*All at once cry out and wring their
hands*—Q1 : SD) till the Friar cuts through their confused and exaggerated
babble—"Peace ho, for shame! Confusion's cure lives not / In these confusions" (4.5.65–66). Inevitably, attempts like S. Franco Zeffirelli's to play
this scene seriously have failed.[31]

As Juliet's intended wedding in 4.5 turned into funeral, her and Romeo's
real deaths in act 5 should likewise poignantly recall the wedding bed.
Shakespeare draws on several elements of staging to stress this: costume,
props, lights (as we have already seen), and the disposition of his characters.

It is clear that Juliet should be immured in the Capulet monument in all
the finery that should have been hers at her wedding. This is twice, quite
explicitly, demanded by the Friar, first when he describes his plan to Juliet:

> Then, as the manner of our country is,
> In thy best robes, uncovered on the bier,
> Thou shall be borne to that same ancient vault
>
> [4.1.109–11]

The same orders are then made to her family when they discover her
corpse:

> Dry up your tears, and stick your rosemary
> On this fair corse, and as the custom is,
> And in her best array, bear her to church;
>
> [4.5.79–81]

As in the source, she lies on an open bier in the Capulet monument,[32] not
only in her best attire, but surrounded by the flowers and herbs with which
the Elizabethans customarily strewed both the beds of marriage and of
death. Hence the Friar's direction here for rosemary; hence, too, Paris's

entry in the last act, *"with flowers and sweete water"* (Q1 : I4v) with which he, too, wishes to strew her:[33]

> *Paris.* Sweet flower, with flowers thy bridal bed I strew—
> O woe, thy canopy is dust and stones!
>
> > [5.3.12–13]

It is, indeed, an irony of ceremony often remarked upon, for instance by Gertrude as she scatters flowers on Ophelia's open grave: "Sweets to the sweet, farewell! . . . I thought thy bride-bed to have deck'd, sweet maid, / And not have strew'd thy grave" (*Hamlet* 5.1.243–45). It is an irony played in happy reverse by Perdita, during her flower-distribution at the sheep-shearing festival,

> *Perdita.*   O, these I lack
> To make you garlands of, and my sweet friend,
> To strew him o'er and o'er!
> *Florizel.*   What, like a corse?
> *Perdita.* No, like a bank for love to lie and play on;
> Not like a corse; or if—not to be buried,
> But quick and in mine arms.
>
> > [*Winter's Tale* 4.4.127–32]

But it is only in *Romeo and Juliet* and *Othello* that Shakespeare stages the poignant ambiguity in which bride bed and death bed actually unite, and one looks like, or even is, the other.[34] Indeed, Perdita's speech recalls more than one of the paradoxes of Romeo and Juliet's deaths. Juliet is buried, "quick" and alive; Romeo, conversely, drinks off the poison, praising it in the same words, but with opposite intent: "O true apothecary! / Thy drugs are quick. Thus with a kiss I die" (5.3.119–20). And Romeo and Juliet are also buried in each others' arms, as the dialogue makes clear at several points. When Romeo first hears of Juliet's supposed "death," in Mantua, he resolves with quiet determination, very different from his earlier hysterics: "Well, Juliet, I will lie with thee to-night" (6.1.34). That pun is precisely what Shakespeare stages in his final tableau. Romeo's fulfilment of his promise is evident from a rejected line from the Second Quarto, as he lies beside Juliet on the tomb to take his poison: "Come lye thou in my arme" (Q2 : L3). The line was rejected because Shakespeare expanded on the speech, not because he changed his mind about its staging. The staging is reaffirmed by the Friar's line to Juliet, on her awakening: "Thy husband in thy bosom there lies dead" (5.3.15). There can be hardly any doubt that, after the Friar has left, Juliet should die, like Romeo, in her lover's arms—a tableau, incidentally, also described in Shakespeare's source and specifically detailed in Cibber's version.[35] So the play ends with the most poignant paradox of all, as love and death unite, and one visibly looks like the other.

The fusion of love and death has its origin, of course, in the old Elizabethan pun on death as sexual climax. But with Romeo and Juliet the cliché comes true. Given the enmity of their families, the only union Romeo and Juliet can enjoy is the consummation devoutly to be wished, to die to sleep together. So they find peace in the very end that Friar Lawrence warned them against:

> These violent delights have violent ends,
> And in their triumph die, like fire and powder,
> Which as they kiss consume.
>
> [2.6.9–11]

Theatrical interpretations of Shakespeare's plays raise two questions. First, the author's intentions and contemporary theatrical practice. Second, the arguable relevance of such interpretations to the theater today. As for the first, I would argue that my reading simply spells out a unified motif that is indicated by the play's language, imagery, narrative structure, and the staging implicitly suggested by the dialogue, and explicitly demanded by the stage directions, which happen to derive both from the author himself, in the second Quarto, and from his theater, in the First Quarto. With modern productions, of course, one cannot and should not legislate for any one particular reading, however, "right" it may seem. Academic interpretations with pretensions to theatricality are generally dismissed by the professional director, perhaps with reason. As Jonathan Miller said, in interview:

> There are points which come out much more clearly in a literary analysis. Once you start to strain after those in the action, you get bogged down in a fantastic amount of exegesis which holds up the action. . . . You really have to take things in the long phrase or paragraph . . . and get some overall image or metaphor.[36]

Yet this is precisely what Shakespeare has done in the sustained realization of Petrarchan paradoxes in this play. Moreover, the modern theater can embody some of these effects (most notably, the lighting) better than the original Elizabethan theater. And failure to accept the comic aspect of the play's middle acts has hampered modern productions of the play, in contrast with its apparently successful tragi-comic presentation in the earliest days of its revival. Ironically enough, it is Jonathan Miller, of all the English directors at least, who is adept at finding the apt stage action to give body to Shakespeare's dialogue. There was a fine example of his tactfully imaginative building on the implications of the dialogue in his 1980 production of *Hamlet* at the London Warehouse. Hamlet returned from lugging Polonius's bloody corpse offstage, casually wiping his hands clean—a natural enough action, the audience thought, but one that then provided him with the ideal image, as he struggled to express his loathing for Guildenstern and Rosencrantz, saw it in his hands, held it out, and squeezed it dripping onto the stage:

> *Hamlet.* Besides, to be demanded of a spunge, what replication
> should be made by the son of a king?
> *Rosencrantz.* Take you me for a spunge, my lord?
> *Hamlet.* Ay, sir, that soaks up the King's countenance, his rewards,
> his authorities. . . . When he needs what you have glean'd, it
> is but squeezing you, and, spunge, you shall be dry again.
> [*Hamlet* 4.2.12–16; 19–21]

Paradoxically, too, the modern theater often turns to significant effect the doubling that was a mere exigency forced on the limited companies of the Elizabethan theaters. They did not use doubling to make a point. We can. Miller doubled Hamlet's father's ghost with the player king and extracted an even deeper vein of affectionate, happy intimacy from Hamlet's scenes with the players, and an obviously more changed quality to the play scene proper. Peter Brooke's celebrated production of *A Midsummer Night's Dream* doubled Titania-Oberon with Hippolyta-Theseus, which allowed Bottom a comic doubletake in the last act, stonily outfaced by Titania-turned-Hippolyta. The implication, once more, was perfectly in the spirit of the play—that our sexual partners can change in an eye-blink, and high and low make no difference to sexual appetite. Similarly, in my ideal production of *Romeo and Juliet,* I would double the Friar and the Apothecary, joint purveyors of drugs and poison, the choking gall and the preserving sweet, so visibly underlining the Friar's crucial homily on man and nature's potential for good and ill. But such doubling would have been highly unlikely in Shakespeare's own theater, according to the scholar of today.[37]

Notes

1. The play's recent editors all comment on the Petrarchan influence; see G. Blakemore Evans in the New Cambridge edition (1984), 11–12; B. Gibbons in the Arden edition (1980), 42–52; T. J. B. Spencer in the Penguin edition (1967), 38. Petrarchanism is seen without irony by M. Praz, "Shakespeare's Italy," *Shakespeare Survey* 7 (1954): 95–106; W. Nowottny, "Shakespeare's Tragedies," in *Shakespeare's World,* ed. J. Sutherland and J. Hurstfield (London: E. Arnold, 1964), reprinted in *Twentieth-Century Interpretations of "Romeo and Juliet,"* ed. D. Cole (Englewood Cliffs, N.J.: Prentice-Hall, 1970), 49–51; M. Mahood, "Unblotted Lines: Shakespeare at Work," *British Academy Lecture* (London: Oxford University Press, 1972), 4–5. Uncontrolled shifts between "old" and "new" styles are seen by H. Granville-Barker in *Prefaces to Shakespeare Imagery* (London: Batsford, 1972), 300–349; W. H. Clemen, *The Development of Shakespeare's Imagery* (New York: Hill and Wang, 1951), 64; G. B. Evans, New Cambridge ed., 17, 18; Spencer, Penguin ed., 38; and R. O. Evans, *The Osier Cage: Rhetorical Devices in "Romeo and Juliet"* (Lexington: University of Kentucky Press, 1966), 24, 40, 44. However, R. O. Evans correctly identifies oxymoron as the play's central trope in a preeminently linguistic study, as is W. Draper's less suggestive "Patterns of Style in *Romeo and Juliet,*" *Studia Neuphilologica* 21 (1948–49): 195–210. Parodic Petrarchanism is identified by D. Cole, *Twentieth-Century Interpretations of "Romeo and Juliet,"* 7, and intermittently acknowledged by J. H. Steward, *Tragic Vision in "Romeo and Juliet"* (Wilmington, N.C.: Consortium Press, 1973), e.g., 67, 69, 76. It is seen as part of a controlled development of style in the two most interesting, primarily linguistic studies of the play: H. Levin, "Form and Formality in *Romeo and Juliet,*" *Shakespeare Quarterly* 11

(1960): 3–11, and I. Leimberg, *Shakespeares "Romeo und Julia": Von der Sonettdichtung zur Liebestragödie* (Munich: W. Fink, 1968), 126–207.

2. Wyatt's "My galley charged with forgetfulness," translating Petrarch's *Rime* 189.

3. Clemen, *Development of Shakespeare's Imagery*, 64.

4. "Well, well, I see / I talk but idly, and you laugh at me" (*Richard II* 3.3.170–71). Like Romeo's "Dost thou not laugh?", this is an implicit internal stage direction suggesting the reaction of the stage audience.

5. Both Sidney and Shakespeare are parodying Petrarch's *Rime* 134, as translated, for instance, by Wyatt: "I find no peace and all my war is done." For other analogues, see H. H. Furness's New Variorum edition of *Romeo and Juliet* (Philadelphia, 1878), 22.

6. "The necessity of loving creating an object for itself, etc." S. T. Coleridge, *Shakespearean Criticism*, ed. T. M. Raysor (London: Dent, 1960), 1:6.

7. Otway and Cibber's versions both jettison Rosaline; Garrick retained her in 1748, then reversed the popular decision in his version which held the stage from 1750 to 1845. See G. B. Evans, New Cambridge ed., 36, and G. W. Stone: "*Romeo and Juliet:* The Source of Its Modern Stage Career," in *Shakespeare 400*, ed. J. G. McManaway (1964), 191–206.

8. For the 1662 revival of *Romeo and Juliet*, see J. Downes, *Roscius Anglicanus* (1708), ed. M. Summers (n.d.), 22: "When the Tragedy was Reviv'd again, 'twas Play'd Alternately, Tragical one Day, and Tragicomical another; for several Days together." Several critics have seen *Romeo and Juliet* as an experiment with genres. For some it is a failure, e.g., R. O. Evans, *Osier Cage*, 31; H. B. Charlton, "*Romeo and Juliet* as an Experimental Tragedy," *Annual Shakespeare Lecture* 26 (1939). Others argue for a tragicomic reading, notably S. Snyder, "*Romeo and Juliet*, Comedy into Tragedy," *Essays in Criticism* 20 (1970): 391–402; Cole, *Twentieth-Century Interpretations*, 5ff.; J. Wain, *The Living World of Shakespeare* (New York: St. Martin's Press, 1964), reprinted in Cole, 104–5; F. M. Dickey, *Not Wisely but Too Well: Shakespeare's Love Tragedies* (San Marino, Calif." Huntington Library Publications, 1957), reprinted in Cole, 72–75, and for an exemplary piece by C. B. Lower, see n. 31 below. The relative dating of *Romeo* and the *Dream* are still disputed, though the most recent editors agree that they are close in time. H. Brooks, Arden ed. *A Midsummer Night's Dream* (1979), inclines to it being the later play, but dates it 1594–96 (see xliii, lvii), which puts it before G. B. Evans's dating of *Romeo* late in 1596.

9. G. Bullough, ed., *Narrative and Dramatic Sources of Shakespeare* (London: Routledge, 1964), 1:350, ll. 2507ff. "In steade of mariage gloves, now funerall gloves they have, / And whom they should see maried, they follow to the grave."

10. W. H. Auden's incredulity that Juliet should have such lines, in his Laurel Shakespeare, ed. F. Fergusson (New York: Dell, 1958), 26, is well answered by Levin, "Form and Formality," 5: "When Juliet feels at one with Romeo, her intonations are genuine; when she feels at odds with him, they should be unconvincing."

11. E.g., 1.4.106ff, 1.5.87ff, 136ff, 2.2.117ff, 2.3.91ff, 2.6.9ff, etc.

12. I follow B. Gibbons, Arden ed., 1–23, in the identification of Q1 as memorial reconstruction, and Q2 as deriving from foul papers.

13. *Prefaces*, 318, noting "the continuity of action, with its agonies and absurdities cheek by jowl."

14. E.g., G. B. Evans, writing about Juliet's soliloquy as she takes the sleeping draught, points out her speech "is a pastiche of bits and pieces re-arranged from . . . Brooke's poem [but] neither the additional material nor the speech as a whole rise imaginatively or emotionally much beyond Booke's merely competent level. Somehow the moment failed to involve Shakespeare creatively" (New Cambridge ed., 18). Similar discomfort is expressed by Granville-Barker about the mourning in 4.5; it "does jar a little," but Shakespeare "is working here in a convention that has gone somewhat stale with him, and constrainedly" (*Prefaces*, 319).

15. This detail of staging is kept by T. Cibber in his *Romeo and Juliet, a Tragedy* (1748, facsimile; London: Cornmarket Press, 1969), 33, and its irony is noted by Granville-Barker, *Prefaces*, 311.

16. E.g., *All's Well* 1.3.450ff (line reference is to Charlton Hinman's Norton Facsimile of *The*

First Folio of Shakespeare [New York: W. W. Norton, 1968]. Other examples of such apparently "early" entries in plays arguably set up from authorial copy can be found in *2 Henry IV* 1.1.Q:A3, 4.5.Q:H4, 5.3.Q:K2; *Othello* 1.2.Q:B4, 2.1.Q:D4, 2.1.Q:E-E, 3.3.Q:H2, 3.4.Q:I, 4.1.Q:I4 (all "corrected" in the Folio texts). It would seem that W. W. Greg was wrong to assume that such supposedly anticipatory entries were indications of prompt copy, though he admits "the inference may not be a very strong one." See *The Shakespeare First Folio* (Oxford: Clarendon Press, 1955) 138–39.

17. Outstanding among these is Seward, whose condemnation of the lovers is surprisingly categorical, in an otherwise minute and often suggestive study.

18. Stage directions quoted from Q2:C, C3. I assume half-masks were used, so that the lovers could kiss with them on; they are also suggested by "beetle brows" (l. 31). Brooke's maskers unmask at l. 170; Granville-Barker assumes Shakespeare's Romeo does too (*Prefaces,* 305).

19. This hypothesis was questioned by some participants at the Berlin World Shakespeare Congress. Of course the lines need not be staged for their point to be made. But there seems no cogent argument against their staging. A temporary wall was not problematic for the Elizabethan stage, and the dialogue seems to allow for it. The Chorus preceding 2.1 gives fourteen lines for it to be set up; Friar Lawrence's soliloquy following the lovers' scene gives twenty-two lines before Romeo's reentry for it to be removed again. Such dialogue provisions are common: Hosley gives statistics for a comparable use of dialogue and sustained sound effects to cover the actors' ascent and descent from the gallery, which takes eight to ten seconds on modern replicas of the Globe and Fortune stages. See R. Hosley, "Shakespeare's Use of a Gallery over the Stage," *Shakespeare Survey* 10 (1957): 78, 86–87, nn. 10–12. T. W. Craik, in *The Tudor Interlude* (Leicester: Leicester University Press, 1958), 107–8, argues for such structures elsewhere and their parody in *A Midsummer Night's Dream.* Brooks, Arden ed., xliv, n. 5, concurs, following M. C. Bradbrook and C. L. Barber in suspecting the *Dream* to be parodying this moment in *Romeo and Juliet.* G. B. Evans (New Cambridge ed., 30–31) and Gibbons (Arden ed., 123) both argue against a property wall, assuming it would obscure the audience's sightlines and be "distractingly ridiculous," but neither would necessarily be the case. Sight-lines would not have been obscured if the temporary wall ran, for instance, outwards from one of the pillars suggested by De Witt's drawing of The Swan, to the edge of the stage, or outwards and backwards to the tiring house wall.

20. M. P. Tilley, *A Dictionary of Proverbs in England in the Sixteenth and Seventeen Centurie* (Ann Arbor: University of Michigan Press, 1950), N 167, and see C. F. E. Spurgeon, *Shakespeare's Imagery* (Cambridge: Cambridge University Press, 1965), 310–16.

21. The distinction between the traditional associations for night and dawn are made in *Richard II* 3.2.36–46 and *Tempest* 5.1.64–68.

22. Tilley C 51.

23. For instance: *Romeo.*   come she will.
                  Friar. I gesse she will indeed,
                        Youths loue is quicke, swifter than swiftest speed.
(Replacing Shakespeare's: Therefore love moderately: long love doth so;
                        Too swift arrives as tardy as too slow.)
                        Enter Juliet somewhat fast, and embraceth Romeo.
                                                    [2.6.14–15, Q1:E4]

24. Cibber, *Romeo and Juliet* 17–18.

25. Levin, "Form and Formality," rightly relates this book image to a series of others in the play, identifying its overall movement as "this recoil from bookishness." There is a similar recoil from bookishness to actuality when the Petrarchan sonneteers' clichés are replaced by the genuine sonnet Romeo and Juliet create between them in 1.5.93–107, and the intimacy this act of poetic collaboration implies is emphasized by their physically intensified involve-ment, as they move from holding hands to kissing in the course of the sonnet.

26. Leimberg, "Shakespeares *"Romeo und Julia,"* 198–200, also notes the enactment of the

lovers' light imagery at the ball and in the tomb (but not in the balcony scene), and suggestively relates the final tableau to Sonnet 116. Candlelight shines in the tomb in Brooke also, ll. 2695, 2707, 2794.

27. Compare Coleridge: "The spring and winter meet, and winter assumes the character of spring, spring the sadness of winter" (*Shakespearean Criticism*, 11).

28. Granville-Barker, *Prefaces*, 316. N. Coghill, *Shakespeare's Professional Skills* (Cambridge: Cambridge University Press, 1964), 31, notes a similar staged juxtaposition as the lovers first kiss: "A kiss is the visual symbol of love, the simplest, the oldest, the most beautiful . . . here . . . we see this kiss, instantly following upon Tybalt's rage, juxtaposed images of the two great passions that power this play, and which in the end destroy one another. It is a meaning that can be *seen*."

29. *Hamlet* 1.1.Q2:B3, probably authorial SD: "*The cocke crows*" and the ghost disappears. Clocks toll for the rising of Hamlet's ghost and chime before Caesar's assassination; a bell summons Macbeth to murder and owls hoot and crickets jar as the deed is done. Hieronymo instructs the Painter depicting his discovery of his murdered son: "Let the clowdes scowle, make the Moone darke, the Starres extinct, the Windes blowing, the Belles towling, the Owle shriking, the Toades croaking, the Minutes ierring, and the Clocke striking twelue . . ." (*Spanish Tragedy*, 1602, ll. 2220ff).

30. Granville-Barker also notes the ironic misplacement of the sound effects (*Prefaces*, 327), as does Levin, who argues uncertainly for an *entr'acte* with Peter's merry dump ("Form and Formality," 11 and n. 12). Cibber also keeps the dialogue demanding Paris's wedding music as Juliet's "corpse" is found (*Romeo and Juliet*, 54).

31. C. B. Lower, "*Romeo and Juliet*, IV.v: A Stage Direction and Purposeful Comedy," *Shakespeare Studies* 8 (1975): 177–94. For Zeffirelli, see J. R. Brown: "S. Franco Zeffirelli's *Romeo and Juliet*," *Shakespeare Survey* 15 (1962): 147–55, esp. 151–52. Cole, *Twentieth-Century Interpretations*, 7, also notes actors' and actresses' difficulties with "the laboured lamentations of Romeo and Juliet in Act Three." Shakespeare implicitly directs a critical onstage response similar to that noted in n. 4 above, by the Friar and Nurse's responses in both scenes (3.3.52ff, 85ff, 4.5.65ff).

32. Brooke, ll. 2523–25.

33. He is not actually able to do so, being killed by Romeo outside the tomb.

34. Shakespeare does more to make death bed *look* like the bridal bed in *Romeo and Juliet;* in *Othello* there is a more effective linguistic stress on the wedding sheets covering the bed where Desdemona dies: the point is made more dramatically but less obviously visually. The same duality is used to very different ends in Middleton and Rowley's *The Changeling* 5.3.114–41. Several critics note the dualities in Romeo and Juliet's bridal death without identifying their stage backing. E.g., Gibbons, Arden ed., 52, and Levin, "Form and Formality," 7, noting "Eros and Thanatos, the *leitmotif* of the *liebestod*, the myth of the tryst in the tomb."

35. Cibber has Juliet's death thus (p. 64):

> This is thy Sheath, there rust and let me die?
> 'Tis o'er;—my Eyes grow dim. Where is my Love?
> Have I caught you! now, now, we'll part no more.
> *Falls on Romeo, and dies.*

In Brooke the people find "In clasped armes ywrapt the husband and the wyfe" (l. 2801).

36. See A. Pasternak Slater, "An Interview with Jonathan Miller," *Quarto*, September 1980, 11.

37. T. J. King, "The King's Men on Stage: Actors and their Parts, 1611–1632," *Elizabethan Theatre* 9, ed. G. R. Hibbard (Port Credit, Ontario: P. D. Meany, 1986), examines all ten extant plays that identify King's men in principal parts. King's summary of the evidence about casting shows that only rarely do actors in principal parts double, table 2, pp. 34–35. In a letter King informs me: "It is possible for the actor playing Friar Lawrence to double as the Apothecary, but the Friar is the second largest male role in the play; it is unlikely that the actor in that part doubles."

Changing Images of Romeo and Juliet, Renaissance to Modern

by JILL L. LEVENSON

In each of the sixteenth-century fictions that popularized Romeo and Juliet, the narrative identifies the lovers primarily in two ways: by their positions in the story, and by the narrator's continuing description of their intense passion. But when the protagonists speak, they sound like everyone else in Verona. And because the major fictions are translations of one another, the protagonists and the rest of Verona sound alike in Italian, French, and English. They share the rhetoric and other conventions of the Renaissance novella, where people communicate through reasoned argument or formalized gestures. As a result, we recognize these lovers in their narratives, but we would not recognize them on the street.

When Shakespeare dramatized this well-known fiction, he distinguished the voices of Romeo and Juliet from the others. The comedy and wordplay he added deepen the original narrative, but they do not account for the individuality of the lovers. That distinctiveness arises from Shakespeare's manipulation of conventions from another medium: Renaissance love poetry. Since Nicholas Brooke emphasized the point in *Shakespeare's Early Tragedies,* we all realize "that the experience of the non-dramatic sonnets is involved here, and in fact the play can partly be seen as a dramatic exploration of the world of the love sonnet."[1] If the play as a whole investigates the components of amatory poetry, however, amatory poetry serves as a chief means for distinguishing among the characters and singling out Romeo and Juliet.

As all of the crucial dramatis personae express themselves in the idiom of love poetry, the personalities in *Romeo and Juliet* define themselves especially by the skills with which they manage poetic conventions. Most of Verona betrays a failure of imagination in using the standard conceits and commonplaces of love, laboring the familiar, saying nothing original; and in this ordinariness, most of Verona remains constant. Yet Mercutio speaks his anti-Petrarchan strain with a creative difference. More important, Romeo and Juliet disclose their special qualities—and their everyday qualities as well—through the modulations of their verse.

151

Variations in the poetry reveal variations in the protagonists: the lovers' changing moods, perceptions, intensities. In later tragedies, Shakespeare would employ less contrived means for portraying character. But here, changes in the verse from moment to moment convey the shifting contours of personality. Immediately after Romeo's banishment, for example, at the beginning of 3.2, Juliet's prothalamium quickly shrinks to mere wordplay and sound effects as she glimpses calamity in the Nurse's report, the swift reduction implying that absolute grief has arrested Juliet's imagination. Yet shortly, as she begins to recover from shock and learns the truth, her verse expands again with typical Petrarchan devices. She describes Romeo in a catalogue of oxymora that do not fit their subject accurately:

> Beautiful tyrant! fiend angelical!
> Dove-feather'd raven! wolvish ravening lamb!
>
> [Ll. 75–76]

At this moment, the formal, imprecise figures of speech indicate Juliet's unreadiness for this first encounter with sorrow and disillusion. Her lexicon for making distinctions cannot verbalize the true nature of either her husband or her experience. Within a few minutes, though, her diction changes again, and as it does, it communicates that her vision is clearing. Less figurative, more prosaic, it simply analyzes the bleak reality just disclosed:

> Some word there was, worser than Tybalt's death,
> That murd'red me; I would forget it fain,
> But, O, it presses to my memory
> . . . .
> "Tybalt is dead, and Romeo banished."
>
> [Ll. 108–12]

As the tragedy takes its course, modulations like these—as well as the more striking poetic changes that occur between scenes, early and late— add up to our impressions of Romeo and Juliet. The sense that their passion for each other is extraordinary, and that it transforms them from typical adolescents into patterns of love, arises especially from the way they speak. Their soliloquies do not analyze these developments, nor do the assessments of other characters. Nothing in the text explicitly remarks how the lovers have grown from ordinary to archetypal. But the variations in their poetry signify both transformation and, finally, uniqueness. Like some of Shakespeare's other plays from this period, *Romeo and Juliet* makes a connection between qualities of love and qualities of imagination. Sexual passion sparks imagination and vice versa; the more sensual and genuine the feelings, the more original and lyric their expression. In this tragedy, the playwright fuses these qualities in verse at times so wonderful that it seems to embody the emotion itself: the garden and balcony passages express transcendent love in transcendent poetry.

In contrast with their fictional prototypes, then, Shakespeare's Romeo and Juliet do not simply mark key episodes in a famous narrative. They are also verbal creations, poetic conventions dynamically changing, inspiration working its way through platitudes. And they assumed physical presence on the Elizabethan stage in the young male actors who vocalized their words. As Alfred Harbage describes them, Elizabethan actors "were craftsmen of the theatre, and . . . theirs was a craft of intercession."[2] Apparently their mediation depended on studied elocution as well as stylized, graceful movement. The developing actors who performed Romeo and Juliet must have relied on prosody, stage directions, content, and perhaps Shakespeare himself as they translated the text into living impressions. Essentially, they projected character from verse, rounding out their impersonations with formal gestures. If the actor's presence gave the character physicality, his delivery of the lines conferred more specific traits: imagination, sensuality, youth, impulse, and gender. Through the actor's person, the dramatist's abstract conception materialized.

With his verbal constructs, Shakespeare evidently gave the young male actors who played Romeo and Juliet everything they needed to produce the illusion of reality on the Elizabethan stage. But he did not provide for the future. By the time of the Restoration, performance had lost the key to Shakespeare's depiction of the lovers, and since then, instead of looking for it, actors and producers have usually replaced the lock. Of course, changing mores and tastes have influenced these performance strategies, as we shall see from glancing at five decisive moments in the tragedy's theatrical history. Although Romeo and Juliet have remained stylized through all the versions of Shakespeare's play, in the passage of time they have absorbed and reflected fashions in the performing and fine arts more than literary trends. With one or two exceptions, later productions have substituted new means of stylization, nonpoetic means, and they have generated impressions of Romeo and Juliet different from those signified by original texts.

David Garrick recast Shakespeare's young lovers for the eighteenth-century stage because the originals held little appeal. By 1748 he had modified both the protagonists and the tragedy to meet his patrons' standards for decorum in the theater. As a result—in his highly successful script that lasted for ninety-seven years—Romeo and Juliet not only speak, but also act differently from their Elizabethan counterparts.

Towards elegance of tragic diction, Garrick first cleared the play of "jingle" or rhyme. This procedure satisfied the eighteenth-century criterion for blank verse as the proper medium of tragedy, but it also collapsed several of the poetic forms supporting the original play and its characters. Thinning the Petrarchan content, Garrick also trimmed the remaining conceits to check any persistent flights of fancy. And when the poetry became flatter, so did the lovers. Additional cuts by 1750 made the tragic figures conform to acceptable stereotypes. As George C. Branam explains in *Eighteenth-Century Adaptations of Shakespearean Tragedy*, "the mood of high seriousness with which the eighteenth century approached tragedy encouraged the idealization of characters and the exaggeration of 'noble' qualities."[3] In short, Romeo's less-than-noble change of heart disturbed his tragic image: it disappeared, along with Rosaline, from Garrick's text, and Romeo met a Juliet he already loved at the Capulet ball. Juliet appeared as unblemished as Romeo: Garrick removed all sexual innuendo and other subtleties from her speech, transforming her into a perfectly innocent heroine.

So Garrick changed not only the lovers' idiom, but also their places in the narrative sequence. In fact, he changed the sequence itself. As he cut the text for staging, he also produced a lucid narrative format corresponding with that of eighteenth-century pathetic drama, the genre that centers on the trials of its victimized protagonists. With his additions—particularly the seventy-five-line dialogue he created for the lovers' death scene—Garrick replaced the individuality of Shakespeare's protagonists with the quality of pathos. According to a contemporary article in *The General Evening Post*, Shakespeare had neglected to fill his catastrophe with as much distress as it could hold; Garrick supplied the missing agonies.[4]

In the process he created a performance script radically different from Shakespeare's. While Garrick disposed of improprieties, he also revised the text as a vehicle for two performers; and with his modifications, he allowed performance to impose a whole new dimension on the figures of Romeo and Juliet: a dimension that materialized from the star actors' understanding of the roles. Although the new eighteenth-century acting style fell short of Stanislavsky, it depended on the actor's conception of his character rather than eloquent delivery of the playwright's words. It may have shared a degree of formality with Elizabethan practice, but in the end it interpreted character rather than transmitting it.

On the eighteenth-century stage, therefore, Garrick's *Romeo and Juliet* became a tragedy of character interpreted moment by moment, in the current performance style, through the actors' voices and gestures. One mid-eighteenth-century document, MacNamara Morgan's *Letter to Miss Nossiter* (published anonymously in London 1753), describes a young actress's rendering of Juliet at Covent Garden. Clearly idealized, this exhaustive account reveals the age's criteria for successful enactment of dramatic texts in general and this Shakespearean tragedy in particular. The perfect rendition assigned the appropriate gesture and tone to every line, sometimes to every word, and at least to every idea in every sentence (p. 16). In performance, a drama conceived as pathetic tragedy demanded not only thoughtful inflection of its blank verse, but also unstinting effusions of its pathos. As Miss Nossiter performed Juliet in the third act of her ideal rendering, for instance, her constantly changing deportment played variations on the theme of heartbreak.

Thus eighteenth-century performances of Garrick's *Romeo and Juliet* constantly restated the lovers' passion, in both senses of the word *passion*. The audience witnessed a finished and controlled performance, an unequivocal if melancholy statement of what the play meant. During the first half of the nineteenth century, that picture sent revivals of the tragedy into decline. In particular, the emotional writhings now associated with the character of Romeo discouraged male actors. Charles Shattuck explains, for example, that "the regular actor of Macbeth and Othello would find embarrassingly womanish that passage in Friar Lawrence's cell where Romeo is called upon to tear his hair in grief and throw himself upon the ground."[5] Although these players envisioned a boy in the part, it was a woman who finally enacted it: Charlotte Cushman, now regarded by scholars like Shattuck as the greatest American actress of the nineteenth century, created a sensation in London during the 1845–46 season with her portrayal of Romeo. Arousing curiosity and attracting crowds, her interpretation excited more response than the breeches role itself.

Theater historians know Cushman as the actress who discarded Garrick's script of *Romeo and Juliet*—for a while, anyway, restoring Shakespeare's plot. But she made enough changes to produce her own version of the narrative. Many cuts abridge her text, some intended to accelerate performance, others to conform with Bowdler's *Family Shakespeare*. Although these reductions frequently correspond with the eighteenth-century cuts, Cushman's script out-Garricks Garrick in eliminating impracticalities and indecencies. The Cushman version does restore a modicum of Shakespeare's wit to *Romeo and Juliet* by reintroducing many of his words. At the same time, it reconstructs a number of the original poetic forms. Nevertheless, despite these gestures towards authenticity, Cushman's text—like Garrick's—simplifies Shakespeare's original composition; and in the end, it too remains a decorous star vehicle that forgoes poetic subtleties to enhance the lovers' passion. If Garrick reworked Shakespeare's script as a vehicle for two star actors, however, Cushman arranged its performance as a vehicle for one. With her, *Romeo and Juliet* became *Romeo and Romeo*.

By the time she played the young lover, Cushman had become a polished, all-purpose actress with an unusually eclectic style combining eighteenth-century conventions for performing tragedy, the new American style of diction, and naturalistic techniques—all fused by the influence of William Charles Macready. From Macready she also learned to analyze character, identifying with the personality she conceived and projecting it as a unified whole. According to one recollection, "[she] impersonated, she did not recite."[6]

Reviews and other accounts indicate that Cushman impersonated Romeo with all the professional resources she had acquired to date. They also reveal that her performance raised to the level of brilliance an otherwise humdrum (or worse) production: plain and inconvenient staging; careless blocking; ungifted supporting cast. How did she conceptualize Romeo to overcome these obstacles? Unlike her predecessors who wrung pathos from every line, Cushman emphasized the energy and intense feeling released by passion. Her ardency issued with such abundance that it not only vitalized the rest of the performances, but generated an interpretation of the entire tragedy.

Again and again, critics praised the "reality" of Cushman's performance with enthusiasm like that of James Sheridan Knowles, the playwright amazed by her Romeo in the Friar's cell after the sentence of banishment: "It was a scene of topmost passion; not simulated passion—no such thing; real, palpably real; the genuine heart-storm was on,—on in wildest fitfulness of fury."[7] According to the reviewers, the character of the young lover had lately declined into a mere "convention," "a collection of speeches," or worse, "an unfortunate and somewhat energetic Englishman." They found Cushman's portrayal "a creative, a living, breathing, animated, ardent human being," or more specifically, "a living, breathing, burning Italian."[8] Cushman had seized on an abstraction in the original text, an emotional state, and made it an objective reality on the stage through her performance style. For twenty-three years she continued to project this uncomplicated Romeo to admiring crowds, taking over the whole tragedy with her expression of his most obvious traits.

In the work of Garrick and Cushman, early audiences found images of Romeo and Juliet that satisfied not only their tastes, but also their fantasies. Even though both versions petered out in their latter seasons, each enjoyed decades on the stage. Since the mid-nineteenth century, however, no theatrical production of the tragedy has resulted in such long-lasting conceptions. Major revivals came and went in the years after Cushman's performances, series of tableaux that reduced even Henry James to boredom.[9] Once the century turned, theater became increasingly restless and began to experiment with the various components of dramaturgy. As time passed, new media fed into those components and other arts furnished additional means for invigorating old conventions. A new breed, the director, sifted among the growing number of available styles and techniques, determining a fresh concept of production for each play he staged. Caught in this flux, the Shakespeare canon has responded to the pulls of many different performance trends, from Elizabethan authenticity to wholesale dispatch of previous traditions. No image of *Romeo and Juliet* has lasted on the stage more than a year or two against this constantly changing theatrical backdrop.

Before mid-century, two distinctive productions of the tragedy illustrate the current range of performance styles and the sorts of protagonists they fostered. The young John Gielgud, alternating the roles of Mercutio and Romeo with the young Laurence Olivier, produced the play in 1935 for a commercial run at the New Theatre in London's West End. A critical and box-office success, this revival attempted to honor Shakespeare's intentions and his verse. Twelve years later, a very young Peter Brook mounted *Romeo and Juliet* as his second production for the Royal Shakespeare Company. Audiences came in large numbers, but the critics resisted this iconoclastic version, which interpreted the original through techniques from cinema and the fine arts.

Gielgud's production also reflected contemporary influences, but here they negotiated a compromise between Elizabethan conventions and the modern stage, as well as its audience. With attention to the play-text and great ingenuity, the design team Motley devised a streamlined set that imitated Shakespeare's theater, allowing for continuous action—at filmic speed. Costumes, inspired by Italian Renaissance paintings, gave visual expression to features of characterization inherent in the verse. Working with the electrician, Gielgud tried to suggest hot Verona summer through lighting, but unsophisticated equipment made the atmosphere seem overcast. More reliable, the canned incidental music—in the style of Purcell—discreetly sustained the tragic mood.

For Gielgud, these effects advanced his major purpose: restoring the format and poetry of Shakespeare's play. Toward this end he rehearsed from an almost uncut Temple edition, shaping an ensemble production rather than a star vehicle. He did not impose a reading on the text or engage in theoretical discussions of its meaning. Rather, he emphasized skillful delivery of the lines among the actors, most of them classically trained and ideally matched up with their parts. As Margaret "Percy" Harris of Motley recalls, this group had no problem with the silliness of the narrative and little difficulty with the wordplay. "When you do it for the verse, you find a meaning in it. At least when John speaks it, you do." In an interview during rehearsals, Gielgud stated his main purpose in terms of the poetry:

> . . . I want to set Romeo and Juliet in contrast to the other characters—poetry in contrast to prose. I want to set them almost on an operatic plane, so that they shall *sing* those marvellous duets while the other characters *speak* their lines.
> They must not only be Romeo and Juliet: they must be symbolic, immortal types of the lovers of all times.[10]

In this production, therefore, Romeo and Juliet rejoined the larger scenario that had contained them on the Elizabethan stage. Echoing the old tradition, actors drew their characters from the playwright's verse rather than their own conceptions or the producer's; and they spoke their lines as precisely as they could. As a result, critics evaluated their performances according to the ways they sounded: most thought Gielgud conveyed the most elegant Romeo and Mercutio, eliciting characterization from every line: Olivier, not "superb as a noise,"[11] evidently tried to compensate in gesture and intensity what he lacked in elocution; and Peggy Ashcroft made almost all of Juliet's expression both comprehensible and genuine, although she had trouble with the stylized outbursts of 3.2. Keyed to the lines, color in this production—the sets, props, and especially costumes— pointed essential features of the verse, even its modulations. All in all, as new conventions supported old in Gielgud's *Romeo and Juliet,* the protagonists sounded impassioned, looked young and beautiful, and carried out Shakespeare's entire plot.

Apparently unaware of Gielgud's production, Peter Brook viewed his own as a complete departure from precedent: "It is our job . . . to forget the conventions of painted curtains and traditional "business," . . . and endless scene-changing. . . . We must make you feel this is not the "Romeo and Juliet" you have all loved and read, but that you have come into an unknown theatre in an unknown town prepared for a new experience." Toward this end, Brook emphasized the visual elements of theater: "We must . . . keep you in [the] picture," he told the Playgoers' Society at the Birmingham Repertory, and he stressed the "picture" from rehearsals on. The actors worked "in a small room, in close physical contact, so they could watch intently reactions to . . . the words they spoke."[12] In reviews, the visuals repeatedly attracted more attention than the performers, and critics continually drew analogies with painting, cinema, and ballet.

Rolf Gérard created the remarkable sets that were impressionistic, small pieces of architecture, "little bits of isolated realism bathed in translucent light." Crafted from light, shadow, space, texture, and mass, Gérard's blocks and screens adapted to various effects. Cleared, the stage produced a mood of desolation especially appropriate to the idea of banishment. Filled, it enhanced the action that took place in glorious color: the brawling crowd scenes; the fatal duel treated in the manner of ballet; the cinematic torch-lit masque of Capulet's feast. Costumed in crimson, black, gold, and blue, the characters looked less romantic than passionate and violent. When pencils of light isolated individuals and groups against a Mediterranean blue backcloth, the whole composition appeared more cinematographic than theatrical. According to the *New Statesman,* lighting "destroy[ed] the stage as stage, that is, as a square, confined space." The stage assumed other functions with Brook, as one representative critic summarized: "One feels that to him the stage is alternately a gallery in which to display his paintings, then a screen on which to outmove the movies. It seldom fails to fascinate the eye."[13]

It generally failed to fascinate the ear, however, despite the assistance of Robert Gerhard's original score. If the music picked up emotional and poetic cadences, the lead actors lost them. Daphne Slater, eighteen years old and "dewy from RADA,"[14] and Laurence Payne, twenty-seven years old and a relative newcomer, acted out Brook's conception of "two children lost in the maelstrom around them."[15] In the process, a sympathetic viewer recalls, "one way and another, hallowed lines seemed constantly to be . . .

spoken out into the wings or head downwards."[16] *The Evening Standard* described the balcony scene as "splendidly, indomitably British." Payne behaved "like an undergraduate turned sentimental on Boat Race night. Neither of them made any attempt to sing the lines."[17] "It was, many said, the play without the lovers."[18]

Although it took as long to perform as Gielgud's version, about three and a half hours, it was also the play without much of the fourth and fifth acts; even the reconciliation between Capulets and Montagues was omitted. Brook excused his cuts—and other decisions—in public forums arranged for the purpose. He found Shakespeare's dramaturgy wanting in the last part of the tragedy, and he felt it morally wrong to emphasize the verbal elements of drama—"the last decadence."[19] In later years, Brook would explain his youthful point of view to Ralph Berry from his mature perspective: "I had always wanted to direct films, and in fact I started in films before going into the theatre. A film director shows his pictures to the world, and I thought a stage director did the same in another way."[20] When he gave this interview in the 1970s, Brook recognized the danger in moving Shakespeare's words and scenes around. With his second Shakespearean effort, however, he envisioned and projected tragic protagonists who looked and sounded plain in a dynamic environment that coordinated pictures, colors, mood, and action.

Brook's early production and ambitions lead conveniently to my final illustration, Franco Zeffirelli's film of *Romeo and Juliet*. This cinematic version carries Brook's methods—and Zeffirelli's 1960 theatrical production—to their logical conclusions; and it provides an appropriate stopping place for at least two other reasons: it remains the most popular and commercially successful rendition of the play during the twentieth century, and it converts the Romeo and Juliet narrative to another genre, as Shakespeare did in the late sixteenth century and at the start of this paper. Whereas Shakespeare translated fiction into theater through verse and dramatic conventions, Zeffirelli turns theater into cinema through all the resources of the new medium. Shakespeare borrowed plot and character from his predecessors; Zeffirelli uses key events and characters from the play as well as one-third of Shakespeare's dialogue.

We can see how the film "absorbs" the play by glancing at two touchstone passages in Zeffirelli's script, a blueprint that agrees closely with the finished product. What happens, for instance, to Juliet's characterization at the beginning of 3.2, after the fatal duel and before her wedding night? In the right-hand column of the script, which gives instructions for "SOUND," dialogue and effects read thus (n.b., the Nurse does not actually speak the bracketed words in the film):

> *Nurse (off).* Oh, Tybalt.
> *Nurse.* [Tybalt! Tybalt!

                                   The best friend] I had,
                                   Oh, courteous Tybalt, honest gentleman,
         Nurse (off-sobs).   That [ever] I should live to see
                                   thee dead!
                   Juliet.   Oh, God!
                                   (Sobs-off)
                                   Did Romeo's hand shed Tybalt's blood?
            Nurse (off).   It did, it did, alas the day, it did!
                  Juliet   (overlapping).
                                   Oh, Nurse,
                                   Oh, serpent heart, hid with a flow'ring face!
                                   (Sobs)
                                   Was ever book containing such vile matter
                                   So fairly bound?
                                   Moans and sobs (off)

The accompanying left-hand column of the script specifies an "ACTION" for each "SOUND" and a setting: the Nurse leans against and then moves foreword right along a dresser in the Capulet house. While she sobs, Juliet looks right, then rushes right, the camera panning with her. As they overlap verbally, she and the Nurse embrace in a medium shot, and then they sink to the floor as the camera tilts down. Finally Juliet throws herself left, exiting foreground left for the closing moans and sobs.

Zeffirelli has siphoned the anguish from this part of the narrative, conveyed it through gestural and sound effects, set it off with the camera, and produced the impression of an adolescent sorely disappointed and oddly formal in her expression of grief. He creates a similar impression of Romeo in Friar Lawrence's cell, a scene introduced as tolling bells and murmuring fade after the Prince's sentence. During the whole sequence, Romeo speaks thirteen Shakespearean lines; the Nurse speaks the same number; but Friar Lawrence speaks three dozen. While the Friar admits the Nurse to another tolling bell, and they both admonish Romeo, the young lover fills out his performance with sobs (there are as many directions for sobs as lines of dialogue), grunts, pants, thumpings, grappling, and general commotion.

Romeo and Juliet look beautiful in this film, and they carry on against a gorgeous and authentic Mediterranean backdrop. Nino Rota's score emphasizes the melancholy aspects of their love—of *all* young love. And as Albert R. Cirillo has demonstrated in a long, sympathetic analysis of Zeffirelli's method, visual and aural effects often work together to project multifaceted images of the protagonists and their relationship, especially their communication through physical action and gesture. But if the director uses "sight, sound . . , color, photography, pictorial composition—in the way that a poet uses rhythm, rhyme, and recurrent imagery,"[21] the cinematic results vary significantly from the poetic. Shakespeare's Romeo and Juliet sound different from the rest of Verona as they express themselves in skillfully managed verse; Zeffirelli's Romeo and Juliet sound different because they speak less—and less articulately—than the others. Zeffirelli's characters therefore lack the imaginative qualities that distinguish Shakespeare's; and his visual and aural effects, superimposed, do not replace the lyricism that identifies Romeo and Juliet in the original dramatic text. So we recognize Zeffirelli's Romeo and Juliet by their places in the narrative and by the ways the actors make them look and sound to fit the director's "controlling image." We perceive contemporary, lovely, strikingly young figures, Renaissance in dress and awkward in diction, a conflation of the very old and the very new. In this age of advertising and technology, we recognize them today even outside the film, on posters and in television guides: they are Leonard Whiting and Olivia Hussey almost twenty years ago, literal translations of Romeo and Juliet into flower children of the aging twentieth century.

Notes

The content of this paper will appear fully elaborated in my book about *Romeo and Juliet* in performance to be published by Manchester University Press in 1987. Material on Shakespeare's poetry and sources has already been published in *Shakespeare Studies* 15 (1982): 21–36, and *Studies in Philology* (Summer 1984): 325–47.

1. (London: Methuen & Co., 1968), 80.
2. Alfred Harbage, *Theatre for Shakespeare* (Toronto: University of Toronto Press, 1955), 59.
3. (Berkeley and Los Angeles: University of California Press, 1956), 116.
4. S. H. and A. K., 17–19 October 1771.
5. *Shakespeare on the American Stage* (Washington, D.C.: Folger Books, 1976), 93.
6. Emma C. Cushman, "Charlotte Cushman: A Memory," 1918 typescript at the Library of Congress, 7.
7. Quoted in Emma Stebbins, *Charlotte Cushman: Her Letters and Memories of Her Life* (Boston, 1879), 63.
8. *The London Times*, 30 December 1845, and an unidentifiable review, 13 January 1846, in Cushman's scrapbook at the Library of Congress.
9. See E. J. West, "Irving in Shakespeare: Interpretation or Creation?" *Shakespeare Quarterly* 6 (Autumn 1955): 419.
10. Quoted in *The Evening Standard*, 10 October 1935.
11. *The Sketch*, 30 October 1935.
12. Quoted in *The Birmingham Post*, 10 March 1947.
13. *Time and Tide*, 12 April 1947; *The New Statesman*, 18 October 1947; *The Evening Standard*, 11 April 1947.
14. *The News Chronicle*, 28 November 1946.
15. Quoted in *The News Chronicle*, 8 April 1947.
16. *Time and Tide*, 12 April 1947.
17. 11 April 1947.
18. *The Daily Telegraph*, 7 October 1947.

19. *The Stratford-on-Avon Herald,* 18 April 1947.

20. *On Directing Shakespeare: Interviews with Contemporary Directors* (London: Croom Helm, 1977), 117.

21. "The Art of Franco Zeffirelli and Shakespeare's *Romeo and Juliet,*" *TriQuarterly* 16 (Fall 1979): 92.

"Your Sense Pursues Not Mine": Changing Images of Two Pairs of Antagonists

by HERBERT S. WEIL, JR.

Perhaps the most familiar attitude toward antagonists in Shakespeare's plays tells us that the stronger we cast Claudius, the stronger we make Hamlet. This will hold true for the reader's conceptions of hero and villain as well as for the spectator. If we think of antagonists not only through images of warfare, murder, and revenge, but also through those of sports, political debates, or judicial pleading, we realize that strengthening the hero may be a kind of idealized poetic justice—not a practical certainty. In the simplest skeletal sense, Hamlet will kill Claudius, no matter how each character is portrayed. But not every athlete or every actor can rise to the test and play his or her best against the most skilled opponent. On our opponent's best day, we—unlike Hamlet—might lose. For character—and for actor—performing most strongly when most challenged, then, becomes a very useful ideal, not a universal truth.

The most interesting antagonists in Shakespeare, I think, both do and do not play the same game. In some sense both must agree—and someone must win—no matter how arbitrary or lucky, rather than earned, may be the victory. But in other senses, strength does not go against strength, speed against speed, nor guile against guile. Richard and Ann, Othello and Iago, Coriolanus and Aufidius, perhaps Hal and Falstaff, all repeatedly play games other than—or in addition to—those that their opponents or dupes can recognize.

Few continue to compete throughout a play. Shakespeare's technique seems to set characters sharply against each other in one sequence and then to change their relationship. Furthermore, we often find, as in *Henry IV*, one of the old pair often turns to a new conflict, or even two new antagonists altogether. Sports fans will readily recognize parallel images in substitutions within a single game, or with trades of players before the next contest. Comparisons between sport and drama can be helpful if we treat the one-on-one competition as intermittent and if we remember that opposition can coexist in drama with moments of cooperation, of fear and hope.

Of Shakespeare's plays, *Measure for Measure* I think presents the most challenging pairings—meetings that excite and then frustrate us. Noticing such patterns and combinations will help make clear both the potentialities and the limitations of my analogies between plays and sports. Furthermore, in the last thirty years interpretation has increased and changed more for *Measure* than for any other of his plays. Not only have critical views changed radically, but also unpredictably fluctuating images of characters during the play itself—long absences, newly presented figures, shifting textures, roles, and credibility—have led to many negative judgments.[1]

It seems not inaccurate, if crude, to summarize the scholarly attitude current in 1960 as one that praised or deplored Isabella, Angelo, and Claudio as naturalistic characters, and the Duke as either a largely symbolic one or as an afterthought based upon a familiar folktale type. Not surprisingly, there was almost no consideration of how the whole play could work on stage (particularly Isabella's becoming a depersonalized symbol in order to wed the Duke), nor upon the personal qualities of the Duke, nor upon the roles and traits of Lucio, Pompey, Elbow, and Mariana. Not until the five-year period beginning in 1961 did close readings by A. P. Rossiter, Ernst Schanzer, and J. Walter Lever try to explain rather than explain away passages that did not fit the author's thesis.[2] Most exciting and influential recent work has tried to expand our sense of unity and control, to discuss harsh juxtapositions of character and mood, changing emphases, intentional anticlimax, and to focus upon problems rather than upon satisfactory resolutions. Their concerns are unlikely to inspire agreement, but they do lay a foundation for an understanding of ways in which the characters seem to be created and developed according to different rules.

I want to consider four sets of antagonists: first, Isabella and Angelo, who have captured the excitement not only of those who love the play, but also of many who do not; second, Isabella and Claudio, who intensely, but in an even more localized passage, serve as a sort of transition; third, Lucio and the Duke, whose repeated bickering had thirty years ago been important for Tyrone Guthrie and William Empson, but for few others.[3] The fourth set of antagonists must be more conjectural. In the long single scene of act 5—most of which the Duke has tried to script—despite many pairings, few feel that he convincingly resolves all discord. But how many agree as to which oppositions become primary and which subordinate?

In the first major opposition, when Isabella meets Angelo, *Measure for Measure* explodes into a new emotional and intellectual vigor. Her first interview with the deputy becomes, I feel, the most exciting scene in Shakespeare's comedies (perhaps the most immediately forceful and ultimately resonant such dispute in any of his plays). Almost every reader and spectator—whatever our sex, whatever our attitudes toward sexual license or to sudden enforcement of long-dormant laws—strongly supports Isabella. Although both are extreme and hyperbolic, particularly if compared with their prototypes (although Shakespeare almost seems to have created both character and situation in terms of extreme hypotheses: what sort of woman would be least likely to submit? what sexual offense would clearly violate the law, but be as minimal a violation as possible?) most respond to both Angelo and Isabella as creditable mimetic figures. In fact, one aspect or pole of characterization challenges the spectator as profoundly as it does Angelo. When, just before Isabella enters, Escalus asks the deputy:

> That in the working of your own affections,
> Had time coher'd with place, or place with wishing,
>
> . . . .
> Whether you had not sometime in your life
> Err'd in this point which now you censure him. . . .
>
> [2.1.10–15]

every spectator is encouraged to ask himself or herself the same question.

Because most can understand Angelo's self-image and his temptation—while the situation has been shaped so that none wish him to succeed—there have been less drastic changes in his psychologically convincing representation. Moral judgments range from the extreme villainy found by Samuel Johnson, "Every reader feels some indignation when he finds him spared," to the "soul large enough for tragic intensity" seen by Winifred Dodds.[4] Recent refinements include a precurtain dumb show (Monmouth, 1977), displaying Mariana, which made Angelo a hypocrite from the start, and the very credible, weak man whose fears became his dominant quality for Adrian Noble (RSC) in 1984.

Sympathy for Isabella seems unaffected by the divergent responses that her personality has inspired. Initially, most conceive her in one of two images: either she is deeply and devoutly committed to the convent *or* she is very young and innocent, but lacks knowledge of her real passionate self. Martha Henry, the most impressive of twelve Isabellas I have seen, played her as a woman almost forty years old, coming late to a firm decision that she will renounce the secular. Henry was very severe, wearing glasses, revealing only when impassioned a very surprising beauty. The actress, at the Folger Library, argued that this first scene with Angelo so changes the novice that she cannot return to the convent. For her, it provided a subtext that required a decision: "Where will I spend the night before I return to learn what Angelo will do?" In the last thirty years, three striking views have come to the fore; first, the harsh and egocentric side, as well as the idealistic, of Isabella's first statement ("I speak . . . wishing a more strict restraint / Upon the sisterhood, the votarists of Saint Clare"—1.4.3–5). Second, a recognition of the qualities that Isabella shares with Angelo (though few point out, also with the Duke): idealism, a hatred of "the vice that most I do abhor," an egocentric insistence, "I have the spirit to do anything that appears not foul in the truth of my spirit." John Bayley (1976) found Isabella and Angelo "two strong characters, who do indeed seem made for each other, and who in confrontation have been compelled to realize the truth about their natures—a realization which hovers on the dangerous edge of intimacy."[5]

Third, conversely, moments of early tolerance and compassion in Isabella have become more widely recognized. She promptly acknowledges Juliet, "O, let him marry her!" then more resonantly (and repeatedly) Lucio—when one would in respect to the moral fable as well as in analysis of personal traits surely suppose him to be her main antagonist. These overlapping, perhaps contradictory, qualities create a personality for Isabella far more rich, complex, and fluctuating than that of Angelo.

He, like the Duke, tries to insist upon a second pole of his personality. His first statement in response to Isabella's pleading concludes, "Mine were the very cipher of a function / To fine the faults . . . / And let go by the actor" (2.2.39–41). Angelo resists any appeal to himself as an individual that can be sufficiently deep or disturbing to make a difference. Whether or not her character changes as her arguments tumble out, it becomes very clear to the audience just when Angelo changes and why. After Isabella enters, she and the deputy each speak fourteen times, alternating, except for the brief asides. After Angelo's repetitious, "Be satisfied; Your brother dies to-morrow; be content" (2.2.104–5) he remains silent through nine distinct speeches. By Angelo's next statement, his first aside, he is lost. "She speaks, and 'tis such sense that my sense breeds with it" (ll. 141–42) uses its image with the greatest agony. No longer can he reject his own feelings in order to promote his function. In this world of debate, not Isabella's beauty, but her speaking, has seduced Angelo. However much we may understand the deputy, our partisan feelings are triumphant and clear—perhaps for the last time in the play.

When Isabella returns all the rules have changed. Isabella thinks that she is playing the same game. But Angelo, shattered by the self-image that he could not and would not imagine, now transforms a debate between two conflicting idealists (who share many of the same principles) into a melodramatic effort at seduction. The crucial line comes after Isabella promises to assume upon her soul any sins caused by charity, and the impatient, perhaps enraged, Angelo argues, "Your sense pursues not mine. Either you are ignorant, / Or seem so craftily," adding, almost as if he has become a stock villain, "and that's not good" (2.4.74–75) We, like Isabella, still clearly oppose Angelo; but what do we support? Very few can share with the heroine the certainty that she is making the right decision. When Isabella can no longer evade Angelo's sense, ["gentle my lord, / Let me entreat you speak the former language"—(ll. 139–40)] she will neither submit nor find any language to engage in this new debate. Among the strange aberrations of critical history are the frequent statements that the tormented Isabella wrestles painfully with her choices. Many of us do struggle and debate, but the problem of our sympathies for either antagonist here are severely confused—intentionally, I strongly feel—by Isabella's refusal even to consider the possibility of submitting and by the consequent language she uses against her condemned brother. Never again do we feel the unity of spectators all strongly backing their own side—no matter what our reservations or even dislike for some of the individuals who are competing for our team.

Can we recapture the surprise that we must have felt as we first read or watched this play when, in the next scene, Isabella suddenly turns into the antagonist not of Angelo, but of Claudio? This anger, this bitterness, is amazingly one-sided and brief. Perhaps the most intense opposition in the entire play comes this sole time when brother and sister speak to each other. Even here, the opposition flames out for only brief moments in a very long scene. In half-lines, Claudio asserts, "Thou shalt not do't" and "Thanks, dear Isabel"—and weakens only in the short span of forty lines. To her devastating final words,

> Mercy to thee would prove itself a bawd,
> 'Tis best that thou diest quickly
>
> [3.1.149–50]

he replies, "Nay, hear me Isabel," which, moments later, he makes completely unambiguous, "Let me ask my sister pardon." Hearing Isabella curse her condemned brother, many of us feel as if our favorite player were suddenly traded to the team that has been our worst enemy—or even more horrifying, that she *chose* to go over to the other side. When the Duke tells her, "the hand that has made you fair has made you good" (ll. 180–81), he seems a manager or coach giving an alibi for a star player's bad day. If our sympathies become progressively less secure in the three debates of Isabella, we can at least always recognize firmly opposed antagonists, clearly arguing in an effort to help determine a coherent end: the pardon of Claudio or the sacrifice of Isabella. But in the ensuing dialogue when the disguised Duke participates, we feel as if we are watching not only new players—as if both teams have made substitutions—but also a new match or contest, perhaps a new sport with new rules.

That, in the second half of the play, the Duke comes to the fore, now seems generally accepted as part of a coherent design, not as an afterthought. An overview will show that Vincentio, as Duke or as Friar, confronts twelve different characters individually and repeatedly engages Isabella, Angelo, and Lucio. Most critics now agree that the exchanges between the disguised Duke and Lucio provide the most significant conflicts after midplay. We can see that the bantering by this strange character—no mere comic relief—leads the Duke to reveal many of the personal traits that he would hide from himself, from his subjects, and from us.

To notice how clearly this antagonism echoes those most prominent in the opening half can tell us a great deal about both the virtues and the limitations of emphasizing the structures of substitution. The Duke shares with his deputy Angelo vital qualities of personality and of function. Like Angelo, he was idealistic, thought he knew himself well, thought himself immune to sexual temptation. In fact, we can almost hear the deputy, his image captured by such phrases as "His blood is snow broth," "His urine is congeal'd ice," speaking his ruler's ugly self-description, "Believe not that the dribbling dart of love can pierce a complete bosom."

The parallels between Isabella and Lucio at first seem less apparent. Shakespeare constructs his play so that their roles and functions reinforce each other although neither directly changes the very different personality of the other. He makes Lucio, like Dogberry, necessary to resolve the action when such a character was not vital in the sources or the basic story. Isabella and Lucio oppose rulers who need not even listen to their arguments. There can be no contest, no debate unless Angelo and the Duke permit. The rulers can lose only if they permit a resolution, if, in effect, they defeat themselves.

Although the Duke clearly manipulates most events and he speaks many more lines than any other character in Shakespeare's comedies, he achieves neither a rich and complex personality nor a finally revealed clear essence. I think that Shakespeare wrote his part so large because he was playing with different possibilities for his main character—a theory that will hardly provide much comfort for director or actor. Efforts to make the Duke symbolic, or even consistent, required deletion of many recalcitrant lines. We now watch the Duke more often as a well-meaning bumbler (Sebastian Shaw [Barton, RSC, 1970]), or William Hutt (Ontario, 1975) than as an impressive leader. Adrian Noble's 1984 RSC production repeatedly strengthened awareness of the Duke and his concern with his own image, starting with a silent opening sequence in which, standing before a pair of large mirrors, he made much of his costume. Some productions stress his meditation, his search to understand himself (Pennington, RSC, 1978), but many no longer pretend that he succeeds. For Robin Phillips, the Duke really seemed to know "some feeling of the sport," for the production encouraged us to open—and then to leave open, said Phillips—the possibilities that the Duke was having an affair with Mariana, as well as one with her young boy. For both Jonathan Miller (Greenwich, 1975) and Michael Bogdanov (Ontario, 1985) the Duke became primarily a manipulating Machiavel. Peter Brook's Duke (in 1979 at the Bouffes du Nord)[6] allegedly showed a strong homosexual desire for the highly praised proletarian Lucio, a far cry indeed from the same director's famous version at Stratford-on-Avon in 1950 with Harry Andrews as a providential figure—an interpretation in which Brook cut many of the Duke's more self-revealing lines altogether.[7]

His antagonist, Lucio, has been even more difficult to place in the world of Claudio and Isabella. Some directors, recognizing that Lucio seems created in a different mode, have often made him so sexually diseased that one cannot understand how Isabella could accompany and later defend him. Others have presented him as a well-dressed lounge lizard, as a gossip columnist, or as a public relations man. Few have gone as far as Neville Coghill, who in 1953 described Lucio as the Spirit Sinister or Satan, thus explaining how he sees through the Duke's disguise.[8] No production, however, has made convincing Lucio's disrobing the Friar if he has recognized the Duke throughout. In fact, no naturalistic explanation has worked for both the strong loyalty of Lucio to Claudio and Isabella and his cruel treachery to Pompey and Mistress Overdone. Yet we all have experience with persons who manipulate their power according to their whim.

The most immediate theatrical inconsistency can be made to work if we recognize the images and the rhetoric of teasing. Among many lines which indicate that these two characters not only fail to play by the rules of the same game, but also seem to inhabit different social, moral, and epistemological worlds, my own favorite comes in Lucio's intended compliment to the "absent" Duke, "He had some feeling of the sport and that instructed him to mercy." The disguised Duke angrily rejects any such praise (" 'Tis not possible" and "You do him wrong surely,") leading Lucio to conclude this vein, "This I can let you know: the greater file of the subject held the Duke to be wise." When the Duke gratuitously defends his absent self, "Wise? No question but he was," Lucio completely reverses his praise, "A very superficial, ignorant, unweighing fellow" and then in the very next line again reverses his field, "Sir, I know him, and I love him" (3.2.149).

In the theater, on the page, the immediate effect of the repartee dominates. Only later do we remember that Lucio is meeting the Duke-Friar for the first time—as Isabella had met Angelo (and then the Duke) for the first time. The skillful adapting of their arguments to the responses of Angelo and Vincentio could not be based upon any well-grounded knowledge of their antagonists—or upon treatment of ruler and deputy as types. Instead Lucio and Isabella embody very alert (and at times sympathetic) insight into the hidden but essential qualities of their opponents.

Through the center of his play, Shakespeare has made both his controlling character and Lucio much more lively and clear figures in relation to each other than as coherent, understandable individuals whose essence we can discover. Lucio and the Duke, unlike Isabella, really compete for an aesthetic, rhetorical victory, for the support that the audience can choose to give. Shakespeare has carefully insured that no spectator can treat Lucio as a model to be copied. He finally is a character without a core, a reflector even when he initiates, one who leads the Duke to reveal himself. Lucio, like Falstaff, like Feste and Lear's fool, relies on the goodwill of the character he baits because that figure holds power. But unlike Falstaff or Feste, Lucio has neither the real nor the pretended friendship of his antagonist. Unlike them, Lucio does not know that his antagonist holds power—but we do.

Does the unusually long unit of act 5 have significant antagonists? Isabella's dispute with Angelo surely no longer unifies the action. When she falsely accuses him, she is speaking lines that the Duke has scripted. The Duke even refuses Isabella's plea that he spare Angelo, a refusal the implications of which most have sidestepped. No speech takes us into the feelings of Angelo, who must remain silent for over 160 lines while first Isabella and then Mariana accuse him. Can he, any more than the informed audience, believe in the Duke's outrageous command, "Punish them to the height of your pleasure"?

Nor does antagonism continue between sister and brother. Among important studies, only Richard Wheeler in his psychoanalytically oriented book disagrees, asking, "Can she forgive Angelo so easily because she is in some sense relieved that Claudio is dead? . . . Is she right in thinking that her 'brother had justice'?"[9] Each production I have seen, however, adds business to the text so Isabella and Claudio embrace warmly, usually in act 3, where they badly dilute the force of her concluding curse, and again, more justifiably, in act 5.

One conflict clearly endures through the fifth act. Lucio continues to embody for the Duke the one character who cannot be tamed. Usually unbidden, he has twenty-seven speeches before he pulls off the Friar's hood. When he interrupts Isabella, the heroine publicly supports him, but the Duke ignores her, attempts to silence Lucio, and violates his own alleged character to wish that Lucio were drunk. (So much for impartiality, justice, and mercy.) Perhaps most significantly for a final sequence in which Angelo, Claudio and Isabella remain silent, the Duke has the last word, but Lucio has the next-to-last word. Even more important thematically, Lucio's plea that the Duke not make him a cuckold leads his ruler to the brilliantly comic self-contradiction: five lines after telling Lucio, "Thy slanders I forgive," the Duke compels him to marry a punk, because, he says, "Slandering a prince deserves it."

Yet, to ask this incongruous final example of antagonism to do too much will topple its brilliant but secondary function. If the antagonist of the controlling character must be told, "Sneak not away," we do not have at the climax a satisfactory image of a worthy opponent. If we are to concentrate on Lucio's punishment, we have indeed a disproportionate moral and theatrical structure.

Although their opposition offers yet untapped possibilities, at least four recent productions concluded by suggesting a new antagonism. Until John Barton's 1970 RSC version, no widely discussed staging and few scholars had made much of Isabella's silence in response to the Duke's "Give me your hand and say you will be mine." Invariably earlier business gave her a sufficiently positive and forceful response to the first request so that few in the audience noticed her failure to comply with the second. Barton's Estelle Kohler stood surprised and confused while the disappointed elderly Duke and all other characters quietly exited. Barton argued that he created an "open" ending.[10] The effect on stage, I felt, was not openness but rejection. But three major directors have gone much further. Jonathan Miller's Penelope Wilton (Greenwich, 1975) carefully prepared us with "consistent icy disapproval for the Mariana intrigue. . . . At the Duke's proposal, she backs away from him in nerveless horror, plainly heading for the convent, never to re-emerge."[11] At Ontario in the same year, Robin Phillips's Martha Henry had clearly moved away from an unusually forceful commitment to "the life removed," but, even so, she could only gasp in revulsion as William Hutt's Duke—who, we recall, had apparently been the lover of both Mariana and the boy who sang to her—suddenly let his Friar's habit open to reveal a huge potbelly. Most extreme of all, in the summer of 1985, again in Ontario, Michael Bogdanov's Isabella, no frigid prude, but from her first appearance dressed in a very modern habit, and never shrinking from touch or even kiss, was so stunned by the proposal that she stood still and alone. Suddenly she—and we—saw, to the rear of the stage, spotlit faces behind bars, suggesting a final image either of madness or of being imprisoned with all the bawds and pimps in a world she never made. One scholarly variant came in 1985. Kathleen McLuskie hypothesized "a radical production" that might "celebrate Isabella's chastity as a feminist resistance, making her plea for Angelo's life a gesture of solidarity to a heterosexual sister."[12] How Isabella should respond to the proposal, the author leaves implicit.

From such stances, we retain little doubt how deep and unresolved is the antagonism between heroine and ruler. In none do we feel that Isabella wins. Whether the Duke wins is another matter. (And one can surely imagine another slight turn that would make Isabella a triumphant martyr.)

I doubt seriously if these recent images will long satisfy. But they do, at least, bring out one side, long noticed but rarely developed with care. And so far, like most earlier stagings, they do shake us at the end with the unexpected—which Ernst Honigmann rightly reaffirms as essential to the play.[13] At least no director has yet tried to prepare us in an explicit manner for Isabella's nontextual physical and psychological revulsion toward the

Duke.[14] Inappropriate as their marriage may be for characters conceived at least partly to embody richly textured mimetic qualities, we should be jarred, jolted, even shocked by the conclusion—however it is played. Firm rejection of the proposal, like docile acceptance, mutes, limits, and reduces the rich problematic nature of these characters and of the play.

When Angelo angrily told Isabella, "Your sense pursues not mine," she at least knew the purpose for which she opposed the deputy. But when Lucio met the disguised Duke—and when Isabella, in these recent examples, conferred with him—they did not, until very late in act 5, know that the Duke was their antagonist. As each competes for our sympathy, rather than for any agreed-upon prize or victory, the role of the spectator becomes more vital. We realize that not only does the Duke misinterpret the sense of Lucio's compliment; in the final speech of the play he might well say to both Lucio and Isabella, "Your sense pursues not mine."

Notes

1. In the mid-1950s *Measure for Measure* was infrequently performed; it had almost no significant published stage history. Scholarly works, almost without exception, argued one of two incompatible positions: in the more common view, Shakespeare was writing a play mainly about Isabella, and *Measure* fell apart early in the third act when the Duke stepped in to interrupt her angry attack on Claudio. Perhaps most representative was Hardin Craig, who in a widely adopted text edition (Chicago: Scott Foresman, & Co., 1951) asserted, "When Shakespeare with his constant faith in the chastity of women, considered Whetstone's story of Cassandra, he decided that she would never have yielded up her honour. . . . After writing two acts at the very highest level, Shakespeare became perplexed and changed his whole conception of the characters." The only influential alternative (especially as argued by G. Wilson Knight and F. R. Leavis) unified the play upon the Duke, treating him as a figure for Providence, for the ideal ruler, perhaps for the new King James—not necessarily claiming that this made the work a success or even a stimulating failure.

2. *Angel with Horns* (London: Longman, 1961); *The Problem Plays of Shakespeare* (London: Routledge & Kegan Paul, 1963); ed. New Arden Shakespeare (London: Methuen, 1965).

3. Guthrie described his earlier opinions and productions in a letter (1967) to this writer; Empson, *The Structure of Complex Words* (London: Chatto, 1951).

4. *Modern Language Review.* Dodds, 41 (1946). The production at Monmouth (1977) is discussed by Herbet S. Weil, Jr., *Shakespeare Quarterly* 29 (1978): 226–27. All other productions discussed in this essay have received readily available criticism in *Shakespeare Survey,* and/or *Shakespeare Quarterly,* which often may be supplemented by three thorough and helpful chapters: Jane Williamson, "The Duke and Isabella on the Modern Stage," in Joseph Price, ed., *The Triple Bond* (University Park: Pennsylvania State University Press, 1975); Ralph Berry, *Changing Styles in Shakespeare* (London: Allen and Unwin; 1981); and Philip C. McGuire, *Speechless Dialect* (Berkeley and Los Angeles: University of California Press, 1985).

5. *The Uses of Division* (London: Chatto, 1976), 246.

6. Wolfgang Solich, *Comparative Drama* 18 (1984): 54–81.

7. Herbert S. Weil, Jr., "The Options of the Audience," *Shakespeare Survey* 25 (1972), a paper delivered at the World Shakespeare Congress in Vancouver, 1971. Brook's production,

the one before 1970 that is most cited, provides a convenient contrast for "changing images of character."

8. *Shakespeare Survey* 8 (1955): 14–27.

9. *Shakespeare's Development and the Problem Comedies* (Berkeley and Los Angeles: University of California Press, 1981), 10–11.

10. In a discussion at the Shakespeare Institute, Stratford-upon-Avon, published in *Shakespeare Survey* 25 (1972).

11. Berry, *Changing Styles,* 45.

12. "The Patriarchal Bard" in *Political Shakespeare,* ed. Jonathan Dollimore and Alan Sinfield (Manchester: University of Manchester Press, 1985).

13. "Shakespeare's Mingled Yarn and *Measure for Measure,*" in *Proceedings of the British Academy,* vol. 67 (London: Oxford University Press, 1981).

14. Most productions before 1970 (and many after, such as that by Barry Kyle [RSC, 1978]) tried to "prepare" the audience for the Duke's marriage proposal, often by embraces and clutchings between "Friar" and novice. Whatever slim success they achieved, of course, reduced the impressions of harsh juxtaposition and discordance.

"The Emperor of Russia Was My Father": Gender and Theatrical Power

by KATHLEEN E. McLUSKIE

Considerations of gender and power in early modern England must base themselves firmly on the incontestable fact that men had power and women did not. Women are indeed absent from all but the rawest data of historical inquiry and though social historians can reconstruct them lactating, prophesying, rioting, or slandering,[1] they never find them determining the contexts and the meaning of power. To be sure the annals are full of stirring or pathetic tales of resistance and contest: women threatened the patriarchal ideal with every strategy from mockery to murder.[2] However, that very resistance was directed against male power firmly in place, securing its position there by every means at its disposal.

And yet the paradox persists:

> If woman had no existence save in fiction written by men, one would imagine her a person of the utmost importance . . . in fact she was locked up and beaten and flung about the room.

Virginia Woolf's own resolution of the paradox was characteristically tart:

> Women have served all these centuries as looking glasses possessing the magic and delicious power of reflecting the figure of man at twice its natural size.[3]

Virginia Woolf's opposition between fiction, fact, and fantasy is extremely suggestive, embodying as it does the important distinction between "woman" the subject of representation and "women" the historical beings lactating, prophesying, and on and on.

In the early modern period the absence of women from the records is amply compensated by overrepresentation of "woman" in all kinds of texts.[4] In particular, in the drama, "woman" is omnipresent in the narrative and indeed on the stage and yet "women" nowhere appear. Perhaps because of the convention of boys playing women's parts, "woman" is quite explicitly a constructed category in the drama of the period and it is worth reflecting on the power of these constructions to move and convince, to function as "the body to be looked at, the place of sexuality and the object of desire."[5] In part, of course, these fictions of woman are projections, as Woolf suggests, of the fantasies of their creators. Nevertheless fictions and fantasies do not bear any such fixed relationship to fact as the notion of reflection suggests and it is the internal dynamic of key images of women and their relationship to dramatic narrative that will repay attention.

When Hermione reminds her audience "the Emperor of Russia was my father," when Cleopatra claims that she is "no more but e'en a woman," or when Lady Macbeth remembers how she has "given suck and know how tender 'tis to love the babe that milks me," we see some of the most powerfully affecting images of woman in Shakespearean drama. They establish the characters' identities by providing them with authenticating existence outside the confines of the plot; they provide the stories that give the characters life. The dramatic power of these stories is not that they are pejorative or laudatory: it is rather that though they are entirely convincing, none of them is verified or needs to be verified. They have a literary and dramatic autonomy generated by a set of internal oppositions between the image on stage and the claims of the language, between the particular and the conventional, between essential and contingent notions of womanhood.

For each of these dramatic images contains a paradox that is perhaps most clearly defined in Cleopatra's assertion of her essential femininity. She is, she says,

> No more but e'en a woman, and commanded
> By such a poor passion as the maid that milks
> And does the meanest chares.
>
>   [4.15.73–75]

It is an image that is powerfully overdetermined[6] in that it gains its meaning from a number of familiar associations and connections that carry ideological force. The parallel of queen and milkmaid has its historical analogue in the apocryphal story of the young Princess Elizabeth in prison hearing the milkmaid sing and owes a good to the tradition of royal pastoral.[7] However, the fantasy of essentialism, the assertion of the common lot of all women, transcends the particular historical context and is central to the notion of "woman" for misogynists and feminists alike. In the particular context of Cleopatra's lament for Antony the image depends for its power on a combination of that ideological heritage with the terms of its internal paradox. It is an image that has no power at all in the mouth of a milkmaid: it is for queens to assert their essential femininity and thus confirm their special status and power. The paradox is furthermore enacted on stage as the regal figure of Egypt's ruler asserts her womanliness in answer to Iras's anxious "Royal Egypt, Empress!"

In each of these powerful images of woman there is a tension between representing these figures as essentially "woman" and their particular identity as individuals between the fixed value system that attaches to certain notions of femininity and the narrative dynamic of the stories of particular women. The effect is to disrupt the codes of femininity and to reveal gender as both essential and contingent at the same time. Since the essential characteristics of each gender are manifest in the other on particular occasions, the exact location of gender is called into question and the uncertainty can be manipulated for a powerful effect. Camden, for example, described Queen Elizabeth as "a Virgin of a manly courage,"[8] thus conceding both weakness essential to her gender and asserting her own particular strength. Similarly Lady Macbeth's plea to be unsexed depends for its dramatic power on the striking image of essentially feminine nurture, the nursing mother. It is not simply that Queen Elizabeth or Lady Macbeth are exceptional women; it is that their exceptionalness is best expressed by a challenge to the essential qualities of womanhood itself. Women characters become the most powerful image of "woman" by a strategy in which conventional images of woman are contested and affirmed at the same time. When Hermione, for example, is first accused by Leontes, she responds with an assertion of her difference from other women:

> I am not prone to weeping, as our sex
> Commonly are, the want of which vain dew
> Perchance shall dry your pities; but I have
> That honorable grief lodg'd here which burns
> Worse than tears drown.
>
> [*The Winter's Tale*, 2.1.108–12]

Her denial of her sex's frailty grants her dramatic power and distinguishes her from the weaker women who surround her on stage—"Do not weep good fools." However that dramatic power depends upon a set of rhetorical oppositions—"vain dew/honorable grief," burning and drowning—of which woman/not woman is only one. Hermione's denial of her gender is, moreover, given further dramatic twist by succeeding on a stage image in which she is the center of domestic harmony as she listens to her son's whispered story.

The conflict between essential and contingent notions of "woman" is particularly suited to dramatic representation, which can create complex effects by the shifting relationship between visual and verbal and between narrative and individual scenes. Nevertheless while recognizing the role of rhetorical and theatrical effects in constructing images of women we must also recognize that the power of these effects is further determined by the cultural assumptions that inform them. The long tradition of the *querelle des femmes* and the untiring efforts of Elizabethan pamphleteers provide a vast store of more or less repetitious, more or less anxious, more or less informed attempts to capture the essence of sex and gender. As Linda Woodbridge has shown, the very frequency and all-pervasive character of this polemic could render it conventional, available simply as rhetorical gesturing, yet in particular circumstances it also had the power to define and constrain. This double-edged effect of images of woman is acted out, for example, throughout *Othello*. The purely conventional and rhetorical character of the currently available images is demonstrated in the curious "filler" scene while Desdemona, Iago, and Emilia await the arrival of Othello in Cyprus. When Iago is mockingly called on to give his opinion of womankind he resorts to the literary tradition of witty misogyny:

> If she be fair and wise: fairness and wit,
> The one's for use, the other useth it.
> . . . .
> If she be black, and thereto have a wit,
> She'll find a white that shall her blackness [hit]
> . . . .
> There's none so foul and foolish thereunto,
> But does foul pranks which fair and wise ones do.
>
> [2.1.129–42]

The self-enclosed, paradoxical character of these maxims is reinforced by the patness of the rhyme: the images, as a result, do not engage with any referent outside themselves at all. As Desdemona says, "These are old, fond paradoxes to make fools laugh i' th' alehouse" (ll. 138–39). They have no theatrical power to refer to the woman characters in the action and their misogyny carries no threat. Iago, after all, can, in the next speech, turn his inventiveness to a parallel list of positive womanly attributes and then turn the argument again into a joke. The virtuous woman, like the foolish, the fair, or the foul serves only "to suckle fools and chronicle small beer" (l. 160). Even the evident contempt for women's work implied in the final judgment is mitigated by its rhetorical function as the jokingly unexpected finale of the poem.

This short episode can work at the level of a joke because *at that moment* no power is being contested. The trivial game of defining woman in the self-enclosed rhetoric of joke and paradox takes on a different theatrical force when it is inserted into the meaning of a particular narrative: when notions of *"woman"* are applied to women in particular. For within the action Desdemona is defined not according to the generalities of the *querelle des femmes* but according to the needs of those who have or wish to have power over her. She is the object of Roderigo's lust, Iago describes her as the victim of miscegenous rape, Brabantio as a fantasy of filial obedience (1.3.94–98), and Othello as the idealized audience for his construction of himself. These conflicting meanings of "Desdemona" are played out before the figure who carries their theatrical meaning appears on stage. When she does so, it is in the context of the most explicit contest—between Brabantio and Othello. The language of Desdemona's speech then shifts the context from opposing fantasies to the cultural sanctioned meaning of woman as the object of exchange between husband and father:

> My noble father
> I do perceive here a divided duty:
> To you I am bound for life and education;
> My life and education both do learn me
> How to respect you; you are the lord of duty;
> I am hitherto your daughter. But here's my husband;
> And so much duty as my mother show'd
> To you, preferring you before her father,
> So much I challenge that I may profess
> Due to the Moor, my lord.
>
> [1.3.181–89]

All of the images imposed on Desdemona—or rather that construct Desdemona, for she has no existence outside them—are drawn from custom or convention or indeed from literary tradition. Cassio, for example, describes her as beyond customary images:

> a maid
> That paragons description and wild fame;
> One that excels the quirks of blazoning pens,
> And in th' essential vesture of creation
> Does tire the ingener.
>
> [2.1.61–65]

The denial of convention is itself conventional and places Desdemona firmly in the literary tradition of mistresses with faces nothing like the sun.

However, in the course of the action, we see dramatized the process by which conflicting meanings come to define and constrain. By act 2 Iago has been established as the most fertile creator of meanings (the inventive details of his imagery of miscegenation) and the most effective underminer of others' views of the world ("Virtue? a fig!"). In 2.1, immediately after the playful banter around the images of women, we see his technique at work. After the rhetorical game Desdemona turns to Cassio, they move upstage where they are held in dumbshow while their action is "read" by Iago: the stage is divided into observer and observed, language and action. Cassio performs the actions dictated by Iago's speech and Iago interprets the meaning that they will have for the particular action of the narrative:

He takes her by the palm; ay, well said, whisper. With as little a web as this will I ensnare as great a fly as Cassio. Ay, smile upon her, do; I will gyve thee in thine own courtship. You say true; 'tis so indeed. If such tricks as these strip you out of your lieutenantry, it had been better you had not kiss'd your three fingers so oft, which now again you are most apt to play the sir in. Very good; well kiss'd! an excellent courtesy! 'Tis so indeed. Yet again your fingers to your lips? Would they were clyster-pipes for your sake! [2.1.167–77]

The power of Iago's images are, of course, resisted throughout the play. His efforts to engage Cassio in locker room banter after Desdemona and Othello have gone to bed are met with polite demurrals, and the whole of the great temptation scene of act 3 is a contest between Othello's and Iago's fantasies of womanhood played out on Desdemona. The narrative power of act 3 lies in the psychological detail of Othello's growing jealousy combined with the audience's superior knowledge of the true state of affairs. On its own the narrative drive of the sequence is trivial—let housewives look to their linen—a tale of domestic misunderstanding. A good deal of its dramatic energy comes from Iago's comic ability to wriggle out of exposing his lies by inventing new ones. However, its emotional power depends upon the characters' investment in their views of the situation. With each of Desdemona's appearances the titanic contest between man's definitions of sexuality, love, and the object of that consuming attention is returned to focus. There is an almost total split between the Desdemona of the dialogue, irritatingly insistent on her suit, showing wifely concern for Othello's health, and the silent figure of Desdemona, seen and read by the two men. For the physical figure of Desdemona on stage is again and again established as iconic, exemplary, the site of meanings generated by others. At Desdemona's first exit Othello indicates the blasphemous degree of significance that he accords her:

> Perdition catch my soul
> But I do love thee! and when I love thee not,
> Chaos is come again.
>
> [3.3.90–92]

But for meaning to exist it must be endorsed by a community of understanders; Iago can easily disrupt that meaning by his refusal to answer Othello's questions. By the end of the sequence Iago's apparently unconventional understanding has gained power over Othello's simple one and Othello is resolved to "whistle her off, and let her down the wind / To prey at fortune" (ll. 262–63). At this moment Desdemona's physical appearance on stage is enough to change his mind, though once again it is to do with her iconic exemplary power: she appears upstage (in Elizabethan theater conditions at any rate) and Othello observes to the audience,

> Look where she comes:
> If she be false, O then heaven mocks itself!
> I'll not believe it.
>
> [3.3.277–79]

The structure of this first sequence makes the temptation scene similar to parallel scenes in morality drama with Iago and Desdemona cast as evil and good angels. However, since this is not a morality play, the iconography of sainthood that attaches to Desdemona's physical appearance is overlaid with fantasy images of her status in Othello's world—the beloved hawk he would be content to lose—and with the fantasy of sexuality conjured up by Othello and Iago both:

> I had been happy if the general camp,
> Pioners and all, had tasted her sweet body. . . .
>
> [3.3.345–46]

In this contest over the truth of Desdemona's sexuality, Othello is frustrated by the increasingly apparent arbitrariness of the relation between signifier and signified. He asks:

> Make me to see't; or (at the least) so prove it
> That the probation bear no hinge nor loop
> To hang a doubt on.
>
> [3.3.364–66]

Iago revels in just that ambiguity, grossly punning

> but how? How satisfied, my lord?
> Would you, the supervisor, grossly gape on?
> Behold her topp'd?
> . . . .
> It were a tedious difficulty, I think
> To bring them to that prospect.
>
> [3.3.394–98]

The dramatic power of Iago's imagery of sexual transgression depends upon language alone and though an audience knows it to be "untrue" in narrative terms, it has all the erotic appeal of the "dreams" of pornographic fantasy.

Throughout the rest of the action Desdemona is constructed in Othello's language and her physical presence, her beauty, her clothes, her demeanor has less and less corrective influence. The "fond paradoxes" of female duplicity create a double bind that separates appearance from perceived reality and leave fantasy and dream as the only truth.

In 4.1, while contemplating the murder, Othello declares, "I'll not expostulate with her, lest her body and beauty unprovide my mind." There is already no room for the reality principle, and in the following "brother scene" Desdemona's self-defense speaks from a totally different discourse of honesty and sin and the rules of evidence, which has no point of contact with sexual fantasy:

Desdemona. I hope my noble lord esteems me honest.
    Othello. O ay, as summer flies are in the shambles,

> That quicken even with blowing . . .
> . . . .
> *Desdemona.* Alas, what ignorant sin have I committed?
> *Othello.* Was this fair paper, this most goodly book,
> Made to write "whore" upon? What committed?
> Committed? O thou public commoner,
> I should make very forges of my cheeks,
> That would to cinders burn up modesty,
> Did I but speak thy deeds.
>
>   [4.2.65–80]

By the end the fantasy need not even be spoken and in the final scene Desdemona's role as the recipient of images, fantasies, meanings that exist only in language is given physical embodiment. Asleep on her bed, center stage, she is a monument to others' projected meaning. To the audience she may appear a sacrificial victim, an image of innocence wronged, in Othello's language she is both the deceptive image of "monumental alabaster" emptied of sexuality but she is also the rose to be plucked. Above all she is representative, exemplary, the "cunning'st pattern of excelling nature."

As the emblem on stage, glossed by Othello's language, Desdemona provides a focus for the combination of violence and reverence that informs pornography.[9] Nineteenth-century theatrical tradition, recognizing the sexual import of this scene, hid the strangling behind the bed curtains.[10] More recent productions from Maggie Smith in the 1960s to the 1985 production at the RSC openly offer up the figure of Desdemona to the audience's view, placing her center stage on a structure that is part bed, part altar. The place of Othello's fantasy is shared with the audience, enforcing Othello's imagery of defloration and sacrifice in the image on the stage. The suggestive gap between the action seen and the action described that existed in act 2 has been finally closed.

The play, of course, does not end there and the scene cannot remain simply pornographic. The simple fulfillment of Othello's desired ending— "I will kill thee and love thee after"—is disrupted as Desdemona struggles for life and sacrifice is revealed as butchery. Moreover, even after Desdemona's death, the struggle for meaning continues in the argument between Othello and Emilia, the tedious explications of purposes mistook, and the dramatic confusion of the final moments. Nevertheless, the power of Othello's impositions of meaning have taken their toll both in the dramatic action and in the audience's response to it.

The power of Othello's meaning over an audience's response is not a matter of narrative—we know throughout that Iago is lying—but a matter of the success with which Desdemona is seen as an appropriate focus for the emotional power of the play. As a result she needs no narrative of her own. Othello's account of their love affair before the action began is of the stories *he* has told. Even the clinching evidence that Iago produces is a story of Cassio's dream, not Desdemona's response to it, far less her action in it.

What is at issue is not the action of a particular woman but a conflict over reading woman as a sign.

This conflict over signs and meanings is rendered quite explicit in *The Winter's Tale*, where the construction of the scenes once more exposes the potential contradiction between visual and verbal signs. In 1.2 the two modes are separated—as in the Othello example—with a dumb-show collo-quy between Hermione and Polixenes and a commentary from Leontes, the looker-on:

> But to be paddling palms and pinching fingers,
> As now they are, and making practic'd smiles,
> As in a looking-glass; and then to sigh, as 'twere
> The mort o' th' deer . . .
>
> [1.2.115–18]

The scene raises problems of theatrical meaning that have to be closed off by directorial decisions but the question of the gap between signifier and signified persist throughout the action.[11]

Leontes' language of sexual mistrust has a dramatic autonomy that does not depend on the presence of its object on stage. Indeed when Hermione and Polixenes leave the stage, they free Leontes to construct a narrative of their adultery out of the known and familiar stories of deception:

> There have been
> (Or I am much deceiv'd) cuckolds ere now,
> And many a man there is (even at this present,
> Now, while I speak this) holds his wife by th' arm,
> That little thinks she has been sluic'd in 's absence,
> And his pond fish'd by his next neighbor—by
> Sir Smile, his neighbor.
>
> [1.2.190–96]

The power of that tradition, the vividness of the imagery, the generaliza-tion implied in the allegorical name, make Leontes' story convincing as an emblem if not in relation to the particular narrative in hand. The fantasy of dispossession is no less powerful for being based, as Leontes himself para-doxically describes, on nothing:

> Is whispering nothing?
> Is leaning cheek to cheek? is meeting noses?
> Kissing with inside lip? . . .
>
> . . . .
> Why then the world and all that's in't is nothing.
>
> [Ll. 284–86, 293]

The fallacy of Leontes' syllogism is no longer made evident by the correc-tive image of figures on the stage; there is nothing to stop the progress from "paddling palms" to "kissing with inside lip." In the source story for the play, Pandosto fears that preoccupation with the cares of state has left his wife free to philander, but in Shakespeare's version the language and narrative of jealousy have no circumstantial constraints.

Moreover as the action proceeds, the question of the relationship between Leontes' version of events and the image seen by the audience becomes more complex still. In 2.1, when Hermione is first accused, the stage is divided once again. On one part is the static emblem of Hermione as mother, being told a tale of sprites and goblins, on the other Leontes is being told the tale of Camillo's escape. As in the case of Sir Smile, the tale of one treachery encourages him to see treachery everywhere and he can confidently invite his courtiers to share his interpretation of the signs: "Look on her, mark her well." His confidence comes from his ability to penetrate beyond Hermione's "without door form" to a complex understanding that "all's true that is mistrusted."

This tendency to read a particular image with a code based on a view of the general is shared by the courtiers. They do not share Leontes' view of Hermione but when they protest her innocence their assertions are couched in the rhetoric of mistrust:

> Be she honor-flaw'd,
> I have three daughters: the eldest is eleven;
> The second and the third, nine and some five;
> If this prove true, they'll pay for't. By mine honor,
> I'll geld 'em all; fourteen they shall not see
> To bring false generations. They are co-heirs,
> And I had rather glib myself than they
> Should not produce fair issue.
>
> [2.1.143–50]

Once again the argument proceeds by a syllogism: Hermione, chaste or false, cannot be Hermione; she must be representative, exemplary, and on her action depends the fragile relationship between male power to do violence ("I'll geld 'em all") and male anxiety about their rightful progeny.

At her trial Hermione tries to assert her particular situation, her particular circumstances:

> my past life
> Hath been as continent, as chaste, as true,
> As I am now unhappy; which is more
> Than history can pattern, though devis'd
> And play'd to take spectators.
>
> [3.2.33–37]

Just as her assertion that she would not weep was different from other women, so her particular story is more than history can pattern. Nevertheless the terms of her self-defense soon slide from her particular circumstances to her construction as woman:

> For behold me,
> A fellow of the royal bed, which owe

> A moi'ty of the throne, a great king's daughter,
> The mother to a hopeful prince . . .
>
> [Ll. 37–40]

Moreover, the dramatic construction of the scene make her the center of attention in a way that makes her part of a paradigm of dramatic images of women, the image of innocence abused. Her dramatic and theatrical power at that moment depends upon a confluence of narrative meaning—the pattern of action would make guilt on her part a surprising twist[12]—and ideological meaning—wives and mothers are by definition chaste. When Leontes continues to deny the power of such familiar tokens, insisting that such signs cannot be read at face value, the effect verges on bathos. The logic of his position is that nothing can be known and the action collapses completely when Leontes will not even believe the unequivocal statements of the oracle at Delphi herself.

Leontes is convinced of the truth soon after but only by the news of Mamillius's death and Hermione's collapse. Once again the relationship between signs and truth is completely arbitrary; within the narrative Mamillius's death is real but Hermione's turns out to be false. Leontes, moreover, is restored to his wife in a denouement that on the one hand is a completely unexpected resolution to the story but on the other has a dramatic structure that resolves contradiction. Hermione is once more the center of attention but even more than at her trial or in her dumb show with Polixenes, she is there to be looked at and to be read: "Comes it not something near?" (5.3.23). Leontes' reaction is carefully and slowly orchestrated by Paulina's instructions, and when the statue finally comes to life and embraces her husband, Leontes becomes part of her image, the sign of matrimony restored to be read by the others on stage:

> *Polixenes.* She embraces him.
> *Camillo.*   She hangs about his neck.
>   If she pertain to life, let her speak too.
> *Polixenes.* Ay, and make it manifest where she hath liv'd,
>   Or how stol'n from the dead.
>
> [5.3.111–15]

Camillo and Polixenes gloss the action in the simplest descriptive terms and give voice to the audience's own surprise. The disturbing gap between words and action, between the view of the audience and the view of the onstage audience, is closed and the action resolved. But this consummation is achieved, like Othello's calm before the silent, still figure of Desdemona, by turning the woman into a figure cut in alabaster,[13] the emblem where appearance and reality might comfortably coalesce, the essential woman be manifest in the woman on the stage.

This contest over signs and meanings, over the essential and the contingent is not, of course, restricted to questions of gender in Shakespeare.

The search for the sign of "that within which passes show," the anxiety over whether a king could be "unkinged" or a woman could be "unsexed," the nature of subjectivity itself, recur as motifs in the drama of the period.[14] Nevertheless the narrative resolution of many of Shakespeare's plays depends upon sexual identity. The question of gender and the appropriate signs for distinguishing true from false love are obvious features of the comedies, and from the problem comedies on these questions are built into the dramatic structures in an increasingly problematic way as we contemplate the paradox that "this is, and is not Cressid" or witness the complex maneuverings required to turn maids into wives.

In all of these cases it is important to note that the question of identity is locked into stories that lie behind the images: Desdemona is the inheritor of new comedy stories where lovers deceive their parents but the story also carries disturbing echoes of January and May. Hermione at her trial carries with her a host of images of female martyrs tried before pagan kings. The woman from the late plays who is neither maid, widow, nor wife may make a statement about the limited social roles available to women, but she is also a magical problem-solver from folk tales,[15] and the final acts of the plays in which she appears involve peeling off layers of other possible stories of ladies at a casement, of betrothals betrayed, of assignations in a secret garden and treasure lost at sea. For the problem with women in Shakespeare (or any other mode of representation) is not that his power as author obscures the identity of some notional "real" woman but that they are part of the contemporary experiments with dramatic representation that are circled round in prologues and plays within plays.

The cultural origins of such concerns are rather less easily identifiable. It is true that the concern with subjectivity and in particular gendered subjectivity are paralleled in other writing in the period and it has been variously suggested that sexual relations were a "site of struggle," part of the ideological conflict of the time. Social historians have investigated the extent to which the latter part of the sixteenth century and the seventeenth century witnessed "the construction of new mechanisms of power," including "a movement to establish firmer social and personal control over the body of the individual."[16] It would be possible to see in this movement an interesting analogue to the dramatic constriction of women characters into static postures of icon and exemplum. The argument by analogy, however, is suspiciously pat. The "repression" thesis is increasingly contested, first by the difficulty of locating a historical epoch in which the tension between repression and deviance did not occur, and second by the sheer variety of evidence that is available.

For when we turn to those other stories of women prophesying, rioting, slandering, analogies are harder to sustain. Court depositions in marriage causes and cases of defamation and sexual slander offer an embarrassment of evidence for the social lives of historical women. The vividness of these accounts, transcribed *viva voce* from the hearings, presents tantalizing echoes of the stories of unhappy marriages and of the violence wrought on women by men.[17] They show the need for women to maintain their reputations as honest, of the damage that an aspersion of whoredom could inflict; they show the importance of language and symbolism for real social and sexual relations as for fictional ones.

However, when individual narrative—the stuff of documentary drama—is carried back into the mass of evidence dealt with in social analysis, the image of women submitting to patriarchal control, fixed in the images and language of others, becomes less clear. The very existence of the depositions shows that women had access to the courts as a means of self-defense and did not have to submit actually or symbolically to fixed images imposed on them by others' words. Moreover, as J. A. Sharpe has shown, men as well as women were accused of sexual misdemeanor in the form of adultery and fornication and it was as important to them as to women to defend themselves through the courts. It is hard to dissent from Susan Amusson's conclusion that though an important element of social identity, gender was not paramount but was part of a network of social relations that included patronage and service as well as sex and marriage.

For the crucial difference between "woman" and "women" is that in the main traditions of storytelling, woman's principal narrative relations are sexual. Women as servants, women as workers, women's contributions to the gross domestic product, are not the stuff of dramatic narrative.[18] Like the variety of material from the depositions, such themes are shapeless, offer less possibility for confrontation, dénoument, image, and sign. It is hardly surprising that Shakespeare, like the storytellers who preceded him, uses his authority to tell once again the story of women as mothers and lovers. As critics we must beware that in analyzing the construction of "woman" in Shakespeare even under the rubric of "gender and power" we do not too readily construct "women" in the same image, but keep ever before us the salutory warning of Virginia Woolf's sketch "Professor von X engaged in writing his monumental work entitled, *The Mental Moral and Physical Inferiority of the Female Sex.*"[19]

Notes

1. See Mary Prior, ed., *Women in English Society 1500–1800* (London: Methuen, 1985), passim; Christine Berg and Philippa Berry, "Spiritual Whoredom: An Essay on Female Prophets in the Seventeenth Century," in *1642: Literature and Power in the Seventeenth Century,* ed. Francis Barker et al., (Colchester: University of Essex, 1981), 37–54; and J. A. Sharpe, *Defamation and Sexual Slander in Early Modern England,* Borthwick Papers no. 58 (York: University of York, 1983). See also the bibliographical essay on women in early modern Europe by Olwen Hufton in *Past and Present* 101 (November 1983): 125–40.

2. On mockery see Martin Ingram, "Ridings, Rough Music and Mocking Rhymes in Early Modern England," in *Popular Culture in Seventeenth Century England,* ed. Barry Reay (London:

Croom Helm, 1985), 166–197. On murder see Catherine Belsey, "Alice Arden's Crime," *The Subject of Tragedy Identity and Difference in Renaissance Drama* (London: Methuen, 1985), chap. 5.

3. Virginia Woolf, *A Room of One's Own* (New York: Harcourt Brace Jovanovitch, 1929), 45, 35.

4. See Linda Woodbridge, *Women and the English Renaissance Literature and the Nature of Womankind 1540–1620* (Urbana and Chicago: University of Illinois Press, 1984).

5. Teresa de Lauretis, *Alice Doesn't: Feminism, Semiotics, Cinema* (Bloomington: Indiana University Press, 1984), 4.

6. The term used by Alessandro Serpiere, "Reading the Signs: Towards a Semiotics of Shakespearean Drama," in *Alternative Shakespeares,* ed. John Drakkis (London: Methuen, 1985), 119.

7. See Louis Adrian Montrose, "'Eliza, Queene of Shepheardes' and the Pastoral of Power," *ELR* 10 (1980): 153–82.

8. William Camden, *History of the Most Renowned and Victorious Princess Elizabeth,* ed. Wallace T. MacCaffrey (Chicago and London: University of Chicago Press, 1970) 25.

9. For a sophisticated analysis of the semiotics of pornography and the source of its power see Rosalind Coward, "Sexual Violence and Sexuality," *Feminist Review* 2 (June 1982): 9–22.

10. See A. C. Sprague, *Shakespeare and the Actors: The Stage Business in His Plays 1660–1905* (Cambridge: Harvard University Press, 1945), 214.

11. The problems of reading this scene for the critic are evident in Howard Felperin's anxiety over verification in his essay "'Tongue-tied our queen?': The Deconstruction of Presence in *The Winter's Tale,*" in *Shakespeare and the Question of Theory,* ed. Patricia Parker and Geoffrey Hartman (London and New York: Methuen, 1985), 3–18.

12. Compare for example the complex dramatic image that Webster creates in the trial of Vittoria by presenting her theatrically as innocence abused while making her unambiguously guilty in the narrative.

13. The words are, of course, the Duchess of Malfi's. I have addressed the similar tension between action and monuments in Webster's play in "Drama and Sexual Politics: The Case of Webster's Duchess," in *Themes in Drama* ed. James Redmond (London: Cambridge University Press, 1984), 7:77–91.

14. See Belsey, "Alice Arden's Crime."

15. See, for example, Peele, *The Old Wives Tale,* in which Sacrapant's magic glass can only be broken by "she that's neither wife, widow, nor maid."

16. Martin Ingram, "The Reform of Popular Culture? Sex and Marriage in Early Modern England," in *Popular Culture,* ed. Reay, 130. Ingram discusses the theories of Foucault and Muchembled with particular reference to the local variety of evidence in England.

17. These cases are discussed in Sharpe, *Defamation and Sexual Slander,* and Susan Amusson, "Feminin/Masculin: Le Genre dans l'Angleterre de l'epoque moderne," *Annales: Economies Sociétés, Civilisations* 40 (1985), and I am particularly indebted to the thesis by Virginia Savage, "Women and the Social Order in Sixteenth-Century England: The Evidence of Kentish Ecclesiastical Depositions 1585–1603," M.A. thesis, University of Kent, 1984.

18. There are, of course, interesting exceptions in Elizabethan/Jacobean drama. I have discussed the formal problems posed by so-called domestic drama in "'Tis but a woman's jar': Family life and Kinship in Elizabethan Domestic Drama," *Literature and History* 9 (Autumn 1983): 228–39. Other plays that would repay attention would be *The Old Wives Tale* or *Bartholomew Fair.*

19. Woolf, *A Room of One's Own,* 31.

The Comedies in Historical Context

by MARILYN L. WILLIAMSON

Shakespeare's comedies, especially the romantic comedies, have customarily been assumed by critics to be fantasies remote from history and questions of power. For Frye and Barber they are excursions into green and golden worlds where conflicts from the sere world are resolved, and all—or almost all—atone together. Sexuality is natural, universal, life-giving, temporarily constrained by the senex, but released in the green world, as the plays drive to marriage. In this paper, with *As You Like It* and *Measure for Measure* as examples, I propose to use the theories of Michel Foucault to relate the comedies and their fantasies to history, to Elizabethan and Jacobean social structures, and to contemporary ideas about power. In Foucault's thought, sexuality is neither natural nor universal, but a social construct transmitting cultural power:

> Sexuality must not be thought of as a kind of natural given which power tries to hold in check, or as an obscure domain which knowledge tries gradually to uncover. It is the name that can be given to a historical construct: not a furtive reality that is difficult to grasp, but a great surface network in which the stimulation of bodies, the intensification of pleasures, the incitement to discourse, the formation of special knowledges, the strengthening of controls and resistances, are linked to one another, in accordance with a few major strategies of knowledge and power.[1]

If we read the comedies through these concepts, we may trace the evolution of sexuality from a remedy for social conflicts in *As You Like It* to the source of major social problems in *Measure*. In *As You Like It* power is ratified by nature; in *Measure* power is justified by social corruption. Although both plays are defined as comedies, we may account for their profound differences through history and we may invoke Foucault's theories to explain their strategies as well.

> From tyrant Duke unto a tyrant brother.
> But heavenly Rosalind!
>
> [1.2.288–89]

As You Like It begins with a set of male social problems. Orlando, a younger son, has inherited a paltry legacy, and his brother violates their father's will by keeping Orlando no better than oxen or horses and by not providing Orlando with an education suited to his gentility.[2] It is part of Shakespeare's ironic wit that he begins a pastoral play with Orlando's declaration, "You have train'd me like a peasant, obscuring and hiding from me all gentleman-like qualities" (1.1.68–70). We soon learn, however, that "pastoral" has a different meaning for each of the social classes represented in the play. The second major conflict is, of course, also between brothers: Duke Frederick has usurped Duke Senior's rule. Although the usurpation appears a mutation of Oliver's mistreatment of Orlando, both actions are violations of the father's will. The usurpation is a rebellion Orlando might be tempted to, were he as ambitious as Oliver says. Yet the effect of the usurpation is muted because we hear about it from Rosalind and Celia in a scene where Celia assures Rosalind that she will return to Rosalind the dukedom Frederick "hath taken away from thy father perforce" (1.2.19–20). Here, as elsewhere in the play, Shakespeare conceals the power relationships that drive *As You Like It.* Foucault observes, "Power is tolerable only on the condition that it mask a substantial part of itself. Its success is proportional to its ability to hide its own mechanisms. Would power be accepted if it were entirely cynical? For it, secrecy is not in the nature of abuse; it is indispensable to its operation."[3]

And so this play artfully translates the social issues with which it begins into two kinds of discourse that conceal power: the Petrarchan and the pastoral. Orlando's double courtship of Duke Senior and Rosalind reveals the parallel function of the two modes. By idealizing the powerless, both conventions understate or deny the true operations of power evident in *As You Like It.* And the Petrarchan and pastoral also provide the mechanisms whereby male conflicts are resolved and patriarchal forms of power are restored.

The Petrarchan code is somewhat less complex than the pastoral. Rosalind manages this discourse that begins, however, before she and Orlando meet in the forest. Celia, Touchstone, and Rosalind have already overheard Silvius confessing to Corin his love for Phebe, and that encounter gives Touchstone a chance to parody the effects of love that is defined as natural: "as all is mortal in nature, so is all nature in love mortal in folly" (2.4.55–56). The Petrarchan conventions supply the folly of love with its vocabulary, of which Phebe and Silvius become extreme examples. Before Rosalind is aware of it, Orlando has already begun to write sonnets about her and tack them to trees in the forest. She has only to step into the role of the mistress to whom her lover "would live and die her slave" (3.2.154). The language and themes of the code provide the illusion that Rosalind is the center of the play while containing her power and presence in the male-dominated structures that conclude the drama.[4] The erotic relationship of

Orlando and Rosalind offers a solution to the discrepancy between his gentle birth and his oppressed fortune; in fact, their love overcompensates for Orlando's past suffering: he marries the heir to the realm and becomes the Duke's designated successor. All without ambition, but simply through love. The Petrarchan idealization of the lady, combined with the temporary equality of the forest exile, both reveals and conceals the difference in their social stations. It largely conceals Rosalind's rank, and her many fictional roles hide her subordination at the end as she arranges her own exchange from father to husband. She tells Phebe that marriage is a market, while Silvius remains self-inscribed in the Petrarchan discourse.

The play's insistence that sexuality is a natural given ratifies the class sexualities[5] we find in *As You Like It,* where the complexity and range of the Orlando-Rosalind courtship contrast with the fixed roles of Phebe and Silvius, and with Touchstone and Audrey among the country copulatives. These highly socialized and largely artificial differences are made to seem natural by the pastoral mode and setting, and the range of differences implies the universality of love, while at the same time tolerating deviancy in Jaques. Through the same trick of the pastoral, moreover, nature restores the patriarchal structures Frederick has disrupted as the play opens. Duke Senior is able to set up a gentle alternative court in the forest,[6] the benevolence of which contrasts with Frederick's unnatural tyranny. Duke Senior's style of ruling "finds tongues in trees, books in running brooks, / Sermons in stones, and good in every thing" (2.1.16–17).[7] Like the erotic relationships that flourish in the forest, patriarchal power seems natural, and Orlando's double courtship connects the erotic and the patriarchal. Arden proves worthy of Duke Senior's faith in that the forest provides Frederick a father who converts him "both from his enterprise and from the world" (5.4.162). Earlier Orlando, having felt the effects of the forest, yields to kindness and nature in saving Oliver's life: "Twice did he turn his back, and purpos'd so; / But kindness, nobler ever than revenge, / And nature, stronger than his just occasion, / Made him give battle to the lioness" (4.3.127–30). Thus an efficacious nature rectifies two unnatural conflicts between brothers to reestablish the patriarchal regime in which the eldest son becomes the father to his sibling. We notice that Orlando immediately begins to behave as father to Oliver as soon as the latter announces his intention to give Orlando "my father's house and all the revenue that was old Sir Rowland's." Orlando replies to Oliver's intention to wed Aliena, "You have my consent. Let your wedding be to-morrow" (5.2.10–11; 14–15). The brotherhood restored at the end of *As You Like It* resolves through nature the intense male rivalries for power and the world's goods. They are hidden in the forest, just as Duke Senior seeks to conceal in the pastoral community his resumed power:

> First, in this forest let us do those ends
> That here were well begun and well begot;

> And after, every of this happy number,
> That have endur'd shrewd days and nights with us,
> Shall share the good of our returned fortune,
> According to the measure of their states.
> Mean time, forget this new-fall'n dignity,
> And fall into our rustic revelry.
> Play, music, and you brides and bridegrooms all,
> With measure heap'd in joy, to th' measures fall.
> [5.4.170–79]

The varied meanings of *measure* in this speech show the degree to which social issues are masked by the pastoral conventions and the love stories.

We are beginning to understand, then, that *As You Like It* is as much about male rivalry as about Rosalind's wonderful wit and charm. The play is a tissue of male wish fulfillments, but without ambition, which is always denied in the pastoral. A younger brother, tyrannized by family and state, becomes heir-apparent, but only after replacing his elder brother as his father's heir by the brother's wish. Another younger brother—the very term became identified with "the unpropertied, unfranchised social classes"[8]—has displaced his father-brother but finally sees the error of his ways. Thus the fear of sibling rivalry that Elizabethan social structures would inevitably produce can be evoked and then resolved. In addition, the social hierarchies among the lovers balance the rustic equality of the pastoral. As L. A. Montrose writes,

> Without actually violating the primary Elizabethan social frontier separating the gentle from the base, the play achieves an illusion of social leveling and of unions across class boundaries. Thus, people of every rank in Shakespeare's heterogeneous audience might construe the action as they liked it.[9]

The focus on younger brothers in *As You Like It* makes sense when one remembers that the practice of primogeniture was increasing in England during the Elizabethan and Jacobean period, largely among gentry and lesser landowners. As a result, hardships and abuses produced "a literature of protest by and for younger sons."[10] We should also recall that enormous increases in the population of England—from three million in 1500 to four and a half million in 1600—meant that the number of young people in Shakespeare's potential audience could outnumber the adults.[11] Younger sons therefore could easily be overrepresented in groups frequently mentioned in Shakespeare's audiences such as students at Inns of Court, apprentices, soldiers, merchants, and shopkeepers, among others.[12] Such elements within an audience could find the problems represented in *As You Like It* resonant with meaning.

Yet Shakespeare's naturalization of the power structures in *As You Like It* is essentially conservative. The play represents patriarchy as natural in accordance with political theory of Shakespeare's time. Jean Bodin says, for example, "The power of the Father over his children is the onely naturall power."[13] Making any particular power structure seem natural, as Barthes has taught, makes it myth and therefore unchangeable.[14] So the effect of the play is to reconcile potentially hostile elements of the audience to the patriarchy by showing them a younger son who prospers and another who repents his ambition in an immutable but benevolent political structure. The presence of Rosalind, who has wooed and distracted countless audiences from these issues, should not surprise us either, for in the midst of Shakespeare's highly patriarchal society sat a reigning queen who was herself a grudging source of favors to still another burgeoning group of rival males who yearned for a dwindling number of posts at court, preferments, and titles.[15] The nineties were the bottleneck years, when too many well-educated men lusted for too few appropriate positions.[16] Written at the end of the long reign of an unmarried queen who eroticized relationships with her subordinates, *As You Like It* exploits the Petrarchan codes to which Elizabeth's style of ruling gave currency.[17] Just as she used erotic language to disguise power relationships, so *As You Like It* employs love to transform profit, nature to translate power. Social status gained through sexuality is natural and therefore not the product of ambition and not to be questioned. The woman represents the fulfillment of male desire, even if she is subject to patriarchal structures. Idealization masks her lack of real power. When she was truly powerful, as Elizabeth was, the pastoral code could give the appearance of self-effacement.[18]

> Our natures do pursue,
> Like rats that ravin down their proper bane,
> A thirsty evil; and when we drink we die.
>
> [*Measure,* 1.2.128–30]

With the death of Elizabeth in 1603, the Petrarchan structures emptied of their meaning, but preexisting social problems remained to give other kinds of fantasies more urgent significance. Although these changes should not be defined mechanically, there seems little question that the sky has changed from *As You Like It* (1600) to *Measure for Measure* (1604). The plays represent very different constructions of sexuality and patriarchal power. Women, therefore, have a vastly different role in the world of the play. These differences may be related to the historical context of *Measure.*

In *Measure* male sexuality exploits women and is a threat to the social order, a construction that justifies coercion of male and female sexuality by the ruler through the bed trick and enforced marriage. No longer a relationship of trust based on wooing, marriage is a contract that may be compelled by deceit or a means, albeit an inadequate one, of regulating sexuality. Men see women as corrupting objects of consuming lust or obstacles to fulfillment, and women accept men as flawed by their social irresponsibility.

Measure may be read as part of a crisis in the relation of authority to personal life. Although it was performed at court in 1604, it is too simple to read *Measure* as only a play for James I.[19] It is one of a subgenre in which a disguised authority figure—a husband, parent, ruler—spies upon the sexual behavior of wife, children, subjects in order to control that behavior. There were many such plays written about the same time as *Measure*: *The London Prodigal* (1604), *The Malcontent* (1604), *The Phoenix* (1604), *Law-tricks* (1604), *How a Man May Choose a Good Wife from a Bad* (1604–5), *The Honest Whore II* (1604–5), *The Fawn* (1605), *The Fleire* (1606), *West-Ward Hoe!* (1607), *Humour Out of Breath* (1608). The spying on society, especially on the young, which the disguises make common to all these plays, represents a deep anxiety of authority about sexuality. Here we should recall Foucault's observation that the forms of power appropriate to sexuality are largely regulatory rather than punitive:

> The law always refers to the sword. But a power whose task is to take charge of life needs continuous regulatory and corrective mechanisms. It is no longer a matter of bringing death into play in the field of sovereignty, but of distributing the living in the domain of value and utility. Such a power has to qualify, measure, appraise, and hierarchize, rather than display itself in its murderous splendor; it does not have to draw the line that separates the enemies of the sovereign from his obedient subjects; it effects distributions around the norm.[20]

Although Shakespeare shows a sensivity to Foucault's generalization by moving his play from the threat of death to the use of surveillance as a control mechanism, Shakespeare seems to press the limits of the intrusion of state power into subjects' sexual life, not only through the threat of death for Claudio, but through the action of the real authority, Vincentio, who forces both coupling and marriage of those in no way related to him. *Measure* is unique among the disguised-authority plays in representing the death penalty for fornication and the Duke's behavior.

To understand what may have led Shakespeare to these bleak representations, *Measure* should be related to a complex political debate within Parliament and the public about the legal regulation of personal conduct at the turn of the century. The conditions that inspired this crisis may be summarized. As we have said, the population of England had increased by 50 percent during the sixteenth century, and by the end of the century there was genuine fear of the "wandering poor" and their getting of superfluous offspring.[21] To cope with the numbers, some members of Parliament advocated colonization;[22] others argued for enclosing forests and wastes;[23] still others lamented the growth of the London underworld and called for stricter law enforcement.[24]

Bastardy, moreover, had doubled during Shakespeare's lifetime, peaking in 1604.[25] Historians account for the increase, not from the "bastardy-prone sub-society," but from intended marriages of socially acceptable citizens delayed by economic conditions.[26] These increases attracted the attention of reformers like Philip Stubbes, who saw male irresponsibility at the root of bastardy:

> It (whoredom) is so little feared in Ailgna, that untill every one hath two or three Bastardes a piece, they esteeme him no man (for that, they call a mans deede) insomuch as every scurvie boy of twelve, sicteen or twenty yeares of age will make no conscience of it, to have two or three, perad-venture half a dozen severall women with childe at once, and this exploite being doon, he showes them a faire pair of hæles, and away he goeth.[27]

The law grew more harsh with women, who were more frequently whip-ped and carted than in the sixteenth century.[28] Some thinkers, like Stubbes, translated problems of bastardy into those of fornication, for which Stubbes would invoke the death penalty.[29]

Shakespeare's representation of this social crisis is closer to the actual circumstances of English life than most of the disguised-authority plays. Vienna, like London, is a city of widespread immorality, with suburbs full of brothels. The city hosts a large subculture in Lucio, Kate Keepdown, Mistress Overdone, Pompey, and the denizens of Overdone's brothel. Lucio has fathered a bastard on Kate, whom he now perceives as a "rotten medlar," to whom he has shown a fair pair of heels. Vincentio tries to force Lucio to marry Kate at the end, but she, like the other prostitutes in the world of *Measure,* is invisible. This play resembles *As You Like It* in dealing primarily with male fantasies that control female roles. During his experi-ence in the prison, Vincentio moves from being concerned about bastards to a tyrannical control of marriage.

Juliet's plight conforms with remarkable similarity to historical condi-tions in that she and Claudio are gentle folk whose marriage has been interrupted by her lack of dowry, an exact parallel to the relationship of Angelo and Mariana. The other parallel of the Juliet-Claudio relationship is Kate-Lucio, and the audience is aware that despite his genuine commit-ment to Juliet, Claudio must suffer for Lucio's defiant profligacy, which provokes but escapes the law. Claudio's exclamation that forms the epi-graph to this discussion illustrates the fact that in plays like *Measure,* male desire constrained by society becomes negative by the coercion and the guilt of irresponsibility, and consequently this negative attitude is projected on women and the desire for them.

The relationship of Angelo and Isabella is the center of this degraded notion of desire and the demeaning attitude toward women. In his attempt to use state power to force himself upon Isabella, Angelo is the extreme form of male rejection of social constraint and responsibility—sex turned to male violence. He intends, he tells Isabella, to use her lack of social power to deny any responsibility to her after he has used her. Her fierce virginity protects her from his assault on her identity, but also becomes a mirror of the destructive impulse in her rejection of Claudio's pleas and her condemnation of his lust. Isabella accepts Angelo's definitions of law and desire; she truly believes Claudio did the thing he will die for. In their reaction to the intensity of negative desire, both become dehumanized and render others worse than they can be. Because she has only the power to withhold love, the play allows Isabella to change her attitude while it must compel Angelo's behavior.

Desire, however, is not the only cause of problems in *Measure:* the play is part of a debate about laxity and law enforcement at the time. Observers believed that the large immoral subculture, already mentioned, was quite immune to the law.[30] They perceived the justices and constables as incompetent, impoverished, and partial.[31] The new king had more interest in hunting than ruling, however insistent he was on his prerogatives. James's clemency quickly became legendary, and his court just as quickly notorious for sexual license.[32]

The sense of laxity from top to bottom produced a general wish to regulate personal conduct, particularly sexual offenses. Local authorities gradually became stricter.[33] In addition, from 1576 to 1628 Parliament proposed and debated ninety-five measures that would control personal conduct, including regulation of dress, drinking, swearing, bastardy, church attendence, and profaning the Sabbath.[34] Members' concerns about the bills sound many themes of *Measure.* They wished to distinguish between the father of a child who would support it, presumably Claudio, and another, like Lucio, who would leave it to the care of the parish. Members showed little concern for women, to be sure, but they worried greatly about the impact of legislation on the social order—would gentlemen be abused by their social inferiors, justices who might act from malice, self-interest, or passion? Parliament assumed that social problems were created almost entirely by the poor, and so bills were designed to be class-conscious because members feared that gentlemen, like Claudio, would suffer from laws aimed at rogues like Lucio. Parliament also feared the partiality of magistrates. One speaker might have been describing Angelo: "For magistrates are men, and men have alwayes attending on them two ministers, *libido* and *iracundia.* Men in this nature do subjugate the free subject."[35] Commentators also worried that a reaction to previous laxity might result in the hunting of sin and partial justice, particularly among the Puritans, who were sponsors of many of the regulatory bills.[36]

Measure represents many of these issues about the relation of law to personal conduct. The Duke's desire for greater severity after his previous laxity is his announced motive for placing Angelo in the role of deputy. We watch Escalus discovering that Elbow is no match for the likes of Pompey, but Elbow is the only man in his ward willing to serve as constable. Angelo's reform movement quickly evolves into partiality, sin-hunting, and disruption of the social order. Instead of concentrating on the irresponsible subculture of Vienna, Angelo, driven by *libido* and *iracundia,* pursues

Claudio and Isabella, who mirror in their differing ways Angelo's own flaws. Shakespeare stresses the social disruption of tightened control through Angelo's attempted victimization of Claudio and Isabella and through the theme of no difference.

Shakespeare builds the theme of no difference into a terrifying idea as he associates the law, sex, and death as elements that obliterate identity, the distinctions among persons. Angelo reminds Isabella that the law effaces individuality: it deals with classes and actions. The Duke-friar's substitutions link the law, death, and sex in this suggestion of no difference. He uses substitutes to replace Angelo's intended execution of Claudio with one who has died naturally because Angelo will not tell one head from another disguised by death. Abhorson explains the mystery of the hangman to Pompey in terms of no difference between the clothing of the true man and the thief. The theme is most powerfully evoked, however, in the bed trick, where there must be no difference between one woman and another to the lustful male in the dark.[37] The trick is a true mirror of Angelo's attempt to use the power of the state to rape Isabella, for it intrudes the state directly in sexual intercourse, which is "rendered transparent to the eyes of the sovereign and the audience."[38] The autonomy of the individual is lost to the design of the ruler, and male desire is used to compel its own conformity. In thinking he is committing a mortal crime, Angelo is consummating a marriage he had rejected.

In *Measure* only Claudio and Juliet make their own marriage; the Duke makes all the others through deceit or force. Marriage is radically divorced from desire, and the intrusion of the state into the relationship makes marriage unstable. As a single institution to regulate the complexities of desire, marriage is subject to almost intolerable strains. Once marriage ceases to be the fulfillment of desire, especially for the male, and becomes a regulatory agency in society, usually on behalf of women, it overtly intrudes power into sexuality. For Mariana and Angelo marriage becomes "a vow'd contract" fulfilled by the bed trick, a deceit rationalized by Angelo's lack of faith. The Duke accents this relationship by his intention to force Lucio to marry Kate, the clearest example of marriage as a social agency of the ruler: "Marrying a punk, my lord, is pressing to death, whipping, and hanging" (5.1.522–23). The invisibility of Kate reveals how in this context marriage is an affair between men, using women, not as a means of exchange, but as a means of enforcement of the subject's will to the ruler's design. These forced marriages should be read against the outrage voiced in contemporary literature at forced marriage and the ample evidence in plays of forced marriage that the husband invariably rebels against the union, causing much suffering for the family.[39] Thus, *Measure* ends with the strong suggestion that constraint of sexuality by patriarchal authority is largely illusory, that sexuality is the "worst case" for testing the limits of state authority in regulating personal conduct.

These forced marriages are but a prelude to a final unanswered proposal of marriage that reveals how tyrannical Vincentio has become. His repeated proposal to the entirely silent Isabella seems particularly callous because it substitutes himself for Angelo after Claudio's life has been saved. Because Vincentio controls all else, he expects Isabella to abandon, casually, because he wishes it, the celibate identity she was unwilling to sacrifice for her brother's life.[40] The Duke's proposal reveals how he pushes all his subjects toward a sexual norm as it violates Isabella's celibate deviancy. But, more important, it is also a sign of Vincentio's abuse of patriarchal power. By splitting the ruler into duke and friar, Shakespeare at once gives the ruler enormous power and exposes the tyrannical nature of that power. The disguise allows Vincentio to be invisible to his subjects while their most private lives are visible to him.[41] The Duke-friar is frightening because at the end he blends the private, religious power of the friar and the public power of the duke without the constraints of either one. As duke he lacks knowledge of his subjects' passes, and he rules visibly within the law. As friar he is ruled by his holy vows; he acts in accordance with divine authority, subduing his own interests, all earthly passions. His actions, like power divine, may be invisible. The composite of the Duke-friar approaches James's definition of the king in the *Basilicon Doron*,[42] but by splitting the figure Shakespeare shows how this concept of the ruler confuses being a man of god with being like a god, and how it justifies control of the subject's intimate life according to the ruler's design. It also illustrates the truth of Foucault's observations about the visibility of power: much of the Duke's providential control comes from the friar's invisible substitutions and manipulations. Although the friar's substitutions result in some mercy, they also use the women he seems to protect in order to coerce the men. Vincentio becomes tyrannical as he uses the friar's role to extend his power beyond the law and as he becomes like Angelo in yielding to his desire for Isabella.[43]

We may now better understand why James could find *Measure* appealing, while most audiences find it disturbing, why it is one of a subgenre, yet seems unique. The play accords enormous power to a ruler, who meddles in the lives of his subjects in ways that James endorsed.[44] The puritanical Angelo is shown to be inferior to his sovereign. All reservations about Vincentio's conduct are subversive elements within the text, and James was tolerant about criticism even if it was quite blatant. But *Measure* was not designed for James alone; it was part of a debate that had much wider implications than Stuart conceptions of the monarchy. The issue is the public regulation of personal conduct. *Measure* clearly represents many topics of the public debate on this question and questions the efficacy of moral reform. By representing the patriarchal ruler as tyrant, willing to exceed the law in coercing his subjects' most private actions, Shakespeare presses to its limits the question of the relation of state authority to personal life. *Measure* has always been a disturbing play; reading it from its historical context helps us understand why.

Such radically different representations of sexuality, marriage, and men and women in two comedies of the same author separated by a few years attest to the truth of Foucault's theories that sexuality is not a natural given, but a historically contingent social construct. Clearly, notions of power, concepts of the ruler, definitions of patriarchy are also historically contingent and as deeply embedded in the comedic genre as in tragedies or history plays. A historical approach to Shakespeare's comedies does not exclude recognition that they are complexly woven from antecedent literature, myth, holiday custom, folkloric ritual, but such an approach will account for the changes in Shakespeare's comedic practices, as the interests and anxieties of his audiences changed. Years ago Maynard Mack said that Shakespeare "keeps up an elusive but fascinating traffic between the world of history and the world of art," and "our chances of learning more about his achievement in the latter depend in large part on our learning more about the former."[45]

Notes

1. Michel Foucault, *The History of Sexuality*, trans. Robert Hurley (New York: Vintage, 1980), 105–6.

2. For a detailed discussion of this theme, see L. A. Montrose, "'The Place of a Brother' in *As You Like It*: Social Process and Comic Form," *Shakespeare Quarterly* 32 (1981): 28–54.

3. Foucault, *History of Sexuality*, 86.

4. See Peter Erickson, *Patriarchal Structures in Shakespeare's Drama* (Berkeley and Los Angeles: University of California Press, 1985), 22–25.

5. See Foucault, *History of Sexuality*, 127.

6. See Erickson, *Patriarchal Structures*, 28–31.

7. For a good discussion of this "second-world strategy" and the Nature-Fortune opposition in *As You Like It*, see Elliot Krieger, *A Marxist Study of Shakespeare's Comedies* (New York: Barnes and Noble, 1979), 70–96.

8. Montrose, "'Place of a Brother,'" 35.

9. Ibid., 33.

10. Joan Thirsk, "Younger Sons in the Seventeenth Century," *History* 54 (1969): 359.

11. Paul S. Seaver, introduction to *Seventeenth-Century England: Society in an Age of Revolution* (New York: Franklin Watts, 1976), 8.

12. Alfred Harbage, *Shakespeare's Audience* (New York: Columbia University Press, 1941), 53–91; the point is also made by Montrose, "'Place of a Brother,'" 33.

13. Jean Bodin, *The Six Bookes of Commonweale*, ed. K. D. McRae, Facsimile of English Translation of 1606 (Cambridge: Harvard University Press, 1962), 20.

14. Roland Barthes, "Myth Today," in *A Barthes Reader*, ed. Susan Sontag (New York: Hill and Wang, 1982). A complete discussion of the process of making political structures seem natural and therefore immutable in Shakespeare's romances is contained in my book *The Patriarchy of Shakespeare's Comedies: The Plays in History* (Detroit: Wayne State University Press, 1986).

15. It is significant, I believe, that the political structures represented in Shakespeare's comedies do not become thoroughly patriarchal until after 1603. Gordon Schochet explains

that the progress of patriarchal thought was briefly slowed by the presence of women rulers during the Renaissance. With the accession of James in England, its moment came. See his *Patriarchalism in Political Thought: The Authoritarian Family and Political Speculation and Attitudes, Especially in Seventeenth-Century England* (Oxford: Blackwell, 1975), chap. 1. For issues of patronage, see Wallace MacCaffrey, "Place and Patronage in Elizabethan Politics," *Elizabethan Government and Society: Essays Presented to Sir John Neale*, ed. S. T. Bindoff, Joel Hurstfield, and C. H. Williams (London: Athlone Press, 1961), 95–126; Lawrence Stone, *The Crisis in the Aristocracy: 1558–1641* (Oxford: Clarendon Press, 1965), 385–504.

16. Antony Esler, *The Aspiring Mind of the Elizabethan Younger Generation* (Durham, N.C.: Duke University Press, 1966), 51–86; Richard Helgerson, *The Elizabethan Prodigals* (Berkeley and Los Angeles: University of California Press, 1976), 41–42; Lawrence Stone, "Social Mobility in England, 1500–1700," in *Seventeenth-Century England*, ed. Seaver, 43; idem, "The Educational Revolution in England, 1560–1640," *Past and Present* 28 (1964): 41–80.

17. Leonard Foster, *The Icy Fire: Five Studies of European Petrarchanism* (Cambridge: Cambridge University Press, 1969), 122–47; Roy Strong, *The Cult of Elizabeth: Elizabethan Portraiture and Pageantry* (London: Thames and Hudson, 1977); L. A. Montrose, "Celebration and Insinuation: Sir Philip Sidney and the Motives of Elizabethan Courtship," *Renaissance Drama*, n.s., 8 (1977): 3–35; A. F. Marotti, "'Love Is Not Love': Elizabethan Sonnet Sequences and the Social Order," *ELH* 49 (1982): 396–428.

18. See L. A. Montrose, "'Eliza, Queene of the Shepheardes,' and the Pastoral of Power," *ELR* 10 (1980): 153–82.

19. Two such discussions are J. W. Bennett, *"Measure for Measure" as Royal Entertainment* (New York: Columbia University Press, 1966), and Jonathan Goldberg, *James I and the Politics of Literature: Jonson, Shakespeare, Donne, and Their Contemporaries* (Baltimore: Johns Hopkins University Press, 1983), 231–39.

20. Foucault, *History of Sexuality*, 144.

21. John Howes, "Famyliar and Friendly Discourse Dialogue Wyse," in *Tudor Economic Documents*, ed. R. H. Tawney and Eileen Power (1924; reprint, New York: Barnes and Noble, 1961), 3:421.

22. Robert Gray, "A Good Speed to Virginia," in *Seventeenth-Century Economic Documents*, ed. Joan Thirsk and J. P. Cooper (Oxford: Clarendon Press, 1972), 757.

23. "Statement of the King's surveyor (1612)," in *Seventeenth-Century Economic Documents*, 117.

24. Edward Hext, "Letter to Burghley on the Increase of Rogues and Vagabonds," in *Tudor Economic Documents*, 2:342.

25. Peter Laslett, *Family Life and Illicit Love in Earlier Generations* (Cambridge: Cambridge University Press, 1977), 113; Maurice Ashley, *The Stuarts in Love* (London: Hodder and Stoughton, 1963), 57.

26. Peter Laslett, "The Bastardy-Prone Sub-society," and David Levine and Keith Wrightson, "The Social Context of Illegitimacy in Early Modern England," in *Bastardy and Its Comparative History*, ed. Peter Laslett, Karla Oostererveen, and Richard M. Smith (Cambridge: Harvard University Press, 1980), 217–46; 170–72.

27. Philip Stubbes, *The Anatomy of Abuses* (London: Richard Jones, 1583), chap. 3.

28. William Hunt, *The Puritan Moment: The Coming of Revolution in an English County* (Cambridge: Harvard University Press, 1983), 76.

29. Stubbes, *Anatomy*, chap. 3.

30. See Howes, "Discourse": Hext, "To Burghley"; and Henry Arth, "Provision for the Poor," in *Tudor Economic Documents*, 3:421; 2:342; 2:453–54.

31. Hext, "To Burghley," 2:344.

32. Richard Ashton, ed., *James I by His Contemporaries* (London: Hutchinson, 1969), 6, 10, 66; G. B. Harrison ed., *A Jacobean Journal: Being a Record of Those Things Most Talked of During the Years 1603–1606* (London: George Routledge, 1941), 86–89; Lady Anne Clifford, *The Diary*, ed. Vita Sackville-West (New York: George Doran, 1923), 16–17.

33. Levine and Wrightson, "Social Context," 173–74.

34. Joan Kent, "Attitudes of Members of the House of Commons to the Regulation of Personal Conduct in Late Elizabethan and Early Stuart England," *University of London Bulletin of the Institute of Historical Research* 46 (1973): 41–71.

35. Ibid., 52.

36. Howes, "Discourse," 3:441–42.

37. For comments on this theme, see the discussion of *Measure* in Meredith A. Skura, *The Literary Use of the Psychoanalytic Process* (New Haven: Yale University Press, 1981).

38. Franco Moretti, "'A Huge Eclipse': Tragic Form and the Deconsecration of Sovereignty," *Genre* 15 (1982): 23.

39. Glenn H. Blayney, "The Enforcement of Marriage in English Drama 1600–1650," *Philological Quarterly* 38 (1959): 459–72; in a source for *Measure,* George Whetstone describes contemporary reaction to forcing marriage: "I crye out uppon forcement in Marriage, as the extreamest bondage that is: for that the ransome of liberties is y death of the one or y other of the married. The father thinkes he hath a happy purchase, if he get a riche young Warde to match with his daughter. But God he knowes, and the unfortunate couple often feele, that he byeth sorrow to his Childe, slaunder to himselfe, and perchaunce, the ruine of an ancient Gentleman's house, by the riot of the sonne in Lawe, not loving his wife." *An Heptameron of Civill Discourses* (London: Richard Jones, 1582), Sig. F1.

40. Goldberg says, "The Duke's wooing of Isabella, even though he offers marriage, seems at least as much an assault upon her integrity as Angelo's proposition" (*James I and the Politics of Literature,* 235).

41. See Foucault's description of the Panopticon in *Discipline and Punish: The Birth of the Prison,* trans. Alan Sheridan (New York: Vintage, 1979), pp. 195–228.

42. James says, "God gives not Kings that stile of *Gods* in vaine, / For on his throne his Scepter do they sway: / And as their subjects ought them to obey, / So Kings should feare and serve their God again" (*The Political Works of James I,* ed. C. H. McIlwain [Cambridge: Harvard University Press, 1918], 3). Goldberg discusses "the stile of *Gods*" at length in *James I and the Politics of Literature,* 27–54.

43. See Moretti, who says, "Beginning with the figure of the protagonist, the legitimate holder of supreme authority, Shakespeare's Duke or Marston's Altofront, we notice that his fundamental characteristic is *not to be subject to the passions.* This separates him from the other characters, who are notably weaker in this respect, and designates him as the sovereign of the Elizabethan utopia, dedicated to the public weal insofar as devoid of personal interests." ("'A Huge Eclipse,'" 21.) Shakespeare represents this idea through the disguise of the friar.

44. Goldberg's arguments demonstrate the sense in which Jacobean ideology is based on invasion, as we would see it, of the personal by the state, "that the body is consumed for the sake of ideology." He says, "Donne's lovers in bed alone; Donne himself in bed in illness; Stuart families in the intimacy of marriage, procreation, and death: the net of political discourse encompasses this territory" (*James I and the Politics of Literature,* 88, 55).

45. Maynard Mack, "Rescuing Shakespeare," *International Shakespeare Association Occasional Paper No. 1* (Oxford: Oxford University Press, 1979), 30.

The Changing Role of Eloquence in Shakespeare's Comedies

by DAVID P. YOUNG

Progress in understanding Shakespeare's development as a writer of comedy has been marked enough in the past fifty years or so that one may now begin an essay of this kind with some sense of shared assumptions: that Shakespeare's ability to write stage comedy did not, as once held, deteriorate or go sour; that his tendency to experiment and test the limits of genre is everywhere evident in his comedies, but especially pronounced in the later ones; and that the fruitful tension in Elizabethan and Jacobean drama between word and deed, language and action, style and structure, is much in evidence in Shakespeare's comedies, early to late.[1]

We may later wish to challenge and test these assumptions, but it is with them as background that I undertake to consider the changing function of eloquence in Shakespeare's comedies. I take eloquence to suggest those moments that attract our attention, as readers or spectators, by their relative length, their poetry, their ability to achieve overviews of dramatic action and memorable summaries of meaning. They are descendants of the "set speech," related to the arias of opera, and in drama they generally involve, as we might expect, an element of persuasion. I contend that the relation of eloquent passages to action and plot grows more questionable and ironic as Shakespeare develops as a writer of comedy, so that its evolving role can be taken as an index or litmus for the patterns I described above. The three plays *The Taming of the Shrew, As You Like It,* and *Measure for Measure* will serve well as test cases.

The Taming of the Shrew would never be described as one of the most poetic plays in the canon, but its love of language and thus potential for eloquence are in evidence from the moment the Induction gets under way. As Christopher Sly's sensibility and diction suggest, much of the play's eloquence is to be of a deliberately prosaic sort, and the first example I wish to examine is Biondello's prose speech describing Petruchio's approach as a bridegroom.

Why, Petruchio is coming in a new hat and an old jerkin; a pair of old breeches thrice turn'd; a pair of old boots that have been candle-cases, one buckled, another lac'd; an old rusty sword ta'en out of the town armory, with a broken hilt, and chapeless; with two broken points; his horse hipp'd, with an old mothy saddle and stirrups of no kindred; besides, possess'd with the glanders and like to mose in the chine, troubled with the lampass, infected with the fashions, full of windgalls, sped with spavins, ray'd with the yellows, past cure of the fives, stark spoil'd with the staggers, begnawn with the bots, sway'd in the back, and shoulder-shotten; near-legg'd before, and with a half-cheek'd bit and a headstall of sheep's leather, which being restrain'd to keep him from stumbling, hath been often burst, and now repair'd with knots; one girth six times piec'd, and a woman's crupper of velure, which hath two letters for her name fairly set down in studs, and here and there piec'd with packthread. [3.2.43–63]

Eloquence serves dramatic action nicely here. No persuasion is involved, simply an anticipation and reinforcement of Petruchio's unconventional program for taming Kate. While his appearance will presumably confirm the description of his outfit, a parody both of bridal superstitions (something old, something new, and so on) and of the epic arming of the hero, no ingenuity of stagecraft will be required to bring his horse before us, since no real animal could assume such legendary proportions through its multiple ailments and its inappropriate bridling and saddling. The bravura quality of this little passage involves tension with the progress of the dramatic action only in the most minimal sense, that it arrests events momentarily to divert us with description and create a sense of anticipation.

Similar observations seem to be in order concerning Kate's famous wager-winning speech at the play's close. I will quote the opening lines rather than the whole speech:

> Fie, fie, unknit that threat'ning unkind brow,
> And dart not scornful glances from those eyes,
> To wound thy lord, thy king, thy governor.
> It blots thy beauty, as frosts do bite the meads,
> Confounds thy fame, as whirlwinds shake fair buds,
> And in no sense is meet or amiable.
> A woman mov'd is like a fountain troubled,
> Muddy, ill-seeming, thick, bereft of beauty,
> And while it is so, none so dry or thirsty
> Will deign to sip, or touch one drop of it.
>
> [5.2.136–45]

Modern productions often interpret the speech as ironic, but the text scarcely supports such a choice, understandable as it is for the sensibilities of twentieth-century actors and audiences. We *can* suggest that Kate's exaggerated account of male dominance in marriage is aware of its exaggeration and playful rather than dead serious, but we must also recognize that the speech wins the wager, resolves the problems of Kate's shrewishness, sums up a view that was very dear to its contemporary audiences, and brings the play to a harmonious close. Here too, then, verbal eloquence serves the needs of dramatic action. Whether or not Kate persuades the women around her to behave differently, she does convince us and her auditors that she has changed, and for the better. We need not return to Sly to feel that the play has ended satisfactorily.

That such a speech can be interpreted ironically is perhaps partly a reading back from later Shakespearean practice, where eloquence is not always so neatly fitted to the needs of plot, character, and action. *As You Like It* shows an intermediate stage where eloquence's relation to action has become more problematic and oblique. The two work together, but at some cost. Dramatic incident in this play is, as is often remarked, considerably reduced, relegated to a perfunctory background role, and eloquence—love of language, wordplay, speech for its own sake rather than some practical end—is often the culprit. It slows and inhibits possibilities of event, protracting scenes and insisting on a leisurely pace. As eloquence moves into the foreground, we relish it, but recognize uneasy implications in its dominance. Rosalind's verbal mastery could well jeopardize her courtship, but does not. Jaques' satirical articulations could puncture the pastoral daydream, but are instead safely contained within it. The consequences of eloquent speech are generally checked and tamed, either as practical achievements or as hindrances to effective action. Both negative and positive possibilities seem to be held in balance by the play's atmosphere and design.

We may begin with another prose passage. Orlando has just protested to the disguised Rosalind that if his Rosalind will not have him, he will die. Speaking as Ganymede playing Rosalind she separates the love and death conflation deftly:

> No, faith, die by attorney. The poor world is almost six thousand years old, and in all this time there was not any man died in his own person, *videlicet*, in a love-cause. Troilus had his brains dash'd out with a Grecian club; yet he did what he could to die before, and he is one of the patterns of love. Leander, he would have liv'd many a fair year though Hero had turn'd nun, if it had not been for a hot midsummer night; for, good youth, he went but forth to wash him in the Hellespont, and being taken with the cramp was drown'd; and the foolish chronicles of that age found it was—Hero of Sestos. But these are all lies: men have died from time to time, and worms have eaten them, but not for love. [4.1.94–108]

Does this pail of cold water threaten true love or the dramatic action? Not really. It is true that it requires explanation and disarming. Orlando responds, "I would not have my right Rosalind of this mind, for I protest her frown might kill me." Since the right Rosalind is in fact of this mind, her answer needs both to reaffirm what she has said and to reassure us and Orlando: "By this hand, it will not kill a fly." Her tongue is one thing, her hand and frown another, she tell us. At the same time, she reminds us that love is not as deadly as Orlando likes to imagine. It will not kill a fly. We come to recognize that love is validated by its testing in such moments, not only by affirmations like Rosalind's but by eloquent exploration of love's limits and hyperboles. Ultimately, then, this eloquence supports the ends of dramatic action, the courtship of Rosalind and Orlando, but only when we have had some time to recognize the roundabout means it uses.

If we turn to the play's most famous flight of eloquence, Jaques's "Seven Ages of Man" speech, we may discover a number of interesting features by asking about its relation to dramatic action and characterization. The first, perhaps, is the fact that it nearly always comes, in production, as a somewhat awkward and intrusive moment, welcome, to be sure, but such a deliberate shift of pace, attention, and tone that its arrival creates a mild discomfort. I used to think, watching actors playing Jaques struggle to introduce it with a minimum of fuss and fanfare, that this discomfort stemmed from its fame, everyone saying, "Oh, here comes that famous speech." That may be part of the difficulty, but I think the speech's "intrusion," as I have termed it, would strike even an audience unfamiliar with the play and the speech's fame. It *feels* like a set-piece, and it resists casual handling. It is an eloquent moment that calls itself and its special status to our attention.

So does its immediate dramatic function. The speech is used to cover the short interval in which Orlando fetches Adam from offstage, and it does that job effectively, but we need only a moment's reflection to recognize that Shakespeare was capable of handling this kind of dramatic need much more unobtrusively. The patent function of the speech as a bridge or a distraction may add to the slight sense of discomfort I cited as associated with the speech in production.

The metatheatricality with which it opens serves to reinforce these effects. We are now so used to recognizing this effect that we may be in some danger of taking it for granted. When the Duke says, "Thou seest we are not all alone unhappy: / This wide and universal theatre / Presents more woeful pageants than the scene / Wherein we play in," and Jaques responds, "All the world's a stage, / And all the men and women merely players," they shift our attention to art and artifice, and they blur the distinction between reality and metaphor. Their world turns into a theater, which it is, and then that theater turns into our world. Life becomes artifice, a series of precast roles, and that notion affords Jaques a plausible foundation for the claims he is going to make.

The idea that all human behavior can be effectively contained in seven categories is of course reductive. There is room to amplify it and explore it within the pastoral mode, which affords contemplation, but it implicitly contradicts the self-fulfillment and, if you like, self-fashioning that pastoral romance offers its heroes and heroines. There is no room in Jaques's speech for Rosalind's individuality or, as commentators have noted, Orlando's humanity and Adam's distinctive old age. The satirical reductiveness of the speech is a testing of pastoral in the same way that Rosalind's satirical view of love and death is a testing of her courtship and imminent marriage. And pastoral survives partly by providing hospitality to such questionings and challenges, by its liberality and tolerance.

By taking us to the end of man's life, to "mere oblivion," the speech also introduces mortality into Arcadia, insisting on death's inevitability even in this golden world of sojourn and carelessness. We know by now how the "et in Arcadia ego" notion belongs to pastoral and validates it by relating it more effectively to reality. But the end of Jaques's speech might be said to threaten the cessation of action by its emphasis on closure and finality: "Sans teeth, sans eyes, sans taste, sans every thing." Is there anything that can be said to follow this effectively? The answer is not a speech but an action, an iconic stage image created by the entrance of Orlando with Adam on his back. Two of the seven ages of man are fused in this image, which recalls Aeneas and Anchises, Christ and Saint Christopher, and may even take us, when we recall Adam's name, all the way back to our first father and the burden of humanity he left us, the sins of the fathers carried by their sons. These associations are momentary and interpenetrating, while the main effect of what we see in the play's response to the speech's striking summary is, as others have pointed out, a contradiction to solitary or meaningless oblivion, a human community of relatedness and cherishing that is not negated by aging and death. What follows is a feast, a sharing of nourishment, and a song. The song's content echoes Jaques's bitter sentiments, but its lyric effect also distances them, and Jaques himself is silenced for the remainder of this scene, his cynicism disarmed by the hospitality and mutual care that he has not acknowledged as values to range against the progression toward death.

Here again, then, there is a "fit" of eloquence to action and plot when we look closely at the apparent inconsistencies and problems. It remains to add that the two instances of eloquence in *As You Like It*, like the two in *Shrew*, are "in character," that is, consistent with what we know about the characters elsewhere. Again, a slight tension is evident in the resolving of this question, especially in relation to Kate and to Rosalind. Their speeches raise questions about their characterizations, and the answers to the questions extend our sense of what the characters are like by showing them capable of saying things we might not have expected them to say but that, on reflection, we recognize as appropriate. Biondello and Jaques are more squarely "in character," though we might wonder whether it is temperamentally appropriate for Jaques to be quite as elaborate and formal as he proves to be in the Seven Ages of Man speech. These issues are mainly worth noting,

however, as an indication that Shakespeare is still keeping eloquent utterance and characterization closely allied. In plays to come he will risk that
tie as well.

When we turn to *Measure for Measure* we can see almost immediately that
we are in a new phase with regard to the use of eloquence. This play
contains some of the most beautiful and memorable speeches Shakespeare
ever wrote, but their relation to dramatic context is problematic in almost
every way: with regard to their function and effect within the action; with
regard to character; with regard to genre; and with regard to the value of
language, both within the drama and beyond it. I say "problematic" not as a
criticism or reservation but to remind us that the difficulties of interpretation that led to the term *problem plays* for the late comedies are clearly
reflected in these speeches and their places in the play.

Isabella's plea to Angelo, beginning "O, it is excellent / To have a giant's
strength; but it is tyrannous / To use it like a giant," rises to an unforgettable
crescendo:

> but man, proud man,
> Dress'd in a little brief authority,
> Most ignorant of what he's most assur'd,
> His glassy essence, like an angry ape
> Plays such fantastic tricks before high heaven
> As makes the angels weep.
>
> [2.2.117–22]

This is surely one of the finest statements of its kind ever made, memorable
and moving and widely applicable. It is worth noting, then, how it operates
in its context. Instead of persuading Angelo of the need for humility and
mercy, it fires his lust and tempts him to use his power to seduce Isabella.
The effect is deeply ironic. As a speech by a young woman about to enter a
convent, it is remarkably worldly; we almost need to think of Isabella as a
vehicle for insights she scarcely understands in order to make the speech
one that can plausibly issue from her lips, especially since she will prove
unable to act according to its wisdom in her dealings with her brother
shortly afterwards. The speech's climatic flourish—angels weeping—threatens to move us from a comic perspective to a tragic one, and its reversal,
"who, with our spleens, / Would all themselves laugh mortal," does not so
much restore comedy as argue its relativity and cruelty: we can laugh only
because we do not understand the consequences of human pride and folly
as fully as the angels do.

Actually, Isabella continues for many more lines. She is, as my students
would say, "on a roll." And the effects I have been describing continue to
mount. We are in a world where eloquence misfires badly, creating the
opposite of its intended effect. The more true and moving the utterance,
somehow, the less likely it is to persuade, and the more deeply ironic its

relation to character, to action, and to genre. The overall effect opens up the old disjunction between verbal rodomontade and the demands of dramatic action that characterized Elizabethan drama in its early stages, a problem that Shakespeare himself had helped to solve. As a problem it takes on a more sophisticated form here than it did in Marlowe or Kyd or Greene, but the echoing seems almost deliberate, as though the invocation or re-creation of a dramatic and artistic dilemma was being used to mount a criticism of life. We are right, I think, to suspect a kind of pessimism about language and poetry and literary genre in such moments, a questioning of their value that darkens the world of this play and the other late comedies very perceptibly.

My other example, from the many that I might have chosen in this play, is the Duke's speech to Claudio that begins "Be absolute for death" (3.1.5–41). I do not know of a better statement of the set of attitudes associated with despising life and accepting death, the *contemptus mundi* and *ars moriendi* traditions, though Webster does a splendid job with comparable material he gives Bosola to use on the Duchess in *The Duchess of Malfi*. The Duke's speech is beautiful, lengthy, and extremely persuasive. And, in its context, it seems for the moment to work. Claudio is won over: "To sue to live, I find I seek to die, / And seeking death, find life. Let it come on." For the moment, that is. No sooner does Isabella tell him of the disgraceful means by which he might be saved than he is on his knees to beg for life, demonstrating to the overhearing Duke that the effect of his astonishing persuasiveness was, either skin-deep or of such short duration—about two minutes—as to be worthless. Claudio himself is moved to stirring eloquence in his own plead-ing ("Ay, but to die, and go we know not where," 3.1.117–31) and typically, his persuasive words move Isabella not to the sympathy he wants but to anger and contempt ("O you beast! / O faithless coward! O dishonest wretch!")

The effect of eloquence, then, is once more sharply disfunctional and arrestingly ironic. In addition, difficult questions surround the whole mo-ment. Is it plausible for the Duke to speak at such length in favor of death when he expects and intends to save Claudio's life? Is he "acting" in his part as a monk and thus not necessarily sincere, or is he speaking from the heart, giving voice to sentiments that will help us understand his reason for leaving his city and returning in disguise? These questions are virtually impossible to answer with assurance, though they are fun to speculate about. We may also want to ask about generic appropriateness; is not this rather somber and melancholy material to be taking up thirty-five lines in the middle of a comedy? We may appreciate the thoughtful note while wondering about appropriateness of context. And, once more, since per-suasion fails so utterly to accomplish its task, we may be tempted to ask whether language and speech have very much value in this world. It may be very lovely to say things like "Thou hast nor youth nor age, / But as it were an after-dinner's sleep, / Dreaming on both," but if the words do not accomplish the purpose of persuading the character at whom they are aimed of their truth, they threaten to turn to expendable ornamentation rather than meaningful dramatic utterance.

I, of course, feel that *Measure for Measure* is the richer and deeper for its ability to raise such questions again and again, risking its genre and its very means, language and action, to set before us a mirror of human thought and behavior that is very troubling to gaze into. I would not alter Shakespeare's course of development a jot, though I suspect that he may have stopped writing comedy and eventually any kind of drama as one consequence of these experiments.

The logical next stage of this pattern I have been tracing lies in the dramatic romances. What becomes of eloquence there? I will not attempt to answer the question here, but it may engender some interesting discussion. I suppose I should also ask, in closing, whether I have been using a "new approach" to Shakespearean comedy. I think all new approaches build upon old ones and are usually less novel than they like to pretend. What earlier considerations of the comedies have made possible, as I tried to suggest at the outset of this essay, is a kind of shorthand, based on shared assumptions, that allow this kind of investigation of stylistic and structural interactions. I do not think I am simply repeating what has been said before, but I am obviously in debt to my predecessors, and gratefully so.

Notes

1. For an overview of these issues, see my "Shakespeare as a Writer of Comedy," in *William Shakespeare: His World, His Work, His Influence,* ed. John F. Andrews (New York: Scribner's, 1985), 2:489–503.

Tragedy and Laughing in the Wrong Place

by JULIET DUSINBERRE

On 4 September 1667 Samuel Pepys saw a performance of Fulke Greville's tragedy *Mustapha*, acted by Betterton at the Duke of York's playhouse, "which," he noted in his *Diary*, "the more I see, the more I like; and is a most admirable poem—and bravely acted; only, both Batterton [*sic*] and Harris could not contain from laughing in the midst of a most serious part, from the ridiculous mistake of one of the men upon the stage—which I did not like."[1] Pepys's brief but vivid evocation of a moment of alienation of the actors from the tragedy they enact, and of the audience who witness it, suggests a related problem that tragic dramatists must always have faced, of how to stop the audience laughing in the wrong place.

The genre of tragedy does not preclude laughter; indeed the grotesque, the satiric, and the incongruous were for the Greeks integral to a mode distinguished by its catholicity.[2] But in Greek drama the vital interplay between comic and tragic in both kinds of writing did not appear to disturb the aesthetic identification of either, which depended on a strict observation of decorum. Horace claimed that as "a theme for comedy refuses to be set forth in verses of tragedy; so the feast of Thyestes scorns to be told in everyday tones that almost suit the comic stage."[3] When the Greek audience heard the elevated discourse of the tragedian it presumably adjusted its behavior accordingly, and if it expressed merriment did so within the context of tragic emotion. Clytemnestra's grim irony at the Chorus's expense in the *Agamemnon* might raise a laugh, but it could never upset an audience's immediate apprehension of dire consequences hanging in the air. Similarly the Porter in *Macbeth* may provide relief from the spectacle of the Macbeths' self-torment before the murder, but his humor is more likely to intensify the audience's suspense than to relax it. These effects of incorporating figures from the comic mode into the tragic are well known, and Wilson Knight's essay "Lear and the Comedy of the Grotesque" in *The Wheel of Fire* (1930) cut new ground not in its identification of the Fool's essentially comic function transposed into a tragic setting, but in its recognition of a deep competition in *Lear* as a whole between tragedy and comedy—"a dualism continually crying in vain to be resolved" (p. 176)—which violently unsettles the audience's minute-to-minute perception of kind and makes it as a body self-conscious and apprehensive of disintegration in its corporate reaction. As Knight observes: "In the theatre, one is terrified lest someone laugh" (p. 180).

The way in which this acute perception is phrased is revealing. Knight, though painfully alive to the comic incongruities and indignities foisted on Lear during the course of the play, does not actually laugh. His horror comes from a fear that others less finely tuned to the ebb and flow of contrary emotions will do so: "To the coarse mind lacking sympathy an incident may seem comic which to the richer understanding is pitiful and tragic" (p. 175). Two assumptions lie embedded in Knight's analysis. First, the problem is brought to light by theatrical performance. The reader cannot spoil the drama's balance between comic and tragic because his reactions are private. It is only in the public arena that an unthinking burst of laughter can excite the horror of other participants. Secondly, the oscillation that the dramatist allows himself between the comic and the tragic divides the audience into the sensitive and the insensitive, giving the coarse observer a fatal power to destroy the pleasure of his more discriminating neighbor. Caviar to the general, as one might say.

Shakespeare himself seems to have been well aware that he depended on the goodwill of the general quite as much as on that of the caviar-eater. His tragedies never suffered the fate of Jonson's *Sejanus* of failure on stage because Shakespeare never indulged in contempt for the dramatic tastes of the motley multitude. He may perhaps have attempted to educate its palate by winning its love for a Prince whose own drama is self-evidently more exciting and more real than the Senecan rhetoric which that same Prince enjoyed so much more than the general listener. The dramatist seems to observe that after all, Hamlet only admired a play, whereas his own groundlings can watch a real Prince working out his destiny. As Partridge in *Tom Jones* remarks after Garrick's performance of Hamlet, there was nothing to it, the renowned actor behaved exactly as he, Partridge, would have behaved had he seen a Ghost, whereas it was plain to all that he who played Claudius was a fine actor. But the very fact that *The Murder of Gonzago,* a play conceived in the same mode as the Player's "Hecuba" speech, occupies such a central place in the play of *Hamlet,* demonstrates Shakespeare's conviction that the ultimate power of tragedy lies in the reactions it excites in the audience. The guilty King does rise, does call for light, does display the guilt that he recognizes in the performers on the stage. Claudius's susceptibility to what he sees has a long classical ancestry. It could be argued that the single factor of audience response has remained from ancient times the one constant in any analysis of tragedy as genre.[4]

The Greeks judged a work in terms of its power over the listeners. Plato believed that tragedy stimulated emotions that were socially disruptive, and Aristotle that it provided a valuable outlet for those emotions, but neither doubted that the arousing of them in the audience by the tragic dramatist was the ultimate mark of his power, which had the same impact as the oratory of the rhetorician.[5] Oliver Taplin remarks that for Gorgias the rhetorician—whose identification of the tragic emotions of pity and terror preceded Aristotle's—"outgoing emotion, as opposed to introverted self-absorption, is characteristic of Greek tragedy, and of most (perhaps all) great tragedy."[6] In *Hamlet* the player's capacity not only to represent Hecuba's grief, but to feel it himself,[7] is for Hamlet a proof of proper tragic emotion. Herington in *Poetry into Drama* draws attention to Plato's dialogue *Ion* in which the rhapsode feels the emotion that he represents: "When I speak (lego) one of the pathetic episodes, my eyes brim over with tears; and when I speak one that is filled with fear or dread, my hair stands on end with fright, and my heart pounds" (p. 11). This is the condition of Macbeth, presenting to himself the spectacle of his own murderous actions, "the swelling act / Of the imperial theme":

> why do I yield to that suggestion
> Whose horrid image doth unfix my hair
> And make my seated heart knock at my ribs,
> Against the use of nature?
>
> [1.3.134–37]

Socrates asks Ion the rhapsode whether he realizes that he must recreate in the audience passions that he himself experiences while presenting a tragic narration. He replies: "Each time, from up there on the platform, I spot them crying, and taking on dreadful expressions, and matching all that is spoken *(tois legomenois)* with their wonder. In fact, I'm obliged to pay the closest attention to them, the reason being that if I make them cry I shall laugh, because I get money; but if I make them laugh I shall cry, because I lose money" (quoted in Herington, *Poetry into Drama*, 11). The rhapsode's emotion suffers a crude translation into commercialism as he becomes the slave of responses that, to be successful, he must control. Pepys was not pleased when the laughter of the coarse-grained disrupted the tragedy of *Mustapha*. Although he later arranged for his wife and Deb Willett to go to the play, he voted his own disapproval with his feet and, contrary to his usual practice when he enjoyed a play, did not go again himself.

It is no longer possible in a world distanced from the Greek by language and culture to identify places in its drama where an audience might have laughed in the wrong place. No doubt the moment in Euripides' *Hippolytus* when the slain Phaedra is borne on to the stage on the *ekkyklema* would, in performance in the original language, have been one of intense horror.[8] But it seems doubtful that even on the stage, as opposed to in the study, the dithering banalities of the Chorus could have failed to arouse embarrassing mirth when the Chorus Leader announces the news that everyone, both on and off stage, already knows: "It is done, she is hanged in the dangling rope. / Our Queen is dead." The women of the Chorus embroider this theme relentlessly, until one of their number concludes: "From what I hear, the Queen is dead. They are already laying out the corpse."[9] It might just be possible to gabble the Chorus's lines in production so that the whole scene passed with merciful celerity. In reading, the mind can only boggle over the leisurely tautologies that the dramatist saw fit to introduce[10] and at the strange artistic judgment that either ignored the bathos of the Chorus's speeches or decided that Phaedra's death must be savagely undercut in order to provide for that of Hippolytus, itself described at such gruesome length that it too can become laughable. The dilemma is the opposite of that outlined by Wilson Knight in his discussion of *Lear,* in that theatrical performance of Euripides' play might validate a text that mere reading seems to undermine, whereas in *Lear,* as Lamb declared when he argued the play's unfitness for presentation on the stage, performance can fatally disrupt an audience's perception of tragedy.

Euripides suffers from accidents of time and circumstance, from changes in theatrical convention as well as in lack of cultural correspondence in the language into which his play is translated. In the case of Seneca's version of the *Hippolytus* the position is different. Seneca's dramas were not meant for performance. The crisis of the play is conceived differently from its counterpart in Euripides' version. Hippolytus's death precedes Phaedra's; she dies confessing her fatal calumny. Audience reaction to her death is swallowed up in Theseus's immediate and lengthy lament for the son on whom he has wrongfully avenged himself, which culminates in an attempt to reassemble his son's corpse:

> Bring me those remains
> Of his beloved body, though the parts
> Be heaped in no right order.

He pieces it together as best he may: "What part of you it is I cannot tell, but it is part of you."[11] The reader laughs at the imaginary action. But solitary risibility lacks the anarchic potential that any member of an audience possesses in relation to his fellow theater-goers.

The elements of self-parody implicit in Euripides' plays stimulated Aristophanes' mockery of him in *The Frogs.* But the persistent parodying of tragic effects in the Greek New Comedy of Menander, from whom the Roman Terence and Plautus took many of their comic models,[12] may have helped to create a new audience for Greek tragedy, slower to recognize a tragic idiom than the earlier audiences of Aeschylus and Sophocles had been. Euripides seems to have shared his audience's capacity for ambivalent response. His pervasive irony towards his own dramatic creations constitutes one element in his popularity in England during the Renaissance, that supremely self-aware and self-critical period.

Like Euripides, Shakespeare was no stranger to the vagaries of audience reaction. He often incorporates the caprices of the spectator into his plays. The tragedy of Pyramus and Thisbe, "very tragical mirth," excites in Philostrate emotions that would have brought Ion to despair:

> Which when I saw rehears'd, I must confess,
> Made mine eyes water; but more merry tears
> The passion of loud laughter never shed.
>
> [*MND*, 5.1.68–70]

Falstaff often laughs in the wrong place. When Hal makes a glorious martial exit at the end of act 3 of *Henry IV Part I*, proclaiming:

> The land is burning, Percy stands on high,
> And either we or they must lower lie,

Falstaff comments:

> Rare words! brave world! Hostess, my breakfast, come!
> O, I could wish this tavern were my drum!
>
> [3.3.203–6]

Having slain Hotspur, Hal speaks an epitaph over his old friend, the fat knight, who also lies spread-eagled in the dust:

> Embowell'd will I see thee by and by,
> Till then in blood by noble Percy lie.

As the Prince marches triumphantly off a head rises from the ground and a voice retorts in indignant *sotto voce:*

> Embowell'd! if thou embowel me to-day, I'll give you leave to powder me
> and eat me too tomorrow. [5.4.109–13]

Falstaff must be banished from Henry V's court for reasons of law and order, but more urgently because he laughs when he should be serious, and is, moreover, the cause of that laughter in other men. Falstaff is as aware as Ion of the actor's capacity for simulating emotion: "Give me a cup of sack to make my eyes look red, that it may be thought I have wept, for I must speak in passion, and I will do it in King Cambyses' vein" (2.4.384–87). Shakespeare's delight in parodying tragic effects may have been stimulated by an acquaintance with New Comedy,[13] but it also seems rooted in his theatrical experience of the mixed dramatic modes of his own time, of which *Cambyses*

(1569), billed as a "Lamentable Tragedie, mixed full of pleasant mirth,"[14] was a notable example.

Domestic tragedies of the late sixteenth century constantly remind an apparently forgetful audience that it is watching a tragic spectacle. The Prologue to *A Warning for Faire Women* points out that "The stage is hung with black, and I perceive / The auditors prepar'd for Tragedy."[15] In *Arden of Feversham* (1592) the actors refer to the fate that pursues Thomas Arden as his "tragedy." Black Will declares to one of Alice Arden's henchmen that he knows that his own destiny lies in the dispatching of Thomas Arden:

> Thy office is but to appoint the place,
> And train thy master to his tragedy.

He expresses his longing to encounter his victim as that of a parched traveler who

> Ne'er long'd so much to see a running brook
> As I to finish Arden's tragedy.

When Michael, reluctantly an accomplice, imagines being hunted down by Black Will and Shakebag he hears Black Will cry, "Stab the slave! / The peasant will detect the tragedy." Strangely enough, in all these cases the "tragedy" is an action that has yet to happen, the slaughtering of Arden himself. The action witnessed by the audience has almost the status of prologue because Arden's death, the real "tragedy," only happens at the end. At that point the Epilogue explains to the audience that the whole play has in fact been a tragedy: "Gentlemen, we hope you'll pardon this naked tragedy."[16] If they had found it funny, they now realize their mistake.

Even if Shakespeare had not witnessed audience unruliness—or even on occasion been a part of it—he must have meditated, as he embarked on his own career as tragic dramatist, on the necessity of controlling the responses of a very mixed audience who had no real theatrical education in how to behave during a tragic action, such as the Greek dramatists might have expected from their own audiences. *Arden of Feversham* contains marked anticipations of *Macbeth* in imagery, action, and atmosphere, and of *Hamlet* in a plot where the delays of the murderers turn the dilatory Danish Prince into the most efficient of executioners. But the domestic play aspires to a tragic seriousness that it never attains. If Shakespeare saw it—and he may even have acted in it[17]—he must himself have laughed at such interchanges as, in a moment of *Macbeth*-like murk:

Ferryman. Fie, what a mist is here!
Arden. This mist, my friend, is mystical.

[P. 254]

Or at the suddenness with which Arden forgives his rival, Mosbie, and assures him of everlasting friendship, when the audience has just witnessed a passionate love scene between Mosbie and Alice. Or at the long parting between Alice and her husband, when she urges him to stay, hoping meanwhile that he will go so that she can make merry with her lover. Her performance is so convincing that Thomas nearly changes his mind. Business calls, however, and as he leaves the stage his wife remarks to her paramour: "I am glad he is gone; he was about to stay" (p. 217). The actors may be caught up in the raw but powerful atmosphere of violence and subterfuge, but the audience can laugh to its heart's content.

The printing press no doubt created the situation in which Seneca's dramas became popular during the Renaissance, by providing a readership for tragedy rather than merely an audience for it. The ductility of a reader, quietly ensconced in an armchair in the privacy of his or her own chamber, is obviously far more to be counted on than the malleability of a large and disparate audience determined to enjoy itself, if necessary at the dramatist's expense. Shakespeare was too much a man of the theater not to know that the question of whether a play was a tragedy or not would not be determined by the words on the page, however often the word *tragedy* was presented to the audience's attention, but by the collaboration of actor and audience in the theater.

Shakespeare's tragic dramas evince a recognition that the audience may laugh in the wrong place and provide for it in various ways. If the theater audience, or at least its coarse-grained members, mock the extravagance with which Richard II bewails his misfortunes, they are forestalled by a stage audience, of whom the lachrymose king observes: "Well, well, I see / I talk but idlely, and you laugh at me" (3.3.170–71). In *Romeo and Juliet* the Nurse and the Capulets, aided by the full flowers of rhetoric, lament the apparent demise of Paris's bride:

> O woe! O woeful, woeful, woeful day!
> Most lamentable day, most woeful day
> That ever, ever, I did yet behold!
> O day, O day, O day, O hateful day!
> Never was seen so black a day as this.
> O woeful day, O woeful day!
>
> [4.5.49–54]

The audience is placed in the dilemma of finding funny a grief that is real, expressed for a death that is unreal. However, its alienated laughter is allowed for by the Friar's remonstrance:

> For though fond nature bids us all lament,
> Yet nature's tears are reason's merriment.
>
> [Ll. 82–83][18]

By the time of *Hamlet* the dilemma "Of mirth in funeral and dirge in marriage" dominates the play. The Friar's speech has become the property of Claudius and Gertrude, both guilty, according to Hamlet as audience of their actions, of confounding a time to be merry and a time to mourn. This contradiction reaches a climax in the ludicrous spectacle of Laertes and Hamlet wrestling in or over Ophelia's grave, gazed on not only by an amazed theater audience, by the grave-diggers themselves—professional jesters at death—but by the astonished stars who "stand / Like wonder-wounded hearers." By recognizing the disruptiveness of unexpected laughter, Shakespeare makes it part of a new kind of tragic expectation. The supreme tragic experience begins to be located in precisely that anarchic wish to laugh in the wrong place that Wilson Knight analyzes so acutely in his essay on *Lear*.

One may wonder, however, whether Shakespeare was entirely contented with the way in which his audience coped with the demands he made on it. The mad scenes in *Lear* always arouse laughter in the theater from the sensitive as well as from the coarse-grained spectator. Indeed, they seem to call out a coarseness in the tenderest consciousness.[19] The Folio omission of the least controllable part of that scene, the "joint-stool," may have reflected the dramatist's dissatisfaction with the audience's merriment. Certainly the much-quoted speech about the cruelty of the gods—

> As flies to wanton boys are we to th' gods,
> They kill us for their sport.

—provides a painful gloss on the audience's relation to a tragic action in which acute suffering is represented for its entertainment. It is as though the fearful movement between horror and risibility that Knight charts in audience response to Lear, is itself the cause of the tragedy. Without the human capacity to find the torments of its own species laughable there could be none of the opposition between greatness and triviality that forms a far larger element in Shakespeare's tragedies than it ever did in Greek tragedy.

The case of *Othello* is arresting because Shakespeare set himself the task, as Kenneth Muir puts it, of transforming "a sordid story with a commonplace moral into a universal tragedy of love."[20] But this involved a movement from one well-established and recognized genre, in which all the main characters had their counterparts,[21] that of the situation comedy that he himself had exploited in *The Merry Wives of Windsor,* into another, in which, by virtue of its extraordinary protagonists, Shakespeare's play stands alone. The great danger for the dramatist, and one that he must have recognized as the ultimate challenge to his capacities, must have been that under inept handling the play would revert to kind, to the world of Dekker's *Westward Ho* or of Jonson's *Every Man in His Humour* or of many of Middleton's comedies. In theatrical terms, *Othello,* despite the unluckiness of the Scottish play, is the one most at risk from audience reaction,[22] where a skillful and unscrupulous Iago and a poorly acted Othello can return the play to comedy. Catherine Phillips wrote in 1662: "Only the other day, when *Othello* was play'd the Doge of Venice and all his Senators came upon the Stage with Feathers in their Hats, which was like to have chang'd the Tragedy into a Comedy, but that the Moor and Desdemona acted their Parts well."[23] Thomas Rymer's dismissal of the play as a "senceless trifling tale . . . which impiously assumes the sacred name of Tragedy"[24] can be authenticated only too easily by the behavior of the audience in the theater, which may laugh even at Othello's fit. The tendency to ribald reaction must have been more common in the Elizabethan theater than it is now because the behavior of Shakespeare's contemporaries was not conditioned by the reverence that now surrounds the playwright's name.

By the time Shakespeare wrote *Timon of Athens* he had pushed his reflections on tragedy as kind into a new domain. The Poet who plans to describe the fall of the great man from the height of fortune is presented to the audience in the opening scene of the play as a contemptible hack reworking a tired convention. His projected poem hovers in the audience's consciousness during Shakespeare's own reworking of the same convention in presenting the painful spectacle of Timon's downfall. The tragedy of Timon, fooled by all who surround him, creates in the audience if not laughter, a dissociation more marked than in any of Shakespeare's other plays. It is as though the playwright himself mocked his own play, dissipating its seriousness as Betterton dissipated the seriousness of Fulke Greville's tragedy. Did the dramatist tire of watching every expression of the audience's emotion and decide that he, like it, would laugh as he pleased at the passions he represented?

Shakespeare recognized throughout his career, with varying degrees of acquiescence, that it was in the power of an audience to destroy a tragedy through its reaction to it. That destructiveness remains, however, the dramatist's ultimate register of what tragedy is. Laughter in the wrong place implicates the audience in the tragic action because the unreliable response of its members provides a paradigm for the fearful conflict between meanness and nobility, cruelty and compassion, which all Shakespeare's tragedies transfer from the theater of the mind, the solitary consciousness embodied in the reader, to that more turbulent arena, the public theater.

Notes

1. *The Shorter Pepys*, ed. Robert Latham (London: Bell and Hyman, 1985), 827.

2. John Herington, *Poetry into Drama: Early Tragedy and the Greek Poetic Tradition* (Berkeley and Los Angeles: University of California Press, 1985), 69.

3. Horace, *Ars Poetica*, 89–91, quoted in Alastair Fowler, *Kinds of Literature* (Oxford: Oxford University Press, 1982), 65.

4. Fowler, *Kinds of Literature*, 72; Susan Snyder, *The Comic Matrix of Shakespeare's Tragedies* (Princeton, N.J.: Princeton University Press, 1979), 8; Stephen Orgel, "Shakespeare and the Kinds of Drama," *Critical Inquiry* 6 (Autumn 1979): 123; Northrop Frye, *Anatomy of Criticism* (Princeton, N.J.: Princeton University Press, 1957), 246–47; Paul Hernadi, *Beyond Genre: New Directions in Literary Classification* (Ithaca, N.Y., and London: Cornell University Press, 1972), 178, 180.

5. Jane P. Tompkins, "The Reader in History: The Changing Shape of Literary Response," in *Reader-Response Criticism: From Formalism to Post-Structuralism*, ed. Jane P. Tompkins (Baltimore and London: Johns Hopkins University Press, 1980), 202–94.

6. Oliver Taplin, *Greek Tragedy in Action* (London: Methuen, 1978), 168.

7. Emrys Jones, *The Origins of Shakespeare* (Oxford: Oxford University Press, 1977), 22, discusses the Player's emotion in terms of a passage from Quintilian, *Institutio Oratoria*, 6.2.35: "I have often seen actors, both in tragedy and comedy, leave the theatre still drowned in tears after concluding the performance of some moving role."

8. Taplin, *Greek Tragedy in Action*, 115, 11–12: "The *ekkyklema* (literally 'something which is rolled out') was a low platform on wheels which could be extruded from the central doors."

9. *Hippolytus*, trans. David Grene, *The Complete Greek Tragedies*, ed. David Grene and Richard Lattimore (Chicago: University of Chicago Press, 1955), 1 : 195.

10. Bernard M. W. Knox, "The *Hippolytus* of Euripides," in *Oxford Readings in Greek Tragedy* (Oxford: Oxford University Press, 1983), 311–31, presents a fascinating analysis of the play in terms of a choice between speech and silence for all the characters, from which it is tempting to conclude that the Chorus at Phaedra's death made the wrong choice.

11. *Phaedra*, in Seneca, *Four Tragedies and Octavia*, trans. E. F. Watling (Harmondsworth: Penguin, 1966), 149.

12. R. L. Hunter, *The New Comedy of Greece and Rome* (Cambridge: Cambridge University Press, 1985), 114–36.

13. Anne Righter, *Shakespeare and the Idea of the Play* (London: Chatto and Windus, 1962), 43, discusses various aspects of Elizabethan indebtedness to New Comedy.

14. The Arden editor, A. R. Humphreys, p. 77, notes the similarity between the full title of *Cambyses* and the "tragical mirth" of Pyramus and Thisbe.

15. *A Warning for Faire Women*, in *The School of Shakespeare*, ed. Richard Simpson (London, 1878), vol. 2, l. 74.

16. *Arden of Feversham*, in *Minor Elizabethan Tragedies*, ed. T. W. Craik (London: Dent, 1974), 231, 229, 235, 278.

17. *See The Predecessors of Shakespeare*, ed. Terence P. Logan and Denzell S. Smith (Lincoln: University of Nebraska Press, 1973), 241.

18. John Downes, *Roscius Anglicanus*, recollected a production of *Romeo and Juliet* in which Lady Capulet "enter'd in a hurry, crying 'O my dear Count!' " and "inadvertently left 'o' out in the pronunciation of the word 'Count!' giving it a vehement accent" that "put the house into such a laughter that London Bridge at low water was silence to it." Quoted in Gamini Salgado, *Eyewitnesses of Shakespeare* (Sussex: Sussex University Press, 1975), 61. Shakespeare cannot have been a stranger to this sort of incident and this may have made him all the more determined to control his audience's reactions as far as he was able.

19. Snyder, *Comic Matrix*, 164, records that audiences at Gielgud's production of *Lear* in 1940 laughed—as Gielgud himself recalled—at the interchanges between Lear and Kent when Kent was in the stocks [2.4.14–21] "whether they were 'played for comedy' or not."

20. Kenneth Muir, *The Sources of Shakespeare's Plays* (London: Methuen, 1977), 196.

21. Leo Salingar, *Shakespeare and the Traditions of Comedy* (Cambridge: Cambridge University Press, 1974), 86. Barbara Heliodora C. de Mendonca, "Othello: A Tragedy Built on a Comic Structure," *Shakespeare Survey* 21 (1968): 31–38, argues the close relation between *Othello* and the Italian *commedia dell'arte*, as performed in London in 1602. See also Frances Teague, "*Othello* and the New Comedy," *Comparative Drama* 20 (Spring, 1986): 53–64, for analysis of the connections between that tragedy and the New Comedy of Terence and Plautus.

22. Orgel, "Shakespeare and the Kinds of Drama," 122, declares of *Othello* and *Romeo and Juliet:* "Much of the dramatic force derives from the way they continually tempt us with comic possibilities."

23. Letter dated 3 December 1662 in *Letters from Orinda to Poliarchus,* 1705, quoted in Salgado, *Eyewitnesses of Shakespeare,* 54.

24. Quoted in Orgel, "Shakespeare and the Kinds of Drama," 110.

Changing Modes in Hamlet Production: Rediscovering Shakespeare after the Iconoclasts

by WILHELM HORTMANN

The election campaign that took Helmut Kohl and his Christian Democrats into office in 1983 was fought under the battle cry of "spiritual and moral regeneration." The new administration promised to return to the conservative values of stability, tradition, self-reliance, and moral probity, and it was to bring to an end the period of ideological radicalism and social experiment begun in 1968. If one is prepared to take a broad view, a similar reversal can be claimed for the theater. The parallelisms between art and ideology in themselves are perhaps less instructive than it would be to investigate the timelags and countercurrents. However, in the space allotted, only the most general drifts can be charted.

The beginnings of the cultural revolution had been auspicious, in politics as well as in the theater. The vision of a society free from repression fired quests for emancipation in every area of social life. In the theater, it meant a complete reorientation. At the beginning of the 1960s the theater was still looked upon as an institution where good Germans paid their respects to culture and reaffirmed their belief in the values of Christian humanism. Ten years later there was nothing left of all this. The theater had become a battleground, a tribunal, a propaganda forum, a circus—anything but a museum or a high altar. The change was initiated by three emigrants: Bertolt Brecht, Erwin Piscator, and Fritz Kortner, and it was carried out by their disciples, directors like Peter Palitzsch, Egon Monk, Hansgünther Heyme, and Peter Zadek. These young men took Brecht's statement for their motto that some classical works were valuable only as raw material. They handled them accordingly and made them aggressive and dissonant, topical and provocative.

The impulse to wrench the classics from their moorings was not only a German phenomenon; vide Joseph Papp, Charles Marowitz, Edward Bond, and Tom Stoppard. The radical transvaluations that Shakespeare was subjected to in the 1960s and 1970s reflected the progressive schiz-oidism in the world view of Western man, to which the theater reacted with categories of absurdity, irrationality, and fragmentation.

In Germany the movement to reshape the classics was stronger than in most other countries for two reasons. The first is organizational. The subsidized theater allows greater independence from the opinions of the ticket-buying public. Furthermore, municipal vanities began to favor avant-garde directors. Ideologically (and this is the second reason) the revolution in the theater coincided with that angry attack on the restoration of tradi-tional values upon which the Federal Republic had been built. What had made the Holocaust possible? That was the question behind all questions, and it was now asked with greater insistence and acrimony than ever before. A radical process of self-searching was set in motion, with docu-mentary plays about the Nazi past on the one hand and with a critical review of the cultural heritage on the other. In the course of this self-scrutiny, the classics were made to stand in the dock, and Shakespeare as "our" third classical poet next to Goethe and Schiller as one of the accused. Had they not, in the harmonizing endings of their fifth acts, dispensed a spurious justice in the service of the status quo? Had they not lent their powerful authority to support a repressive value-system and thus weak-ened the utopian hope that it might be altered? Traditional reception, it was felt, had harmonized the plays into icons of ultimate reconciliation. But take away this constraint towards affirmation and immediately the classical play will show what it is made of: glaring oppositions and negations, disruptive egoisms, murderous passions in the grip of an incomprehensi-ble, absurd disorder. This was how Jan Kott interpreted Shakespeare as "Our Contemporary" (German edition 1964), and the theatrical avant-garde in Germany soon out-kotted Kott. In the course of this process they arrogated unheard-of formal freedoms in speaking, acting, costume, mu-sic, stage design; they tested new aesthetics of ugliness, violence, absurdity; they made a bonfire of all the old rulebooks and thoroughly thwarted the theater-goer's expectations in sight, sound, logic and sense.

Some brief notes on a few productions must suffice to show how, from the mid-sixties onward, the traditional images of Shakespeare were broken up.[1]

Held Henry ("Harry, the Hero"), directed by Peter Zadek in Bremen in 1964, was the first irreverent break with tradition. Zadek turned *Henry V* into a pacifist collage, an ahistorical multimedia show against heroism and militarism. The text was not greatly changed, but many means were em-ployed to point the message that patriotism is *made* and that the hero is a *product* of a cult and of manipulation. A screen at the back showed Hitler's troops marching into Paris and "Harry" taking the salute; a backdrop showed fifty portraits of kings and queens, some of them changing into the heads of Hitler, Stalin, Billy Graham, football stars, and so on. Henry V was still portrayed as a hero but also as television-conscious, carefully arranging his public appearances while—once in the field—he occasionally relaxed in bed with a French mistress.

The histories were obvious material for debunking presentations. In *Krieg der Rosen,* directed by Peter Palitzsch in Stuttgart in 1967, the central idea was not (as in John Barton's and Peter Hall's *The War of the Roses* of 1964) that of order in nature as well as in the Commonwealth, but that of a grotesque, self-destructive mechanism of feudal power-grasping and power-losing. This mechanism operated in a cannibalistic world whose emblems—skeletons, corpses, hacked-off limbs—were constantly on view in a pictured frieze stretching across the whole width of the stage. Palitzsch, who adapted the text with Jörg Wehmeier, used Shakespeare as "raw material" in the Brechtian sense to point a Marxist lesson (the first of many) about the contradictions and self-delusions of feudal power politics. The appeal was to the intellect, not to the emotions.

Productions "against the grain" were common and often visual impressions contradicting the text were made to convey the message. Thus, in *Troilus and Cressida,* directed by Hans Neuenfels in Frankfurt in 1972, Ulysses gave a perfect rendition of the speech on Degree but his Uncle Sam costume and his cigar-chewing and champagne-swigging revealed the grand performance as cynical exercise in rhetoric, as lip-service to the letter while perverting the spirit.

More brutal shock tactics were employed by Peter Zadek in directing *Measure for Measure* at Bremen in 1967. In this notorious production the Duke was murdered by the people, Mistress Overdone took his place, she had Angelo and Mariana executed and Isabella sent to a brothel. Zadek distrusted Shakespeare's justice. He also distrusted fine language and controlled gesture. Both were abandoned. For example, Isabella to her brother Claudio: "If I hop into bed with Angelo, you're free, Claudyboy. You make me vomit, you're a beast, utter dirt". A correspondingly primitive body language was developed to shock sensibilities into a new kind of awareness. Thus Angelo and Escalus, instead of discussing the right use of power, fought for possession of the Duke's chair, the symbol of power.

Hamlet productions of similar iconoclastic furor did not arrive upon the scene until much later. The most important ones were directed by Peter Zadek at Bochum in 1977, George Tabori at Bremen in 1978, and Hansgünther Heyme at Cologne in 1979.[2]

Zadek's particular kind of theater—roisterous, funny, grotesque, obscene, circensian, poetic—rebelled against the two prevailing modes of the postwar German theater: the spiritual and the political. According to Zadek the theater had to be liberated from the domination of reason. The means he employed to this end included breaking taboos, allowing minor figures in a play lives of their own, dismantling the hero figures, acting out indications in the text in physical terms no matter how odd (physicaliza-

Figure 1. *The Wars of the Roses*, directed by Peter Palitzsch, Stuttgart (1967). *(Courtesy of Schauspiel Stuttgart, Stuttgart.)*

tion), openly showing the theatrical conventions and machinery (the-atricalization), mixing modes and genres (high and low, slapstick, pop, comic strip, Grand Guignol, and realism) to make a "total" theatrical event (spectacularization), in an uninhibited onslaught on the mind and senses. The five-and-one-half hour performance in an unused factory was domi-nated by Ulrich Wildgruber as Hamlet. Fat, zestful, versatile, he upstaged everybody, drowned the audience in his idiosyncratic cascading declama-tion and reveled in mad action such as cutting up Polonius's corpse and throwing the dismembered carcass out of the window. There were further physically garish effects such as Ophelia, who in her madness sees the world as swinish: everyone suddenly wore pig masks; Gertrude, much younger than Hamlet, had her naked breasts painted bright red; Ophelia's petite corpse was not buried in a grave but was literally swept under the carpet. Theatrical conventions were openly caricatured. Thus the Ghost was followed everywhere by a stagehand in overalls operating a fog-ma-chine. Polonius, the Ghost, and Guildenstern were played by women; Rosencrantz, a transvestite, impersonated one.

Critical opinion was divided. The most positive comment was that the production showed the inexhaustibility of *Hamlet*. Others felt that Zadek's provocations were beginning to be a well-oiled routine, that Hamlet as a superentertainer and clown only managed to render the ambivalence of his feelings in the scenes with Ophelia and Gertrude, and that the whole was only a parodistic rehearsal of a play about a play.

Hamlet was Tabori's last production with the Bremer Theaterlabor, an experimental group that he directed from 1976 to 1978. Tabori does not regard himself as a director but as a "playmaker," responsible for creating, together with his actors, a theatrical event from a (not necessarily literary) scenario. He believes in the free play of fancy in associational experiments with the actors, group work, "spontaneous dramaturgy," improvisation, and keeping the production open and unfixed for as long as possible. Tabori, a Hungarian by birth, has worked in England and America and writes most of his experimental plays and film scripts in English. In 1978 he brought out his own *Improvisationen über Shakespeares Shylock* in Munich.

The action took place in, on, around the central bed on an otherwise empty and black stage; Hamlet, ill from the beginning, refused to rise and watched most of the plot against him from the bed. In the Ghost scenes the corpse of Hamlet's father rose from the bed (his grave) and rode on Hamlet's back, the action still taking place in the bed. In the court scene Claudius and Laertes, on hands and knees, were whipped like dogs around the bed by Polonius; Ophelia meanwhile was bound hand and foot like an animal for sacrifice. In the prayer scene Claudius, naked in bed, wrestled with the corpse of his brother. In the closet scene Hamlet and Gertrude undressed and exchanged shirts.

Critics were bewildered by this outré production. They agreed, however,

Figure 2. *Hamlet*, directed by Peter Zadek, Bochum (1977). *(Courtesy of Schauspielhaus Bochum, Bochum.)*

on the central idea, namely that of children as impotent victims of their fathers ("psycho-terror of a super-father") and pointed to Freud and Kafka as the sources of Tabori's inspiration.

Hansgünther Heyme, the most uncompromisingly intellectual among the avant-garde directors, cooperated with Wolf Vostell, a famous arranger of "happenings," to create the first "electronic" *Hamlet*. Bizarre alienation was effected by the set, which included the stuffed carcass of a horse hung by its hind legs and dripping blood into a chalice and a strip of eighteen television monitors and a video camera that actors occasionally turned on each other or themselves and whose pictures then appeared eighteen times in a row on the monitors. Electronic gadgets (transistors, pocket computers, walkie-talkies, microphones, cassette recorders) were handled by the actors during most of the scenes. Mystifying objects, from soup plates to herring, were attached to the costumes. The actors divided their attention between the action itself and the recording and transmitting of it by one of these mediums. The most extreme form of this schizoidism occurred in the figure of Hamlet, who was played by two actors. The Hamlet onstage was almost beyond speech and incapable of contact, lost in the crude sexual fantasies of his subconscious and reduced largely to gestures and to a wondering preoccupation with his own body, which he studied in poses and grimaces in front of the video camera. Meanwhile, his alter ego in the

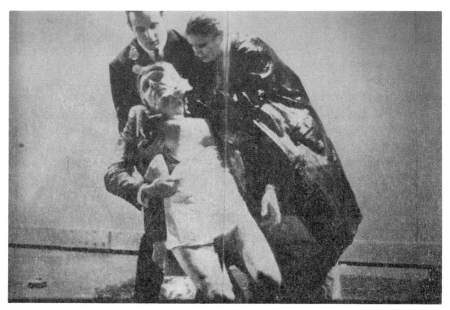

Figure 3. *Hamlet,* **directed by Hansgünther Heyme, Cologne (1979); Wolfgang Robert as Hamlet.** *(Courtesy of Buhnen der Stadt Köln, Cologne.)*

auditorium (the director) spoke the monologues and part of the dialogues over the theater's amplifier system.

Practically every scene showed the dislocation that had torn the play "out of joint." Thus Hamlet's advice to the players was read by an uncomprehending Horatio from a piece of paper picked from Hamlet's pocket while Hamlet himself lay in a swoon. In the burial scene "Hamlet, the Dane," a physical and mental wreck, had to be propped up by Horatio and prompted through his responses. There was, naturally, no wrestling with Laertes in the grave. Nor was he fit to undertake the concluding fencing scene. All the death candidates were abruptly laid out on trolleys, their entrails like so much rotten meat placed on top. Fortinbras, played by the beautiful Ophelia and dressed like a racing driver, stepped from a blinding sun to take possession of Denmark while the current news program was displayed on scores of television monitors.

Critics were surpised at how well the play stood up to the distracting elements of a destructive civilization. They noted many beautiful scenes, but also many gags and inanities.

Iconoclastic productions continued into the early 1980s, although by the end of the 1970s the creative impetus of the movement was dead. The beliefs that had buoyed it up had evaporated. From a euphoric trust in global revolutionary solutions the disappointed utopians fell into resignation and pessimism. Many gave up politics altogether, retreated into the long-maligned inner world, and rediscovered the value of individualism and private life. They found solace and inspiration in beauty, yoga, sectarian cults, and also—with many misgivings—in history and tradition. Perhaps history was after all more than a bloody charnel house and a record of gigantic errors; perhaps tradition had other uses than to be held up to enlightened scorn.

But exactly what position concerning history and tradition was the disaffected intellectual to take? Rejecting history out of a sense of ideological superiority would no longer do, neither in politics nor in the theater. The antiauthoritarian movement had served its purpose; it had released a flood of experiments and had given us some of the most exciting moments in the theater imaginable, but it was obvious that keeping the classical work strapped to the operating table to be brainwashed or dissected could no longer be justified. It had resulted in enormous losses; politically orthodox messages had been bought at the price of historical truth, psychological complexity, and depth of meaning. In the hands of lesser-gifted directors the newly gained aesthetic liberties were an excuse for incompetence and insensitivity. Further reductionism was impossible.

But how was one to get back to Shakespeare? The Schaubühne in Berlin did the job most thoroughly. In 1976 they put themselves and their audience through a nine-hour marathon called *Shakespeare's Memory* with a medley of texts by Elizabethan and Jacobean authors in order to illustrate the social and political background and the intellectual climate of Shakespeare's age. The vast area of the C.C.C. film studios in Berlin-Spandau was filled with various constructions from a colossal Ship of State to pulpit, platform, and stage on which actors simultaneously did acrobatic acts, gave musical performances, or lectured, harangued, and entertained a public that was free to wander from one attraction to the next. The purpose of this interdisciplinary exercise was to recover a sense of history, to regain a feeling for its texture, and at a time when others were still busy denouncing tradition in the name of social criticism. On one point, however, the Schaubühne's position was utterly uncompromising: history and tradition can only be made to live in art, as aesthetic reenactments, not as political manifestos. And they began to prove their point in one breathtaking production after another. For *As You Like It* (1977, directed by Peter Stein) Karl-Ernst Herrmann designed uncannily beautiful sets, a scene of cold cubist abstraction for Duke Frederick's palace, a dark maze for the spectators to squeeze through before they were allowed to see the Forest of Arden, a varied arcadian landscape and a suggestive locus for a play full of refined nostalgia and symbolic tableaux.

Hamlet (1982, directed by Klaus Michael Grüber) was an equally sophisticated *Gesamtkunstwerk*. It presented traditional elements in so self-conscious and deliberate a manner that the whole appeared both as a homage to history and as a final proof that the past—at least as a vital, living force—is irrecoverable. It was a *Hamlet* of superlatives. Performed by an all-star cast that used the uncut text in the longest German *Hamlet* production ever (six and one-quarter hours), every word and syllable was accorded its own weight, fully preserving the aura of the hallowed classical heritage. At times it left the impression of a deliberate exercise in poetic archaeology, as a last, lingering, savoring of a never-again-to-be-recaptured excellence. It was a *Hamlet* that could be recorded on a gold disk and sent into space on the last rocket to leave earth. Every movement and gesture was carefully choreographed, every attitude was designed to create a visual event, which frequently alluded to the Renaissance or baroque paintings that had also served as models for the sumptuous costumes.

Against the overpowering odds of so much calculated beauty, Hamlet's anguish of soul failed to arouse compassion. What remained was the image of the play as nostalgic artifact: every speech was a poem, the full text was its own anthology of purple passages.

What is to be done with *Hamlet* on the postmodernist stage? K. M. Grüber solved this problem by producing the play as an aesthetic recapitulation of the cultural impact of its reception since Goethe, the performance of *Hamlet* as the monument of its former magnificence.

Holk Freytag at the tiny Schloßtheater in Moers (1982) used the new freedoms differently. His answer was to make the play gripping as total

Figure 4. *Hamlet*, directed by Klaus Michael Grüber, Berlin (1982); Bruno Ganz as Hamlet. *(Photo courtesy of Ruth Watz.)*

theater—as a system of interlocking fictions and theatrical cross-references. The idea was to make the audience see *Hamlet* with new eyes. To this end, auditorium and stage were rebuilt to create an oblong arena with the audience looking down into it from three sides. As the company was too small for a full cast, each actor had to take several roles. Some of these doublings gave rise to interesting speculations: for example, Claudius playing the Ghost and Player King (i.e., murderer doubling as victim) or Hamlet playing Lucianus. Others were dictated by necessity. All of them required changes in the text. In the production the undisguised switch from one character to the next by the same actor stressed the underlying idea that theatrical communication is an agreement about roles. The cuts and alterations, though severe, did not touch the core. There was no absurdist reshuffling or collage of the Marowitz type. The soliloquies were given their full weight, the standard of delivery was high. Alienating elements to jolt the audience into a new awareness consisted largely of enigmatic actions and included the use of the amplifyer system or the use of venetian blinds to indicate isolation or deception. The most striking allusion to recent theater history was the costuming of the Player King and the Player Queen in *Endgame* dustbins, their texts drastically cut to provide ping-pong repartee marked by a spotlight that switched rapidly from one to the other. At the end of the fencing march Hamlet did not stab the King but only his gigantic shadow, a teasing conclusion.

Klaus Michael Grüber and Holk Freytag provided two radically different answers to *Hamlet* on the postmodern stage—each in his different way showing the existential German problem of coming to terms with (their nation's) history. The Schaubühne performance exaggerated its weight and importance. It totally immersed the play in its past. It focused the performance not on Hamlet the prince in an existential personal and political dilemma, but on *Hamlet* the play as an existential fact in German cultural history. Their intense and deliberate dedication to tradition thus, paradoxically, exempted the Schaubühne from having to take a stand "and unfold" why *Hamlet* matters now. *Hamlet* matters, their sophisticated rationale would seem to say, not for what it presents but for what it has meant. Or, in other words: the theater's concern with history is aesthetic, rather than of political relevance to the present. The Schloßtheater's denial of history was simpler; it was motivated precisely by its concern with fictions, roles, and communicative structures, and it produced intellectual insights at the price of a loss of historical dimension. How to produce *Hamlet* knowing that it has served as a locus of identification for the German mind and soul seems to have been K. M. Grüber's question. Holk Freytag seems to have asked how to produce *Hamlet* in the knowledge of the last thirty years of international theater history.

Other directors have rediscovered Shakespeare in more straightforward ways. Günther Fleckenstein at the Deutsches Schauspielhaus in Göttingen (in 1984) used the more rugged text of the First Quarto in a production called *Hamlet 1603* to perform a play about power politics in which Hamlet and Claudius both drew on large resources of determination, cunning, and hatred. In this play Hamlet could not afford to procrastinate because in Claudius he had to deal with an utterly fearless opponent. Claudius's call for lights in the Mousetrap Scene was a rumbling threat, not the usual indication of fright; of his "rank offense" Claudius spoke not in customary contrition but—champagne bottle in hand and half-drunk—in terms of gross reasoning with a barely respected deity. Against this daunting figure was pitted a Hamlet of slight physique, a bundle of nervous energy with a deep, booming voice, its timbre as commanding as Claudius's imposing presence. A welcome surprise was the rhythmic and meaningful structuring of their lines by the main characters and the great care they took to fit sound and sense to physical action, two arts that were scorned by the iconoclasts and that many troupes are slow to relearn.

Fleckenstein interpreted *Hamlet* as a play about relationships and he was lucky to have a cast who were able to make them come alive. That something so self-evident should need rediscovering shows how far German Shakespeare productions had been dominated by nonmimetic aesthetics. Avant-garde directors still seem to balk at taking what they probably believe to be a step back, although even an out-and-out avant-gardist like Hansgünther Heyme now uses words like "tradition," "history," even "conservative," without blushing. Simply stepping back into a "prepostmodernist" attitude, however, is impossible. It would put them back into line with their Rip van Winkle colleagues in the provinces who had never moved.

The avant-garde director is in a quandary. The old revolutionary certainties are gone; there is no justification for further debunkings; aesthetically, the philosophy of "heterogeneous elements by violence yoked together" will no longer do. What is needed is a new interpretation or vision *and* a corresponding style. But these are nowhere in sight. Consequently directors are casting around for new bearings. They have to find something along avenues they used to scorn, and yet it cannot and must not be what they once, for good reasons, departed from. An almost impossible task.

The result of this dilemma is not a purposeful quest but a disoriented search covering a wide spectrum of approaches, from crude realism to extreme stylization, in which no common ideological or aesthetic denominator can be made out. More positively, one might say, the field is open again.[3] There is no longer a canon of respectably avant-garde methods: neither Brecht's didactic, presentational theater nor Horvath's "popular" theater with its voyeuristic perspective nor Zadek's fireworks of circus effects nor Heyme's intellectual incisions and operations command special respect and preference any more. The field is indeed open once more for discoveries and rediscoveries, but its guiding principles cannot as yet be made out.

The current *Hamlets* (at Frankfurt, Munich, Vienna, and Düsseldorf) exemplify the tentative character of many recent treatments of Shake-speare. At Frankfurt, after a long period of internal ideological dissension that had sent the Frankfurt Schauspiel into artistic decline, *Hamlet* was to mark the turning point. Here, for once, was a Hamlet who would *not* have "proved most royal," but a young man of excitable temper convincingly on the brink of madness and confronted by an impenetrable world. In his efforts to understand it he engaged in futile intellectual skirmishes, scoring brittle academic points off his opponents or even directly off the audience, and argued himself toward baffling conclusions in the soliloquies. Just as Hamlet was preoccupied with himself, so were the others: Laertes and Ophelia with private jokes of their own, Reynaldo overjoyed at his coming trip to Paris, Gertrude with inner terrors that twisted her gold-robed figure into contorted shapes, and Claudius afflicted by his guilt from the begin-ning. Action had to be forced on them from without and it developed almost against their will. The great revelation of this production was nei-ther Hamlet nor Claudius but Polonius. His overruling passion was the theater. The court was to him merely a stage on which to arrange im-pressive scenes if the protagonists would only let him. He welcomed the players as colleagues, enumerated their qualifications ("tragical-comical-historical-pastoral") with the air of a connoisseur, he lipspoke Hamlet's and the First Player's Pyrrhus lines and even so far forgot himself as to carry the latter's suitcase off the stage. In the mousetrap scene he was as anxious for the success of the performance as if he had staged it himself. To the end he remained pitifully ignorant of the fact that the scenario had changed and that he had become an expendable extra in someone else's act. The overall impression was of a play in which every figure spun in its own orbit and everyone was immersed in his own problems and, in spite of intense exchange, there was no communication.

The other current productions (Vienna, directed by Hans Hollmann, Hamlet: Klaus Maria Brandauer; Munich, directed by B. K. Tragelehn, Hamlet: Peter Brombacher; Düsseldorf, directed by Michael Gruner, Hamlet: Hans Diehl) support the impression that there is little common ground, that every director is pursuing ideas and forms incompatible with those of his neighbor, and that critics disagree to an unusual extent. To some the Vienna *Hamlet* was the great achievement of a homogeneous cast with star actor Klaus Maria Brandauer in the title role scoring triumphs in disciplined delivery and presenting the contradictions of a character caught between reason and emotion. Other critics saw the same production as an unwarrantable reduction of Hamlet to the psychological dimension with a particular stress laid on an incestuous mother fixation, and they deplored

Figure 5. *Hamlet,* directed by Holger Berg, Frankfurt (1985); Martin Wuttke as Hamlet. *(Courtesy of Schauspiel Frankfurt, Frankfurt.)*

the omission of the Fortinbras action and the nonappearance of the Ghost. Others again failed to see a directorial conception at all, spoke of star cult and the embarrassing spectacle of elegant Vienna onstage and in the stalls.

Where Hollmann in Vienna suppressed the historical dimension altogether, B. K. Tragelehn in Munich used *Hamlet* principally to air his and his translator Heiner Müller's (both are East Germans) pessimistic convictions about history. Fortinbras, who arrives for the takeover like the junta general of a banana republic and puts his dirty boots on the desk, is sufficient guarantee that the senseless mechanism will continue. What is the quintessence of history? Dirt, earth, dust, rubbish. The Munich stage was covered in it ankle-deep: dirt and earth for the men to drag their feet through, for Ophelia in her madness to wallow in and to form phalluses and breasts with, for the clowns to shovel onto the dead Ophelia. Hamlet's problem would seem to have been to clear away that mass of dirt, to clear up that mess called history—an impossible task for someone enmeshed in words, caught in a father fixation, incapable of love (either for Ophelia or his mother) and generally psychotic, harrassed, petulant. One critic saw the production inspired by the black pessimism of Heiner Müller's seven-page monologous text and scenario *Hamletmaschine* (1978), an unrelievedly reductionist *Endgame* version of *Hamlet,* and therefore regarded the deliberate presentation of repulsive details as justified. Another rejected this as an all-too-easy and cheap interpretation of history.

After grimly meaningful ugliness in Munich came a meaningless feast to the eyes in Düsseldorf. Critics were unanimous in their praise of the costumes, of the fencing match, of Horatio, even of Hildburg Schmidt as Gertrude transmitting tremors of power, but the rest was "words, words, words" and fine poses. Michael Gruner, the director, wanted to avoid any one-sided interpretation—being conscious, as the program explained, of the history of *Hamlet* reception and of *Hamlet* the play, representing a world in transition and crisis. Yet nothing of this came across. Too much respect for booklearning and a kind of historical self-consciousness made him lose the obvious truth that "the play's the thing."

Several other important *Hamlet* productions have been announced, and 1986 will enter Shakespearean theater history as the year of the German directors' struggle for *Hamlet.* The issue may be very much in the balance but it is already clear that the iconoclasts among them will fight no more than a rearguard action.

Notes

1. A full theater history of the 1960s and 1970s is yet to be written. The nearest approaches are Günther Rühle's two volumes, *Theater in unserer Zeit* (Frankfurt: Suhrkamp, 1976) and *Anarchie in der Regie?* (Frankfurt: Suhrkamp, 1982). There are also many collections of

documentary material, essays, interviews, and so on, such as *Deutsche Dramaturgie der Sechziger Jahre,* ed. Helmut Kreuzer (Tübingen: Deutscher Taschenbuchverlag, 1974). There is also a mass of material in theater journals, notably *Theater heute,* and the review columns of the important dailies and weeklies, not to forget the theater programs themselves in which directors and dramaturges, without fear of contradiction and lack of space, propounded their new ideas. With reference to Shakespeare, scholars such as Ulrich Broich, Manfred Pfister, and Horst Prießnitz have dealt with individual aspects of this movement while a comprehensive presentation of the fate of Shakespeare during the two decades of radical experimentation is still to come.

2. Grateful acknowledgment is made to the editor of *Shakespeare Quarterly* for permission to reprint excerpts from my reviews of various *Hamlet* productions (31:410ff; 34:236–38; 36:346ff).

3. An idea first propounded by Günther Erken, "Theaterarbeit mit Klassikern. Erfahrungen eines Dramaturgen bei Hansgünther Heyme," in *TheaterZeitSchrift* 11 (1985): 5–21.

A *Spate of* Twelfth Nights: *Illyria Rediscovered?*

by MAIK HAMBURGER

Records tell us that *Twelfth Night* has always been by far the most frequently acted Shakespeare comedy in Germany.[1] It belonged to the standard fare of the former German Stadttheater and is still a staple item in the repertoire of theaters in both German states. The stage history has shown that more than any other Shakespeare comedy this play lends itself to the manufacture of stage stereotypes—sentimental lovers, romantic twins, the drunkard, the simpleton, the bureaucrat—which appear to be the price Germans have had to pay for the transculturation to the German theater. Any new approach has to reckon with clichés that have pervaded hundreds of productions and formed a kind of traditional crust around the play.

In the past fifteen months there have been six productions of *Twelfth Night* in the German Democratic Republic, which is an unusually high incidence even for this comedy. I would like to make some remarks about these productions and consider whether this sudden spate can be attributed to any particular reason and whether any common factors may be discerned.

For reasons that will become apparent, I cannot and will not attempt a critical appraisal of these stagings but will try to assess from conversations with the directors and from stage performances what ideas went into the productions of this particular play and which visual and metaphorical vehicles were employed in mounting them. It should be made clear that directors' concepts are never fully realized in production; most of the directors I talked to estimated they had fulfilled about 30 percent of their intentions. In fact a concept is never just turned into theater, in the course of rehearsals it is transmuted into something new and often strange.

In the seven years previous to the period under consideration, i.e., from 1978 to 1984, a total of ninety-one productions of Shakespeare's plays were put on. These included twelve stagings of *Twelfth Night,* which as usual led the comedies, the runners-up being *The Taming of the Shrew* with eleven and the *Dream* with ten productions. The average then was thirteen Shakespeares a year and 1.7 *Twelfth Nights.* The early 1980s were conspicuous for a number of avant-garde, modernistic Shakespeare productions. After the highly original stagings of the *Dream* in Berlin in 1980,[2] there were two productions of *Twelfth Night* in 1981 also notable for their deconstructive approach and their emphasis on disharmony and disjunction of human relationships. A critic of the Brandenburg staging entitled his review "The nasty people of William Shakespeare" and described as a prominent item of the décor a toilet bowl that was widely used for fecal stage-business. Love and desire, the critic states, are reduced to sex and lechery.[3] The Berlin staging in the same year mounted by the Hungarian István Iglodi also stressed the nastiness of Shakespeare's people projecting the disruption of human relationships through an exposition of man's selfishness and culminating in a deeply pessimistic ending.[4] These performances were radical attempts to break up the traditional patterns of Shakespeare reception; they can be interpreted as a violent reaction to preceding productions, whose harmony was evidently no longer considered valid as awareness grew of the contradictions men and women were involved in today.

In the five most recent productions of 1985 and 1986, to which I will devote the rest of my paper, there has again been a shift of emphasis.

In Cottbus, a company of twenty-eight actors puts on Shakespeare regularly every two years in a magnificent Art Nouveau theater. Here *Twelfth Night* had its premier on 19 May 1985, directed by Renate-Louise Frost. The ambience of the comedy here is a southern fairy-tale land bounded right and left by pinkish-white palisades, behind which wiry palm trees stand out like skinny white hands. The costumes are selected eclectically, ranging from Renaissance elements through Biedermeier to present-day casual sportswear. Olivia first appears in an elaborate Queen Elizabeth dress in black and silver, a wealthy matron with a lorgnon who forces her household to observe mourning. After her meeting with Cesario we see her totally transformed as a young woman in a long white chiffon gown and flowing chestnut hair. The projection of Olivia as the Virgin Queen who is allowed to act out the erotic fantasies denied to her in real life on the throne is indebted to the interpretation of André Müller, according to which Olivia's suitors represent the various social classes currying for the Queen's favor; thus Belch stands for the impoverished landed gentry, Orsino for the degenerating aristocracy, Malvolio for the Puritans.[5] However, these parallels are not driven too far and most of the action is in comic clashes between stage personalities. Feste provides an exception: he is an old man looking ludicrous in an immaculately white harlequin's costume, whose antics for the delectation of his superiors provide a pathos as moving as anything in the production.

In line with the André Müller reading, there is no harmonious ending: Olivia's disappointment with the substitution of Sebastian for Cesario is evident. The theme of this production is the contradiction between seeming and being, between appearance and reality in the characters' relationships to one another, in the characters' projection of themselves and their interaction with the audience.

The production used a new translation by B. K. Tragelehn that was considered to be sharper and more colloquial than the classic Schlegel text and gave the characters a more pronounced social delineation. Most of the young actors, I was told, feel uncomfortable with the classic translations, which they find difficult to bring to life for young audiences.

The Friedrich-Wolf-Theater in the Mecklenburg town of Neustrelitz, with a company of about twenty actors, put on *Twelfth Night* on 27 October 1985. The play was directed by Roswitha Schubert, a recent graduate of the Berlin Institut für Schauspielregie.

Illyria here has an Italianate air. The set consists of a tentlike edifice made of white canvas in the center of the revolve and a campanile with a bell towering in the middle. The festive character of the play is underscored by a group of masked revelers entering like a Venetian masquerade through the auditorium. They provide the music for Orsino and are present as onlookers during a number of scenes. From the revelers, Belch, Aguecheek, and Feste are seen to emerge, merely pushing their masks up to play their parts and disappearing again in the anonymous carnival. The costumes were vaguely inspired by Italian dress—the lavishly uniformed aristocrat, the carabinieri, the priest—without becoming too specific. Aguecheek's broad-shouldered suit, on the other hand, suggested a ranger's uniform, and the actor played the part with the impish impertinence of a well-to-do visitor from across the Atlantic.

The central issue of the Neustrelitz production happened to crystalize during the course of rehearsals: the theme of personal loneliness and isolation due to a fear of living out one's emotions, a loneliness that is gradually overcome by a growing capability for emotional exchange. However, emotional opening-up also means vulnerability. Olivia, who goes all the way to total emotional engagement and whose degree of commitment is regarded as an utopian ideal, suffers absolute loss at the end of the play when her husband Sebastian turns out to be no more than a hollow replica of the person she had really given her love to. Illyria is conceived by this director as a portmanteau word coined out of illusion and lyricism.

Unlike most GDR theaters, Neustrelitz had no continuous Shakespeare tradition, its speciality hitherto being modern drama. Thus the actors had little exprience with verse and encountered the same difficulties described by John Barton at this congress and more explicitly in his book *Playing Shakespeare*[6]—the difficulties of an actor accustomed to working in a contemporary idiom when confronted with the complex poetic language of the Elizabethan, albeit in the modern Tragelehn translation. The director also admits to problems with the actors of the Belch troupe, who tended to cling to the reliable clichés of low comedy.

In Altenburg, an old ducal seat in Saxony, the Intendant Achim Gebauer and his ensemble of some twenty actors put on *Twelfth Night* on 2 February 1986. The costumes were adapted from the dancehall and nightclub of the 1950s—i.e., a period that permits a showy opulence and is neither contemporary nor historical. Cesario and Sebastian wear white tailcoats, Sir Toby appears in a glittering pink jacket like a barkeeper, and Orsino sports a gold embroidered waistcoat.

Gebrauer's staging concept was to let the play emerge from the actors and their text alone, so that apart from the odd desk or bed there was no scenery. On the empty stage the play was run through at a furious pace, with the revolve helping to accelerate the actors' exits and entrances. The intention was to give the production an orgiastic quality based on the premise that the whole play was constructed like a love act, moving from the erotic overtures with growing intensity to the final eruption. In this production there is no hesitation, no doubting, no retarding element. The driving force of the characters is taken from the German title of the play, *Was ihr wollt* (What You Will, or rather, What You Want). Each person knows what he or she wants, be it power, love, life, and they all reach their objectives although the unpredictable relations they have to take up with others to follow their aims leads to quite unexpected results. For the director the message of this play is the emancipation that derives from the liberty of admitting one's submerged desires and actually trying to live them out. Malvolio represents the forces of convention and repression that run counter to this process of self-fulfillment.

The sensual, almost hedonistic attitude projected into the characters is coupled with a sense of transitoriness of the Illyrian world. With a feeling of time slipping away, the production resembles a dance on a volcano. "What's to come is still unsure" is the most highly emphasized line in the play. (The German "Wer weiß, wo mir morgen sind" intensifies this sense of insecurity.) For all that, Illyria is an attractive place as long as it lasts, and the audience is invited to take part in the fun.

For this production, a new translation by Eva Walch was selected after a test in which a number of unnamed translations of key passages were allowed to circulate among the actors. This was the first staging of Eva Walch's translation.

In the three productions just described the casts were predominantly young, most of the actors being in their early twenties. Orsino, Olivia, Viola, and of course Sebastian were all of an age, as were Malvolio, Belch, and Aguecheek. The directors were in their thirties. Although the productions abounded with ideas, there was no attempt to build up a coherent historical or metaphorical idiom. The directors were not primarily interested in projecting Illyria as a particular model, be it Arcadian, Utopian, geographical, or metaphorical. Instead of seeking such a medium that would heighten and distance the action as a whole, they were more concerned with the direct involvement of audiences in the network of dramatic relationships between people. Although the productions moved in a modern idiom and employed anachronisms without compunction, there were no modernistic shock-effects of the kind seen in 1980/81, and the possibility of meaningful human intercourse was implicit.

The modern quality of these productions lay in the uninhibited way young people acted out and reacted to emotional situations. All three stagings were extroverted, outspoken, spontaneous, and direct. The more leisurely, self-conscious forms of articulation were externalized, there was no reflection or introspection. The self-questioning soliloquies of Olivia and Viola were not given as asides but addressed immediately to the audience. All productions were, indeed, profoundly influenced by Robert Weimann's investigations of actor-audience relationships on the Elizabethan stage.[7] The downstage (platea) mode of audience contact was preferred to an extent not always warranted by the specifics of the actual text.

The central character in every case was Olivia, whose courage to enter human relationships was seen as the most important statement of the play, although in two of the three productions she suffered dire disappointment as a consequence. Viola and Sebastian, on the other hand, tended to be rather single-layered. There were rigid attempts to discard the roisterous drunkard and simpleton clichés for Belch and Aguecheek but no really convincing alternatives were discovered.

In line with the tendency to externalize and depsychologize, the stage music, written by bandleaders or composers of popular music, aspired in each case towards a modern, slangy mood. The songs were treated in a very casual way, and often the text was merely spoken to accompaniment. The languishing atmosphere customarily associated with this play was supplanted at all levels by a vital activism.

The last two productions I would like to discuss differ in some basic ways from those described hitherto. The towns of Görlitz and Zittau in the far southeast of the GDR are both played to by an acting ensemble resident in Zittau. *Twelfth Night* had its premiere there on 7 June 1985. As the director of that production, I am a generation older than the directors considered up to now. The setting of the play was a large black cubic space behind a proscenium arch depicting the sky in hues of blue and gold. The orchestra pit was used as a forestage where the below-stairs characters literally surface from below through a set of steps. The scenery actually stood for the physical boundaries of Illyria. When people arrived from elsewhere, as Viola and Sebastian do, the backdrop was lifted and the actors entered from the brick firewall at the back, stepping from the real theater into the theatrical fiction of Illyria. The costumes combined Renaissance dress with modern casual wear. As the actors playing Viola and Sebastian were of extremely different stature and appearance, the twinning was performed by a second set of faces in the costume: their bright red leather waistcoats bore identical pairs of appliquéed eyes.

Illyria was projected as a sensual, languishing Arcadia: all modes of erotic communication are feasible but they generally remain in the realm of fantasy because noone is prepared to make the effort to opt for one concrete partner at the expense of the hundreds of partners of his imagination. Orsino, generally wheeled onto the scene reclining on a couch, longs for Olivia but at the same time fears her accepting him and consoles himself with his servant-boy Valentine—here played by a girl. There are no external hindrances to love as in *Romeo and Juliet* and the *Dream;* the obstacles lie in the melancholic luxury of nonproductive self-reflexivity.

In line with the life of fantasy, role-play is an essential component of life in Illyria. Not only do Orsino and Olivia play their well-known parts; the three men in Olivia's household, who all seek to depose her on the strength (or weakness) of her sex, embody three types of male role-play. Belch adopts the part of the macho, the dominant, riotous male. The motif of topsy-turvydom, of the Lord of Misrule inherent in the festive component of the play, here attains sinister overtones as Belch's revolt against Olivia could tip over to a radical right-wing coup d'état. Aguecheek is the corresponding Boy Scout youngster trying in vain to emulate his masculine companion, and Malvolio plays the role of the efficient man of affairs. Feste makes an exception in so far as role-playing is part of his job; he is the only professional among amateurs, consequently he is the only one who does not confuse role-play with reality.

Viola plays her role out of dire necessity. Taking a clue from the law of Ephesus from the *Comedy of Errors* and from Marina's predicament in *Pericles,* I assumed that Viola alone in a strange country would be a girl in acute jeopardy. Luxurious Illyria can be a poisonous flower that destroys intruders—as it does not only Antonio, who disdains to play a role, but also the Captain, who is arrested for no apparent reason at all. Viola has to play a role to survive but her interaction with the Illyrians induces them to discard their illusionary roles and discover their true feelings. However, that means saying goodbye to the elegiac luxury of fantasy. Only when they enter into real love relations do the Illyrians learn what real pain, jealousy, and disappointment are. Olivia is mortified by the deception practiced upon her by Sebastian, with whom she had an intimate rendezvous, and is provoked to box his ears.

The production in Zittau attempted to show a coherent Arcadian world that possessed the lethargic comforts of a sophisticated Schlaraffenland or Cocaigne but was endangered by the belligerent male Belch troupe. The stage world of Illyria was broke open so as to admit Viola and Sebastian, who gradually stirred up the Illyrians to more real and active relationships. In the end, Feste sings the play out of Illyria back to everyday life, where the rain it raineth every day. The lyrical mood often evoked was supported by the use of the original music where available, occasionally countered by loud blasts from Pink Floyd.

The last production of *Twelfth Night* to be discussed here was mounted at Weimar on 20 March 1986. The company of about thirty-five at the Nationaltheater in Weimar, the seat of German classics and scene of the annual GDR Shakespeare Conference, is naturally very well versed in Shakespearean acting. After doing a highly modernistic, deconstructive *Measure for Measure* two years ago, the team of directors, Peter Schroth and Peter Kleinert, now produced a *Twelfth Night* that is conjunct and closely adhering to the Shakespearean structures, albeit in a startlingly original interpretation.

The setting suggests a holiday resort in Morocco, although again many elements of the production point to Latin America. White palm trees meet the eye, far upstage there is a suggestion of a beach, and a number of white camels recline on the floor to provide atmosphere and seating accommodation; a Mediterranean-blue backdrop completes the picture. A world of sun, leisure, and holiday is conjured up. Orsino, a latinate figure in red tails, ecstatically conducts an invisible orchestra that provides the "food of love." Belch, enormously fat and mustachioed, is modeled on some Latin American entertainer. Aguecheek, on the other hand, is a visitor from Europe wearing a tropical hat and carrying an umbrella. The troupe around Toby Belch dance and skip uninterruptedly to the rhythms of South American percussion instruments; they are raised onto a separate plane that serves as a commentary and foil to the main action. In the drinking scene the entertainment cliché is unashamedly exploited: Belch and Aguecheek sing their canons to popular tunes through microphones, a lit-up pleasure steamer crosses upstage, and Malvolio interrupts from the auditorium, protesting on behalf of the venerable theater.

This lifting-out of the Belch plane permits some remarkable scenic effects. In the eavesdropping scene the secret spectators are distanced from Malvolio by their empathy with the music to which he does not react. This suffices to establish a convention of nonvisibility, so they do not have to hide from Malvolio at all; only when in their excitement they fall out of rhythm does discovery become imminent.

A prominent feature of the main plot is that Viola and Sebastian are played by one and the same actor. This has, of course, been done before; but what we see here is not merely one actor doubling for two parts but in fact accomplishing a fusion of the genders, becoming an androgynous being with the ability to communicate erotically with either sex. The blond ephebic youngster in a white gown oscillates between male and female until the borders become blurred. In 2.4 it is he who sings "Come away, come away death," beginning (as Cesario) in a tenor voice and gradually rising to a soprano (as Viola). The directors write in their program notes:

Viola expresses her love for Orsino as Cesario. In Shakespeare there is no transformation from boy back to girl. The disguising-game is a prank with a deeper meaning. Orsino has learned to love Viola as a boy, so that her personality, not her sex, determines his affection. The same happens to Olivia. She falls in love with the servant Viola-Cesario. An Utopia has taken shape in their minds. Traditional sex-roles are being abolished or questioned, the borders dissolved—one of the fascinations of the play. . . . In the end Olivia and Orsino are happy. In our play Viola and Sebastian fuse theatrically into one character, Violasebastian. . . . That is a dream, an Utopia—here hidden wishes are fulfilled in theatrical fiction.[8]

Indeed this is the only production with an unequivocally happy ending. During Feste's song we see the three lovers perform an exhilarated dance behind a curtain of gauze.

Illyria is regarded as an island where everbody's sole aim is to realize his or her own love; there are loving relationships between Antonio and Sebastian, even between Belch and Aguecheek. It is also an island of superfluity where social distinctions are of secondary importance. Although it evokes melancholy undertones, the production is in fact extroverted. The directors see the comedy as a night-play, a nocturnal Utopia, a realm far away from the realities of daytime. I should add that the production is more evocative of the bright nights of Palm Beach than of nocturnal lyricism.

Schroth and Kleinert also played the Tragelehn translation, which for them provides a contemporary sense of life through the present-day understanding of the language; consequently the meaning of the text and the undertext can be conveyed without applying external pressure. The directors felt this text enabled them to be modern without being modernistic. The Schlegel version would have tempted them to mount a more modernistic production to counteract the more archaic language.

Weimar and Zittau thus concur in attempting to build up a heightened artificial stage world to provide a coherent image for Illyria, a wishful Utopia contrasted to the more inhibited and humdrum modes of everyday life. They are also ready to readmit an elegiac or melancholy mood as against the starkly activistic productions of Cottbus, Neustrelitz, or Altenburg. Whereas the trend towards explicit sexual activities on the stage is more or less followed everywhere, Illyria in Weimar and Zittau is at least in part used as a metaphor for overt, free relationships involving spiritual and physical interdependence.

Although the spate of *Twelfth Nights* seem to have come into being more by accident than by concerted artistic purpose (only two directors deliberately opted for the title), the eagerness with which directors and actors grasped the opportunity hints at some significant implications that may be conveyed by this comedy today. After GDR theater had explored questions

of political power and social processes in numerous presentations of other
Shakespeare plays, interest now centered on the possibility of multiple,
uninhibited, and enriching relationships between individuals in their endeavors to attain some degree of human sovereignty. Such a focus means
that credible characters have to be built up, acting in a comprehensible
network of relationships. Hence a reversion to the more orthodox structures of theater occurs. This would also explain why all recent productions
elected to play modern translations; a theater performance aiming to speak
immediately to its audience on the subject of modalities of behavior between people will try to reduce as far as possible the language barrier
between the actor and the spectator. From these stagings of *Twelfth Night* it
would appear that Shakespeare's visions can be made to bear very immediately on the intricate complexities of our own lives and emotions; Illyria is
being discovered, as it were, in our own heads, hearts, and bellies.

Notes

1. See, for instance, Ina Schabert, ed., *Shakespeare-Handbuch* (Stuttgart: Kröner, 1978).
2. At the Deutsches Theater, directed by Alexander Lang and at the Maxim Gorki Theater,
directed by Thomas Langhoff. I discuss these productions in an unpublished paper, "New
Concepts of Staging and Translating *A Midsummer Night's Dream*," read at Seminar 24, "Current Trends in Non-English Shakespearian Performance," at the Second Congress of the ISA,
Stratford-upon-Avon, 6 August 1981.
3. Achim Gebauer, "Die hässlichen Menschen des William Shakespeare," *Theater der Zeit* 37
(1882), 12 (translated by Maik Hamburger). Quoted from Armin-Gerd Kuckhoff, "Shakespeare auf den Bühnen der DDR im Jahre 1981," *Shakespeare Jahrbuch* 119 (1983): 144.
Gebauer's own production is discussed later in this paper.
4. See, for instance, Armin-Gerd Kuckhoff, "Shakespeare auf der Bühnen," 145.
5. André Müller, *Shakespeare ohne Geheimnis* (Leipzig: Reclam, 1980).
6. John Barton, *Playing Shakespeare* (London and New York: Methuen, 1984).
7. Robert Weimann, *Shakespeare und die Tradition des Volkstheaters* (Berlin: Henschelverlag,
1967). English translation 1978.
8. Deutsches Nationaltheater Weimar, Programmheft zu *Was ihr wollt*, Heft Nr. 11 der
Spielzeit 1985/86. (Translated by Maik Hamburger)

"Bless Thee! Thou Art Translated!": Shakespeare in Japan

by TETSUO KISHI

In the Japanese production of *Macbeth,* which was a sellout as well as a critical success at the 1985 Edinburgh Festival, there is a scene which is aesthetically puzzling if theatrically effective. For this particular production, the entire stage was transformed into a huge Buddhist altar, complete with a set of double doors that are the first objects the audience sees when it enters the auditorium. When the performance starts, two old women appear at the rear of the auditorium, slowly walk toward the stage, reach the stage, and then open the double doors. This marks the beginning of the play proper. Throughout the performance the women remain crouched on each side of the forestage, and when the play of *Macbeth* is over, they stand up and close the double doors. In other words, Shakespeare's *Macbeth* is made into a play-within-a-play, or more specifically, into a pseudoreligious experience of the old women that the audience seems to be expected to share. The action is confined within the Buddhist altar, and the double doors function as the fourth wall, which for once is not transparent but visible. In one scene toward the end of the play, however, Malcolm's soldiers enter the auditorium from the rear, just as the old women do at the beginning of the performance, and rush to the stage with a loud war cry.

The production that one British critic called "Kabuki ritual"[1] was actually realistic and modernistic in its fundamental approach, in spite of the medieval Japanese costumes the actors wore. The scene I referred to was not consistent with the basic concept of the production because it drastically changed the nature of the acting space. At the same time, this scene was quite refreshing as momentarily it freed the audience from a claustrophobic feeling that pervaded most scenes. For a brief moment the production became peculiarly Elizabethan. As we all know, Shakespeare's plays were performed on a nonrepresentational open stage. It is true that the actors did not exactly play their scenes in the pit but it is also true that the staging had absolutely nothing to do with the idea of the fourth wall.

The case is no doubt a minor one, but I think it involves the kind of problems we have to cope with when Shakespeare is produced in a country such as Japan, which has a long theatrical tradition with its own semiotic system and at a time such as the late twentieth century when the sensibility of the audience is attuned to aesthetic principles different from those of Elizabethan England.

When the works of Shakespeare were first introduced to the Japanese public sometime after the so-called modernization of Japan in 1868, by far the most popular type of theatrical art in the country was Kabuki. As many scholars have pointed out, Kabuki shares a number of characteristics with Shakespearean drama. Apart from an obvious similarity such as the playing of female roles by men, there is an important factor that both are performed on an essentially "open" stage. It is true that the Kabuki stage has a curtain, but it also has a *hanamichi*, a long elevated passageway running from the main stage to the rear of the auditorium on which some of the most impressive scenes are played. It is true that many Kabuki plays, unlike Shakespearean plays, rely on the use of elaborate scenery, but this scenery is often changed in full view of the audience. Thus the curtain of a Kabuki theater is totally different from the curtain of modern realistic drama, which functions as the fourth wall. We must also bear in mind that the style of language used both in Shakespearean drama and in Kabuki varies from an extremely formal verse to colloquial, naturalistic prose. This means that the style of acting also runs the whole gamut from the stylized to the realistic. Most important, both Kabuki and Shakespeare are fundamentally "audience-conscious" types of theater. By this I mean that both accept the existence of the audience as an indispensable element of dramatic experience, while modern realistic theater is based on a false assumption that the audience belongs to a different world from that of the play, requiring actors to behave as if the audience was simply not there. In the end, neither Shakespearean drama nor Kabuki tries to create an illusion of mundane reality on the stage. This is clearly reflected in the nature of the dramatic language. Both in Kabuki and in Shakespeare many speeches are delivered as a direct address to the audience. But Kabuki goes a step further. In a production of many if not all Kabuki plays, a small dais is placed on the left side of the forestage on which a narrator and a musician take their seats. The narrator gives comment on the action of the play, describes the emotion and inner feeling of the characters, and sometimes even chants the kind of speeches that in realistic drama would be spoken by the actors themselves. What we hear is, if I may use T. S. Eliot's definition, the second voice, the epic voice or the voice of the poet addressing the audience, rather than the third voice, the dramatic voice or the voice of the poet addressing the audience through imaginary characters. The closest we have in Shakespeare would be the Chorus in such plays as *Romeo and Juliet* and *Henry V*. But if we examine Shakespearean texts carefully, we will find an amazing number of speeches, including of course soliloquies and asides, which have a distinctly choric nature. In Shakespeare the relation between speech and speaker is certainly more complicated than in Ibsen or Chekhov. All this points to the fact that Shakespearean drama has a strong narrative element that modern realistic drama lacks and in that sense has a close affinity with Kabuki.

Strangely enough, this affinity was not always understood by the Japanese who were first exposed to Shakespeare. Obviously this was partly due to the way Shakespeare was being produced in the then contemporary England. The time was the 1880s. After all it was as late as 1894 that William Poel organized the Elizabethan Stage Society to restore what he thought was the Elizabethan staging of Shakespeare. What those few Japanese who were fortunate enough to visit England in the 1880s or earlier saw must have been the Victorian productions of Shakespeare, which very probably did not pay much attention to what I called the narrative element in Shakespeare. But to most Japanese, Shakespeare meant literary texts. Here again we have to bear in mind that the modern principles of textual criticism had yet to wait for universal acceptance. The editions of Shakespeare they had access to would have been mostly those full of stage directions added by later editors. We cannot really blame the Japanese intellectuals of the 1880s if they failed to understand Shakespeare within the context of dramatic history.

But the reason for this failure was actually more serious and is relevant to the nature of modern Japanese culture in general. The feeling shared by a large number of Japanese intellectuals around the 1880s was that traditional Japanese culture was fundamentally inferior to Western culture. To them the only way to "improve" and "reform" Japanese culture, whatever those words may mean, was to "modernize" and "Westernize" it, again whatever those terms may mean. They tried to "catch up" as quickly as possible. In the field of theater, this produced a group of critics active in the 1880s who advocated the "reformation" of Japanese drama with Western drama, especially Shakespeare, as the model. They thought, rightly, that Shakespeare was the pinnacle of Western drama, but also thought, wrongly, that Shakespeare was more than anything else the pioneer of modern drama, or more specifically realistic drama, which was then popular in European countries. This was the original image of Shakespeare in Japan, as the master of modern drama, though of course it was to be modified later.

Not surprisingly, this led to a confusion. One advocate[2] of reformation of the theater maintained that the *hanamichi*, the long passageway in a Kabuki theater, should be abolished because no Western theater had it. It seems that to him a proscenium arch stage was the only type of stage that was "civilized" enough. He did not realize that it was not the type of stage used for the original productions of Shakespeare. The same critic defended the use of the three unities. Certainly most Kabuki plays obey none of the rules of the unities, but neither did Shakespeare. This critic also rejected the use of female impersonation in Kabuki. Obviously he was ignorant of the Elizabethan convention of boy actors. Most seriously, he condemned the use of a narrator in a Kabuki production, and interestingly enough, suggested that it should be replaced by an extensive use of soliloquies and asides. He was aware at least vaguely that they fulfill a similar function, but because the former is Japanese, he rejected it and preferred the latter, the Western convention. He was not aware, however, that the use of asides and soliloquies is not quite compatible with the use of a proscenium arch stage with an invisible fourth wall. The argument is almost pathetic in its lack of historical perspective, but it was by no means exceptional.

Fortunately, not all the critics were so naive as he was. Shoyo Tsubouchi (1859–1935), who later translated the complete canon of Shakespeare, refuted the argument of the so-called reformers, and rightly pointed out that soliloquies and asides are, as a dramatic device, just as "unnatural" as the use of a narrator in Kabuki. Tsubouchi's knowledge of Kabuki was vast and his understanding of it was accurate, and while he realized the affinity between Kabuki and Shakespeare, he felt that the Kabuki actors lacked the kind of training necessary for a performance of plays with a high literary quality depicting complex human psychology. In 1906 he founded the *Bungei Kyokai* (Literary Society) to start the training of amateurs. Its activity, together with that of the *Jiyu Gekijo* (Free Theater) founded in 1909, led to the establishment of a totally new theatrical genre called Shingeki, the literal meaning of which is "new drama" or "new theater." The first play the Free Theater produced was *John Gabriel Borkman* (1909), and two of the earliest productions of the Literary Society were *Hamlet* (1911) and *A Doll's House* (1911). It may sound strange, but the two dramatists who played vital roles in deciding the course of Shingeki were Shakespeare and Ibsen. It is doubtful how well the early Shingeki artists realized the difference between these two playwrights, but the fact remains that these two very different writers together contributed to the "modernization" of the Japanese theater. This was all because Japan was very suddenly exposed to the flow of Western culture after more than two centuries of self-imposed isolation. In a way it was unfortunate to Westerners as well, because the same lack of historical perspective is often detectable in the Western understanding of the Japanese theater. To Japanese, Noh and Kabuki are two different genres of drama, but Westerners often speak of the two in the same breath.

In any case, since Shingeki was closely modeled on the contemporary Western theater, it was destined to be realistic more than anything else. It must be mentioned that even today any Western play, from *Oedipus Rex* to *Waiting for Godot*, is automatically accepted as part of the Shingeki repertoire. This is unfortunate because the Shingeki actors and directors tend to adopt an essentially realistic approach not only to Ibsen and Chekhov but to such diverse writers as Sophocles, Molière, Brecht, Beckett, *and* Shake-

speare as well. This causes no small difficulty when Shakespeare is produced in Japan. For instance the Shingeki actors try to treat soliloquies and
asides as an expression of the inner thought of a character rather than a
message to the audience. They tend to emphasize individual characters
rather than the whole action and try to explore the psychological motivation of each character.

In this, the recent well-received production of *Macbeth* was no exception.
To play *Macbeth* as a play of feudal Japan certainly made it more congenial
to the Japanese audience, but the aesthetic concept of the production was
strictly modernist. In its treatment of the acting space and in its understanding of the nature of the dramatic language and the stage-audience
relationship, it was neither Kabuki nor a ritual, as one British critic thought
it was.

I do not know whether or not the director Yukio Ninagawa had a
Western audience in mind when he first conceived the production—probably not, because the production originally opened in Tokyo in 1980 with
no prospect of touring to other countries—but frankly it fits the image of
"the Japanese Shakespeare" a little too comfortably. I do not mean to say
that the director consciously modified his production of *Macbeth* so that it
might become readily acceptable to the Western audience. What I do say is
that, when a theatrical production is "exported," whether from Japan to the
West or vice versa, there is always a danger of making it fit the preconceived
image the audience has.

I think it is time that the non-Japanese audience, especially the Western
audience, stopped expecting the Japanese theater, including the Japanese
Shakespeare, to be Japanese in the way they imagine it to be Japanese. In
my opinion many so-called Kabuki-style productions and Noh-style productions are actually extremely realistic in their aesthetic concept. The
audience tends to be misled by such visual elements as costume, make-up,
and the actors' movements, and sometimes by such aural elements as music
and declamation. But more often than not what is really important is
neither visible nor audible. In this sense, *aesthetics* may be a better term to
use than *style*. One always has to examine very carefully how the nature of
the acting space, the nature of the dramatic language, and the relation of
the audience to the performance are grapsed in a given production before
forming a final judgment.

So has there ever been a Japanese production of Shakespeare that effectively used the aesthetics of Kabuki? In 1976, a Shingeki director Toshikiyo
Masumi directed a *Macbeth* in which Lady Macbeth was played by a popular
Kabuki actor, Tamasaburo Bando, who specializes in playing female roles.
But what is more relevant is that the production when it played in a Kabuki
theater in Kyoto used not only the main stage but the *hanamichi* as well. For
instance, part of Lady Macbeth's sleepwalking scene was played there, right
in the middle of the audience, thus depriving the scene of any sense of

illusion of reality. The distance between the actor and the audience was minimal, and the impact of Lady Macbeth's madness was felt most strongly. In this scene, as well as in other scenes, soliloquies were delivered as direct addresses to the audience. The stage was "open" to the audience and the audience was very much a part of the whole event.

But is this not exactly what happened in the Elizabethan theater? When Shakespeare is produced in a Japanese theater, it can work both as an antidote to the realistically oriented Shingeki and as a means to rediscover the aesthetics of the traditional Japanese theater. After all, the Japanese audience is never antagonistic to such an approach, and when this is achieved, we can happily cry, "Bless thee, Will, thou art translated!", and add, perhaps as an aside, "We hope we haven't made an ass of him."

Notes

1. Stewart Conn, in *The Listener*, 29 August 1985.

2. Kencho Suematsu, in *Engeki Kairyo Iken* (An opinion about the reformation of theater), published in 1886.

Yuri Yarvet's Lear: The Face of Tragedy

by ROBERT F. WILLSON, JR.

When Grigori Kozintsev's 1970 film version of *King Lear* finally reached American movie theaters in 1975, reviews were uniformly favorable, many expressing unqualified praise for the director's interpretation of Shakespeare's timeless tragedy. Several commentaries stressed the film's Russianness: its emphasis on the suffering masses, its operatic style (greatly aided by Dimitri Shostakovich's score), its epic scope. Richard Eder *(New York Times,* 7 August 1975), for instance, lauds the Russian cultural tradition that allows men to express physical emotion more freely than women. Kozintsev's Lear can unaffectedly spit in Kent's face when he banishes him for interceding on Cordelia's behalf, or sensitively lift a tear from his daughter's cheek and wet his lips with it when the two are reunited. Eder also admires the sound of Cordelia's "nichevo," claiming its arresting power exceeds that of the English "nothing, my lord." Believing the film pursues a Marxist-realist line, *New York Post* reviewer Sylvanie Gold (11 August 1975) cites the suffering peasants—seen at the beginning and frequently throughout the film—as the protagonist and not Lear. The lesson taught is that the folly of great ones inevitably inflicts unwarranted pain on those already subjected to misfortune by society and nature. It follows, Ms. Gold argues, that Edgar should shoulder the role as the people's leader at the film's close. Even the acting style has about it a peculiar Russian cinematic quality, according to Stanley Eichelbaum *(San Francisco Examiner,* 15 June 1975). Yuri Yarvet holds back emotion in his portrayal of Lear, making his tragedy "poignant and believable." Even the criticisms of the film in these reviews seem to spring from a preconceived idea about Russian art: one confronts an "occasional excessively operatic overtone" (Eder); exposition scenes are "uncinematic and slow-moving" (Eichelbaum); the lamenting choral accompaniment for the last "collapsing" act is unnecessary (Eder).

These immediate critical reactions were succeeded by more reflective scholarly appraisals in books and cinema journals. Assessments of this kind attempt to place the film in a larger critical context while speaking to a more sophisticated audience. Jack Jorgens stresses the centrality of the director's interpretation to understanding and appreciating Kozintsev's *Lear.* He also

251

conducts a lengthy comparison of this version with Peter Brook's 1970 film. For Jorgens the Russian film is "a Christian-Marxist story of redemption and social renewal."[1] Given that reading, we are equipped to grasp the significance of directorial choices. The excision of Gloucester's grotesquely comic suicide attempt, for instance, suggests that Kozintsev believed such an absurdist episode was out of harmony with the blind man's redemptive struggle. Instead we witness Gloucester's actual death (reported in Shakespeare) as he reaches out and suddenly "recognizes" Edgar's face. This moment of pathos documents the report of how Gloucester's heart "burst smilingly." In addition, the Fool survives his master's death; his more bitter remarks are cut, and he serves as a reliable guide for Lear's journey of self-discovery.

Certain visual images likewise function to buttress Kozintsev's essentially optimistic reading, according to Jorgens. In this regard the film's central memorable scene is the capture of Lear and Cordelia by Edmund's troops (p. 241). Kozintsev makes us understand that even though the prisoners are "encircled by iron, weapons of murder," their innocence and defenselessness reduce their captors to silent respect: "Good triumphs over evil even when about to be destroyed by it" (p. 241). Likewise, Cordelia's death, a scene that many revisers have deemed too horrible to depict, attains a quality of hope here as we glimpse flowing water beyond the tower on which she has been hanged. This water of mercy and forgiveness is symbolicly associated with Cordelia throughout (p. 243). Shakespeare's nihilism has been mitigated, moreover, by the figure of Edgar standing tall among the ruins and looking directly at us, "breaking the fourth-wall convention" (p. 244). He accuses us of not having felt deeply enough but strides confidently away to continue his journey toward a new beginning.

Stressing the centrality of Kozintsev's *mise-en-scène*, Barbara Hodgdon also believes that the director's interpretation must be comprehended in order to explain his cinematic choices.[2] She cites the careful establishment of two worlds—the court and landscape—as evidence that Kozintsev's reading of Lear's tragedy emphasizes the king's role as mediating figure. That is, when the mad monarch loses control of his passions, the two worlds collide: Lear becomes a peasant-sufferer trudging toward an apocalypse of "charred ruins peopled with unseeing survivors" (p. 149). For Hodgdon this collision of peasant and court worlds denies any healing resolution; unlike Jorgens, she finds the ending disruptive rather than redemptive.

Like Hodgdon, James Welsh seizes on images of division in the film, which he argues depicts an essentially Shakespearean interpretation of Lear's tragedy.[3] "Kozintsev does not attempt to Kotterize *Lear*," he claims, praising the director's effort to maintain the play's thematic integrity while translating it to the modern screen. Although the process of division develops through successive shots of king divorced from court, father from child, sister from sister, brother from brother, it leads inevitably to the victory of the worthy over the unworthy, in Welsh's view (p. 151). The conclusion underscores a moral division that embraces the nobility of suffering innocence, a quality symbolized by the Fool and the poignant flute notes he plays over the credits.

While Hodgdon and Welsh explore the film's cinematic technique, Douglas Radcliff-Umstead considers its place in the history of Russian filmmaking.[4] For him, the opening processional of citizens recalls the angry Petrograd masses in Eisenstein's *October* (p. 266), suggesting that the crowd emerges as a "Marxist-realist entity." The peasants, "a great personality inspired by a unified idea," stand as Kozintsev's collective hero, a role they were assigned in such other classics as *Boris Gudunov, Alexander Nevsky,* and Kozintsev's earlier *Don Quixote.* This reading explains the representation of a Lear "among the people," who are both fellow sufferers and opponents. "Whereas Shakespeare intended to bring Lear to an awareness of himself as a kingly man, the socialist filmmaker takes the former monarch down to the level of the masses" (p. 269). As a result, the film allows us to glimpse the promise of renewal in a closing shot of refugees rebuilding their city with hands and hearts. (Kozintsev admitted to being influenced by documentary footage of homeless victims of World War II.) Radcliff-Umstead applauds the director's achievement because he wins his goal without distorting characters or episodes "in the spirit of Marxist criticism of class conflict" (p. 272).

These thoughtful evaluations of Kozintsev's *Lear,* though by no means constituting an exhaustive list, demonstrate the critics' overriding concern for directorial intention. The explications at the heart of each discussion depend upon theses that attempt to capture that intention. Cuts, transpositions, *mises-en-scènes,* symbols, flow from the one inspirational source, the director's reading of Shakespeare's play. In Kozintsev's case, the task of grasping that reading is aided immeasurably by the director's diary, published in 1977 under the title *"King Lear": The Space of Tragedy.*[5] This valuable testament cannot be described as a systematic aesthetic statement of the director's interpretive goals, however. (And most critics cited here do not appear to have made extensive use of it in their discussions of intention.) We learn instead that he attended performances of Noh and Kabuki plays in Japan prior to shooting *King Lear;* that he viewed a number of detective movies, most of which he disliked for their superficiality; that he loves clowns and owns a large collection of books about them; and that he admits to being influenced by such diverse figures as Vsevolod Meyerhold, Sergei Eisenstein, Dostoyevsky, and Peter Brook. The entries are clearly impressions and reflections, a record of Kozintsev's journey over the inner landscape of his artistic world prior to and during the production.

While he adumbrates no theory of the meaning of Shakespeare's tragedy, Kozintsev does outline the kind of film he proposes to make. In a letter to

Peter Brook (himself shooting a film of *Lear* in Jutland at the same time), he declares: "I am trying to find a visual *Lear*. Nature in this case would have to become something like the chorus of a Greek tragedy" (p. 26). To do justice to the tragedy, then, Kozintsev felt the need to represent a Shakespearean landscape rather than a text: "The problem is not to link Shakespeare with art, even the most contemporary art, but with life" (p. 33). These comments explain in large part the Marxist-realist and people-as-protagonist elements pointed out by many reviewers and critics. Yet the central question of Kozintsev's reading of Lear's tragedy does not seem to rest on any political or theological foundation. Indeed, the diary is remarkably free of dogmatic pronouncements of any kind. On the contrary, the director's overriding dilemma is to find "a space of tragedy." The solution was found by locating the action in a kind of timeless locale, in which walking, marching, and running convey a sense of "everything shaken from its place, everything in movement."[6] The goal appears to have been to show that dislocation not only precipitates tragic consequences but is itself a tragic condition. This meant that Kozintsev's protagonist had to be the archetypal outcast, a sufferer in desperate search of forgiveness. That choice had to do more with the face than the space of tragedy.

The director spent months trying to find the right actor to play his dispossessed Lear. The search preoccupied him and delayed the shooting schedule. (As a result he was forced to rush many of the film's final shots.) The diary reveals his frustration as well as information about just what features he was looking for. Kozintsev wanted a Lear capable of displaying "bitter irony, born of suffering, or . . . wisdom, arising out of madness" (p. 75). What made the process so frustrating was that those who tested for the part approached it either with undue reverence or histrionic excess. None of the candidates resembled the Lear Kozintsev had fixed in his imagination; the director's "interpretetion" rested not on a particular philosophy but a specific visage. Here is evidence of a "visual *Lear*" in another sense.

Kozintsev's choice was, finally, an unlikely one. An Estonian actor named Yuri Yarvet had originally been suggested for the part of Poor Tom, the mad beggar's disguise Edgar dons after his banishment. Scanning many screen tests in his studio, Kozintsev was struck by Yarvet's expressive smile, which reminded him of the portraits of Voltaire, "the wit of Europe." In a further test, the director asked Yarvet to blow out a candle, then watch the spiraling smoke and curling wick and think of death. The moment of truth came suddenly: "I looked at Yarvet and recognized Lear. Yarvet looked like him" (p. 76). Complications soon accompanied the selection, however. The actor spoke Estonian and knew little Russian, which meant an elaborate dubbing scheme would have to be devised, further delaying the schedule. But Yarvet proved to have resources beyond his Lear-like countenance. Working with heroic determination he soon learned Boris Pasternak's difficult Russian script; this dedication immediately won the respect of director and cast, a galvanizing event that contributed to the production's success.

Throughout Kozintsev's account of Yarvet's discovery run two constant themes: the riveting quality of his eyes and his "spiritual education." The actor's magnetic eyes were important to Kozintsev because of the restrained manner of performance he hoped to portray. Before shooting the storm, captivity, and death scenes, he wrote to Yarvet: "The stronger the emotion, the more restrained must be the mode of expressing it—only then will your eyes really light up" (p. 232). Shakespeare's iterative imagery of sight and insight was likewise given life by close-ups that looked deep into Lear's spiritual world. Only in this way could the director create a hero whose madness leads not to despair but to self-discovery. To underline the significance of Yarvet's eyes, Kozintsev employs an intriguing analogy: he likens them to the piano in a concerto, giving life to the other instruments in the orchestra (p. 111). The analogy reveals the way in which ocular expression stimulates other elements in the actor's and company's performances. It also explains the prominence of eyes in the film, the way in which even the look of animals—dogs, horses, and so forth—conveys a sense of frenzy or fear. But all these images flow from Yarvet's fountain. Combined with his frail appearance, his enormous peasant's hands, the actor's sorrowful eyes heighten the effect of suffering he is forced to undergo. As Jack Jorgens points out, comparing Yarvet's Lear to Paul Scofield's in the Brook film, this is not a ruffian who overturns tables and looses his men to destroy Goneril's dining hall. His violent responses are "inner ones" (p. 246), and his eyes are the conduits to the source of emotion.

Yarvet's spiritual education, a capacity to understand that Lear's soul shines through even his "coarsest displays" (p. 234), was likewise eagerly accepted by Kozintsev. It is a quality that transforms the opening rejection of Cordelia and Kent into more than a display of anger by a petty tyrant. Perhaps it also accounts for the symbiotic relationship between this Lear and his fool. We come to appreciate that spiritual brotherhood most fully in the director's ingenious rendering of the play's first climactic scene. At Gloucester's castle (2.4) Lear finds himself the object of a cynical game being played by his daughters. Each denies him a larger segment of his knights as he follows them and their husbands along Gloucester's porch toward the door to his main hall. At "What need one?" (l. 263), Regan closes the door in Lear's face, leaving him to deliver the "O, reason not the need!" speech (ll. 264–286) to the heavens above and the Fool below. Kozintsev has perceived an elemental truth about the scene: the daughters do not listen to their father in any case. By placing Lear outside the main hall, the director makes us see how his breakdown coincides with the gathering storm. Yarvet's eyes search the skies for pity, yet his expression reveals that he has felt for the first time the sting of thankless children. He is an outcast, dispossessed of the titles and respect in which he invested so much faith. Now his only "child" is an outcast whose "value" he begins to appreciate. As riders hurry to enter Gloucester's compound, escaping the impending storm, Lear and the Fool rush in the other direction, the courtyard gates closing firmly behind them. Pursuing the device of closed doors, Kozintsev emblemizes the theme of dispossession; his chief actor's capacity for conveying the spiritual damage of that dispossession also assists us in believing him capable of self-discovery and moral reeducation.

The face of Kozintsev's *Lear*, then, is the face of Yuri Yarvet. Without its "very bright eyes," its waif-like smile, its ability to show vulnerability, the film would lose its emphasis on Lear's humanity rather than nobility. Although the direction deftly plays upon the actor's features—close-ups highlight his eyes, medium and long shots trace the "clumsy ceremony" of his walk—camera technique alone cannot fashion a successful film version of a Shakespeare play. (See Franz Wirth's 1960 expressionist interpretation of *Hamlet*.) It is also clear from Kozintsev's diary that a close friendship bloomed between actor and director. This mutual admiration quickly spread to the rest of the cast, easing a tense situation created by shooting delays. More important, the uniform critical praise for Yarvet's performance suggests that whatever the various "readings" of Kozintsev's intention, the actor's interpretation managed somehow to be compatible with them. Thus Yarvet's Lear was embraced as both a redemptive and a despairing hero.

Perhaps the description that best captures the relationship of Yuri Yarvet to the company and to the *Lear* world they created comes from the director on viewing the final cut. This chameleonic personality "was truly great in his parody of a king. Yarvet has a sinewy, wiry body, with . . . peasant hands. He is just like everyone else, and first among other men" (p. 203). The last sentence seems to characterize the man as well as his role. Describing not a philosophical, political, or theological position, the quotation also sheds considerable light on the director's individualized conception of Shakespeare's monumental tragedy of human suffering.

Notes

1. Jack J. Jorgens, *Shakespeare on Film* (Bloomington: Indiana University Press, 1977), 237. Subsequent page references to this and other works cited in this essay appear parenthetically in the text.

2. Barbara Hodgdon, "Two *King Lears:* Uncovering the Film Text," *Literature/Film Quarterly* 11 (1983): 143–51.

3. James Welsh, "To See It Feelingly: *King Lear* Through Russian Eyes," *Literature/Film Quarterly* 4 (1976): 153–59.

4. Douglas Radcliff-Umstead, "Order and Disorder in Kozintsev's *King Lear*," *Literature/Film Quarterly* 11 (1983): 266–73.

5. Berkeley and Los Angeles: University of California Press, 1977.

6. Jorgens, *Shakespeare on Film*, 250.

Images of King Lear *in Czechoslovak Folklore*

by MARTIN PROCHÁZKA

In this paper I shall consider the importance of Czech and Slovak folktale material and the folktale in general in the interpretation of *King Lear,* particularly its thematic structure and some character relationships, scenes, and images.[1] My main point is that the analogies of the play's themes and motifs with folktale themes and narrative patterns[2] help us to understand the modern message of *King Lear* at least to the same extent as the parallels with medieval moralities, parables, and *exempla*[3] or with the popular ceremony and the ritual heritage of folk theater.[4] This hypothesis is based on the assumption that the folktale does not differ from the myth in the basic semantic patterns, but only in the frame of reference: the "universal" of the myth is replaced by the "social" in the folktale. The folktale itself can be understood, analogously to drama, as a process of secularization of myth and ritual: the emphasis shifts from cosmic time to the time of the hero's life, from the preservation of cosmic order to the preservation of a community or even of the life and well-being of individuals.[5] The mythical and ritual patterns of the *Lear* world can be made more meaningful if we realize that they do not refer just to self-enclosed metaphysical truths, but to the images of the life of a social whole that reaches beyond the historically verifiable references of the play to Shakespeare's own time.

The Czech and Slovak folklore material in which I have found images similar to those of the *Lear* world is not very rich, but it includes several representative folklore genres. Apart from a *Märchen* (a tale of magic), whose theme appears in the Aarne-Thompson index under No. 923, "Love like salt",[6] and in the more recent classification under M.21, "short-sighted judgment; King Lear judgment,"[7] there are specimens of folktales of more recent origin, the so-called novellas or romantic tales. And there is also an example of a balladic folk song on the "short-sighted judgment" theme. Topographically, the material represents all the largest national, linguistic, and cultural regions of Czechoslovakia: the *Märchen* coming from Slovakia, the two romantic folktales from nineteenth-century Bohemia, and the song from late medieval Moravian folklore. In analyzing them I shall start from the earliest and, at the same time, thematically and imaginatively most remote specimen: the Moravian balladic folk song.

The song tells the story of a husbandman who divided his estate unequally into marriage portions for his three daughters.[8] The first got "three hundred thalers," the second "two hundred thalers," and the youngest just "bare walls." In return, all of them had promised to take care of him in time of infirmity. But only the youngest one, whom he had beaten most often when she was a child, kept the promise, while the others gave him either a cord to hang himself or a knapsack for begging.

This story appears to be genetically related to the story of King Lear. According to S:mrock[9] and Gebauer, the pioneers of Czech comparative philology,[10] it is based on tale No. 273 of the *Gesta Romanorum* about the Roman emperor Theodosius and his three daughters,[11] which is derived from the Lear story in the *Historia Regum Britanniae* by Geoffrey of Monmouth and from other medieval English sources.

Apart from the connection with the source of *King Lear* and generally with tales having the "King Lear judgment" theme, there are other and perhaps more interesting points. First, the folk song lacks the folktale theme of the "love-test" important for the relationship of *King Lear* to folklore narratives; unlike Lear's realm, the estate is divided only according to the farmer's free will. Second, the Latin story of the *Gesta* was read and related as a parable.[12] The motifs of an unequal division of the realm and of the individual sisters' attitudes to their father used to be interpreted allegorically: in our life we pay most attention to worldly things; less do we care for our blood relationships, and of least concern is our own heart, our inward life, and the value of our personality in relation to God. In the end we are repaid according to the reversed order of values.[13] The important point here is the functional difference of the folk song from the homiletic parable: the allegory of the importance of man's spiritual and worldly cares and needs is replaced by a simple tale of filial love and duty.[14] An analogous difference, or tension, can be observed between the function of the dramatic images of *King Lear* as "visual *exempla*"[15] rooted in the morality tradition and their meaning in terms of the play's dramatic structure.

Like the imagery of the balladic folk song, Shakespeare's dramatic images in *King Lear* do not allegorize abstract and unchangeable truths, but express the essence of actual life. The reproduction of actual life details or even speech has a similar function in both texts, widely different as they are. In a version of the folk song, the originally happy atmosphere of the father's reunion with his dutiful youngest daughter is overshadowed by his sorrow; he cannot eat the offered soup as the memories of the elder daughters' behavior overwhelm him with woe. Such notes, and even more somber ones, can be heard just after Lear recognizes Cordelia:

> If you have poison for me, I will drink it.
> I know you do not love me, for your sisters

> Have (as I do remember) done me wrong:
> You have some cause, they have not.
>
> [4.7.71–74]

Here the meaning and style of Lear's speech directly contradict the "visual," emblematic meaning of the whole scene as a happy reunion and a decisive moment of Lear's healing. The filial bond is restored but the feeling of bitterness and confusion evident from Lear's speeches contradicts the idealizing resolution. Analogously, in the folk song, the balladic themes of the restoration of order and of retribution—one of the evil daughters is turned into a stone—are contrasted with the motif of the father's sorrowful reiteration of grievances.

This folklore parallel shows that the archetypal and parabolic references of the images of *King Lear* do not imply any necessity of interpreting the play in the morality tradition; they mean rather that the general human or even cosmic dimensions of the conflict may often become very specific and individual. As I have already mentioned, this phenomenon is typical of the folktale, being the main sign of the secularization of myth. Yet this process does not destroy the creative function of myth, which continues its existence in the form of mythical poetry.[16] The analysis of folktale parallels to *King Lear* will then be focused both on the general characteristics of the Lear themes and on the specific features of Shakespeare's art as mythical poetry, which "creates a myth out of the manners of its time."[17]

Thus, on the one hand, we may ask about the relation of *King Lear* and its individual themes and images to folktales and their groups that contain the theme and narrative pattern of the "King Lear judgment." This frame of reference does not exist just in the classifying theoretical mind, but may be understood as a constituent of the aesthetic reality of a work of art, inasmuch as the theme and the narrative pattern have a function of aesthetic category.[18] On the other hand, the comparison of the individual *Lear* themes (e.g., the judgment theme, the blinding of Gloucester) with their analogues in Czech and Slovak folktales may reveal specific features of the secularization of mythical images, especially in Shakespeare's conceptions of community life and of the place of the individual within it. Both of these approaches are used in the following comparison of *King Lear* with Czech and Slovak folktales.

The Slovak *Märchen* is called "Salt above the price of gold."[19] It connects the theme of "King Lear judgment" with a simple magic tale narrative pattern;[20] the heroine acquires a magic object vital for the preservation and continuation of communal life. After comparing the love for her royal father to salt, the youngest daughter is expelled and ordered not to return before salt has become more precious than gold. In a deep forest she meets a soothsayer, an old woman who invites her to share her simple cottage and teaches her weaving and sheep-grazing. In return for her diligent service the princess is given a magic purse, always full of salt, and is sent—after "the time has found another time having crossed the whole world"—back to her father's kingdom, which she rescues from an utter lack of salt. After her coronation she opens—by means of another magic object, a rod—wonderful subterranean halls and gardens of salt, transfigured into most beautiful shapes. These deeds and her virtues gain the queen great love of the people and of her father, and the envy and hatred of her evil sisters, who, however, cannot do any harm to her.

Thematically, this tale belongs to the so-called Cinderella group,[21] comprising *Märchen* or novella folktales with evident echoes of ritual themes of initiation and carnival. Some of these tales may even be treated as a specific "reproduction" of wedding ritual.[22] In most tales of this group where the "love-like-salt" theme is present, the prominent motifs are those of the trials of bride and bridegroom. The initial motif of the "short-sighted judgment" of the father and the scene of his final recognition of his daughter at the wedding feast, which may consist of some unsalted dish, are often of secondary importance.

The Slovak *Märchen* is the only specimen of the whole group in which the initiation motifs connected with the heroine have no relation to the wedding ritual. Instead of her being initiated into married life, the princess is taught the tasks fundamental for the life of the whole community. Consequently, her main trial—service to the soothsayer—does not chiefly consist in the change of appearance (e.g., taking on a coat of mice hides, covering the face with a skin of an old woman, being locked into a candlestick, into a chest, etc.), but in her submission to the order of common life, to the rhythm and discipline of labour. And the aim of her suffering is the preservation of the community, rather than the restoration of family relations, wealth, or social rank.

Analyzing the relation of the mythical poetry of *King Lear* to the Slovak folktale, we must take into account both the initiation ritual patterns underlying the thematic structure of the whole group of tales and the specific position of the tale in the group. As far as the patterns typical for the whole Cinderella group are concerned, we may observe the extreme importance of the "love-test" incipit. In *King Lear,* this phenomenon has already been sufficiently explained in terms of dramatic structure: the function of the opening scene consists in stressing the momentous nature of Lear's and Cordelia's choice as sources of potentialities that become realized in the further development of the play.[23] But in terms of mythical and ritual patterns we realize that the emphasis on the initial test itself may imply the crucial value of the sought object, rather than the ritual trial, for the individual and communal life. Thus, by virtue of its opening scene, *King Lear* becomes related to such folktales in which metaphors like "love like salt" become central and which, like the Slovak one, are concerned with the influence of the king's choice on the life of the realm. Interpreting Lear's and Cordelia's acts of choice in comparison with the Slovak tale, we may assume that one of the central problems of the play's opening, and to some extent of the whole play, is the meaning of the "love-test" theme.

It is evident that Lear's "love test" does not have the purpose of finding out how much his daughters love him. Unlike scene 3 of the *True Chronicle History of King Leir*, where the king arranges the trial as a "meanes to rid me of my doubt,"[24] the "love-test" theme in *King Lear* becomes a mere metaphorical parallel to the theme of the division of the realm. The declaration of love is thus equalled by the declaration of loyalty: it is just the words that should give the act an air of "tenderness."

The theme of realm division has apparently no analogy in the Slovak *Märchen*. Instead, the moment of preservation of the community by means of a magic gift is of chief importance. But the function of both heroines and their action is similar:[25] the folktale heroine manages to preserve the life of the community by restoring a missing link in its material basis. A more abstract "missing link," yet by no means less vital, is implied in Cordelia's speeches and attitudes.

Unlike Goneril and Regan, who profess an inexpressible, superhuman, and suprasensuous love for their father, Cordelia's reluctant love proclamation stresses the identity of her relation with a customary idea of "bond," which is considered to be a "natural" (cf. Lear speaking about "the offices of nature, bond of childhood"), self-evident, basic quality of social relations.[26] But in terms of the division of the realm the seemingly natural, customary bond is given another meaning: it becomes the missing link in the basis of communal life. The new sense originates from the dramatic situation in which Cordelia's proclamation of her bond is introduced by the words "Nothing, my Lord" and from Lear's retort, "Nothing will come of nothing." Similar to the lack-of-salt motif in the Slovak tale, these words signal the absence of some vital quality of individual and social relations that may cause the downfall and destruction of community.

What makes the difference here between the mythical poetry of *King Lear* and the folktale is the way in which the social whole is imagined. As Mikhail Bakhtin observes in his analyses of the "Rabelaisian chronotopos"—a complex Renaissance metaphor of community based also on folklore imagination—the social whole is always represented as the "indivisible unity of cosmic, social and bodily qualities," as a kind of a "collective, material body."[27] Such an idea of a "collective body" or "grotesque body" is most often reproduced by means of feast or carnival images. Some echoes of this imagery are still present in the old *King Leir*, for instance in the reunion scene (24), whose setting is a rural feast (though in fact a court masquerade), where Cordella praises the country-folk both for their "industry and paynes" and for their "quirks," which "go beyond the moone."[28] In *King Lear*, however, the images of a "collective body" are virtually missing, leaving only some traces in the speeches of the Fool, who connects Lear's rash judgment with his sexuality (metaphors of the "head-piece" and the "cod-piece," 3.2.25–35) or the unity of Lear's personality and that of his realm (metaphor of an egg cut in half and of the remaining two empty shells, 1.4.158–65).

The community, then, is imagined in different perspectives: from the viewpoint of common sense (the Fool), of mythologized nature (Lear), and of the nature-custom opposition (Edmund). In the first perspective, which is important in relation to the Slovak folktale, the emphasis is put on the nullity of Lear's personality, when its authority has been reduced to less than nothing ("O without a figure") and to the nullity of feudal authority itself. In this context we may find the closest analogues to the Slovak folktale and generally to the folklore theme of salt.

The commonsense standpoint in *Lear* is expressed in a sequence of rhymed proverbs—maxims teaching a simple wisdom of life (1.4.118–27). In the Slovak folktale, there are units of similar function—for instance, the soothsayer's proverb ("the time will meet another time after crossing the whole world") or the riddle-like question that the king cannot answer ("What can salt like salt?"). In his first dialogue with the Fool, Lear rejects the concentrated expression of such commonsense wisdom by words echoing Cordelia's utterance ("This is nothing, Fool.") Then, a riddlelike question follows: "Can you make no use of nothing, Nuncle?", to which Lear can reply only by using the same phrase as in his answer to Cordelia: "Nothing can be made out of nothing." This dictum is afterwards ridiculed, dramatically, in the Fool's rhyme (1.4.140–47). In it Lear is made to "stand for" nobody, to *represent nothing*.

If we want to understand *King Lear* in terms of the folktale world, we should not think that a completely negative image of Lear's kingship directly implies a social satire on the idea of "sacred kingship," which was the most prominent ideological issue of James's reign. Negating the idea of authority based on rank, *King Lear* calls for a different kind of power, but obviously not the same as that which Edmund invokes under the name of "nature" in his first monologue. Whereas in the Slovak folktale the metaphor of such power has a traditional form (magic gift and experience of popular life and its toil), in *King Lear* there is no really concrete solution. As there is no longer any concrete image of social unity, the "missing link" is grasped only in terms of the potentialities of some individual characters. The ideas of authority as something customary, or legalized, as presented in the first monologue of Edmund, can no longer be accepted, yet only Cordelia's and Edgar's attitudes show, in the course of the action, the concrete aspects of an ideal of unsentimental love, which should replace authority. This becomes especially clear in Edgar's case, after his character begins to dissociate itself from the role of "poor Tom" to create a new role in which the dramatic and ideational aspects are harmonized.

Coming finally to the relation of *Lear* themes and imagery to the two Czech novelistic folktales, their main emphasis may be noticed to shift in a similar way to that in the thematic development of the play. In the first folktale,[29] the feast that is a traditional metaphor of the unity of communal life becomes a prelude to the mortal feud between two kings—the princess's father and her bridegroom. The father is then killed by his son-in-law while they fight in a great battle, having joined opposing armies. In the second tale,[30] the feast images, as well as the initiation ritual pattern, are completely missing. They are replaced by the theme of blinding and magical recovery of eyesight typical of the "Verity-Falsity" group of tales.[31] Though the king consents to his daughter's marriage with a poor vagrant, he seeks the means of getting rid of his new son-in-law. Finally he imprisons him and deprives him of sight. The heroine learns what has happened to her husband as well as about the magic remedy for his eyes and the just punishment of the king. All this is imparted to her in a way characteristic of the "Verity-Falsity" theme: under the magic tree she overhears a conversation among ravens; analogous motifs are gallows or a cross and a conversation of animals, hanged men, or good or evil spirits.

What is important when comparing this romantic folktale with *King Lear* is the function the modified "Verity-Falsity" theme has in both cases. In the Czech tale the initiation pattern is abandoned and the heroine herself must liberate her husband from his suffering. Her recognition (learning about the magic remedy) is functionally equivalent to the main test of the heroines of the Cinderella group, but the aim of healing is no longer the well-being of community. If we attempt to view the thematic development of *King Lear* synthetically, forgetting for a while its dramatic structure and the specific functions of the two plots, we may notice a shift in emphasis from the theme of communal unity[32] to that of the individual quest for the basic value of life in the maddening condition of the "gored state." The hero of this quest is obviously Edgar who in his madman's disguise deliberately destroys the illusion of the "stage-managed" scenes[33] to indicate both the depth of his inward, personal sympathy for mad Lear (in the mock-trial scene) and his resolution to persuade his broken, blinded father about the positive value of life even by means of a colossal illusion. In the course of this quest, Edgar's attitudes based on his warm feeling of life ("our lives' sweetness! / That we the pain of death would hourly die / Rather than die at once" 5.3.185–87) are repeatedly subjected to more and more severe tests. In the last scene of the play these tests acquire another function: they become the trials of the spectator's expectation as to the play's ending.

Yet before this change takes place, a scene (5.2) occurs, preparing both the dramatic and the noetic grounds of the play's conclusion. The tree (or "bush" in Q1), which is the central object of the scene, has an evident emblematic meaning. In its shadow, styled by Edgar as "some bidding" or "good host," Gloucester is to wait for "comfort," praying that "the right may thrive." The whole setting and context may be said to resemble the central image of the "Verity-Falsity" folktale group: the miraculous healing of a blind wretch under the magic tree. But this contradicts the brief, again emblematic, action and the disillusive solution of the scene. Obviously we may object that as a dramatic situation "the battle itself is not important."[34] But it achieves some importance both in its contradictory relation to the folktale setting and with regard to the specific theatrical function of the scene. When listening to the sounds of "Alarum and retreat," the audience is found in the same position as the blind Gloucester. This cannot be said about other "trial" or "ordeal" scenes, for example, the storm scenes, mock-trial scene, blinding scene, or Dover cliff scene. Thus Shakespeare's stage-craft deliberately destroys the aesthetic distance of the stage action and invites the audience to participate in Gloucester's ultimate test and in the subsequent tests of the characters' integrity and spectators' expectations in the concluding scene, which are much more effective.

To understand these tests we should realize that the miraculous interven-tion of supernatural and providential judgment, which could be epito-mized both in the battle scene and in Edgar's combat with Edmund, is ultimately excluded. Life is to be endured without any hope in an absolute, metaphysical truth; the only positive value is the quality of our action, its "ripeness" (due to its chiefly social relevance of this value may be contrasted with Edgar's innate feeling of "Our lives' sweetness"). Yet the indisputable dramatic irony of the whole situation in the battle scene implies that ripeness cannot be explained by analogies with Montaigne's thoughts about the will to live or from the meaning of the humanist concept of "maturity" as balanced, moderate action. It may rather be understood as the state of being prepared for suffering, for the efforts to preserve—through individ-ual integrity—the unity of the social whole ("to speak what we feel and not what we ought to say").

Following the thematic analogues of *King Lear* in the Czechoslovak folklore we have noticed similar symptoms of the secularization of myth both in the play and in the folktale material: a shift from cosmic to social and individual values as well as a radical desecration of the king image, typical of the Czech folktales? But the mythical poetry of *King Lear* in its direct appeal to the spectators' imagination goes even beyond that. As is evident from comparison with the central image of the "Verity-Falsity" group of tales, the play deeply transforms general folklore themes and patterns. The disillusionment of individual situations, the baffling of characters' and audiences' expectations, do not become important as myth-destroying devices, but rather as means of acute confrontation of the established, traditional meaning of the play's images as "visual *exempla*"[35] with their new sense developed in the course of individual dramatic scenes. Thus the meaning of the images of *King Lear* as the "metaphysical meta-phors"[36] of the human condition and its ultimate tragic recognitions (the "image of that horror") is transformed into an aesthetically and socially grounded appeal to individual imaginations.

Notes

1. My approach is much indebted to Professor Stříbrný's suggestion to seek the analogies of the imagery and thematic structure of *King Lear* in the folklore tradition. Cf., e.g., William Shakespeare, *Výbor z dramat II, Tragédie* (Selected Plays II, Tragedies) (Prague: Naše vojsko 1957), 720: "the very essence of *King Lear* can be fully grasped only after we abandon the criteria of modern psychological representation and come to understand it as a kind of folktale. As a story at the same time profound, tender, grand, yet quite simple and unsophisticated, a magnificent image of life unconstrained by petty everyday verisimilitudes." I have also used Stříbrný's notes about the relationship of the sources of the play and the Moravian folksong analyzed below. In the Czech context, the *Lear* story was traditionally connected with Holinshed's version. Ladislav Čelakovský, the author of the first printed translation of *King Lear* (1854) had also translated the ballad "King Leir and His Three Daughters" from Percy's *Reliques*, but argued about the dependence of this song on Holinshed and Shakespeare. Cf. *Časopis českého muzea* 29 (1855): 500–504.

2. The importance of such analogies has been discussed in F. D. Hoeniger's article "The Artist Exploring the Primitive: King Lear," in Rosalie L. Colie and F. T. Flahiff, eds., *Some Facets of "King Lear," Essays in Prismatic Criticism* (Toronto: University of Toronto Press, 1974), 89–102. Professor Hoeniger argues that "the story which reached Shakespeare was not only primitive in its setting but also primitive in origin" and "that in transforming simple story into a complex and powerful drama, he [Shakespeare] explored the primitive in all its depths and terror, as the story in the form it reached him certainly did not . . . but leaves us in the end as the civilized witnesses to the conclusion of a stark tragedy" (98). His approach is based on the folklore material collected and interpreted by an Italian ethnologist, Giuseppe Cocchiara/*La Leggenda di re Lear*, Studi di ethnologia e folklore 1 (Torino, 1932). The most important folklore analogies are to be found—according to Cocchiara and Hoeniger—in a folktale from Corsica belonging to the so-called *Cinderella* group discussed below, but including also rare motifs of the imprisonment of the old king by his cruel children and of the king's madness. In another folktale from Cosenza, "the king is abandoned by the elder daughters and left to wander about without companions 'blind, nothing remaining of him' " (99–100). Cocchiara further attempts to trace the common origin of all the folktale versions in the initiation rituals of primitive tribes, mainly in the ritual of puberty. About the relation of the folktale themes and motifs to another kind of initiation ritual, the wedding ceremony, see the following discussion of the Czechoslovak folklore analogies of *King Lear*, especially passages concerning the Slovak folktale.

3. Cf. Maynard Mack, *King Lear in Our Time* (Berkeley and Los Angeles: University of California Press, 1972), 49, a comparison with the archetypal theme of the "Abasement of the Proud King," 78ff and 115: "Though there is much of the Morality play in *Lear*, it is not used toward a morality theme but toward building a deeply metaphysical metaphor, or myth about the human condition, the state of man, in which the last of many mysteries is the enigmatic system of relatedness, in which he is enclosed." For a different interpretation of the mythical images of *King Lear* that is concerned with their function in the ideological context of early Jacobean pageantry see: M. C. Bradbrook, *The Living Monument* (London: 1976), 130ff.

4. See John Holloway, *The Story of the Night* (Lincoln: University of Nebraska Press, 1961), 97, where Lear is likened to "Jack-a-Green, at once the hero and the victim of popular ceremony"; and Robert Weimann, *Shakespeare and the Popular Tradition in the Theater* (Baltimore and London: Johns Hopkins University Press, 1978), 40ff, about the "nonsensical heritage of ritual action" that in the Fool's part, helps to create an "inverted vision of the world" whose main aim is social criticism.

5. Cf. Eleazar Meletinski, *Poetika mifa* (The Poetics of Myth) (Moscow: Nauka, 1976), 262–66.

6. Antti Aarne and Stith Thompson, *The Types of the Folktale* (Helsinki: Suomalainen Tiedeakatemia, 1928).

7. Stith Thompson, *Motif Index of Folk Literature,* vol. 5 (Bloomington: Indiana University Press, 1957).

8. František Sušil, *Moravské národní písně* (Moravian Folksongs), 2d ed. (Prague, 1860), No. 119.

9. Karl Simrock, *Quellen des Shakespeare* (Berlin, 1870), 2:231–34.

10. Jan Gebauer, "Moravská národní píseň o třech dcerách" (Moravian Folksong about Three Daughters), *Listy filologické a pedagogické* 2 (1875): 304–8.

11. Cf. Heinrich Oesterley, ed., *Gesta Romanorum* (Berlin 1872), 671–73.

12. A similar version with a different moral is contained in the early sixteenth-century *exempla* collection by Johannes Pauli, a German Franciscan preacher. Cf. Johannes Pauli, *Schimpf und Ernst,* ed. Johannes Bolte (Leipzig, 1924), 2:358. Cf. also Simrock, *Quellen des Shakespeare,* 2:234.

13. Cf. Oesterley, *Gesta,* 673:

Karissimi, iste imperator potest dici quilibet homo mundanus, qui habet tres filias. Prima filia, que dicit: Diligo patrem plus plusquam me ipsam, certe est mundus iste, quem homo tantum diligit, quod vitam suam circa mundana expendit, sed quando est in necessitate mortis, tunc mundus vix cum omni dileccione quam habuit concedet ei quinque milites, i.e. quinque tabulas ad modum ciste ad involvendom corpus suum sepulcri. Secunda filia, que tantum diligit patrem sicut se ipsam, est uxor tua, filii tui et parentes, qui inveniunt necessaria quousque in terram positus fueris et nihil aliud. Tercia filia que dicebat: Tantum te diligo quantum vales, est deus, que nimis parum diligemus. Sed si ad eo venerimus in necessitate puro corde et munda mente, sine dubio eius auxilio obtinemus. . . .

14. In this respect the Moravian song differs from the English folk ballad published in Percy's *Reliques,* which is largely dependent on the chronicle treatment of the story.

15. Cf. Mack, *King Lear,* 70. Mack emphasizes the role of characters and situations as allegorical representations of some essential qualities of human life: "The characters who are pure states of being, unmixedly good or bad, or the scenes and episodes that have the quality of visual *exempla.*"

16. According to Schelling (*Einleitung in die Philosophie der Mythologie,* 1857) the creative nature of myth consists in the capacity to produce symbolic images, which—contrary to allegorical—can reproduce the whole in its complexity as general in specific and specific in general. In myth, as Meletinski comments on Schelling's theory, the general does not simply *designate* the specific, but *is* the specific. Thus also every myth allows an endless number of allegorical interpretations that alter in the course of cultural development. Cf. Meletinski, *Poetics of Myth,* 19ff.

17. Meletinski, *Poetics of Myth,* 98.

18. Ibid., 120. Meletinski uses the example of the relationship of Shakespeare's Hamlet to the Hamlet stories and finally to the tales of family revenge.

19. Božena Němcová, *Slovenské pohádky a pověsti* (Slovak Folktales and Sagas) 1858; reprint, Prague: Čs. spisovatel, 2:61–68 and 231–39. The original tale narrated by a nurse in an aristocratic family had been retold and probably also remodeled by the author.

20. Propp's classification of folktale narrative patterns lists the basic patterns that occur in this tale under types 11, 12, 13, 14, 23, 27, 31. See Viktor Propp, *Morfologiya skazki* (The Morphology of Folktale) (1928, reprint, Moscow: Nauka, 1969), 40–70.

21. Cf. M. R. Cox, *Cinderella* (London, 1893). Similar tales from all over the world were listed by Johannes Bolte and Jiří Polívka in their commentary to No. 173 of the *Kinder-und Hausmärchen* by The Brothers Grimm (the tale is called "Gänselhirtin am Brunnen"). See Bolte and Polívka, *Anmerkungen zu der Kinder-u. Hausmärchen der Brüder Grimm* (Leipzig, 1918), 3:305ff; also 2:47ff. My analysis is based on a still more detailed list compiled by Polívka in Josef Kubín, *Lidové povídky z českého Podkrkonoší* (Czech Folktales from under the Krkonoše Mountains) (Prague, 1922), 1:610–14.

22. Cf. Meletinski, *Poetics of Myth,* 99.

23. Cf. Mack, *King Lear,* 95, and John Reibetanz, *The Lear World* (Toronto: University of

Toronto Press, 1977) 23. Reibetanz mentions some analogues of the "diagrammatic" first scene of *King Lear* in the works of other Jacobean playwrights.

24. *King Lear,* ed. Muir, appendixes, 222.

25. According to Propp, *Morphology of Folktale,* 23, the functions of folktale personnae and of their actions are decisive for the classification of narrative patterns and themes.

26. Cf. the "love test" in the third scene of *King Leir* where Leir fails to understand that Cordelia refers to the *essence* of their relation, to the *ideal* of filial love: "But looke what loue *the* child doth oue *the* father, / The same to you I beare, my gracious Lord"; "Do you love us as *euery* child doth loue / *Their* father" (my italics).

27. Mikhail M. Bakhtin, *Tvorchestvo Fransua Rable* (The Work of François Rabelais) (Moscow: Khudozh, 1965), 24ff. Cf. also *Román jako dialog* (The Dialogic Imagination) (Prague, 1980 [Moscow, 1973]), 295ff.

28. *King Lear,* ed. Muir, Appendixes, 228.

29. František Popelka, *Pohádky a pověsti* (Folktales and Sagas) (Poličks, 1883), 43ff. The tale is named "Princess in a Chest."

30. Kubín, *Czech Folktales;* 30ff. The tale is entitled "Vagrant Čejka and Princess Amálka."

31. Cf. Václav Tille, *Soupis českých pohádek* (Index of Czech Folktales) (Prague: 1934), 2, pt. 2 : 164, 505. About the theme (Aarne-Thompson Type No. 613, "The Two Travelers") cf., e.g., Stith Thompson, *The Folktale* (Berkeley and Los Angeles: University of California Press, 1977), 80.

32. The absolute destruction of these vital relations and their virtual *inversion* (in comparison with the Rabelaisian image of society as a "collective body") is signaled mainly by the chains of images in Lear's monologues during his madness, especially 4.6.

33. Scenes current in Jacobean drama in which one of the characters acts as a director and which may serve for the "pointed revelation of characters." Cf. Reibetanz, *The Lear World,* 64.

34. *King Lear,* ed. Muir, 197n.

35. Cf. Mack, *King Lear,* 70ff.

36. Cf. Northrop Frye, *Anatomy of Criticism,* (Princeton, N.J.: Princeton University Press, 1957), 212, on the "archetypal human tragedy" in which the hero "enters the world in which existence is itself tragic, not existence modified by an act, deliberate and unconscious." Frye's note refers to the fate of the biblical—and Milton's—Adam. Cf. also Mack, *King Lear,* 110, 115.

Shakespeare's Plays and an Indian Sensibility: A Possible Sense of Community

by S. VISWANATHAN

> Indian Empire will go, at any rate, some day; but this Shake-
> speare does not go, he lasts for ever with us; we cannot give up
> our Shakespeare.

Carlyle's prophecy has proved to be only too true and in a curiously reverse fashion. The beneficent cultural empire of Shakespeare, an empire without *imperium,* has fortunately survived the loss of political empire and happily endures in India as well as elsewhere. Landor's phrase "not our poet but the world's" has again found ample vindication in the by now long and active tradition of loving study and steady performance of the plays in India as well as in several other parts of the "three-nook'd world." There are no less than three copies of the First Folio held in libraries in three corners of India—west, east, and south. The plays have been translated, adapted, and reinterpreted in many Indian languages and on many Indian stages. The changing interpretations of the plays and the varying approaches to them have been relatively quick to find their way into India over the last century and a quarter. We certainly cannot give up our Shakespeare. To mention another prophesy from the past, there is Maurice Morgann's declaration:

> When the hand of time shall have brushed off his present Editors and
> Commentators . . . the Apalachian mountains, the banks of the Ohio,
> and the plains of Scioto shall resound with the accents of this Barbarian.[1]

The prediction is topologically related to the Shakespearean one so ringingly realized in Julius Nyerere's Swahili version of the "lofty scene" in *Julius Caesar:*

How many ages hence
Shall this our lofty scene be acted over
In states unborn and accents yet unknown

[3.1.111–13]

By hindsight, Morgann seems to predict Shakespearean literary-cultural embassage to lands of more than one Indian race. Curiously, Morgann's celebration of Shakespeare echoes the terms of a standard Sanskrit tribute to the revered Indian epic the *Ramayana* as being enduring as the mountains, the rivers, and the fields.

In this paper I will not deal with the ways of teaching and studying Shakespeare through generations in India, nor will I consider the remarkable impact of Shakespeare on Indian literatures—let alone the Indian mind—nor will I outline the history of Shakespeare in performance or Shakespeare in adaptations or translations in the study or in the theater in India. These are large subjects that would each merit more than a single paper or monograph. Instead I shall offer some reflections or perhaps speculations about what I call a possible community of sensibility between the Indian (with his particular cultural heritage) and Shakespearean drama. I will explore briefly and broadly some of the inherent advantages Indians may have in their responses to Shakespeare's plays, thanks to having been born and bred in the popular cultural tradition of Indian theater and performing arts. In general, the Indian, heir to special traditions of drama, art, and culture that are basically similar to Shakespeare's in his time, probably can establish quicker if not fuller rapport with the nonillusionism, conventionalism, and, above all, the "multiconsciousness" (to use that apt expression of S. L. Bethell) of Shakespearean drama than his present-day Western counterpart. Indeed, one can trace a certain kind of cultural similarity between India up to the 1950s and Shakespeare's England, even as striking correspondences may be seen between the India of the 1980s and the England of the early seventeenth century—both societies and cultures in transformation or caught between tradition and modernity. At least it should be relatively less difficult for an Indian than a Westerner to command the historical sense and imagination needed to appreciate certain qualities of the cultural milieu and ethos of Shakespeare in general and the stage conventions and nonnaturalistic art of his drama in particular.

Sir William Jones translated Kalidasa's great play *Sakuntalam* in the late eighteenth century (the Indians called Kalidasa "the Shakespeare of the Indian stage," while a late-seventeenth-century Englishman called Molière "the famous Shakespeare of this age") and discovered Sanskrit drama as he discovered linguistics from the Sanskrit grammarian Panini for the West. Since then Western scholars like Sylvain Levi and H. W. Wells have studied Indian and especially Sanskrit drama texts and have acquainted the West with them, but they have perhaps paid at best only scant attention to Indian theatrical conventions and practices or to their cultural and aesthetic contexts. Classical Sanskrit drama, whether Kalidasa's or Bhavabhuti's or Bhasa's or that of other playwrights like Charudatta or King Harsha, courtly as the plays were in their origin or original production, ultimately can be regarded as a product of a homogeneous culture, a blend of the popular and the courtly and sophisticated, much like the homogeneous culture, relatively speaking, of Elizabethan England. More interestingly, the conventionalistic, nonnaturalistic orientation of Indian classical drama and its roots in popular culture (for all its stylization and courtliness) survived into the later dramatic and theatrical traditions of the country in several languages, especially in Bengal and in the southern part of the country. This occurred in spite of the popular Indian theater incorporating, in the last two centuries, the Western and Parsee influences and resorting to tricks of illusion after the Western fashion. The resulting realism of this popular stage is similar to the patchy realism of the "impure art" of the Elizabethan theater.

Whether it is the staging of ritual reenactment of the deeds of gods and goddesses during religious festivals or staging of regular plays in the folk or professional theater, the conventions of place and time in traditional popular drama in South India are not unlike those of Elizabethan and earlier drama. The actor and the spectator in terms of these conventions achieve a multiple perspective, a "multiconsciousness," which allows them to move with ease in their imagination between historical and ritual times, between the past and the present, and, most of all, between illusion and reality, besides moving between several levels of either. The convention of the boy actor playing a girl's role or a man that of a woman was fairly common on the popular stage in the south until the 1930s. Despite a rudimentary use (in some theaters) of the drop-curtain and a patchy realism in costumes and in some stage properties, the conception and presentation of plays worked in terms of "simultaneous settings," apparently anachronistic topical references, some audience participation, a formalized sort of acting and speaking (which could appear and sound natural if done with skill), and a use of song, music, and dance that suggested the opera and the ballet and sometimes perhaps the music-hall at the same time.

An Indian used to the so-called anachronism of bespectacled gods like Rama, Krishna, and Muruga on the popular stage can hear the clock strike in *Julius Caesar* without feeling a sense of dissonance. Traditions and anecdotes about the villain being really killed by an irate spectator who got too involved are as common in the Indian theatrical tradition as are Western stories about the sailor who climbed the stage to rescue Desdemona or the old lady who shouted at Othello, "You fool! Don't you see?" or the killing of the man who played Judas. According to stage tradition, something like *The Knight of the Burning Pestle* situations have also occurred in the actual theater. But underlying all this, in spite of the crude perversions and the travesties it may undergo, is a sense of communication between the stage and the world, or the stage-world and the world-stage.

That conventional staging and stylized acting marked classical Sanskrit drama, even as Indian dance and music were also marked by stylization, is clear from several authentic texts that outlined the practice, as well as the aesthetics of dance and drama that have come down to us like Nandikesvara's *Abinavadarpana* or *The Mirror of Gesture*[2] and Raghavabhatta's *Arthadvotanika* ('the illumination of meaning'), a commentary on *Sakuntalam*. It is of interest that when William Poel in the late nineteenth-century and later tried to revive the Elizabethan staging of Shakespeare, he produced Kalidasa's *Sakuntalam* several times in Oxford and London, using the convention of *decor simultané,* stylized acting and verse speaking.[3] Early in the twentieth century, in distant Colorado, George Fulmer Reynolds found confirmation of his ideas of simultaneous settings and emblematic staging on the Shakespearean stage from what he heard about the classical Indian stage. Raghavabhatta's directions for the heroine Sakuntala in *Sakuntalam* were detailed, such as "watering a plant in the garden," "ascending a chariot," or "being pursued by a bee." According to these directions, stylized gestures, especially with the hands, like those of the dancer,[4] without the use of props, are to be used to depict action on the stage. Expressing one's fear of a pursuing bee, for example, could instructively parallel the possible ways an actor of Macbeth could enact the "airy dagger" scene without the dagger.

Conventions such as an actor walking from one end of the stage to the other to denote a journey, the aside—though not the soliloquy, and the direct self-announcement or declaration by a character on first appearance (in a manner sometimes but not always out-Heroding Herod "raging in the pageant and in the street") are common on both the classical and popular Indian stage. All these complement and do not damage the ceremony of theatrical presentation, a "ceremony" not unlike that of the Noh or the Kabuki. The conventions of stylized gestures and also a "placeless" and "timeless" stage that could at the same time convey an imaginative impression of a particular place and time are common to Indian dance and drama. Moreover, Indian traditions of dance like Kathak, Bharata Natyam, Kathakkali, Kuchupudi, or Bhagavathamela[5] are also traditions of dance-drama. To cite an example, the use of a traverse (or a curtain known in the theatrical terminology of the Kathakkali dance-drama of Kerala as *tiraseelai*) in this form of drama to this day is not unlike the use that the traverse may have been put to on the early Elizabethan or pre-Shakespearean stage. Two men walk on to the stage, spread and hold a curtain up at opposite ends. A character who is supposed to arrive from a journey walks across the stage in sight of everyone and stands behind the curtain. After being elaborately called upon or heralded, he or she comes forward and presents him or herself as the stagehands fold the curtain and walk off with it. Richard Southern appropriately cites the Kathakkali use of the traverse in his reconstruction of the use of the curtain in *The Staging of Plays Before Shakespeare*.[6]

Yet the final effect of the performance of Indian drama has a way of seeming natural. The hand gestures *(mudras)*, for which detailed directions are set out in the texts I mentioned earlier, remind one of the formal acting advocated as Elizabethan by Bertram Joseph and indeed resemble the pictures from John Bulwer's *Chironomia* and *Chirologia* that Bertram Joseph reproduced in his book *Elizabethan Acting*.[7] But as Ananda Coomaraswamy astutely points out (*The Mirror of Gestures*, p. 19), all the formal acting and gestures produce an effect of being "individual, impulsive and 'natural'" in spite of, rather precisely on account of, their artifice. It is perhaps a factor to be borne in mind in this discussion of the "still-vex'd" question of how "formal" and how "natural" Elizabethan acting was, especially when we find that contemporary accounts of the acting of Alleyn and Burbage acclaim both as acting "to the life."

Stage directions in some of the Sanskrit plays such as "dhyanam notayati" ('He enacts contemplation') in *Karpuramanjari*, 1.26.10, and "dhyanam abhinaya" ('act out contemplation'—in the imperative) in *Kundamala* 1.28, are as formal as such directions as "He falls in love" in Marston's *The Malcontent*. The intermixture of the natural and the conventional in the Indian dramatic tradition that leads, in the final analysis, to an impression of naturalness is based on an abiding sense of a constant interplay between illusion and reality in drama and perhaps in life also, a sense that expresses itself in a similar currency of the world as stage, the *theatrum mundi* idea in the Indian mind as in the Elizabethan.

The love comedies of Kalidasa such as *Vikramo rvasium* and *Malavikagnimitram* provide an experience of lyrical comedy that may serve as good preparation for or confirmation of the impact of Shakespeare's romantic comedies. Kalidasa's *Sakuntala*, Bhavabhuti's *Uttararamacharita* and Bhasa's *Pratima Nataka* ('the drama of the statue' in which Sita's statue suggests Hermione's "statue") provide uncanny parallels with the last plays of Shakespeare. If these are examples of drama "beyond tragedy," tragic feeling and form alike, despite the common generalization to the contrary, are not alien to or unknown in Indian literature and drama, though these are finally contained in the ultimate resolution of divine "comic" providence. Bhasa's *Urubhanga* among classical plays, the drama of *Harischandra* (the witnessing of which inspired the boy Gandhi to a dedication to truth), and the popular version of Ilango's classic poetic drama in Tamil, *Silappatikaram* (under the title of *Kovalan and Kannaki*), are examples of tragic drama. The latter two plays, especially *Harischandra* in its episode of Chandramati's lament for her dead son, incorporate "a tragedy of grief" akin to this subgenre of tragedy as it may have been current in Elizabethan times and can be traced in translations of *Hecuba* and in plays like *The Spanish Tragedy, Locrine, Titus Andronicus, Richard III,* and *King John* with their set lamentations. The half-folk and half-urban popular Tamil stage-comedy *Thooku-thooki* is strikingly similar in mood and tone, character and situations to *The Taming of the Shrew.* To move on to a different level, the dilemmas of Hamlet in the play and of Arjuna, the *Mahabharata* figure in the *Bhagavadgita,* suggest common ground and link them as kindred spirits. But it should not be forgotten that in all these cross-cultural comparative approaches whatever initial, "more-than-phatic communion" the convergence of basic common cultural orientations and predilections may make possible, the cultural and contextual differences are no less strong and no less important.

Western scholars like Richard Lannoy have identified and acclaimed, as he writes, "the unified field awareness of traditional Indian thought processes . . . perception achieved through synaesthesia, cultivation of simultaneous awareness by all the senses . . . [and] an instinctual mode of perception, the unified sensibility which is India's greatest asset."[8] It would be absurd to claim that the average Indian possesses, much less deploys, the gift of "pattern-recognition and multi-sensory perception" (p. 497), the gift of the "instantaneity of mythic thought," of the "simultaneous perception and presentation of cause and effect as in electronic circuitry" (p. 426). But as an Indian I should like to grant the possibility that a mind with such habits of thought and feeling has at least some innate potential to attune itself to Shakespearean ideational complexities, to the complexities of Shakespearean metaphor, imagery, and diction, not to mention the symbolism of the plays and, more certainly, to Shakespearean dramatic and theatrical devices and communication.

Perhaps one may also venture the suggestion that the Hindu Indian with his potential Blakean apprehension of the body-soul relationship as "two distincts, division none," will respond to the "soul-dimensions" of Shakespeare's dramatic verse, to what Wilson Knight called the "body-soul" in Shakespeare or to what he termed "neglected powers" in Shakespeare. For example, the intuitions and intimations of Edgar's "Dover Cliff" speeches in *King Lear,* which go far beyond the limits of word scenery or verbal evocation of visual impressions, or those of Cleopatra's vision of Antony, are engaging to the Indian mind in their contextual and extracontextual multi-dimensionality. After all, the Hindu in his "grace before meat" every time tells himself that he eats for the immortality of the soul, which is the Brahman, the universal soul, as he starts feeding his body. The paradoxes and problems of simultaneous transcendence and immanence are relatively easily absorbed by the Indian mind.

To look in another direction, there are also opportunities for the Indian student to register the total imaginative impression of the individual play and to apprehend its tonality or resonance, using the speculative instruments of the *rasa* and *dhvani* principles of aesthetic response laid down in

Sanskrit poetics. That would, of course, involve the application of Sanskrit concepts and categories of aesthetic experience to the plays, an enterprise to be undertaken with care.

These are some possible opportunities inherited by the Indian equipped with the legacy of his native culture and the traditional and popular theater of his land to work out a certain relationship of "resonance" (to use E. H. Gombrich's word to denote the art-audience rapport) with Shakespeare's plays in their original theatrical context and their poetic-dramatic and theatrical life. The scene changes from the England of Elizabeth I or Elizabeth II, for that matter, to far-off India of the present day or yester-day, itself a rapidly changing place, but in the light of the possibilities I have suggested, the plays, after all, perhaps do not have to change essentially. What I have done, as I have said, is to outline some common cultural factors that should help an Indian today to savor Shakespeare not only as for all time and all climes (which universality of appeal takes care of itself) but at the same time as the soul of his age. However, I do not for a moment underestimate the need to avoid an improper, exclusive assimilation of Shakespeare to Indian cultural and aesthetic interests, and I stress the concomitant need for Indian students to train their historical sensibilities and imaginations for the purpose.

Notes

1. Maurice Morgan, *Shakespearian Criticism,* ed. Daniel A. Fineman (Oxford: Clarendon Press, 1972), 170.

2. Translated by Ananda Kentish Coomaraswamy and Duggirala Gopala Krishnaiah (Cambridge: Harvard University Press, 1917). I cite from the 1936 edition published in New York by E. Weyhe.

3. See Robert Speaight, *William Poel and the Elizabethan Revival* (London: Heinemann, 1954), 122–23, 147, 181–82.

4. In fact, *natya,* the term for dance in Sanskrit, means at once acting and dancing.

5. Bhagavathamela is a sort of yearly Oberammergau, a dance-drama of divine action staged in the village of Melattur in the Tanjore delta by trained amateurs.

6. (London: Faber, 1973), 271.

7. Oxford University Press, 1951.

8. *The Speaking Tree: The Study of Indian Culture and Society,* Galaxy Books (Oxford: Oxford University Press, 1971), 420.

Dance Images of Shakespeare's Characters

by SELMA JEANNE COHEN

Over the years many choreographers have been moved to create theatrical dances based on the plays of Shakespeare. At first glance the challenge might well seem insurmountable. The Bard was a master of words—the very skill that the dance does *not* use. Yet the attraction persists.

The earliest Shakespeare ballet may be a *Romeo and Juliet,* choreographed by Eusebio Luzzi in Venice in 1785. Later that same year Charles Le Picq presented his *Macbeth* in London. Then there is Salvatore Viganò's *Othello,* performed in Milan in 1818, and Marius Petipa's *A Midsummer Night's Dream,* choreographed in Saint Petersburg in 1876. Many other Shakespeare plays have attracted later choreographers, but these four dominate the scene. And of these four, *Romeo and Juliet* is well in the lead. We may ask why. What is it in the nature of this play that makes it not only more attractive, but more amenable to choreography, than some of the others? To answer this question one must first take a brief look at the representative and expressive capacities of dance.

George Balanchine once made a now-famous statement about the limitations of his medium: "There are no mothers-in-law in ballet." Indeed, how can this relationship be indicated by means of movement? Philosophizing also presents a problem that is especially threatening in *Hamlet.* What can a choreographer possibly do with "To be or not to be?" In less serious moments, what can he do with "Benedict and Beatrice between the sheets"?

Of course, choreographers were bound to find a way to circumvent such problems, and they devised some ingenious substitutes for words. The favorite method of the late nineteenth century was to alternate scenes of pantomime and dance. Using a sequence of conventional gestures, the ballerina and her partner were able to discuss their romantic plans: "Soon we will find a way to get rid of that stupid, rich suitor, and then our parents will consent to our marriage and we shall be happy forever." This idea—prettily but quickly and clearly stated with gestures of the arms and hands—provided motivation for the moment the audience was waiting for—the *pas de deux,* which was even prettier and was therefore allowed considerably more time. Logical consistency was not the point in this form of theater, which was intended only to entertain. The plot was a mere excuse, a clothesline on which to hang a variety of pleasing dances. Some earlier attempts, like those of Viganò, to reflect the structure of serious drama and to make all the dancers' movements precisely meaningful, were found static and dull by many audiences. Unfortunately, little evidence has come down about the details of Viganò's choreography, but perhaps we would agree with those of his contemporaries who felt that words told the story better.

In the twentieth century, the Ausdruckstanz in Germany and the so-called modern dance in the United States aimed to create a genre that was interesting both for its formal qualities and for the character and emotion it depicted. The American Doris Humphrey listed some types of subjects to be avoided: propaganda, cosmic themes, and literary imagery were among the objects of imitation that she deemed unsuitable for dance. In *The Art of Making Dances* (New York: Rinehart, 1959), she asked the choreographer to focus on the "part of experience that can be expressed in physical action." Emotional states she found most eminently fitting for portrayal, but warned against the use of very complex plots. The motivation, she claimed, had to be shown before the eyes of the audience; it was not fair to depend on program notes.

Today's choreographers tend to approach Shakespeare in one of two ways. The first, while allowing that some of the subplots and minor characters can be discarded, attempts to incorporate much of the detail of the original text. Conventional mime is now replaced with recognizable though stylized gesture, while staying clear of complicated or intellectual ideas. The hero brandishes a sword—several times and in increasingly larger arcs—as his energy is reiterated in the musical accompaniment. Rather than just wiping away a tear, the ballerina makes her whole body curl in on itself with introverted sorrow; joy, on the other hand, sends her flying across the stage, arms and legs outspread, covering broad reaches of space. The movements serve more than the practical function of depicting character and emotion; they are also interesting in themselves. Or such is the intention, for we must admit that not every dance works in this respect.

Some choreographers are more daring. John Neumeier, who has created a number of ballets based on Shakespeare's plays, claims that a literally detailed following of the text is detrimental to a dance work. The task of the choreographer is not to translate the play, but rather to embody its essence in another medium. Of the Shakespeare dances that I have seen, José Limón's *The Moor's Pavane* comes the closest to achieving this state. Here are only the four main characters, acting out the highlights of their tragedy as they try in vain to follow the paths of social decorum, exemplified by the formal patterns of a stately court dance.

Figure 1. *The Moor's Pavane* (1949). José Limón as Othello, Betty Jones as Desdemona, Pauline Koner as Emilia, Lucas Hoving as Iago. *(Courtesy of The American Dance Festival, Durham, North Carolina.)*

Literary purists may argue, however, that Limón omitted too much of *Othello*. Should "meditations" or "variations" on a theme from Shakespeare still be counted as representations of the play? How much of Shakespeare is lost in the process? Can different kinds of plays require different approaches? If an essence is chosen, is it really the epitome of the play, or has the choreographer betrayed the Bard by imposing too much of himself? These are only a few of the questions to be considered.

Perhaps the choreographer has simply chosen the wrong kind of play to turn into a dance. *Hamlet* has been choreographed, but it has never succeeded in this form. On the other hand, the ballets based on *Romeo and Juliet* have almost invariably found favor with audiences and critics alike. The reasons are not hard to find. In the tale of star-cross'd lovers, the qualities that present the greatest problems to the choreographer are either absent or of minor importance. Why are the Capulets and Montagues feuding? The motivation does not matter so much; in fact, the basic irrationality of the conflict is central to the theme. The feelings of the characters are basic, but—most significantly—they are intense. Throughout most of the play the emotions of the protagonists are at fever pitch. Only in the early scenes of the young lovers, before they face the reality that threatens their happiness, is the atmosphere somewhat calm, the feelings simple and unruffled. Once they have pledged their commitment, passions dominate.

Here we have indeed the part of experience that can be expressed in

Figure 2. *Romeo and Juliet.* The Royal Ballet, Covent Garden (1965). Rudolf Nureyev and Margot Fonteyn. *(Courtesy of The Royal Ballet, London; photo by Frederika Davis.)*

physical action. As Shakespeare resorted to imagery to express intensity of feeling, so the choreographer resorts to dance, to those actions that contain a superfluity of movement in relation to the demands of their practical function, which is simply to identify the emotions of the characters. The choreographer, like the playwright, is not content with simple statements of fact. Stylization—taking the gesture beyond its merely realistic shape by speeding up or retarding its normal tempo, extending or restricting its path in space, repeating or complicating its basic configuration—enables the choreographer to heighten the impact of the portrayal. Then he achieves what Rudolf Arnheim has called "the kind of stirring participation that distinguishes artistic experience from the detached acceptance of information." As Shakespeare turned words into poetry, choreographers turn movements into dance. Then the spectators are no longer merely informed; they are enthralled. The fact of the thwarted love of Romeo and Juliet is quickly stated, the quality of their passion—vividly etched in frantic leaps and desperate pirouettes—continues to suffuse the stage and thrill the audience as the music builds and soars to its romantic climax.

Not only is *Romeo and Juliet* remarkably suitable to choreographic treatment, but it has also prompted a number of diverse approaches. For the Soviet Leonid Lavrovsky (1940), inspired by ballerina Galina Ulanova, the stress was placed on the maturing of the young Juliet from an awkward, playful child to a passionate woman. More objectively, the British Antony Tudor in 1943 visualized the action as a painting by Botticelli, full of undulating, statuesque poses. In 1972 Tom Schilling gave East Berlin a ballet rooted in class struggle: Romeo as a fisherman; Juliet as the daughter of a rich count. And, while most choreographers have had their hero and heroine plunge headlong into their crises, Kenneth MacMillan in 1965 in London let Prokofiev's music rage around the tortured Juliet as she sat motionless, contemplating her flight to Friar Lawrence.

Of course, the possibilities are not endless. At some point Shakespeare will be betrayed. When is that point reached? With a punk-rock version? Or, more subtly perhaps, before that? Or, not impossibly, the punk-rock scene will work while the conservative one does not. How will we know?

Some questions may be asked. What, for example, was most memorable about the performance? The colorful crowds with their intricate patterns so skillfully managed by the sprightly dancers? Juliet's spectacular *arabesque allongée* as she melted into the arms of Romeo? Or that fabulous decor on the revolving stage! If our memories tend to isolate such technical matters, then Shakespeare has been betrayed. But if we were most moved by the plight of the lovers, who somehow touched us more poignantly than ever before as they met in breathless innocence and parted in tragic wisdom, then justice has been done to the Bard. Was it Shakespeare who made us feel this or the choreographer and his dancers? It could have been so magical a meeting of hearts and minds as can only happen in the theater.

Figure 3. *Romeo and Juliet.* **The Royal Ballet, Covent Garden (1965). Christopher Gable and Lynn Seymour.** *(Courtesy of The Royal Ballet, London; photo by Roy Round.)*

Images of Shakespeare's Plays: Contemporary Set Designs

by JAY L. HALIO

Anyone attending the Royal Shakespeare Company's performances of Shakespeare's plays in the last few years will recognize the justice of Ralph Berry's recent comment that designer's theater has taken over from director's theater.[1] The lavish settings, elaborate costuming, and intricate stage business rival all but the most extravagant Victorian representations associated with names like Irving or Tree. Increasingly, as the 1985 season showed, designers—working closely with directors—tend to set the plays in periods far removed from their original historical or chronological period. The design for *As You Like It* emphasized a stylized modern decor with nary a tree in Arden; *Troilus and Cressida* was set in the period of the Crimean War; and *The Merry Wives of Windsor,* as the program format and notes made clear, was set precisely in 1959.

Nor is the Royal Shakespeare Company alone in this tendency. During the same season, Britain's National Theatre production of *Coriolanus* mixed contemporary and traditional Roman costumes on a set that included nearly a hundred seats for part of the audience, who then participated in the crowd scenes. Earlier, the Folger Theater Group staged *Much Ado About Nothing* in the 1930s aboard a luxury cruise ship. And we are all familiar with various attempts to place *The Tempest* in an extraterrestrial setting.

The rationales for these different designs may vary from one specific production to another, but they seem to derive from the same belief that by changing the locale or time period of the play the production will appear fresher and more relevant to present audiences. In addition, the changes will help uncover hitherto undiscovered or unsuspected aspects of the plays as the company gets away from tradition-bound ways of viewing and, hence, performing them.[2] I can recall attending a performance years ago of *A Midsummer Night's Dream* at the Cambridge Arts Theatre staged by a troupe from Howard Payne College in the United States. It was advertised as done in "Texas Western style," appropriately enough, since the college

282

was in Texas. Like many others, I expected a burlesque performance but was surprised and delighted to see how well the cowboy and Indian motif worked—the Athenians were cowboys and the fairies Indians—and how the players brought the play, with its unusual perspective, newly to life.

That was in 1959. A decade later Peter Brook took the same play and transformed it utterly in what is now regarded as a landmark production. The squash court set, the actors as acrobats, the doubling of Theseus and Hippolyta with Oberon and Titania, and other innovations were all designed to destroy at a blow the nineteenth-century staging of the *Dream*, complete with Mendelssohn's music and a literal forest growing from the boards. (As recently as 1952 the Old Vic in collaboration with the Sadler's Wells Ballet had staged such a production, bringing it on tour to New York's old Metropolitan Opera House.) Brook's production was of course more radical than the less ambitious but still effective "Texas Western" production by Howard Payne College. Both had essentially the same purpose: to awaken our sensibilities to aspects of the play that years of traditional staging had obscured or dulled.

Purists, of course, found Brook's staging outrageous,[3] and I doubt that many have forgiven him a decade and a half later, though he has had his imitators. Ron Daniels of the Royal Shakespeare Company felt compelled in 1981 to stage the play in a still different fashion—using extralarge puppets as his fairies, manipulated on stage by unobtrusive actors—partly in reaction to (if not against) Brook's production, which has remained indelibly fixed in the minds of many theatergoers, especially in Britain. He retained the doubling of Theseus and Hippolyta, but in other respects the set design was vastly different, literally a throwback to Victorian settings and, in the opening scene in Athens, Victorian attitudes. Daniels was struggling with two traditions, the one old and venerable, the other new and radical, and apparently trying to find a middle ground between them while at the same time making a statement of his own.[4] For in his view, the characters are so flagrantly manipulated by those in power that he brought the puppets on stage to emphasize the fact to the audience.

Directors and designers (who typically work together in these matters) may, of course, get carried away with their own inspirations. In the process of staging a new production they can (and sometimes do) destroy vital or essential aspects of the play they are presenting. This was clearly the situation when the RSC recently restaged *The Merchant of Venice*, directed by John Caird and designed by Ultz. Three immense caskets, raised or lowered by special levering machines, remained constantly on stage, dominating the set and threatening at any moment to topple off their platforms—directly onto the heads of actors or audience. And Adrian Noble seems to have an affinity to water, as in his productions of *King Lear* and *As You Like It*, which featured what the company fondly referred to as the wading pond at the front edge of the stage. But these kinds of excesses apart, what further defense, if any, can be made to justify the tendency to "update"—and thereby alter the image of—Shakespeare's plays?

Recognizing the important differences between proscenium and open stages that perforce influence set design, Peter Brook has argued vigorously against any set that would "confine the audience to a single attitude and a single interpretation." The plays being so rich in ambiguity, the director and designer's job is to explore the truths within the ambiguity, not to "use" the play for some particular—personal or political or social— interpretation, which makes the play "a vehicle for exploitation." For Brook, "any complete and consistent set of historical costumes is a fantastic imposition" that "forces the play in certain directions" or places it in a straitjacket. "You cannot enter into a play if part of you is squashed into [a] footnoting attitude," he maintains, and concludes: "To put it very simply: the trap is to make statements and to make illustrations."[5]

These are very powerful arguments, but it is not coincidental, I think, that most of the examples Brook gives are from the tragedies. Fifteen years ago, the Regency *Hamlet* with Richard Chamberlain as the Prince focused successfully on certain aspects of the play while it sacrificed others. The point is also demonstrable from the striking differences between Brook's own stage production of *King Lear* and the more realistic, historical setting of his film version. The trade-offs, as Ralph Berry remarks, must be reckoned, especially when modern sets are used: "The danger is always that an immediate point can be made vividly and tellingly, but that it relies on a set of assumptions about our own society that the remainder of the text cannot sustain."[6] On the whole, as Berry says, modernization or adaptation works better for the comedies than for the tragedies, where gains outweigh losses. Why this should be so I am not sure: it may be that in comedy spectacle is less distracting and fanciful design, or outright fantasy, is more easily accepted, as Thomas Clayton has suggested.[7] Or perhaps seeing our own society (or one we are close to) mirrored in the follies of Shakespeare's comedies is more acceptable than seeing it in the tragedies, where we require a less specific, more "timeless" setting—a setting, that is, which helps the play's essential reality to reemerge, unobstructed and unimpeded by irrelevant or unnecessary topicality.[8]

Whatever the case, sharp lines of demarcation possibly should not be drawn; moreover, one of the important gains in transposing settings has not been often enough stressed—that is, the advantage in replacing literalistic attitudes toward the plays and their interpretation with more flexible and versatile ones. While transposing time-periods may require some adjustments in the text, these usually are not serious. Certainly, it is gratifying to see directors willing to credit audiences with more nimble imaginations, linking them closer to Shakespeare's audience. Thus, Peter Hall bravely mixed contemporary and traditional costumes in the National Theatre production of *Coriolanus*. If there was some slight dissonance in viewing Cominius or Coriolanus now in three-piece suit or blazer and slacks, now in Roman helmet and breastplate with sword and buckler, it mattered little in the overall effect the powerful performances produced. It seems we can do without strict historical verisimilitude or consistency, thanks in part to the relaxing of theatrical conventions and of the historicity nineteenth-century productions promoted. The stage set for Hall's *Coriolanus* was itself a model of simplicity and versatility. Borrowing the sand pit from his earlier RSC production of *Troilus and Cressida*, Hall encircled it with a concrete runway and placed two huge doors or gates upstage with several tiers of benches on either side from which the audience/crowd could descend as needed. By using other elements of the Olivier Theatre's open stage, such as the configuration of the stalls and the aisles as entrance ways, Hall succeeded in surrounding the action, thereby drawing the audience further into the play. In fact, the physical staging more than the mixed costume design did much to accomplish this end.

To return to comedy and the more audacious set designs they tend to evoke, consider two American productions of *Much Ado About Nothing*, a decade apart and quite distinctly staged. First, Joseph Papp's production (1972), directed by A. J. Antoon and set in a small American town at the turn of the century, or in the period of the Spanish-American War. Apart from making the play more accessible to American audiences, the design of this production revitalized the play much in the way that Howard Payne College did *A Midsummer Night's Dream*. No violence was done to Shakespeare's basic conception—his Messina of the 1590s and middle-America in the 1890s turn out to have much in common—and very few cuts or other textual alterations appeared necessary. The musical score was completely changed, of course, to one more consistent with the new time and setting and was in itself delightful. Beatrice, played by Kathleen Widdoes, appeared as a sprightly young woman, her outspokenness underscored by her daring to sneak a cigarette and other bits of added stage business. But throughout she remained Shakespeare's Beatrice. Similarly, Sam Waterston as Captain Benedick, in uniform or out, retained all of the essentials of his role. The greatest liberties were taken with Don John, the comic villain, and his cohorts, and with the Keystone Kops who became the Watch. But the liberties were not extreme and they fit nicely into the overall design of the play.

John Neville-Andrews used quite a different design in 1985 for his Folger Theater production, the 1930s cruise ship motif mentioned earlier. His justification for this setting, as stated in the program notes, was a curious mixture of the right thing for the wrong reasons. "The thirties," he said, "was an extremely joyous, optimistic and romantic era, and I saw it as reflecting the spirit of the play. The personality of the period can be evoked by recalling such songs, events and milestones as"—he goes on to list a great many, including Bobby Jones's "Grand Slam" in world golf, the discovery of Vitamin D, the establishment of the forty-hour work week, "I Got Rhythm," nylon stockings, and the launching of SS *Queen Elizabeth!* Now anyone who lived through the Depression years will recall that it was far from a "joyous" or "optimistic" era, however romantic or even idealistic in some respects it may have been. People sought escape from their troubles and found in the field of entertainment a wonderful vehicle. Technicolor movies (an invention not on Neville-Andrews's list) was one such outlet, as were Broadway shows and, for the very rich, Mediterranean cruises. The milieu of *Much Ado,* the tight uppercrust society of Messina, lends itself quite well to the wealthy voyagers on this early version of the "Love Boat," just as it did to the small 1890s middle-American town in Papp's production.[9] Again, Shakespeare's Watch easily transform into the ship's crew, and Don John as a mafia-type villain is comical in ways essentially consistent with the text (except, possibly, for his heavy New York accent). Designer William Barclay performed a minor miracle in converting the Folger's tiny apron stage into the deck of an ocean liner, a bit crowded at times, but not excessively. The pianist in the ship's lounge playing Cole Porter melodies was an excellent period touch. Where Neville-Andrews went wrong was to introduce (for some additional—but quite unnecessary—comedy) an "Unlisted Passenger" aboard the SS *Messina,* a stowaway whose mysterious presence was explained only at the very end when, as an undercover agent for the F.B.I., she apprehended Don John!

Neville-Andrews's *Much Ado,* like the Spanish-American War setting for the play in Papp's production, helped to bring out the timeless quality of Shakespeare's comedy—not by removing all suggestions of time and place but, on the contrary, by being very specific about both. The ideas and attitudes of sixteenth-century Sicily (or England) appear not very far removed, after all, from our own time, though still distanced from us sufficiently to afford an objective judgment that is vital for comedy. What then should we make of Michael Rudman's National Theater production of *Measure for Measure* at the Lyttleton Theatre in 1981? The setting was a contemporary Caribbean banana republic complete with palm trees and calypso music rather than Shakespeare's Vienna. The nearly all-black cast was not an unprecedented novelty, if an interesting innovation for this particular play. The Duke as a very relaxed ruler was perhaps too casual even for Shakespeare's Vincentio, as some thought, but Angelo and Isabella were the puritanical characters of the original. Little of the text was cut, and some songs and music were added.

Although the basic conception for this *Measure for Measure* was plausible and worked fairly well, it was not a smashing success. Why not? Probably because, in this instance, the conception was not exploited fully enough. The taste for a calypso *Measure for Measure* was merely whetted, hardly satisfied. One could see the potential for a rollicking, amoral ambience, but what was presented was—given the conception and its potential—much too restrained, or if not restrained, then underdeveloped. In other words, the transposition was not complete. It was at once too close and too far from Shakespeare's original. The equivalences in setting, characterization, and time were not worked out thoroughly, so that the production still looked like a transplant, not an indigenous flowering.[10] And that is precisely the danger in transposing Shakespeare's settings. The designer and director must go far enough to make the transposition appear not to be what it is—a transposition. The production must seem to be original to the time and place, even though we know it is not.

Finally, a word about the history plays, which would seem, quite rightly, to resist transposed settings of time and place. Yet some interesting attempts to do just this have been made. Not every aspect of *Richard II* quite fits a Marxist interpretation, but when in 1981 the Young Vic staged the play in the costume of revolutionary Russia, with Bolingbroke looking very much like Lenin and Richard like the hapless Czar, a certain point was made and a relevance established that connected the power politics of the fourteenth century (as seen by Shakespeare) with the power struggles among the Russians.

From here it is but a step to more or less complete adaptation, as in *Your Own Thing* (from *Twelfth Night*) or, at the extreme end, Kurosawa's film, *Throne of Blood* (from *Macbeth*). Much can be said that is instructive, as Ruby Cohn has done in her book *Shakespearean Offshoots*. In those cases Shakespeare's plays as we know them almost entirely vanish from sight, transformed into new images, often rich and strange ones. These involve major alterations of the text, not my present concern, which has been, rather, the visual aspects of the plays and their implications. As I have tried to show, they can help freshen our perspectives on Shakespeare's work, emphasizing relevance in startling and original ways that do not necessarily conflict with the essentials of the drama. Or they can so distract or distort that we find the connections between Shakespeare's original and the current production very far removed, so far that we may feel compelled to reject the production altogether. Taste, imagination, and wit are essential along with a deep understanding of—and respect for—the text. For that is always what we come back to in the end, remembering that in Shakespeare's "wooden O" sets as we know them were unheard of, as were lighting and many of the other advantages of contemporary technology. Modern set designers need hardly eschew these advantages; the danger lies when they become the controlling aspects of a production. For then we are indeed, as Ralph Berry warned, in "designers' theater" and no longer in Shakespeare's, where language and action are—and should remain—the primary elements of his dramatic art.

Figure 1. *As You Like It*, directed by Adrian Noble, Royal Shakespeare Company (1985). *(Photo courtesy of Joe Cock's Studio, Stratford-upon-Avon.)*

Figure 2. *Troilus and Cressida*, directed by Howard Davies, Royal Shakespeare Company (1985). *(Photo courtesy of Joe Cock's Studio, Stratford-upon-Avon.)*

Figure 3. *The Merry Wives of Windsor,* directed by Bill Alexander, Royal Shakespeare Company (1985). *(Photo courtesy of Joe Cock's Studio, Stratford-upon-Avon.)*

Figure 4. *Much Ado About Nothing,* directed by John Neville-Andrews, Folger Theatre. *(Photo courtesy of Joan Marcus.)*

Figure 5. *Much Ado About Nothing,* directed by John Neville-Andrews, Folger Theatre. *(Photo courtesy of Joan Marcus.)*

Figure 6. *Measure for Measure,* directed by Michael Rudman, National Theatre (1981). *(Photo courtesy of John Haynes.)*

Notes

This essay also appears in somewhat different form in Professor Halio's book *Understanding Shakespeare in Performance,* published by Manchester University Press.

1. In a seminar entitled "The Royal Shakespeare Company: Retrospect and Prospect," Shakespeare Association of America, Cambridge, Mass., April 1984.
2. Cf. John Barton, *Playing Shakespeare* (London: Methuen, 1984), 186: "I think the great question about changing the period of a play is 'Does it help unlock something that is truly in the text, or does it distort the play?' "
3. Benedict Nightingale considered Brook's *Dream* "perverse": see "Dream 2001," *The New Statesman* 80 (4 September 1970): 281, for the Stratford performance, and "Tripping Gaily," *The New Statesman* 81 (18 June 1971): 858–59, for the one at London's Alwych Theatre.
4. Cf. Gareth Lloyd Evans, "Shakespeare in Stratford and London, 1981," *Shakespeare Quarterly* 33 (Summer 1982): 187–88: "This production was, arguably, a mix-up amalgam of Brook's theatricality, Kott's misguided intellectuality, the RSC's own contemporary obsession with Dickens . . . and a few personal quiddities of the director."
5. In *On Directing Shakespeare,* ed. Ralph Berry (New York: Barnes & Noble, 1977), 124–26.
6. Ibid., 20.
7. In a comment upon a draft of this paper. I am indebted to Professor Clayton for this and many other useful remarks.
8. See Brook, 125, and Barton, *Playing Shakespeare,* 185.
9. Cf. Ian McKellen on John Barton's production of the play, set in the last days of the Empire in India: "I thought that [setting] released my view of the play enormously. It did what you always have to do with that play, which is to to provide a strict social set-up to explain why Beatrice is the woman she is and why Benedick is the man he is, and why they are somehow, despite themselves, trapped in a set of conventions" (*Playing Shakespeare,* 186).
10. Cf. John Elsom's review, "Bless My Soul," *The Listener* 106 (23 April 1981): 582: "It [Rudman's treatment of the play] is potentially exciting and radical, answering many questions posed by this fascinating and troublesome play, casting new light on them and transforming the tone from sombre tragi-comedy towards that of a less flippant *Candide.* The failures come when Rudman lacks the courage of his inspiration, either because he has not thought through the implications or because he was reluctant to carry them out."

Five Women Eleven Ways: Changing Images of Shakespearean Characters in the Earliest Texts

by STEVEN URKOWITZ

Half of Shakespeare's plays were published before the great collection of the 1623 First Folio. Eight of the plays were first printed in versions so different from later editions—in length, in details of plot and characterization, in imagery, verse forms, and vocabulary—that they have been called "the Bad Quartos." For most modern editors, all of the differences found between the early texts of *King Lear, Hamlet, Richard III, Merry Wives of Windsor, Henry V, Romeo and Juliet,* and *Henry VI, Parts 2 and 3* resulted from the activities of theatrical pirates, rogue stationers, small-part apprentice or journeyman players, and intrusive typesetters. Relatively little attention has been paid to the theatrical revisions evident in these textual variants; instead they have been examined primarily as philological or bibliographical accidents that befell supposedly unique Shakespearean originals.

But to understand the past and our perceptions of it, it may help to watch just how any of these texts were transformed by their contemporaries. Someone or other made changes in the extant texts. Rather than simply bewail their incompetence, I propose to look at systematic patterns of change, particularly differences in dramatic characterization as it is revealed by stage movement, physical gesture, and visible signs of a character's social power—issuing commands or obeying them.

Because some of the most striking instances occur among female characterizations, I have chosen variants found in the roles of five women: from the histories, Queen Margaret in two versions of the second and third parts of *Henry VI,* from the comedies Anne Page in the Quarto and Folio texts of *Merry Wives of Windsor,* and, from the tragedies, Juliet and Lady Capulet in equivalent moments as shown in the first and the second Quartos of *Romeo and Juliet,* and Queen Gertrude in Q1, Q2, and the Folio of *Hamlet.* We may find that the alternative "characteristics" may not be imagined with equal ease by readers untrained in the interpretation of theatrical scripts. But in every case each of the variant forms would be immediately recognizable as meaningful by people of the theater—directors, players, and audiences.

First Queen Margaret. In the opening scene of the 1594 text of *2 Henry VI,* at her first meeting with her husband, Margaret characterizes herself with ostentatious modesty:

> *Queene.* Th' excessive love I beare your grace
>   Forbids me to be lavish of my tongue,
>   Least I should speake more than beseemes a woman:
>   Let this suffice, my blisse is in your liking,
>   And nothing can make poore Margaret miserable,
>   Unlesse the frowne of mightie Englands King.
>   [A2v; 1.1.25–30][1]

Her bridegroom invites her to sit beside him; as far as we can tell she accedes; and then, following the King's command, the nobles of England greet the Queen while they stand about the royal thrones:

> *King.* Her lookes did wound, but now her speech doth pierce,
>   Lovely Queene Margaret sit down by my side:
>   And unckle Gloster, and you Lordly Peeres,
>   With one voice welcome my beloved Queene.
> *All.* Long live Queene Margaret, Englands happinesse.
>   [A2v; 1.2.31–37]

Margaret's first moments on stage in this text stress her own decorum, her acquiescence to the King's will, and her position of formal repose surrounded by attentive but upright peers.

The second script of this play, the 1623 First Folio, has Queen Margaret in contrast announce initially her boldness rather than her modesty.

> *Queen.* Great King of England, & my gracious Lord,
>   The mutuall conference that my minde hath had,
>   By day, by night; waking, and in my dreames,
>   In Courtly company, or at my Beades,
>   With you mine *Alder liefest* Soveraigne,
>   Makes me the bolder to salute my King,
>   With ruder termes, such as my wit affoords,
>   And over joy of heart doth minister.
>   [TLN 32–39]

Then, while the nobles salute the Queen, in the absense of any invitation from Henry to Margaret to sit, the Folio has the royal pair remain standing while all others onstage kneel.

> *King.* Her sight did ravish, but her grace in Speech,
>   Her words yclad with wisedomes Majesty,
>   Makes me from Wondring, fall to Weeping joyes,
>   Such is the Fulnesse of my hearts content.

Lords, with one cheerefull voice, Welcome my Love.
All kneel.
Long live Qu. Margaret, Englands happines.

[TLN 40–45]

Margaret's pride of place and her physical or visual dominance of the stage become the signifying gestures in this text, indicated at least as much by the stage movement as by the language.

A later example of variant gesture similarly affects the characterization of Margaret. Commoners appealing for help from the Protector of the Kingdom, Duke Humphrey, inadvertently approach Queen Margaret and her paramour, the Duke of Suffolk. In the earliest text, Suffolk reads a petition against his own actions, tears it, and drives the petitioners away:

> *Suffolke.* . . . Now sir what yours? Let me see it,
> Whats here?
> A complaint against the Duke of Suffolke for enclosing the
> commons of long Melford.
> How now sir knave.
> *1 Petitioner.* I beseech your grace to pardon me, me, I am but a Mes-
> senger for the whole town-ship.
> *He teares the papers.*
> *Suffolke.* So now show your petitions to Duke Humphrey.
> Villaines get you gone and come not neare the Court,
> Dare these pesants write against me thus.
> *Exet petitioners.*
>
> [B2v]

Suffolk explodes in a moment of irritation; his last line quoted appears to be directed to the Queen, the only other noble person onstage. The Folio however also has Suffolk read the misdirected petition, but then—only after a delay of five speeches (during which a different suit is dealt with) in the Folio—Queen Margaret rather than Suffolk tears the papers in what seems to be a meditated rather than eruptive action.

> *Suffolke.* . . . What's yours? What's heere? Against the Duke of Suf-
> folke, for enclosing the Commons of Melforde. How now,
> Sir Knave?
> *2 Petitioner.* Alas Sir, I am but a poore Petitioner of our whole Towne-
> ship.
> *Peter.* Against my Master Thomas Horner, for saying, That the
> Duke of Yorke was rightfull Heire to the Crowne.
> *Queene.* What say'st thou? Did the Duke of Yorke say, hee was right-
> full Heire to the Crowne?
> *Peter.* That my Mistresse was? No forsooth: my Master said, That
> he was, and that the King was an Usurper.
> *Suffolke.* Who is there?
> *Enter Servant.*
> Take this fellow in, and send for his Master with a Pursevant

presently: Wee'le heare more of your matter before the
King.
Exit.
Queene. And as for you that love to be protected
Under the Wings of our Protectors Grace,
Begin your Suites anew, and sue to him.
Teare the Supplication.
Away, base Cullions: Suffolke let them goe.
All. Come, let's be gone.   *Exit.*

[TLN 405–27; 1.3.20–41]

Margaret, not Suffolk, orders the petitioners away, and she further commands Suffolk to let them pass from the stage. Here variants show her
acting with aggressive strength and commanding the movements of others
on the stage.

A third variant presentation of Queen Margaret occurs at the opening of
a scene showing the court returning from a hunt with falcons. In the
Quarto text Margaret addresses her opening speech directly to her husband; she draws our attention almost deferentially towards his response,
and so for the moment Henry functions as a dominant figure in the group
even though Margaret is the one who speaks first.

*Enter the King and Queene with her Hawke on her fist, and Duke
Humphrey and Suffolke, and the Cardinall, as if they came from
hawking.*
Queene. My Lord, how did your grace like this last flight?
But as I cast her off the wind did rise,
And twas ten to one, old Jone had not gone out.
King. How wonderfull the Lords workes are on earth,
Even in these silly creatures of his hands,
Unckle Gloster, how hie your Hawke did sore!
And on a sodaine soust the Partridge downe.

[C1v]

After the first two lines of his speech, during which his own religious
enthusiasm is the primary focus, King Henry turns the conversation towards the Duke of Gloucester.

Margaret in the Folio, however, immediately takes for herself and firmly
holds the center of attention during her opening speech:

*Enter the King, Queene, Protector, Cardinall, and Suffolke, with
Faulkners hallowing.*
Queene. Believe me Lords, for flying at the Brooke,
I saw not better sport these seven yeeres day:
Yet by your leave, the Winde was very high,
And ten to one, old Joane had not gone out.
King. But what a point, my Lord, your Faulcon made,
And what a pytch she flew above the rest:

To see how God in all his Creatures workes,
Yea Man and Birds are fayne of climbing high.
[TLN 715–24; 2.1.1–8]

By addressing everyone in the group at once, the Queen "takes the stage," herself the most important figure. The King seems to wrest attention away from her and immediately directs it towards the Protector, Humphrey of Gloucester. As in the two earlier examples, Margaret is more dominant and more clearly seen in opposition to others in the Folio text than in the Quarto.

One last example of alterations in the character of Margaret can be found in *3 Henry VI*. The Queen arrives at the court of the King of France as a powerless fugitive seeking his help. In a direct recapitulation of the image of her arrival as a bride in the court of England, the King of France invites her to ascend to a throne beside him.

> *Enter king Lewis and the ladie Bona, and Queene Margaret, Prince Edward, and Oxford and others.*
> Lewis. Welcome Queene Margaret to the Court of France,
> It fits not Lewis to sit while thou dost stand,
> Sit by my side, and here I vow to thee,
> Thou shalt have aide to repossesse thy right,
> And beat proud Edward from his usurped seat,
> And place king Henry in his former rule.
> Queen. I humblie thanke your royall majestie,
> And pray the God to heaven to blesse thy state,
> Great king of France, that thus regards our wrongs.
> [C8v; 3.3.1–16]

Like the earlier moment in the first version of *2 Henry VI*, Margaret in the first text apparently joins the royal figure. And like the Folio version of the earlier scene, in the Folio text here Margaret instead has a bolder action. The Folio stage direction makes explicit an action possible in the earlier text: Lewis enters and sits down, only to rise and invite Margaret to join him.

> *Flourish.*
> *Enter Lewis the French King, his Sister Bona, his Admiral, call'd Bourbon: Prince Edward, Queene Margaret, and the Earle of Oxford. Lewis sits and riseth up againe.*
> Lewis. Faire Queene of England, worthy Margaret.
> Sit downe with us: it ill befits thy State,
> And Birth, that thou should'st stand, while Lewis doth sit.
> Margaret. No, mightie King of France: now Margaret
> Must strike her sayle, and learne a while to serve,
> Where Kings command. I was (I must confesse)
> Great Albions Queene, in former Golden dayes:
> But now mischance hath trod my Title downe,

> And with dis-honor layd me on the ground,
> Vhere I must take like seat unto my fortune,
> And to my humble Seat conforme my selfe.

[TLN 1720–35]

"Sit down with us," says the King. She refuses Lewis's offer and instead drops down to the stage floor, "on the ground." Lewis reacts to her move with great sympathy: for a royal person, sitting on the bare earth was a conventional gesture of grave despair (see Constance in *King John* [TLN 990–96; 2.4.114], Richard II ["For Gods sake let us sit upon the ground," F2v, 3.2.155], and King Lear, in the Quarto version of 3.2.42, where Kent says to the King, "Alas sir, sit you here?" [F4]). The king eventually raises her to sit beside him:

> *Lewis.* Why say, faire Queene, whence springs this deepe despaire?
> *Margaret.* From such a cause, as fills mine eyes with teares,
>   And stops my tongue, while heart is drown'd in cares.
> *Lewis.* What ere it be, be thou still like thy selfe,
>   And sit thee by our side. *Seats her by him.*

[TLN 1736–41]

In the Folio text, Margaret arrests and holds our attention even in her moments of political weakness. The thirteen-line interval between his first offer and her acceptance forms a kind of theatrically ornamented excursion out of the simple action of taking a seat.

I chose these four moments from among hundreds of textual variants relating to Margaret's role in the two versions of the *Henry VI* plays. The alternative texts certainly seem to merit our closest attention as plans for theatrical action and as alternative codes for revealing dramatic character. We may not have enough evidence to determine just who was responsible for these variants, but both versions should be analyzed further. The alternative versions certainly appear purposeful and consistent. They reveal the ways stage action and stage dialogue inextricably combine to create what we perceive in the theater as dramatic character.

I will pass very briefly over two further examples of similar character changes in other plays before turning to consider the role of Gertrude in the three *Hamlet* texts. The first of these character variants is found in *Merry Wives of Windsor*. In the Quarto version of 3.4, specific commands in the dialogue direct characters to move about the stage forming whispering groups: "Come hither daughter, Sonne Slender let me speake with you," says Master Page; "Speake to Misteris Page," says Quickly to Fenton; Page again directs further action, "Come wife, you an I will in, weele leave M. Slender / And my daughter to talke together. M. Shallow, / You may stay sir if you please"; and Shallow urges Slender "To her cousin, to her." Only the parents and parental surrogates in this text—Page and Mistress Page, Quickly and Justice Shallow—speak commands that move others around the stage, and in the Quarto text each of their orders is obeyed; those commanded go where they are sent.

Ann Page in the Folio version of 3.4 breaks the "adult" monopoly of movement-commands. She proposes the first tête-à-tête in the scene when she beckons Fenton to move with her out of hearing of Quickly, Shallow, and Slender, saying, "harke you hither" (TLN 1591; 3.4.21), and later she drives Shallow away so that she may speak with Slender alone (TLN 1617–18; 3.4.50–51). Through her control of action and stage movement, Ann Page takes on visible authority as an effective, active person unlike the essentially passive persona of her Quarto equivalent.

Romeo and Juliet offers variant designs for two women's roles, Juliet and Lady Capulet. Variants between the First and Second Quarto of *Romeo and Juliet* systematically increase the coercive pressures mounted by Lady Capulet on her daughter. In the First Quarto text of 1.3, for example, Lady Capulet delicately introduces the topic of marriage to her daughter.

> *Wife.* And that same marriage Nurce, is the Theame
>   I meant to talke of: Tell me Juliet, howe stand you affected
>   to be married?
> *Juliet.* It is an honor that I dreame not off.
> *Nurce.* An honor! were not I thy onely Nurce, I
>   would say thou hadst suckt wisedome from thy Teat.
> *Wife.* Well girle, the Noble Countie Paris seekes
>   thee for his Wife.
> *Nurce.* A man young Ladie, Ladie such a man as all
>   the world, why he is a man of waxe.
> *Wife.* Veronaes Summer hath not such a flower.
> *Nurce.* Nay he is a flower, in faith a very flower.
> *Wife.* Well Juliet, how like you of Paris love.
> *Juliet.* Ile looke to like, if looking liking move,
>   But no more deepe will I engage mine eye,
>   Then your consent gives strength to make it flie.
>   *Enter Clowne.*
> *Clowne.* Madam you are cald for; supper is reddie,
>   the Nurce curst in the Pantrie, all thinges in extreamitie,
>   make haste for I must be gone to waite.
>   [B4v-C1; 1.3.63–105]

Juliet's modest and agreeable reply seems to match the temper of Lady Capulet's gentle presentation.

In contrast, the Second Quarto presents Lady Capulet as a hard-driving advocate for Paris, directing Juliet's responses, and repeatedly demanding an immediate reply to Paris' offer.

>   . . . tell me daughter Juliet,
>   How stands your disposition to be married?
>
> Well thinke of marriage now, . . .

> this then in briefe:
> The valiant Paris seekes you for his love.
>
> What say you, can you love the Gentleman?
>
> Reade ore . . . finde delight, . . . Examine . . . see
> . . . find . . .
>
> Speake briefly, can you like of Paris love?

[B4v–C1]

While Juliet makes the same reply here as in the earlier text, it seems now self-protective rather than excited, a brief three-line reply to a sixteen-line demand, rather than an expansive three-line response coming after a series of single-line comments and questions.

Where apparently the three women exited together in the first text, the second presents an alternative in which, I believe, Juliet hesitates, prompting Lady Capulet and the Nurse to urge her forward.

> *Servant.* Madam the guests are come, supper serv'd up, you
> cald, my young Lady askt for, the Nurse curst in the Pantrie,
> and everie thing in extremitie: I must hence to wait, I
> beseech you follow straight.
> *Mother.* We follow thee, Juliet the Countie staies.
> *Nurse.* Go gyrle, seeke happie nights to happie dayes.
>> *Exeunt.*

Unnecessary if Juliet "followed straight" upon the servant's beseeching, "Go gyrle" and "Juliet the Countie staies" indicate the child's reticence, an unwillingness to plunge into the high-pressure whirl of Veronese sexuality. Both Juliet and her mother perform significantly different actions in these alternative texts.

The last of the five women, the Queen in *Hamlet,* appears differently in the 1603, 1605, and 1623 texts of her play. For example, in the Q1 version (as in the play's sources) Gertrude learns of both the King's murder of her first husband and his intentions to kill Hamlet. In the later texts she knows neither. The three examples I have chosen here give some idea of the "characteristic" differences in a few of the scores of detailed and "theatrically visible" actions found in the multiple texts.

In the first meeting with Rossencraft and Gilderstone in the Q1 version, the Queen stands as a cipher; the King dominates the action, he alone sets the task for Hamlet's fellows, and he promises to reward their labor.

> *Enter King and Queene, Rossencraft, and Gilderstone.*
> *King.* Right noble friends, that ouor deere cosin Hamlet
> Hath lost the very heart of all his sence,
> It is most right, and we most sory for him:
> Therefore we doe desire, even as you tender
> Our care to him, and our great love to you,

> That you will labour but to wring from him
> The cause and ground of his distemperancie.
> Doe this, the king of Denmarke shal be thankefull.
> *Rossencraft.* My Lord, whatsoever lies within our power
> Your majestie may more commaund in wordes
> Then use perswasions to your liege men, bound
> By love, by duetie, and obedience.
> *Guilderstone.* What we may doe for both your Majesties
> To know the griefe troubles the Prince your sonne,
> We will indevour all the best we may,
> So in all duetie do we take our leave.
> *King.* Thankes Guilderstone, and gentle Rossencraft.
> *Queene.* Thankes Rossencraft, and gentle Gilderstone.
>
> [D3]

Gilderstone gives the cue for their exit, and the Queen simply echoes the King's farewell.

In the Second Quarto and Folio texts, however, the Queen acts independently. Instead of simply observing her husband's actions, she rather than the King promises to reward the two young men, and she rather than Guyldensterne commands their exit.

> *Queene.* . . . Your visitation shall receive such thanks
> As fits a Kings remembrance.
>
> . . . And I beseech you instantly to visite
> My too much changed sonne, goe some of you
> And bring these gentlemen where Hamlet is.
> *Guyldensterne.* Heavens make our presence and our practices
> Pleasant and helpfull to him.
> *Queene.* I Amen.   *Exeunt Ros and Guyld.*
>
> [E3]

Here Q2 gives us an active and involved character where Q1 has only the idea or symbol of a Queen and mother, a costumed figure who stands for royalty in her regal costume rather than demonstrates royalty through regal behavior.

Three radically different versions of Ophelia's entrance after she has gone mad give additional alternative character traits for the Queen. The simplest, found in Q1, again shows her as a relatively passive mirror of events, a surface without independent motives for action:

> *Enter King and Queene.*
> *King.* Hamlet is ship't for England, fare him well,
> I hope to heare good newes from thence ere long,
> If every thing fall out to our content,
> As I doe make no doubt but so it shall.
> *Queene.* God grant it may, heav'ns keep my Hamlet safe:
> But this mischance of olde Corambis death,
> Hath pierced so the yong Ofeliaes heart,

    That she, poore maide, is quite bereft her wittes.
  King. Alas deere heart! And on the other side,
    We understand her brother's come from France,
    And he hath halfe the heart of all our Land,
    And hardly hee'le forget his fathers death,
    Unlesse by some meanes he be pacified.
  Queene. O see where the yong Ofelia is!
    Enter Ofelia playing on a Lute, and her haire downe singing.

                      [G4v]

The Queen reports Ophelia's change, and then she announces the girl's entrance. In the equivalent passage in Q2, a Gentleman reports Ophelia's madness to the Queen. She resists any interview with the girl:

    Enter Horatio, Gertrard, and a Gentleman.
  Queene. I will not speake with her.
 Gentleman. Shee is importunat,
    Indeede distract, her moode will needes be pittied.
  Queene. What would she have?
 Gentleman. She speakes much of her father, . . .
        . . . her speech is nothing,
    Yet the unshaped use of it doth move
    The hearers to collection, . . .
  Horatio. Twere good she were spoken with, for shee may strew
    Dangerous conjectures in ill breeding mindes,
    Let her come in.

                      [K4]

Both the Gentleman and Horatio indicate the political need for hearing Ophelia, and finally either the Queen gives her tacit assent or Horatio interprets her silence as assent and gives it for her. ("Let her come in" directed by Horatio to the Queen will lead to one set of possibilities; directed offstage or to the Gentleman the same line takes on other meanings. The text is ambiguous.) Next, it appears that either Horatio or the Gentleman goes out to admit Ophelia, and, as Ophelia stands silently at the entry, the Queen in this text has a four-line aside (marked in the Second Quarto by inverted commas) revealing her own emotional turmoil.

    Enter Ophelia.
  Queene. 'To my sicke soule, as sinnes true nature is,
    'Each toy seemes prologue to some great amisse,
    'So full of artlesse jealousie is guilt,
    'It spills it selfe, in fearing to be spylt.
  Ophelia. Where is the beautious Majestie of Denmarke?

Although the Queen here is in motion, alive and responsive, we see her primarily directed by others, manipulated indeed by Horatio and the Gentleman, men of far lower social status.

 In the Folio text of this passage, only she and Horatio enter, Horatio

taking the speeches assigned to the Gentleman in Q2. Here a more independent Queen herself recognizes the political need to confront Ophelia,
and she commands Horatio to bring the girl in. Further, when he leaves,
the Queen's revery upon her soul changes from an aside on a busy stage to
a full soliloquy.

> *Queene.* 'Twere good she were spoken with,
> For she may strew dangerous conjectures
> In ill breeding minds. Let her come in.
> To my sicke soule . . .
>
>   [TLN 2759–62]

Alone on stage, the Queen has the audience's undivided attention. These
variants make the Queen's character at once more intelligent and commanding, more poignant, and I believe for an audience more troubling
than the equivalents in the First and Second Quartos.

Literary taste finally determines whether variants such as these are
worthwhile examining. Philip Edwards, in his edition of *Hamlet* (Cambridge, 1985), argues: "In order to save on characters, F gives the Gentleman's speeches to Horatio, and Horatio's to Gertrude. This greatly
coarsens the way Ophelia's madness is introduced" (p. 193n). First, I must
note that "saving" characters is not a problem in English Renaissance
stagecraft, only saving actors, scarce commodities only in those scenes and
scene-transitions requiring epic displays of many figures onstage at one
time. This scene is not one of them; literary or dramatic considerations may
underly the variant, but certainly the change does not resemble theatrical
economies found elsewhere in the casting of English Renaissance plays.
Second, Edwards does not explain why an assertive Gertrude, seen alone
making her own politically sagacious decisions, should be necessarily
"coarse." The suppression of the Folio version in Edwards' and virtually all
modern printed texts of *Hamlet* perhaps tells us something about editorial
perceptions of powerful women. It certainly keeps us from thinking about
the shifting potentialities of this moment as they appear in the earliest
printed texts, whoever may have been responsible for them.

My final example shows how early textual variants again create and alter
what we mean by "Shakespearean character." In the climactic duel of the
last scene the Q1 text gives the Queen two actions to play.

> *King.* Here Hamlet, the king doth drinke a health to thee.
> *Queene.* Here Hamlet, take my napkin, wipe thy face.
> *King.* Give him the wine.
> *Hamlet.* Set it by, I'le have another bowt first,
>   I'le drink anone.
> *Queene.* Here Hamlet, thy mother drinkes to thee.
>   *She drinkes.*
> *King.* Do not drink Gertred: O t'is the poysned cup!

                                                            [13]

First she offers her handkerchief for Hamlet to wipe his face, and then she drinks down the poison meant for him. She dooms herself at the same moment her action gives the audience another false hope, like his unexpected fencing victory, that Hamlet may yet slip through the King's snares. But as soon as she drinks off the wine, the subsequent stage action demands that we turn our attention away from her. Hamlet and Laertes must immediately "take the stage" and we necessarily watch them in the vigorous action of the duel.

> *Hamlet.* Laertes come, you dally with me,
>   I pray you passe with your most cunningst play.
> *Laertes.* I! say you so? have at you,
>   Ile hit you now my Lord:
>   And yet it goes almost against my conscience.
> *Hamlet.* Come on sir.
>   [I3v]

As elsewhere in the First Quarto text, during the ensuing sword-play the Queen fades into the background of male-dominated action.

The Second Quarto packs far more movement—many more dramatic incidents—into the equivalent passage, and it gives us more time to be attentive specifically to the Queen's role. As in Q1 the Queen offers her handkerchief to her son. Then, in the same speech, she immediately raises the poisoned cup to salute him. Hamlet acknowledges her gesture before she drinks. The King tries to stop her as in Q1, but the Queen, now caught up in the ceremony of toast and carouse, swallows the draught.

> *Queene.* . . . Heere Hamlet take my napkin rub thy browes,
>   The Queene carowses to thy fortune Hamlet.
> *Hamlet.* Good Madam.
>   *King.* Gertrard doe not drinke.
> *Queene.* I will my Lord, I pray you pardon me.
>   *King.* It is the poysned cup, it is too late.
> *Hamlet.* I dare not drinke yet Madam, by and by.
> *Queene.* Come, let me wipe thy face.
>   [N4v]

Next, the text strongly implies that the Queen must herself offer the lethal cup to Hamlet, prompting his next line: "I dare not drinke yet Madam." If a production follows the cues set in the dialogue, the audience and the King, painfully aware that the Queen must die in a moment, watch her move to caress her beloved son. "Come, let me wipe thy face." This physical touch is the only gentle contact between mother and son dictated by the play's dialogue or stage directions. The touch marks the Queen's ultimate moment of transition, as she skids from life over the brink into death. (I will not speculate what a good Freudian critic might say about this conjunction of a loving touch and proximate death, especially considering that the only other physical contact between Gertrude and Hamlet—during the Closet Scene when, I believe, he reaches out and forcibly constrains her: "Come, come, and sit you downe, you shall not boudge, / You goe not . . ."— immediately precipitates the death of Polonius.) Gertrude's action here, at once maternal and sensual, indicates the great potential for humane emotional expression and its horrid waste in a world armored like rotten Denmark.

After observing these differences, what consequence? The simplest should be that we read, criticize, and perform these multiple text plays in their multiplicity. For starters, perhaps we should all ring up our favorite publishers asking for new facsimile editions of the Quartos, less ponderous, less expensive, and more serviceable than the University of California volume.

But there is a further consequence. Looking only at the poetry, the psychology, or the grand meaning, or the profound sweeping influences of Shakespeare's plays can be very profitable for the teacher or the student or the performer. However, if we notice the kinds of detail thrown into sharp relief by the superposition of the texts—moments like Margaret's greeting to King Henry, or doomed Gertrude's wiping the brow of her doomed son—then these variants seem to demand that we also look more carefully than we ever have at the fleeting experience of stage presentation itself, as it was encoded in the extant scripts printed four centuries ago.

Note

Research for this study was funded in part by a Fellowship from the National Endowment for the Humanities; an earlier version appears in Konrad Eisenbichler and Philip Sohm, eds., "The Language of Gesture in the Renaissance: Selected Proceedings of the Conference held in Toronto, November 1983," *Renaissance and Reformation*, n.s., 10 (1986).

1. I have taken quotations from Shakespearean quarto texts from Michael J. B. Allen and Kenneth Muir, eds., *Shakespeare's Plays in Quarto* (Berkeley and Los Angeles: University of California Press, 1981); those from the Folio are from Charlton Hinman, ed., *The Norton Facsimile: The First Folio of Shakespeare* (New York: W. W. Norton, 1968). I have also used through line numbers from Hinman's facsimile and modern act, scene, and line numbers from *The Riverside Shakespeare*. In all quotes, *u* and *v, i* and *j*, and *s* and long *s*, as well as typographic ligatures and turned letters are regularized according to modern conventions; italicized English words in the dialogue of the original are here given in roman type; stage directions and speech headings originally in roman type are here given in italic.

The Unstable Image of Shakespeare's Text

by STANLEY WELLS

All of us live with multiple images of Shakespeare's texts, images derived from our experiences of his plays in performance as well as on the page. We accept this multiplicity more readily in the theater than in the study, though anyone interested in the history of Shakespeare in performance will be accustomed not merely to hearing heavily adapted versions of Shakespeare's texts, but to reading printed acting versions that consciously diverge from the texts presented to contemporary readers as the genuine article. Theatergoers who saw early performances of Colley Cibber's *Richard III* could also read printed texts of his adaptation as well as the text of Shakespeare's play printed in the Fourth Folio and, later, editions from Rowe's onwards; admirers of David Garrick could see him as Romeo, read his adaptation of *Romeo and Juliet,* and also read Warburton's, Johnson's, or Capell's text. In the late nineteenth century, you could not only see Henry Irving as Hamlet and read the acting text printed as a souvenir of the performance; you could also buy the Henry Irving Shakespeare, in which a text of *Hamlet* is printed to the accompaniment of a variety of algebraical symbols indicating what happened to it when acted (like about half of it being cut), and then, to soothe your beating mind, you could read Edward Dowden's Arden edition straight through. In the present century the practice of issuing acting editions has dwindled but not died out; for instance, the BBC accompanied its television series with reprints of every play from Peter Alexander's edition, also marked up with changes made in production.

In many ways the acting editions—and the unpublished acting versions— are as important as what I will call, for want of a better word, the scholarly editions. Texts of the plays as performed, from the bad quartos printed in Shakespeare's lifetime up to and beyond John Barton and Peter Hall's *Wars of the Roses* (published by the BBC in 1970), tell us as much about the image of Shakespeare that has existed in the minds of civilized persons of the time as the "received" versions, the literary editions unaffected—or only subconsciously affected—by contemporary theatrical practice. For the historian of taste, acting editions can well be the more revealing documents.

It is, nevertheless, the scholarly editions from which the others derive. There they are, all rent to pieces and mounted in the prompt-books in the Shakespeare Centre: cut-up pages from the New Temple, the Penguin, the New Penguin, the Arden, with lines—sometimes lots of them—marked for omission, phrases snipped out, words altered, words—sometimes lots of them—added, arrows marking transpositions: confusing palimpsests, but underneath them, faintly discernible, lie the printed remains of editions over which scholars have labored to establish a text that shall be as close to Shakespeare's final intentions as their efforts, and those of generations of their predecessors, can accomplish.

The contrast between what we accept in the theater and what we read on the page points to a difference in expectation. In the theater we accept fluidity (or we stay away). If we have any sense of the way theater has to work, we grant directors the right to adapt the texts to their particular social and theatrical circumstances. When we judge the results, we may find them wanting; but there can be very few scholars nowadays, even among editors, who insist that when they go to the theater they should invariably hear totally pure texts presented in their entirety. In editions, however, we look for stability. We want texts from which we can quote in the expectation that the words we reproduce will be the same as those in other editions; we want to be able to cite references that can be used with concordances and other works of reference; we want texts that will not confuse our students, that will create for them the image of a Shakespeare who is immutable, constant, solidly *there,* like a national monument or Mount Everest.

This desire is apparent in the search of scholars for a "standard" edition. For a long time they thought they had one. Not all that long ago, the Globe text, dating from 1864, was still regularly used for quotations and references; even now it crops up occasionally: Dr. Rowse reprinted it, whole and entire, for his annotated edition a few years ago. Eventually, Shakespeare scholars were forced to acknowledge that a textual revolution had occurred, and attention shifted to Peter Alexander's one-volume text published in 1951; but this shift was eased by a compromise, because Alexander's text adopts the Globe line-numbering. This works well enough for scenes that are written entirely in verse, but is infuriating for prose: it means, for instance, that if you start counting the lines in Hamlet's "Yorrick" speech forward from the previous line number you find when you have got to line 195 that it is numbered 191; and if you try to count back from any particular number, you arrive at a conclusion different from that reached when you count forwards. That way madness lies.

This compromise is symptomatic of the inhibiting effect on editors of the desire for stability. The peculiar image of Shakespeare as a universal author, and especially as a universal instrument of education, imposes exceptional constraints on editors. On the one hand they know that as scholars their duty is to present the truth, the whole truth, and nothing but the truth—as they see it—about Shakespeare's text. On the other hand, they are made aware that, though they may be allowed some ideas of their own, they run the risk of outraging the scholarly community if the texts that, they believe, conform to truth are more than a little different from those to which we are all accustomed—on the page, though not in the theater.

In case you think I am exaggerating, I should like to give a few examples—first, of some seminal ideas about the text of Shakespeare that have been propounded in comparatively recent years, that have won a degree of scholarly acceptance, but that have nevertheless had no effect, or virtually no effect, on published editions.

Let me start with an uncontroversial example. No one doubts that, in *Love's Labor's Lost,* Biron's great hymn to the power of love, as printed in both quarto and Folio, includes both unrevised and revised versions of one substantial passage. As originally printed, the speech—4.3.285–361—is made up of seventy-seven full lines and two half-lines. In the eighteenth century, Warburton, without comment, omitted three lines that are approximately repeated later. Dr. Johnson restored them, attributing Warburton's omission to "mere oversight"; Capell omitted two passages totaling thirteen lines, but Steevens reprinted the speech in full while commenting, "Perhaps the players printed from piece-meal parts, or retained what the author had rejected, as well as what had undergone his revisal." In spite of Monck Mason's attempt to defend the repetitions on the grounds that "Biron repeats the principal topics of his argument, as preachers do their text, in order to recall the attention of the auditors to the subject of their discourse," the belief that the speech contains first and second drafts took hold and was expressed by the (old) Cambridge editors, who wrote, "There can be no doubt that two drafts of the speech have been blended together, and that the author meant to cancel a portion of it"; but they shied away from doing anything about it: "as there also can be no doubt that the whole came from his pen, we do not venture to correct the printer's error. We would 'lose no drop of the immortal man.'" That attitude would be acceptable from the editors of a facsimile or a diplomatic reprint, but in an edition that overall makes every attempt to correct error—as the old Cambridge edition does—it amounts to a total abnegation of editorial responsibility. Yet it is the attitude that, with one or two exceptions, has prevailed. The next significant stage in treatment of the passage came in 1923, when Dover Wilson worked out that it contains twenty-one consecutive unrevised lines—eight more than Capell had omitted—and this is generally agreed; yet editors continue to print the revised and unrevised versions within the body of the text: sometimes, as in Kittredge and Alexander, the unrevised lines are italicized; other editions, such as Dover Wilson's, Bevington's, the Pelican, and the Riverside bracket them; but to the best of my knowledge only Sisson (in

1954) and John Kerrigan (in the New Penguin edition of 1982) take the unrevised lines out of the text. Of course, the unrevised lines are fascinating, but it seems unfair both to the reader and to Shakespeare to print them as if they were part of a final version of the play.

Let me move to another example affecting brief passages in a single play, this time involving addition rather than omission. I am thinking now of the Hecate scenes in *Macbeth*. It is a rather more complicated matter than *Love's Labor's Lost*, because of doubts about the authenticity of the episodes. There might be a case for removing them altogether, and I think those editors who believe that *Macbeth* as printed in the Folio represents the play as Shakespeare wrote it with simply the addition of passages by another hand should do this; but there are good reasons to suspect that adaptation extends to other parts of the play and is not simply a matter of omission and addition; if this hypothesis is granted, editors may legitimately retain the Hecate scenes (as all of them have) on the grounds that the best we can do is to represent as accurately as possible the text as adapted for performance at some date between its initial composition and its first publication. As you know, that text includes the cue lines for two songs, one beginning "Black spirits, etc.," the other "Come away, come away." These songs are not merely extant in Middleton's manuscript play *The Witch;* they were also used in Davenant's 1672 adaptation of *Macbeth* for which he is highly unlikely to have had access to the Middleton manuscript and so must be supposed to have used theatrical manuscripts associated with pre-Restoration performances of *Macbeth* itself. It is, then, quite possible for an editor to attempt a reconstruction of the Hecate scenes in full, with their songs intact as they were performed by the King's Men; and to do so produces, in my opinion, very interesting results, as I found recently in preparing these scenes for the Complete Oxford Shakespeare. To print the dialogue of the scenes without believing it to be by Shakespeare, but to give only the cue-lines of the songs, as all editors do, seems a feebly half-hearted procedure. The principle was stated by J. M. Nosworthy in 1965 in another seminal remark that has not borne fruit in any edition so far published: "There is every reason why the two songs should be incorporated in the main text since they were clearly an integral part of the play in its later form, and since songs, whether or not Shakespeare wrote them, are normally set out in full in both quartos and Folio."[1]

My examples so far relate to specific passages in particular plays. I turn now to a far more pervasive matter. In 1970 the late, lamented Jürgen Schäfer published a remarkably thorough and scholarly article entitled "The Orthography of Proper Names in Modern Spelling Editions of Shakespeare."[2] Discussing the spelling of proper names that either have historical associations outside the plays or are significant in themselves, he shows, as Richard Proudfoot said in a review, "that recent editors of modernised texts have been thoroughly inconsistent in handling these names and argues that they should all be modernised on the grounds that no consistent Elizabethan form exists and that 'the principle of full modernization, once embraced, has to be applied without exception since it is the only method, paradoxically enough, that is able to reflect the Shakespearian meaning within the new context.'"[3] Proudfoot accepted Schäfer's case. Again, this should have been a seminal article, but most of its seeds have fallen on stony ground: for instance, every edition of *A Midsummer Night's Dream,* and every edition of *Love's Labor's Lost,* except the New Penguin, published since the article appeared still spells "Moth," not "Mote," although as Schäfer claimed, "there is general scholarly agreement that Shakespeare intended *Mote* in both these plays"; the Arden editor of *A Midsummer Night's Dream* (1979) actually writes in a note, "Almost certainly Shakespeare had in mind not moth but mote, of which moth is a regular Elizabethan and Shakespearian spelling," and produces much supporting evidence, yet, although in general his principles of modernization are not particularly conservative of old spellings, he retains the traditional, and misleading, form here.

For the final part of my paper I want to move on to what is, I suppose, the most contentious—and also perhaps the most potentially exciting—issue in Shakespearean textual criticism at the present time. This is the question of whether or not Shakespeare revised his plays, and, if so, whether it is possible to recover any of them in more than one state. For a long time the dominant image of Shakespeare's practice in this respect has been that once he had brought a play to a finished state, he did no more to it. On the whole this has been the orthodoxy of the New Bibliography, and although even so authoritative a figure as W. W. Greg occasionally inclined to the belief that signs of revision can be detected in some texts, such suspicions have so far exerted practically no influence on the editorial tradition. But in recent years the orthodoxy has begun to crumble. The argument centers on four plays: *Hamlet, Troilus and Cressida, Othello,* and *King Lear.* Let me, with all convenient speed, summarize the situation for each of them.

There are two good texts of *Hamlet,* the 1604 quarto and the 1623 Folio. The Folio includes about 80 lines that are not in the quarto, but omits about 230 lines that are there. There are many verbal variants, some easily explained as misreadings in one text or the other—the quarto is particularly badly printed—but enough that cannot so easily be explained as to have given rise to what Harold Jenkins (who is opposed to the idea) calls "the fancy of Shakespearian revision."[4] In 1965 E. A. J. Honigmann proposed that "Despite the multiplicity of patently corrupt variants in *Hamlet* it may be . . . that some of the indifferent or trivial variants are authorial."[5] A major problem, of course, is whether the Folio omissions are the result of accidents in the process of transmission or whether Shakespeare himself authorized them. Philip Edwards, in his New Cambridge edition published in 1985, teeters on the edge of accepting the idea that they are the result of revision; he is convinced that certain passages were marked for omission in Shakespeare's manuscript and exercises considerable ingenuity in exonerating Shakespeare from the accusation of having sought to withdraw them as the result of experience of the play in the theater; finally he prints them in the body of the text (though within square brackets). He admits outright that the fear of being accused of "arrogance and eccentricity" has led him to act against the courage of his conviction that they should be omitted altogether.[6] G. R. Hibbard, in his Oxford edition, throws caution to the winds and relegates these passages to an appendix; the Complete Oxford Shakespeare will adopt the same course. There has been a remarkable swing in opinion in three editions published within five years of one another.

Now *Troilus and Cressida*. There are about five hundred substantive differences between the 1609 quarto and the First Folio; the Folio contains 45 lines or part-lines not found in the quarto. Theories of revision are not new: the old Cambridge editors thought that the Folio represented a revision of the quarto text, and Peter Alexander that the quarto represented the revision. E. K. Chambers, in 1930, denied that either text had been revised,[7] but in 1942 W. W. Greg cautiously admitted the possibility of revision, and in 1955 he posited that the quarto was printed from Shakespeare's transcript of his foul papers, and that in the course of copying he made "many small changes in the text. Whenever he was dissatisfied with an expression he doubtless altered it if on the spur of the moment he could devise a better."[8] This, as you will realize, is a concise summary of the major theme of the book from which I adapt the title of my paper, *The Stability of Shakespeare's Text,* by Ernst Honigmann. Honigmann (in 1965) made an extended statement of the case in favor of Greg's theory and in opposition to Alice Walker's belief "that all Shakespeare's first and second thoughts stood in a single arch-text from which both the Q and F texts derive" (pp. 78–95). In 1982 Gary Taylor returned to the old Cambridge editorial position with fresh arguments that the quarto was printed directly from the foul papers and the Folio from a promptbook, implying that the Folio represents revisions made probably before performance (which might, therefore, even by editors inclined to the view that postperformance alterations are likely to have been forced upon Shakespeare, be supposed to represent Shakespeare's second thoughts).[9] For all this, editors have gone on producing eclectic texts.

The position for *Othello* is rather similar. The quarto lacks about 160 lines printed in the Folio, and there are over one thousand other verbal variants. Again Alice Walker was a doughty opponent of the revision theory, but Greg admitted that the Folio might contain "alterations made by the author or with his authority after his draft had been officially copied."[10] M. R. Ridley, in his Arden edition (1958), argued that the Folio contained "probably a good deal of Shakespeare's second thoughts" (p. xliii), Honigmann sought to establish "a strong presumption that the variants in *Othello* include authorial afterthoughts,"[11] and Nevill Coghill, in what should have been a seminal chapter of his *Shakespeare's Professional Skills*, of 1964, took the argument a step further by proposing that the quarto represents the play as first performed, that Shakespeare "noted certain confusions and weaknesses in the play" and, some years later, "sat down to purge and improve the play in ways he had for some time occasionally meditated."[12] Norman Sanders, in his New Cambridge edition published in 1984, declares his "strong impression . . . that what we are dealing with is Shakespeare's first version of the play (behind Q) and his own transcription of it (behind F), during the process of making which he not only created additions for dramatic clarification or imaginative amplification but was also enticed into changes in words and phrases which appeared to him at the time as improvements on his first thoughts" (p. 207). This is the revisionist position. The logical consequence of it is, surely, that an editor should base his text on one or the other early text, not, like Mrs. Todgers, go "dodging among the tender pieces with a fork." But Sanders conflates the two early editions, claiming that "Providing the editor supplies sufficient collation for the reader to reconstruct Q1 and F in the original form, he is free to offer what he thinks to be a 'best' version of the play in the full knowledge that in fact he is making a third version of it" (ibid.). This is eclecticism run riot.

Finally, it seems necessary only to mention the *cause célèbre* of recent years, the case of *King Lear*, which, since Michael Warren gave his seminal paper "Quarto and Folio *King Lear* and the Interpretation of Albany and Edgar"[13] at the Shakespeare Congress in Washington ten years ago, has become such a battleground for the revisionist cause. It is the most important case, because the sum total of the differences between the two substantive texts of this play (if we accept that there *are* two substantive texts) amounts not merely to a series of local differences but to a substantial shift in the presentation and interpretation of the underlying action. The traditionally conflated text, then, produces not simply a play that is longer than either of the alternative versions, nor one that requires merely the suppression of a number of localized readings from one text in favor of those from another, but a play that contains irreconcilable elements.

I have not, of course, been trying within so small a compass to persuade you of the truth of the revisionist cause. But I hope I have demonstrated that there is at least a substantial, and growing, body of opinion that the two substantive texts of each of, at least, the four plays I have mentioned allow us to see it at two different stages of its composition. The prospect is, surely, exciting: one might even argue that it opens up the most potentially illuminating area of critical investigation of Shakespeare's creative processes that has been available since the plays were first printed. Yet in spite of this editors go on attempting to produce a single text of each of these plays, a text that will inevitably suppress some variants that the editors themselves believe to be authentically Shakespearean. It is understandable that editors of the complete works should feel that they must make a choice, that their readers want to read *Hamlet*, not *Hamlet* Mark 1 and *Hamlet* Mark 2, and it is perhaps understandable that they should therefore base a text on the one that they regard as closest to Shakespeare's final version, while adding to it bits that are present only in the other version. It is, I say, understandable, even though its effect might resemble that which would be achieved by an art expert faced with two versions of a portrait who decided that the best way to represent them would be by superimposing one upon the other, even if in the process he made the sitter appear to possess four eyes. But not all editors of Shakespeare are producing editions of the complete works, and there is surely room, among the many editions that now appear, for some conscious experimentation. Even if it is not absolutely, finally established that we have two independent early texts of *Hamlet, Troilus and Cressida, Othello,* and *King Lear,* surely it would be valuable for some editor to take the risk of offering the reading public a fully edited text based on the supposition that we can recover two different states of each play: a text, that is, which is not eclectic but attempts to represent the play in either its unrevised or its revised state. I say "take the risk" because the matter is not without its commercial considerations. Publishers hope for large sales for their Shakespeare editions, and because the Shakespeare plays that sell best are those that are most often set as examination texts, they prefer them to be as uncomplicated as possible. Even some university teachers blanch at the thought of introducing their students to the complexities of textual criticism and to the subtleties of comparative criticism. It has been seriously presented to me as an argument against including two versions of *King Lear* in a complete Shakespeare that to do so would run the risk of puzzling the reader. So, paradoxically, it is the very commercial profitability of Shakespeare that militates against a reasoned willingness to investigate the independent evidence of distinct texts in favor of a flattening process that seeks uniformity and denies diversity. The editor's task is to provide accurate images of his author's achievements; it is grotesque to suggest that he should pervert the truth in order to supply easy teaching aids.

I have a private title for this paper that I was deterred from using on the printed program by the superior refinement of my colleagues. To myself, I call it "The Shakespearean Vasectomy: Seminality and Infertility in Textual Criticism." I have illustrated a number of ideas that, though they might properly be called seminal, have so far proved wholly or largely infertile. But if you go into a vasectomy clinic you may, I am told, see a drawer in a filing cabinet marked "Reversals." My colleagues and I on the Oxford Shakespeare have been laboring to create fertility where before there was barrenness. I have deliberately confined myself in this paper to ideas that have been propounded by earlier scholars, outside the Shakespeare department of Oxford University Press; but we have had a few ideas of our own, too, many (though not all) of them emanating from the fertile brain of my colleague Gary Taylor. I hope the results of our efforts will be an edition that, though it may be accused of "arrogance and eccentricity," will visibly display the courage of our convictions and will come to be seen as an attempt to present readers with a truer image of Shakespeare's texts than would have been possible had we not garnered and planted the seeds sown by our predecessors and colleagues.

Notes

1. J. M. Nosworthy, *Shakespeare's Occasional Plays* (London: E. Arnold, 1965), 53.

2. *Studies in Bibliography* 23 (1970):1–19.

3. *Shakespeare Survey 24* (1971):176.

4. Arden edition (1982), 60.

5. E. A. J. Honigmann, *The Stability of Shakespeare's Text* (London: E. Arnold, 1965), 78, summarizing Peter Alexander's conclusions in "*Troilus and Cressida,* 1609," *The Library* 4 (1928–29):267–86.

6. New Cambridge edition, 32.

7. E. K. Chambers, *William Shakespeare: A Study of Facts and Problems,* 2 vols. (Oxford: Oxford University Press, 1930), 2:441.

8. W. W. Greg, *The Editorial Problem in Shakespeare* (Oxford: Oxford University Press, 1942; 3d edition, 1954), 113–14; *The Shakespeare First Folio* (Oxford: Clarendon Press, 1955), 347–48.

9. Gary Taylor, "*Troilus and Cressida:* Bibliography, Performance, and Interpretation," *Shakespeare Studies* 15 (1982):99–136.

10. Greg, *First Folio,* 369.

11. Honigmann, *Stability,* 110.

12. Nevill Coghill, *Shakespeare's Professional Skills* (Cambridge: Cambridge University Press, 1964), 201.

13. In *Shakespeare: Pattern of Excelling Nature,* ed. David Bevington and Jay L. Halio (Newark: University of Delaware Press, 1976), 95–107.

German Shakespeare Translation:
The State of the Art

by PETER WENZEL

Almost universally, histories of translations have a tendency to degenerate into petty complaints about failures, aberrations, and bad taste, and this is small wonder, since for centuries translation at large has been viewed as an unreliable, imperfect, if not fraudulent art.

Of course there are historical reasons for these views. As Hans-Georg Gadamer has stressed,[1] translation is a hermeneutical task. It rests upon general assumptions about the aims of interpretation and the nature of literature, and since until recently these assumptions were focused on the authors rather than the recipients and on the timeless rather than the historical aspects of great works of art, it was quite natural that the only acceptable goal in translation was the ideal version, rendering the original without any losses, once and for all.

It is for this reason that past discussions on Shakespeare in German have usually resulted in an attempt to define the optimum translation of his works and provide a definitive answer to the question "What is the genuine, the original Shakespeare?"[2] Correspondingly, the history of Shakespeare translation in Germany was expected to be an evolutionary development, coming closer and closer to the original,[3] or else dismissed as a failure and a disparagement of the Bard.

Now, far from suggesting that such criteria as authorial intention and closeness to the original are unimportant for judging the merit of a translation, I think that this approach to the problem is no longer feasible. Under the influence of new paradigms in the theory of literature,[4] recent theories of translation have provided us with more appropriate concepts of what translations can reasonably achieve. A translation can never be a timeless, perfect equivalent of the original; rather, it must be evaluated according to its purpose,[5] and this purpose may vary depending on the particular historical situation out of which the translation arises and the group of people to which it is addressed. Under these conditions, optimum translations are no longer ideal versions, but "such translations as meet communicative demands of a certain society at a certain time in the best possible way."[6]

It is from this revised standpoint, then, that I shall try in my paper to sketch the situation of Shakespeare translation in Germany and analyze its present problems and needs.

For more than 150 years, the German Shakespeare has been regarded as largely identical with the romantic Shakespeare translation by August Wilhelm Schlegel, Ludwig Tieck, and their collaborators. And I think that in fact, the Schlegel-Tieck version can be called both an achievement and a legend in the history of German Shakespeare translation. It was an historic achievement because Schlegel, proceeding on the romantic assumption that the reader of a translation should remain fully aware that he is reading a work of foreign origin,[7] created an astonishingly accurate version of Shakespeare's plays. This is confirmed, for instance, by the fact that in a recent linguistic study in the reliability of five German Shakespeare translations, Schlegel still comes off better than two of the modern translators.[8] From a different viewpoint, however, the matchless brilliance of Schlegel's translation is also a legend. For in the course of the almost two hundred years that have passed since Schlegel began his translation, the German language has inevitably changed. Thus, many words and syntactic structures in Schlegel-Tieck do not sound natural any longer, but somewhat antiquated or even strange, particularly on a modern stage.[9] Moreover, scholars generally agree nowadays[10] that Schlegel and Tieck could not avoid being influenced by the aesthetic conventions of their own age and therefore tended to reduce the linguistic audacity of their original, tempering and generalizing its meanings and toning down the immediacy and sharpness of its expressions. In Schlegel-Tieck, for instance, the rhythm is much more regular than in Shakespeare, and so is the syntax. The strangeness of Shakespeare's images is often blunted, his puns are bowdlerized, and some of his ambiguities are dissolved. What was for a long time seen as a timeless all-purpose translation, then, turns out to be the translation of a particular age aimed at a particular audience—namely the readers of romantic poetry.

In view of these findings it appears quite logical that modern German Shakespeare translators, when vying for the attention of the public, have usually tried to improve on Schlegel-Tieck in one of the above-mentioned respects. But what they ultimately achieved was in reality not very different from the translation of their famous predecessors.[11] For like them, they tried to create an ideal all-purpose version that would meet the demands of both the theater and the readers, and in doing so, they all too often fell between two stools.

The most typical example of this is the fate of the much-disputed Shakespeare translator Hans Rothe, who in trying to make the German Shakespeare more speakable and more appropriate for the stage, was not afraid to take great liberties with Shakespeare's texts such as altering their tone, simplifying their diction, and cutting or adding individual lines or even scenes.[12] And in fact, this earned him a considerable influence on the stage. But as Rothe would not content himself with creating a version only for the purposes of the theater, he began to defend his alterations with untenable theories about the textual history of Shakespeare's plays, and in doing this he incurred the anger of many Shakespeare scholars.[13]

In summary, then, the recent history of Shakespeare translation in Germany confirms the necessity to create different translations for different purposes. And I think that this necessity will become even more urgent in the future. For it appears to me that the so-called crisis in modern German Shakespeare translation[14] is largely due to the fact that the interests of the two major customers of Shakespeare translations, the reading public and the theater, are developing more and more into different directions.[15] While the readers, who often have an elementary command of English themselves, usually want to study the plays in detail and thus call for a semantically accurate translation rendering all the subtleties, ambiguities, and complexities of Shakespeare's language, the theater demands a more stagy translation that sounds at least tolerably natural, is easily speakable and not too difficult to understand. And I think that the only way to satisfy these divergent interests of the readers and the theater will be to concede each group its own version of the plays.

For readers the most suitable version will consist in bilingual editions with the original text printed on the one side and a fairly literal prose translation on the other. Such editions have been provided in recent years in the course of two study-projects that are so important that it is worth discussing them in some detail.[16]

The two projects were initiated, independently of each other, by two pilot study-groups at the Universities of Bochum and Basel, who developed the overall concepts and the guidelines for the new prose translations. The translations themselves were then carried out in English departments of various universities and published in two series, the one under the patronage of the *Deutsche Shakespeare-Gesellschaft West*, the other by the Reclam publishing house.

The series of the *Shakespeare-Gesellschaft*, which is the more scholarly edition, comprises seven volumes so far, namely *Measure for Measure, Othello, Richard II, The Merchant of Venice, The Comedy of Errors, Troilus and Cressida*, and *The Winter's Tale*. Further volumes are in preparation, though their publication is not financially easy, since naturally the German market for a Shakespeare edition of that size is not particularly large. The Reclam series is better off in this respect since its volumes are much smaller, cheaper, and therefore easier to sell. This edition, which is often used in the classroom, comprises fifteen plays so far, among them all of the great tragedies, the more important comedies, and three histories. And again, the publication of further volumes is intended.

In all cases, it is the aim of the new translations to render the originals in a prose version as closely as possible, without claiming any poetic qualities, and thus to assist the semibilingual reader in struggling through Shakespeare's texts on his or her own.[17] As the German versions are complemented by footnotes and, in case of the *Shakespeare-Gesellschaft* edition, by a running commentary, the function of the new translations is not very different from that of a modern English edition in the New Arden or Oxford series.

Without carrying praise too far, it can be said that the new prose translations have got a very positive reception from both the critical and the general reading public. Many of the new translations have been reviewed favorably and are frequently used in teaching at schools and universities.[18]

Nevertheless, the new translations leave open a number of questions. For it becomes clear at a somewhat closer inspection that among the individual prose translators, the consensus on basic principles of translation is in reality much smaller than one would have supposed. Although they all seem to agree that semantic accuracy should take priority in their translations, they obviously differ on the question of how far that priority should go. There are translators, for instance, who confess in their prefaces that in spite of the primacy of sense equivalence, they have tried to maintain certain features of the original's formal structure, such as alliteration, consonance and assonance, anaphora, and other rhetorical devices.[19] Another point of considerable disagreement among the new prose translators is the problem of how to treat such key words as, let us say, "honest" in *Othello* and "bond" in *The Merchant of Venice*. There are translators who think that such terms, due to their importance in critical discussions of the plays, should be rendered by one and the same expression in German,[20] while others prefer to look for different equivalents depending on the particular context in which the key words occur. The full dimensions of this problem become clear, for example, when we imagine what would be lost in Othello's jealous exclamation "I think my wife be honest" (3.3.390)[21] if one tried to replace the word "honest" by such English synonyms as "upright" or "trustworthy."[22]

Now, my own view of these problems is that most of them could easily be solved if translators reflected more carefully on the purpose of their translation. For if one proceeds on the assumption that it should be the primary aim of a prose translation to help the semibilingual reader in deciphering the sense of the original, then it is certainly better to search in each case for the closest semantic approximation than to bother about rhymes, verbal patterns, and other poetic features of the text that a skillful reader will be able to follow up by himself.[23]

If, on the other hand, it is the purpose of a translation to serve as a text for the stage, the formal structure of the original, including rhyme and verse, must definitely not be ignored. For it is quite clear that the linguistic audacities of Shakespeare's style will only sound acceptable when embedded in verse[24] and that similar systems of versification will be more likely to produce a similar effect upon a stage than an original and its exact prose equivalent.[25] These considerations, then, lead me straight to my final topic—Shakespeare translations for the present-day German theater.

Of the almost three hundred Shakespearean plays performed on Austrian, Swiss, and West German stages from 1978 to 1983, nearly seventy-five—that is, roughly speaking, one quarter—still follow the classical Schlegel-Tieck version.[26] A second quarter is made up by the cases in which the director or a member of his staff makes up his own version, usually on the basis of Schlegel-Tieck, sometimes on the basis of some early prose translation. This leaves about another half of the acting texts to the modern translators, with Frank Günther, a newcomer to the business, being surprisingly more than twice as popular as Hans Rothe, who is closely followed by two other fairly recent Shakespeare translators, Erich Fried and Wolfgang Swaczynna. In addition, there are a fair number of translators whose versions were performed less than ten times in the period in question, among them Richard Flatter, Rudolf Schaller, and several other East German translators.

This account is remarkably similar to the situation in the GDR, where Schlegel-Tieck still make up one-fifth of the translations and where the growing influence of fairly recent translations like those of B. K. Tragelehn and Maik Hamburger is equally conspicuous. The most important result of this statistical survey—apart from the durability of the Schlegel-Tieck translation—is the rise of a new generation of Shakespeare translators— Frank Günther, Erich Fried, and Wolfgang Swaczynna on the one side, B. K. Tragelehn and Maik Hamburger on the other, which has begun to outstrip such translators as Rothe, Flatter, and Schaller, who are still regarded as the most important modern translators in the literature on the subject.

What is even more surprising is the fact that there seems to be considerable consensus among these recent translators on the major objectives of a modern Shakespeare translation. Thus, they all voice the idea that a modern translation, though it should be well adapted to the demands of the stage, must never try to simplify Shakespeare: speakability and clarity are important aims of a good translation, but the complexity of Shakespeare's texts must not be abolished.[27] Second, they all seem to agree that a modern translator should not follow the blank verse pattern too slavishly, since Shakespeare himself handled this pattern much more flexibly than Schlegel-Tieck and their immediate successors.[28] Third, all of the very recent translators try to write in contemporary diction so that one is much less likely to come across archaisms, weird poeticisms, and trivial metaphors in their translations than in the versions of the translators working some decades ago.[29]

At a closer analysis, however, it becomes obvious that in spite of these common features, there is also a considerable degree of plurality in the recent approaches since each of the new verse translators has his individual preferences and ideals. Frank Günther, for instance, who within a few years has become the most popular translator on the stages in the West, is particularly interested in wordplay, phonological repetitions, verbal patterns, and other complexities of Shakespeare's language. If he does not succeed in rendering such devices directly, he is not afraid to resort to the principle of dynamic equivalence, inventing new wordplays or inserting equivalent phonological repetitions in different places.[30] Erich Fried, the Austrian poet and Shakespeare translator, matches Günther in his efforts to stress the linguistic audacity of Shakespeare's texts and has rightly been praised for the outstanding faithfulness of his versions,[31] but he keeps closer to the elevated diction of traditional Shakespeare translations. Wolfgang Swaczynna[32] moves along very different lines: he is often particularly literal in his renderings of short phrases and quick repartees, thus managing to convey something of the immediacy and sharpness of Shakespeare's language that the traditional translations tended to gloss over. Moreover, he cuts all stage directions, act and scene divisions, uses rhythmical rather than grammatical punctuations, splits up long sentences, and is thus most successful in clearing the German Shakespeare of the long-windedness and heaviness that the more progressive directors so often complained about.[33] However, by his intention to demystify Shakespeare, he is often tempted into skipping the more daring linguistic features of the originals, especially their startling images and freshly coined words. Contrary to such tendencies, the East German translators are not afraid to confront their audience with an unfamiliar language. Drawing on the model of the socialist verse drama in the GDR, they handle the blank verse flexibly but pay particular attention to the metrical density and rhythmical peculiarities of Shakespeare's lines.[34] To make the rhythm of their translations correspond as closely as possible to the originals, they resort to the unusual device of forcing the German language into the English syntax, which is usually done by anticipating verbs, postponing adverbials or attributes, and using many participle and infinitive constructions.[35]

Whatever one may think of all these strategies, at least one result seems to emerge from the above discussion: there are no longer any reasons to speak of a crisis in German Shakespeare translation. Rather, we have a plurality of new and promising approaches that are all useful in their different ways since they illustrate various possibilities of going beyond the classical Schlegel-Tieck version. Nor must the plurality of the new approaches be interpreted as a sign of uncertainty and confusion because in their variety one can also spot certain spheres of agreement. Thus both the new prose and the new verse translators seem to share the opinion that sense equivalence is more important than harmony of form; that if formal devices are important, they must never be allowed to adopt the function of a straitjacket; and that a good translation should not try to normalize Shakespeare, but fully render the variety and audacity of his style.

In summary, then, it appears that German Shakespeare translation today does not lack orientation and fresh ideas. What would be desirable, however, is a somewhat broader discussion of its ideas. Not very much academic work has been done so far, especially in the West, in the recent translations, and the translators themselves rarely have the opportunity to exchange their views. Nor do I think that under the present circumstances a renewed debate between scholars, translators, and directors on the problem of Shakespeare translation could lead to a revival of the animosities that such debates sometimes produced in the past, especially if all participants keep in mind that Shakespeare translation is not a matter of discovering the ultimate truth about the Bard, but of rendering his works for the particular needs of a particular audience in a particular historical situation, so that many translations have a right to exist.

Notes

1. Hans-Georg Gadamer, *Wahrheit und Methode: Grundzüge einer philosophischen Hermeneutik* (Tübingen: Mohr, 1960), 365.

2. Cf. Willy Jäggi, forward to *Der deutsche Shakespeare*, Theater unserer Zeit, No. 7 (Basel: Basilius, 1965), 7: ". . . immer wieder [haben sich] Männer daran gesetzt, einzelne Stücke oder das gesamte dramatische Oeuvre des Briten neu zu übertragen. . . . Welches aber ist der echte, der ursprüngliche Shakespeare?"

3. On this evolutionary model of the history of translations (and the opposite, more modern view that translations should mainly conform to the particular needs of their age) see Ulrich Suerbaum, "Shakespeare auf deutsch—Eine Zwischenbilanz," *Deutsche Shakespeare-Gesellschaft West: Jahrbuch* (Heidelberg) (1972): 42–66, especially 43–44; for a nice formulation of the evolutionary view of translation, see Walter Jost: "Stilkrise der deutschen Shakespeare-Übersetzung," *Deutsche Vierteljahrsschrift für Literaturwissenschaft und Geistesgeschichte* 35 (1961): 1–43: ". . . So stellt sich die Frage: ist der deutsche Geist auf gutem Wege—näher zu Shakespeare?" (quotation from p. 2).

4. I am mainly referring here to the epistemological innovations caused by Marxism, Structuralism, and Reception Theory.

5. See, for instance, Katharina Reiß and Hans J. Vermeer, *Grundlegung einer allgemeinen Translationstheorie*, Linguistische Arbeiten, No. 147 (Tübingen: Niemeyer, 1984), 96, 100, and 123.

6. R. van den Broeck (1980), quoted in Reiß and Vermeer, *Translationstheorie*, 141; for a similar definition, see Eugenio Coseriu, "Falsche und richtige Fragestellungen in der Übersetzungstheorie," in *Theory and Practice of Translation: Nobel Symposium 39, Stockholm, September 6–10, 1976*, ed. Lillebill Grähs, Gustav Korlén, and Bertil Malmberg (Bern, Frankfort on the

Main, and Las Vegas: Lang, 1978), 17–32, esp. 32, and Rudolf Zimmer, *Probleme der Über-setzung formbetonter Sprache: Ein Beitrag zur Übersetzungskritik*, Beihefte zur Zeitschrift für Romanische Philologie, No. 181 (Tübingen: Niemeyer, 1981), 165, who supports Coseriu's views.

7. On the romantic ideal of a literal, non-"naturalizing" manner of translation, see Winfried Sdun, *Probleme und Theorien des Übersetzens in Deutschland vom 18. bis zum 20. Jahrhun-dert* (Munich: Hueber, 1967), 37ff and 49ff; Karl Maurer, "Die literarische Übersetzung als Form fremdbestimmter Textkonstitution," *Poetica* 8 (1976): 233–57, esp. 242–45; and Armin Paul Frank, "Theories and Theory of Literary Translation," in *Literary Theory and Criticism: Festschrift Presented to René Wellek in Honor of his Eightieth Birthday*, Part I: *Theory* (Bern, Frankfort on the Main, and New York: Lang, 1984), ed. Joseph P. Strelka 203–21, esp. 205.

8. Norbert Hofmann, *Redundanz und Äquivalenz in der literarischen Übersetzung: dargestellt an fünf deutschen Übersetzungen des "Hamlet"*, Studien zur englischen Philologie, n.s., no. 20 (Tübingen: Niemeyer, 1980). The five translations compared with each other were Schlegel, Rothe, Flatter, Schaller, and Fried, with Fried coming off best before Schaller, closely followed by Schlegel and far ahead of Flatter and Rothe (see 224–25).

9. For the discussion of a few examples, see Eike Gramss and Frank Günther, "Shake-speare übersetzen—Shakespeare inszenieren," *Deutsche Shakespeare-Gesellschaft West: Jahrbuch* (1984): 13–31, esp. 16ff.

10. See, for instance, Margaret E. Atkinson, *August Wilhelm Schlegel as a Translator of Shakespeare: A Comparison of Three Plays with the Original* (Oxford: Basil Blackwell, 1958), 8–50; Rudolf Stamm, "Probleme der Shakespeare-Übersetzung" (1963), in Rudolf Stamm, *Zwischen Vision und Wirklichkeit* (Bern and Munich: Francke, 1964), 63–84, esp. 70–71; P. M. Daly, "Die Schlegel-Tieck-Übersetzung von *Hamlet*," in *Der deutsche Shakespeare*, 75–93; Ulrich Suerbaum, "Der deutsche Shakespeare, 75–93; Ulrich Suerbaum, "Der deutsche Shakespeare: "Über-setzungsgeschichte und Übersetzungstheorie," in *Shakespeare: Eine Einführung*, ed. K. Muir and S. Schoenbaum, trans. O Weith and D. Klose (Stuttgart: Reclam, 1972), 259–74 and 284–88, esp. 270; and Martin Lehnert, "Shakespeare in der Sprache unserer Zeit," *Shakespeare Jahrbuch* [GDR] 114 (1978): 65–69, esp. 66.

11. Cf. Suerbaum, "Shakespeare auf deutsch," 60.

12. Rothe's alterations of Shakespeare's texts are so fundamental that in a recent critical study his work has been placed near the modern Shakespeare adaptations (see Horst Zander, *Shakespeare "bearbeitet": Eine Untersuchung am Beispiel der Historieninszenierungen 1945–1975 in der Bundesrepublik Deutschland*, Tübinger Beiträge zur Anglistik, No. 3 [Tübingen: Narr, 1983], 102–8).

13. A fair impression of the acrimony with which Rothe's Shakespeare was disputed can be obtained from some of the papers collected in *Der deutsche Shakespeare* (cf. esp. Rudolf Frank, "Geflügelte und beschwingte Worte: Zu den Übersetzungen von Hans Rothe," 109–19, as against Rudolf Stamm, "Der elisabethanische Shakespeare?", 128–40); on the debate in general, see Ruth Freifrau von Ledebur, *Deutsche Shakespeare-Rezeption seit 1945*, Studienreihe Humanitas (Frankfurt on the Main: Akad. Verlagsgesellschaft, 1974), 52 and 117.

14. Cf. the title of Jost's essay: "Stilkrise der deutschen Shakespeare-Übersetzung," and Ulrich Suerbaum, "Shakespeare-Tagung in Frankfurt 1970: Bericht der Arbeitsgruppe zum Thema 'Probleme der Shakespeare-Übersetzung,'" *Deutsche Shakespeare Gesellschaft-West: Jahr-buch* (1971): 11–17, esp. 11.

15. Cf. Suerbaum, "Shakespeare auf deutsch," 47–50.

16. For previous discussions of the two projects, cf. Suerbaum, "Shakespeare-Tagung 1970," 12–17; Jörg Hasler, "Shakespeare in German," *Shakespeare Quarterly* 23 (1972): 455–57; and Rüdiger Ahrens, "Moderne Shakespeare-Übersetzungen in Prosa," *Der fremdsprachliche Unterricht* 15 (1981): 298–301.

17. For brief descriptions of the aims of the two projects, cf. Werner Habicht, Ernst Leisi, and Rudolf Stamm, "Vorwort der Herausgeber," reprinted in all volumes of the *Shakespeare-*

Gesellschaft edition, and Ulrich Suerbaum, foreword to W. Shakespeare, *King Lear/König Lear: Englisch und Deutsch,* ed. Raimund Borgmeier and Barbara Puschmann-Nalenz (Stuttgart: Reclam, 1973), 3–10; for a detailed discussion of particular problems of translation that the new prose editions will be able to solve, see Norbert Greiner, "Purpose and Problems of a New German Shakespeare Translation," in *En torno a Shakespeare: Homenaje a T.J.B. Spencer* ed. Manuel Angel Conejero (Valencia: Universidad, 1980), 159–85.

18. Reviews of the new translations are to be found in the yearbooks of the two German Shakespeare societies: *Deutsche Shakespeare-Gesellschaft West: Jahrbuch* (1974): 245–47; (1977): 167–77; (1978–79): 328–33; (1984): 245–50; and *Shakespeare Jahrbuch* [GDR] 114 (1978): 172–74; 116 (1980): 155–56; 118 (1982): 169–70; 120 (1984): 183–86).

19. Cf. Dieter Hamblock's preface to his translation of Marlowe's *Edward II,* which has appeared in the same series as his Shakespeare translations (Stuttgart: Reclam, 1981), esp. 4–5.

20. Cf. Hamblock's preface to his translation of *Othello* (Stuttgart: Reclam, 1976), 4–5.

21. Quoted from the New Arden edition.

22. Accordingly, the new prose translators try different solutions to the problem. Thus Hamblock keeps to the principle of rendering "honest" as "ehrlich" without bothering about the question of semantic accuracy, while Balz Engler in the *Shakespeare-Gesellschaft* edition of *Othello* (1977) uses "ehrbar" when referring to Desdemona and "redlich" when referring to Jago without bothering about the unity of the pattern. However, it is the translator of the *Shakespeare-Gesellschaft* edition (Ingeborg Heine-Harabasz, 1982), who has the most consistent solution to "bond" in *The Merchant of Venice* (namely "Schuldschein"; only initially "Bürgschaft"), while the translator of the Reclam edition (Barbara Puschmann-Nalenz, 1975) varies her translations continually ("Verpflichtung"—"Vertrag"—"Pfand"—"Anspruch"—"Vertragsverpflichtung").

23. For a similar view, see André Lefevere, *Translating Poetry: Seven Strategies and a Blueprint,* Approaches to Translation Studies, No. 3 (Assen and Amsterdam: Van Gorcum, 1975), 97. The point that readers, even if they have little or no knowledge of the language being used, will still be able to understand the formal patterns in a text is nicely made by Geoffrey N. Leech, *A Linguistic Guide to English Poetry* (London: Longman, 1969), 85.

24. This is rightly stressed by Balz Engler in Raimund Borgmeier, Balz Engler, Karl Maurer, Ulrich Suerbaum et al., "Shakespeare-Übersetzungen (Text und Bochumer Diskussion)," *Poetica* 4 (1971): 82–119, esp. 111.

25. Cf. Suerbaum, "Der deutsche Shakespeare," 263.

26. The numbers are based on the annual records in the yearbooks of the two German Shakespeare societies.

27. Cf. Günther, "Shakespeare übersetzen," 17–19; Erich Fried, "Möglichst nah am Original," *Theater heute* 4, no. 6 (1963): 30–31; Wolfgang Swaczynna, preface to his translations (published by the Bärenreiter-Verlag in Kassel); Eva Walch, "Zwei neu deutsche Übersetzungen von Shakespeares *The Tempest,*" *Shakespeare Jahrbuch* [GDR] 116 (1980): 101–19, esp. 101 (on Tragelehn and Hamburger).

28. Cf. Fried, "Möglichst nah am Original," 31; Swaczynna, preface to his translations, s.v. "Der shakespearesche Versrhythmus;" and Heiner Müller, Maik Hamburger, and B. K. Tragelehn, "Shakespeares Stücke sind komplexer als jede Aneignung—man braucht zu verschiedenen Zeiten verschiedene Übersetzungen: Ein Gespräch," *Theater heute* 16, no. 7 (1975): 32–37, esp. 34–35.

29. On archaisms, weird poeticisms, and trivial metaphors in the translations of Rothe and Flatter, cf. Ingeborg Heine in "Shakespeare-Übersetzungen (Diskussion)," 106–7, and Suerbaum, "Shakespeare auf deutsch," 60.

30. For a justification of these strategies, cf. Günther, "Shakespeare übersetzen," 20–26.

31. Cf., for instance, Rudolf Stamm, "Erich Fried als Shakespeare-Übersetzer: Bemerkungen zum ersten Band seines Übersetzungswerkes," *Deutsche Shakespeare-Gesellschaft West: Jahrbuch* (1971): 23–34, and Hofmann, *Redundanz und Äquivalenz,* 224.

32. For a detailed and well-informed discussion of Swaczynna's achievement, cf. Volker

Schulz, "A New German Shakespeare Translator: Wolfgang Swaczynna," *Shakespeare Transla-tion* 4 (1977): 71–97. Schulz is certainly right in putting Swaczynna above the previous translators in many respects, but I think that he fails to recognize Swaczynna's tendency to temper the linguistically difficult passages in Shakespeare.

33. Cf., for instance, the voices in favor of Rothe in *Der deutsche Shakespeare*, 148–56.

34. Cf. Walch, "Zwei neue deutsche Übersetzungen," 103 and 112ff.

35. For a detailed description of these devices, which are more typical of Tragelehn than of Hamburger, cf. Rainer Priebs, "Syntaktische Abweichung als Wirkungsmittel in der Shake-peare-Übersetzung B. K. Tragelehns," *Shakespeare Jahrbuch* [GDR] 114 (1978): 131–41.

Editing Shakespeare for "Foreigners": The Case of the English-German Studienausgabe *of Shakespeare's Plays*

by KLAUS BARTENSCHLAGER

The years since 1976 have seen the publication of several volumes of the *Englisch-Deutsche Studienausgabe,* which will eventually be a complete edition of Shakespeare's plays in English for German readers. Shakespeareans in seven universities in the Federal Republic of Germany, Switzerland, and Austria are collaborating on this project, which is being carried out under the general editorship of W. Habicht, E. Leisi, and R. Stamm and the patronage of the West German Shakespeare Society.[1]

The obvious question is why a German edition of the whole canon should be produced at all. More and more English editions are being published all the time, and these are not only of a high scholarly standard, but are also cheaper than the *Studienausgabe* can ever be, with its comparatively small potential market. A broad answer to this question is contained in R. B. McKerrow's remark that there might "be at least half a dozen editions of the works of Shakespeare executed on quite different lines, each of which, to one group of readers, would be the best edition possible."[2] One such group would certainly be readers whose native language is not English, with their specific premises and their particular difficulties in reading Shakespeare. The *Studienausgabe* may deserve to be brought to the attention of non-German Shakespeareans for its general implications in the editing of Shakespeare for foreigners.

The edition was not, however, initially conceived with such general principles in mind. It was undertaken as a direct response to the crisis in German Shakespeare translation and the treatment of Shakespeare's texts on the German stage in the fifties and sixties. At the time there was widespread dissatisfaction with the classical Schlegel-Tieck translation, which at that time—even more so than today—was thought to be dated because of its mellowing of Shakespeare's verse, style, and realism to fit the ideals of the age of Goethe. There were many new attempts at a new

German Shakespeare, but the only ones to hold the stage were Hans Rothe's versions, which were both extremely free and philologically irresponsible. Home-made translations and adaptations were the order of the day. The German Shakespeare Society entered the lists under the banner of "Fidelity to the Text" (Werktreue), and an embittered, sometimes polemical debate ensued about an authentic German Shakespeare for our time. It was the more considerate men of the theater who squared scholarly reproaches by asking for a scholarly contribution to a better understanding of Shakespeare's plays, reminding German Shakespeareans that since Nicolaus Delius[3] in the nineteenth century they had not produced an edition catering for the special needs of and making the results of modern scholarship available to a German readership. In a proposal to the Shakespeare Society Hans Schalla, the director of the Bochum Schauspielhaus, presented the idea that what the theaters needed was not so much a new poetic translation of the plays but rather an exact prose version with a thorough commentary to provide a sound basis for translators and theater people.

This idea was taken up and a bilingual edition with a moderately scholarly commentary was projected. Squabbles over the concept[4] and its commercial prospects led to a most unfortunate split right at the start, which by necessity brought about a polarization of concepts. While the *Reclam Shakespeare*[5]—without a general editor and a recognizable concept—skimmed the cream off the market with cheap and basically unscholarly editions of only the more popular plays,[6] the *Studienausgabe* had to define its concept all the more carefully.[7] By the time the first volume appeared it had become much more ambitious than what had been planned at the outset.

Asking for the concept of an edition is the same as asking for its intended readers. The audience that the *Studienausgabe* aims at consists not so much of professional Shakespeareans but rather of nonspecialist German readers with a sufficient grasp of English, and willing (or forced) to tackle Shakespeare seriously in the original language. These are mainly people of the theater, translators or translation critics, students, high school teachers, and a certain number of enthusiasts. The *Studienausgabe* wants to serve readers like those better than English editions can, for, after all, the project can only be justified if it accomplishes what English editions cannot, or do not to the same extent, and if these differences result from the particular needs and interests of German users. In effect two specific problem areas are added to the general problems of presenting Shakespeare's text and providing adequate help for the reader's understanding of it. First, problems arise from the fact that the intended readers' native language is not English. Second, problems come from the fact that the readers belong to a specific cultural milieu in which Shakespeare's works have for over two hundred years played an enormous role that is quite different from the one they have had in Britain or America.

In the field of linguistic competence obvious facts like the continuous faultiness of German translations or the almost unsurmountable difficulties that even university students have with Shakespeare's language reveal the problem. Whether we like it or not, most German readers of English editions find English commentary notes quite as difficult as Shakespeare's text itself. And it is not just the vocabulary of textual and literary technicalities but quite as often the simple glosses and paraphrases that they cannot exactly understand without thumbing a dictionary, something which they, more often than not, hesitate to do. The objection that at least students of English should learn by using English editions is debatable. Considering, however, the dwindling role literary studies play in our curricula, the time left for reading Shakespeare might be turned to better use by concentrating on Shakespeare's English without the distraction of perfecting one's modern English at the same time. It is basically for this reason that courses on English literature are conducted in German in most German universities.

Therefore the fact that the *Studienausgabe* is written in German is important, although, of course, this is not sufficient justification for its production. If it were only a question of linguistic competence it might be just as good to translate the New Arden Shakespeare or any other of the new editions, which on the whole are very good, and which, in spite of their claiming that they approach the problem of editing Shakespeare in a new, fresh, and different way, are growing more and more similar, if not interchangeable.

There are, however, whole areas where the commentary of English editions is simply not sufficient for foreign readers. An example of this from the area of language is the insufficient treatment of Shakespeare's wordplay. Where the native reader very often needs but a hint, the foreigner needs an explanation. The clearly observable tendency of recent English editions to replace explanation by glossing and paraphrasing, on which more must be said later on, is a further point in question. Finally, instead of references to books not easily obtained in German libraries, a reader might want more self-sufficient annotation, and, where possible, references to German publications.

This leads up to the problems of editing Shakespeare for a non-British cultural milieu. Generally speaking, one might say that secondary education in England or America provides a basic knowledge of Shakespeare, his plays, and their literary and historical context that cannot be presupposed in foreign readers of otherwise comparable schooling. More particularly, the background for the history plays, more or less familiar to educated Britons, would need more elucidation for a foreigner. Finally, it must be enough only to hint at Shakespeare's place in the history of German literature and literary theory, his influence on drama from Lessing to Brecht, his presence on the German stage (year after year he is still the most frequently played author in the German-speaking countries), his role in the history and theory of translation (comparable to the Bible itself), and last but not least at the tradition of German Shakespearean studies. All this provides a context for reading Shakespeare of which English editions cannot even take notice, but which it seems worthwhile and desirable to present to German readers.

The *Studienausgabe* tries to achieve its aims partly by new means and partly by conventional means, which are, however, somewhat modified and adapted to their special purpose. Shakespeare's words are elucidated by a German prose version and supplementary linguistic notes. A variety of literary and other topics are treated in a general introduction, numerous commentary notes, and an additional running commentary explaining and interpreting the play scene by scene.

If the intentions behind the *Studienausgabe* are now to be considered in more detail, it may be noted that most of them have been part of the concept from the beginning, while others have been developed by individual editors and might be worth being considered for integration in future volumes. For reasons of clarity—and at the risk of some rather too sweeping generalizations—I want to contrast the *Studienausgabe* with recent English editions. I will begin with the core of the edition, text, prose version, and commentary notes.

The development of English scholarly editions over the last few decades, as analyzed by Marvin Spevack,[8] has been somewhat paradoxical. The reasons for this may be sought in their intended audience, since all of them, in order to be commercially successful, depend on the college market. A look at the latest volumes of the New Arden Shakespeare—apart from the New Variorum Shakespeare the most scholarly editions available at present—shows that on the one hand the treatment of Shakespeare's text has become more careful and thorough, as documented in complex textual and bibliographical discussion and the ever-growing numbers of variant readings and textual notes. On the other hand, the annotation of Shakespeare's language has clearly developed towards a simplistic kind of glossary, consisting mainly of modern English synonyms and paraphrases. While the textual side of editions has become more and more scholarly and exclusive, that is to say addressed to and even readable for fewer and fewer people, the linguistic commentary has become less scholarly and tries to provide for the widest possible readership. Dover Wilson's New Shakespeare started this development and later editors followed suit. Ridley, in his preface to the New Arden *Othello* (1958), confesses construing notes with a "marked lack of erudition" (p. vii) and thinks numerous and even repetitive glosses necessary for the modern reader. S. Wells, when talking about "shifts in pedagogical techniques," notices "far less emphasis on philology in modern editions than there was in editions such as the Pitt Press and the Warwick

Shakespeare."[9] The most recent—post-New Arden—series of Shakespeare editions seem to introduce some changes in the situation.[10] But for New Arden it does not seem totally unfair to say that the majority of volumes serve textual critics better than readers interested in Shakespeare's language.

There the *Studienausgabe* differs markedly from English editions. Without being content "to have any kind of a text" just as "a peg on which to hang [one's] annotations"—as Fredson Bowers once complained[11]—the editors' efforts are concerned to help the German reader to understand Shakespeare's text and not to a fresh establishment of this text.

Without doubt the *Studienausgabe* ought to be based on a scholarly sound text. And indeed the general editors in their preface claim to offer an "authentic" text. So far this means, for the majority of the plays, the text of the single-volume *Pelican Shakespeare*.[12] The copyright for this edition was acquired at a time when the *Riverside Shakespeare* had not yet appeared. This is definitely not a solution that meets with everybody's satisfaction. It is, however, not the general abandonment of editorial originality, which seems problematic. Considering the negligible role of textual criticism in German Shakespearean studies during this century, where should the required number of bibliographically experienced editors come from, anyway? For a number of plays the Pelican text may be as defensible as any other, for others it is probably not, particularly since for quite a few plays the textual discussion has been reopened during the last decade. We may reasonably expect that the general editors may be forced very soon— probably with the appearance of the single-volume *Oxford Shakespeare*—to reconsider their initial decision.

For the time being the pragmatic and less ambitious solution seems reasonable, particularly since all individual editors give an account of the textual situation in the introduction, offer an ample choice of semantically relevant variant readings in the critical apparatus, and discuss them in their notes. Besides, editors are free to establish their own text, and some of the German collaborators have decided to do so. Since a "new" text—as we all know—by no means guarantees a better text, the painstaking job of producing a "new" text would only seem to make sense in those cases where a far-reaching change in textual theory and editorial practice has taken place since the Pelican Shakespeare, and where, therefore, the notes suggesting that the Pelican text is unsatisfactory would be too numerous.

As for the ways the *Studienausgabe* helps German readers to understand Shakespeare's words as exactly as possible, I am convinced that it has its advantages over English editions. These advantages lie basically in the interaction of prose version and annotation—both together are the commentary. The prose version aims at the greatest possible exactitude, at a degree of literalness that the structural difference of the two languages will just about allow. Although "unforced modern German" is the stylistic mode envisaged by the general editors, no autonomous status as aesthetic translation for reader or actor is intended. The well-known semantic losses of poetic translation are to be minimized. The loss of meaning incurred by the loss of form is calculated (although only hesitatingly accepted by reviewers). There is no denying the fact that the first editions went too far in the direction of uncouth word-for-word renderings. But K. von Tetzeli's edition of *The Comedy of Errors* (1982) has already proved that philological exactitude and readable fluency need not be mutually exclusive. It has certainly set a standard for future volumes.

It is not to criticize but rather to explain the particular possibilities and intentions of the *Studienausgabe* that I want briefly to come back to the English editions. According to Marvin Spevack's count,[13] about 65–80 percent of the notes in English editions are linguistic notes. The bulk of them are semantic and render the meaning of Shakespeare's words. Recently—probably as a consequence of the wish to make editions accessible to a wider public—they have acquired an increasingly more diachronic perspective; that is to say, the emphasis in annotation is laid not so much on Shakespeare's language per se but on linguistic change, on the differences between Shakespeare's and modern English. Glosses replace quotations of contemporary parallels, paraphrases replace the explanation of syntactical difficulties. On the whole Shakespeare's grammar is hardly the subject of annotation any longer. To summarize: Shakespeare's text is not so much explained in the context of his language, as translated—sporadically—into modern English. A radical consequence of this tendency would seem to be Rowse's modernized—that is, translated—Shakespeare. As Spevack says about modern linguistic commentary: "The grand assumption underlying the whole scheme is that once the fossils have been identified or explained or replaced, early modern English becomes modern English."[14] This is obviously true as far as modernizing the accidentals of Shakespeare's text is concerned.[15] But for the substance of Shakespeare's words the principle cannot work. To select for annotation what is unusual today may be unavoidable, but by becoming the dominant principle combined with glossing and paraphrasing as the dominant mode of assistance to the reader it runs counter to all professed intentions of "modernizing" editors. Instead of familiarizing the reader with Shakespeare's language, it rather emphasizes the fact that Shakespeare's language is archaic. And what is more, glosses and paraphrases hinder a full linguistic and stylistic grasp of the old text. Spevack's verdict seems generally valid that "the farther the information from the immediate Shakespearean linguistic and cultural surroundings, the more imprecise and indeed more misleading it becomes."[16] The fact that a word or a phrase is uncommon in modern English does not indicate anything about its status in or about 1600.

The situation is worsened by the fact that such "popularizing" annotation very often offers pseudoexplanations that suggest to the reader an unjustified security and prevent him from seeing in how many instances our understanding of Shakespeare's words is quite uncertain. Quite often problems are muffled, new questioning of old cruxes is thereby hindered, and sham solutions perpetuated—a method clearly in opposition to the aims of scholarly commentary.[17] Compared to how much published thought goes into the presentation of Shakespeare's text, very little discussion of the method and rationale of scholarly commentary has found its way into print. What is chosen for comment, why and how it is commented on, seems to be left mainly to the editor's taste and intuition. To take a random example: the Chorus sonnet in *Romeo and Juliet* is not thought worth a single note by the New Arden editor (1982), whereas the New Cambridge editor thinks his reader might need not less than nine linguistic elucidations (1984). It is a telling fact that reviews of editions normally treat the commentary notes very cursorily, although they are one of the largest sections of an edition, the most important source of information for the majority of readers, and definitely the part of an edition where the author can still make a contribution of his own to our fuller understanding of the poet.

The *Studienausgabe* approaches these problems somewhat differently through its combination of German prose version and annotation. This— and the bilingual character—seem to have certain advantages that, it is true, were not fully realized at the beginning of the project. But years of mutual cross-reading and discussion resulted in principles appearing that might well be summed up to form a working theory and so be applied more consistently in the future.

First of all, the German prose version does the same thing for German readers as glosses do for the English: it translates Shakespeare into the reader's language. But it also differs in various ways. The confrontation of two different languages prevents the possible partial misunderstanding implied in the interference of two historical stages of the English language. Above all, the foreign language does not—as English glosses do—accentuate the feeling that Shakespeare's language is a conglomerate of archaisms—a feeling less strong in most foreign readers anyway, but innate, so to speak, in a native reader. Against the objection of one reviewer that the prose version distracts the reader from the original, one might therefore argue that it does so rather less than modern English glosses. To a greater extent than they can, it preserves the integrity of the text because it does not permanently suggest that what is written there on the page "actually" means something else.

Then, of course, the prose version translates more consistently than English notes: it translates the whole text and it translates more exactly—it cannot evade into paraphrase. Translation enforces a decision on the meaning of every single word, and so, more often than mere reading experience and tradition, produces that "semantic discomfort,"[18] which is usually an indication of deficient understanding. The need for a philologically exact word-by-word translation prevents the editor from taking over accepted explanations without fresh questioning and often sharpens his awareness of unsolved or even undiscovered problems—and, if he is lucky, clears the path to a better understanding of words, phrases, and passages.[19]

The prose version, furthermore, has consequences for the selection and the nature of commentary notes. First of all, it replaces a great number of semantic notes, theoretically wherever an exact translation is possible. In practice some compromises may be advisable, particularly in those cases that we might call false friends, where the changed modern meaning of current words—such as *still, odour,* and so on—might provoke the reader's resistance against the translation. The remarkable reduction of the number of semantic notes leaves ample space for nonlinguistic annotation, of factual, literary and theatrical problems. Such notes may be related by cross-references to the scene-by-scene commentary. The selection of items and the depth to which they are treated depend on the concept of this running commentary and its interrelation with the commentary notes. Here the individual editor enjoys the freedom of presenting whatever he or she thinks relevant to the understanding of his play.

Then, of course, the nature of remaining linguistic notes is changed by their interrelation with the prose version. From the beginning the editors stuck to the principles of "transparency" and "presentation of problems" (Problematisierung). The prose version is made "transparent" by being supplemented or justified in a note wherever necessary. Philological, literary, or interpretative presuppositions that fashion the translation are documented. Where the German version cannot render the original meaning (e.g., wordplay, proverbs, untranslatable connotations, and so on) a note will be necessary. In this way the prose version becomes plausible and, at the same time, its limitations are made visible.

Similarly, the limits of our understanding of Shakespeare's text are laid open. This cannot only be a task for the New Variorum Shakespeare—even if we should live to see its completion. Unsolved problems will be marked again in the *Studienausgabe*. The notes give a brief critical account of relevant rival explanations and try to evaluate their pros and cons. This is to provoke further thought and to leave the reader room for his own decision instead of insinuating, by the authority of print, unjustified security.

Finally, since a German edition need not mediate between Shakespeare's and modern English, the *Studienausgabe* attempts to forsake the predominantly diachronic perspective of current English annotation and to try explanation with relation to Elizabethan English, and in particular to Shakespeare's English. As far as the semantic treatment of Shakespeare's language is concerned, the *Studienausgabe* is based on E. Leisi's method of semantic analysis as developed in his old-meaning edition of *Measure for Measure* and described in his *Praxis der englischen Semantik*,[20] which means among other things that for the commentator the Shakespeare Concordance is a more important instrument than the *OED*.

Not being forced to explain Shakespeare's deviations from modern English, the *Studienausgabe* has room to indicate any stylistic values of Shake-speare's language. However difficult this may prove in practice, it is never-theless true that for the foreign reader it is more interesting to know whether a word or a phrase was archaic in Shakespeare's time, or, for that matter, quite new, rather than to know that it is archaic today. Instead of modern synonyms the indication of typical collocations should teach the reader something about Shakespeare's usage or the connotations of a word.

As for grammar, the foreign reader, usually lacking experience of histor-ical forms of English, will require more explanation than an English reader. This is—as we all know—no easy task for an editor, particularly since research on early modern English syntax is not yet available to the non-specialist reader. But at least a number of German publications, among them the yet unrivaled Shakespeare grammar by W. Franz,[21] is accessible to all German editors, which seems no longer the case with all English-speaking editors.

Some brief remarks may suffice to show the orientation of the other parts of the *Studienausgabe* towards its audience of German nonspecialist readers. The introduction is conceived in a fairly traditional way. The problems of date, text, sources, and transformation of sources are covered. As in recent English editions, theatrical aspects and instructive moments of stage history are sketched. On the other hand, the introduction offers no individual interpretation of the play but is a selective survey of the more important chapters in the history of its interpretation up to the present day. One reviewer's criticism, namely that the aim of the edition is not to carry scholarship further but to present a critical recapitulation of its present state, is to my mind not a reasonable objection but rather a reasonable concept. Besides, the remark is neither justified for all parts of the edition nor for each individual volume. Information, presentation of "safe" knowl-edge, and introduction to problems and open questions are, however, definitely the main target.

In any case, there is the scene-by-scene commentary, which, as a part of an edition, is not just a formal but also a methodical novelty. It is an introduction to the individual play that—in accordance with modern views of drama—stresses its processual character more than traditional "spatial" interpretations do. It should not be confused with pedestrian study aids, since it treats problems of the play's interpretation abreast of modern criticism. Besides, it leaves room for various questions of detail (concerning structure, rhythm, style, verse, and so on) that would explode the commen-tary notes. In this part there is hardly any limit (except for space) for the editor in the presentation of his critical individuality and talents.

Finally, as has been indicated, the *Studienausgabe* has to take into account the German reception of Shakespeare. Emphasis there will change from play to play according to what aspects of the play's reception may be of interest to the modern reader. German Shakespearean studies have ob-viously been included from the start. And indeed this seems essential, since the majority of Anglo-Saxon scholars have given up reading or referring to them since the First World War. The New Arden editor of *Richard III*, for example, does not even mention W. Clemen's commentary to that play,[22] although it has appeared in an English translation. Stage history, of course, is another case in point. Many plays of Shakespeare have had their own "national" career in the German theater. And where, to give an example, should a German reader find a handier sketch of the German theater's struggles with *The Merchant of Venice* than in the *Studienausgabe?*[23]

Beyond criticism and stage history much more may be done with regard to adaptation, novelistic and operatic metamorphosis, musical composition, and particularly in the field of translation. On the basis of thorough semantic analysis the *Studienausgabe* of *The Comedy of Errors* has begun a consistent discussion of interesting errors and solutions in German translations. This may be continued. In one way or the other, information about existing translations of the play should be part of the edition, be it only as a bibliography, which, to my surprise, is not the case in the first volumes. The *Studienausgabe* will certainly play an important role in this field; translators from in and outside the theaters are even trying to get their hands on the unpublished manuscripts.

Critical analysis of the volumes published so far may make some adjustments and additions desirable. But there can be no doubt that, ten years after the appearance of the first play in the series, the *Studienausgabe* has shown what services it can do to readers of Shakespeare in the German-speaking countries. After years of misunderstanding and reserve, reviewers from academic and nonacademic circles have begun to acknowledge the basic soundness of the concept and the high quality of individual volumes. If their echo could increase the sales, the *Studienausgabe*, which cannot possibly be a bestseller but will certainly be a long seller, is bound to become a success. If not, I hope that sponsors will be found in a country that is proud of the oldest Shakespeare Society in the world and where Schlegel's Shakespeare is—with less irony than conviction—constantly referred to as one of the classical authors in the mother tongue. Less worthy projects have found their subsidized way into print.

Notes

1. The following editions have appeared so far at Francke Verlag: *Othello*, ed. B. Engler (Bern, 1976); *Measure for Measure*, ed. W. Naef and P. Halter (Bern, 1977); *Richard II*, ed. W. Braun (Bern, 1980); *The Merchant of Venice*, ed. I. Heine-Harabasz (Bern, 1982); *The Comedy of Errors*, ed. K. Tetzeli von Rosador (Bern, 1982); *Troilus and Cressida*, ed. W. Brönnimann-Egger (Tübingen, 1986); *The Winter's Tale*, ed. I. Boltz (Tübingen, 1986); *Julius Caesar*, ed. T. Pughe (Tübingen, 1986); *The Taming of the Shrew*, ed. T. Rüetschi (Tübingen, 1987).

2. R. B. McKerrow, *Prolegomena for the Oxford Shakespeare*, (Oxford: Oxford University Press, 1939), 1.

3. *Shakspere's Werke,* ed. N. Delius (Elberfeld, 1854), which saw numerous reprints during the nineteenth century.

4. For the conflicting concepts cf. "Bericht der Arbeitsgruppe zum Thema 'Probleme der Shakespeare-Übersetzung', " *Deutsche Shakespeare Gesellschaft-West: Jahrbuch* (1971), 15–17. See detailed report in "Shakespeare-Übersetzungen (Text und Bochumer Diskussion)," *Poetica* 4 (1971): 82–119.

5. *Der Neue Reclam Shakespeare* (Stuttgart: Reclam, 1973–). So far *AYL, Ham., JC, H5, Lr., R2, R3, Mac., MV, MND, Rom., Tmp.,* and *TN* have appeared.

6. An exception is H. Klein's unwieldy and possibly overlearned two-volume edition of *Hamlet* (Stuttgart, 1984) with its almost seven hundred pages of commentary notes.

7. Aspects of this discussion are published in the contributions of B. Engler, R. Scheibler, E. Leisi, K. Bartenschlager, K. Büchler, and D. Daphinoff to *Deutsche Shakespeare Gesellschaft-West Jahrbuch* (1975).

8. M. Spevack, "A New Shakespeare Dictionary (SHAD) and the Notes on Language in Editions of Shakespeare," *Studien zur Englischen Philologie, Edgar Mertner zum 70. Geburtstag,* ed. H. Mainusch and D. Rolle (Frankfurt/M.: P. D. Lang, 1979), 123–34; "Shakespeare Synchronic and Diachronic: Annotating Elizabethan Texts," *Festschrift für Karl Schneider,* ed. K. R. Jankowsky and E. S. Dick (Amsterdam: J. Benjamins, 1982), 441–53; "Shakespeare: Editions and Textual Scholarship (I)," *Deutsche Shakespeare Gesellschaft-West Jahrbuch* (1983), 221-41.

9. *Re-editing Shakespeare for the Modern Reader,* (Oxford: Oxford University Press, 1984), 2.

10. The *New Cambridge Shakespeare* tries no longer to inform completely about the textual situation, and the (unpublished) "Guidelines for Revision of Arden Shakespeare: 'Arden 3' " aim to avoid "comment by paraphrase without indication of the source of difficulty" (quoted from "Guidelines" as presented by R. Proudfoot at the seminar "Images of Shakespeare's Texts" at the World Shakespeare Congress Berlin, p. 9.

11. "Some Relations of Bibliography to Editorial Problems," *Studies in Bibliography* 3 (1950–51): 61.

12. *William Shakespeare, The Complete Works,* ed. A. Harbage (London: A. Lane, 1969).

13. "A New Shakespeare Dictionary," 126.

14. "Shakespeare Synchronic," 443.

15. Cf. S. Wells, *Re-editing,* 13.

16. "A New Shakespeare Dictionary," 131. Spevack's statement is a summary of A. Friedman's "Principles of Historical Annotation in Critical Editions of Modern Texts," *English Institute Annual, 1941,* (New York: AMS Press, 1942), 115–28.

17. To give only a few examples: In the New Arden edition of *Romeo and Juliet,* ed. B. Gibbons (London: Methuen, 1980), apodictical pseudoexplanations, some of them clearly wrong, without as much as a hint at controversial explanatory traditions, are used to comment on "draw your neck out of collar" (1.1.4), "fish . . . Poor John" (1.1.30), "propagate . . . pressed" (1.1.185), "wisely too fair" (1.1.219), "on more view . . . reckoning none" (1.2.32–33), "The fish lives . . . hide" (1.3.89–90), and "grandsire phrase . . . The game was ne'er so fair" (1.4.37–39).

18. C. S. Lewis's term. Cf. *Studies in Words* (London: University Press, 1960), 1.

19. For some of my own findings while working on the Studienausgabe cf. "Two notes on *Measure for Measure,*" *Deutsche Shakespeare Gesellschaft-West Jahrbuch* (1976), 160–63, "The Love-Sick Tree; A Note on *Romeo and Juliet* I,1,119 and *Othello* IV,3,39," *English Studies* 59 (1978): 116–18, "Three Notes on *Romeo and Juliet,*" *Anglia* 100 (1982): 422–25.

20. *Shakespeare: Measure for Measure. An Old Spelling and Old Meaning Edition* (Heidelberg: Winter, 1964); *Praxis der englischen Semantik* (Heidelberg: Winter, 1973).

21. *Die Sprache Shakespeares in Vers und Prosa,* 4th ed., (Halle: Max Niemeyer, 1939). G. L. Brook's *The Language of Shakespeare,* (London: Deutsch, 1976) is rarely referred to in recent Shakespeare editions, and whether N. F. Blake's *Shakespeare's Language* (London: Macmillan, 1983) will fare better remains to be seen.

22. W. Clemen, *A Commentary on Shakespeare's Richard III* (London: Methuen, 1968).

23. Pp. 31–33.

"Well, This Is the Forest of Arden": An Informal Address

by ADRIAN NOBLE

Over the last ten days it has occurred to me that I may well never have arrived here because I had a press night two evenings ago of a production of *Mephisto* that proved to be technically a nightmare. One of the lines of that play, which kept ringing in my ears, was by the actor Hendrick Höfgen in parody of Chekhov: "Berlin, when will I get to Berlin?" I am here, and indeed I am absolutely delighted to be here in such a distinguished company of scholars and enthusiasts. What I can bring you, I think, is in no way scholarly: directors don't tend to write books or perhaps directors shouldn't write books; but perhaps what I can offer to this conference is an insight into some of the processes that I have gone through with my actors and designers over the last half a dozen years in Stratford. Indeed, I have to acknowledge the debt I owe to the tradition of the Royal Shakespeare Company, which has now been going for over twenty-five years. Each new generation of directors adds to it, and from it we all gain succor and strength.

Almost twelve months ago to this day, my production of *As You Like It* went into preview in Stratford. It finally opened to what can certainly be called a controversial press. It played at Stratford, then at the Barbican Theatre in London, and when it closed recently—about ten days ago in fact—it had created for itself a very unusual and loyal audience. I chose "Well, this is the Forest of Arden" as a title for my talk because *As You Like It* is still close to me and a production that in a way I am still trying to understand. I am now looking forward to doing the Scottish play and trying to understand what I did last year in relationship to my next piece of work.

When Rosalind says, "Well, this is the Forest of Arden," accompanied by Celia and Touchstone, we must ask ourselves what does Rosalind see when she says that line, and what does the audience see? I believe in those very simple questions lies the challenge, the dilemma of the modern Shakespearean production; albeit, as I am sure John Barton has talked to you about the problem of poetry and the actor these days, I believe the greatest

335

challenge facing the modern director of Shakespeare is coming to terms with the form of his work.

Let's just look at what we know about the Forest of Arden within the play. What sort of place is it? For example, consider the animals: there are rabbits and there are lions; there are snakes and deer. That's a curious mixture for a start. Then there are the people who live in the forest. There's a rather inarticulate young girl who looks after goats; there's an extremely articulate young girl, speaking in quite sophisticated verse, who is supposed to look after sheep (social historians tell us that looking after sheep was a male job and that women were only allowed to look after goats); there's a shepherd who has sufficient financial resources to buy the sheepcote. It's a place to which lovers and exiled dukes and monarchs flee and which attracts the lonely, the dispossessed, the disenfranchised. So what sort of place is this? It doesn't really strike me as the kind of countryside that those of us who live and work around Stratford-upon-Avon know and love. It's not really Charlecote Park, it's not Chipping Campden.

There's an English strip cartoon that is held in great affection in my country called Rupert Bear. Rupert Bear is a lovely character who is a little bear, with a mummy bear and daddy bear, and they all dress up like human beings and they have lots of friends—among them an elephant and a lion— and they live in a little place called Nutwood. Now in this cartoon the interesting thing about the world in which Rupert Bear lives is that it transforms before your very eyes. It is a sunny, benevolent, benign place with nice gentle oaks. If you go round the corner there's an alarming river with a huge, deep, terrifying forest and a seemingly nasty old man who lives in a little sort of gazebo. Now it seems to me that what Shakespeare has done is to write the Forest of Arden rather like the Rupert Bear stories, by which I hope I'm not being facetious, because the forest in the play trans- forms in front of our eyes—not just seasonally but almost according to the inner sensations of the characters and the verse they speak. Indeed, by the end of that short scene which begins, "Well, this is the Forest of Arden," the place has transformed and Celia can say, "I like this place." Now this "problem"—whereby in Shakespeare's time we could believe that the very language could transport us—is no longer a fact upon which the Shake- spearean director can rely. Each of those characters, if you like, has bor- rowed the forest for a short period of time. Indeed, you can say Shakespeare borrowed the forest. It is not a permanent place, so our stage must be susceptible to the transformable powers of the imagination. I shall return to this point a little later.

One of the great challenges of Shakespearean production lies in the chorus of *Henry V:* "And let us, ciphers to this great accompt, On your imaginary forces work. . . . Think when we talk of horses that you see them. . . ." I don't believe that was written by Shakespeare as a challenge— it was simply fact. Our work in production is therefore to liberate the audience's imagination, as quite clearly Shakespeare could do. There's a stage metaphor in *As You Like It,* one that stands in the middle of the play like a large boulder for the actor playing Jaques to trip over. He has to cope with it somehow by giving it central importance to the play and also by making it a logical, psychological and real statement of that man in that position. We felt that the speech "All the world's a stage" is indeed close to the meaning of the play, with the pattern and dance that is unfolded through it. We see this of course in many of Shakespeare's comedies, particularly when you get mass weddings at the end—dubious events at the best of times. And we viewed the whole play as possibly a ceremony or initiation leading towards matrimony and began to see the formality of the play as very positive, a perfect partnering of four and four. The formality comes in Shakespeare's choice of parallel characters, two brothers of each court, in exile and in the city, each having their own satellites, Jaques and Touchstone, Il Penseroso and L'Allegro, both complex characters who aspire to their opposition. And we studied how the meaning of the play could reveal itself through those patterns and rituals, which in fact we tried to formalize. Shakespeare is always particularly interesting when he talks about actors, the job of acting, and the state of acting. There are those wonderful lines from one of his sonnets, "As an unperfect actor on the stage / Who with his fear is put besides his part," that state both an objective and subjective truth about acting. Objectively the audience witnesses a lapse of memory, but as any actor knows, that statement "Who with his fear is put besides his part" very accurately reveals the state of paranoia that drying gives you or the nightmare of entering a stage wearing the wrong costume or not knowing the lines. Shakespeare's life as an actor did not give him stagecraft alone. I believe it gave him a very particular and formal insight into some of his themes.

Another thing an actor does, of course, is to do it every night. You have to repeat it. And there are very few professions that have to do that. Priests have to, politicians do but shouldn't, lecturers do it and probably shouldn't, though I have no right to say that standing on this platform. But actors have to do it every night. Now we took that nightly repetition, which is the very stuff of an actor's life, and the insight we believed seeing the play as a ceremony gave us, and we made the first crucial decision, which was to double the cast—do the play with a reasonably small number of people— and to double the two courts. And as soon as we doubled the courts of the two dukes, every actor in the first court played the identical role in the second court. That made, if you like, our central artistic point, and the play immediately began to talk to itself. It began to create its own conventions and its own rules because disguise was happening within the play; indeed, disguise was happening in a way *about* the play by our decision to double roles. And so, hopefully without becoming self-conscious, that very doubling, I believe, heightened its theatrical artifice and in a way allowed the convention of cross-dressing, breeches-parts, to work more readily. We could immediately make comparisons between court and court. Very early on in rehearsals the actors talked to me about what it meant to go from, for example, the first scene in the forest straight back into the next scene, when the Duke is raging, without a break. We did it simply by having them throw off sheets. And they said, "You cannot play two characters. What happens is that you are playing different aspects of the same person." It meant that a debate followed through the play about, for example, violence. The court seemed to lap up the violence of Charles the wrestler.

There's a very interesting debate in the forest about the killing of the deer in the speech about what happened during the hunt when Jaques was there. That debate is picked up and resolved in the "What is he that killed the deer" scene, when it seems that the courtiers have gone from violence in the court, almost through a vegetarian phase, into an understanding and a harmony with their environment whereby they can kill a deer and be happy. There seems to be some sort of program as soon as you double characters. So we started seeing oppositions, we started seeing mirrors at work within the play. There are of course two wrestling scenes. There's the famous one involving Charles and there's the one we never see that is reported by Oliver—a wrestling match to the death in fact. We started seeing the debate between court rituals and country rituals, between Corin and Touchstone, in a slightly fresher light.

To pick up the play from an actor's point of view and to take it one step further, it has become an almost Royal Shakespeare Company credo—to the point of boredom—that one talks of the journey of the play and the journey of the character. I should like to define this a little for you because it is at the center certainly of our work in Stratford. In a farce it is essential that characters do not go on great psychological journeys. It is essential that they do not change their natures halfway through, because when the woman rushes in and finds her husband in bed with another woman and two chimpanzees, it's crucial that she screams "eek." If she says "that sounds interesting," you have no farce. You have no play. She cannot develop—she is in prison. In Chekhov the world is finite, is closely defined, and within a Chekhov play the character goes on a great psychological journey that changes people. Now in a Shakespeare play, first of all a physical journey very often is undertaken; you can actually go to different places, like Pericles around the Mediterranean, or in *As You Like It* to the Forest of Arden and out again, or Henry V around France, or as in *Measure for Measure,* out of the city and back into it again. There's obviously a physical journey that immediately starts flavoring what one can call the Shakespeare experience. As a member of the audience I can see a battle immediately edited next door to a love scene, immediately edited next door to a chamber scene. Obviously characters go on a psychological journey and are changed. Now consider this Forest of Arden. If you have a forest that does not change—that is, logs and trees with slightly different lighting effects—then I believe you are snookered (I hope snooker is an international game). We are not able therefore to do what Shakespeare could do just through a purely oral work. Let us look again at the original question. What is this Forest of Arden? As soon as we came to the conclusion that the solution was not to put a lot of trees on the stage, we found that we gained a release. We had a sort of motto when one met somebody: "Has he been to the Forest of Arden?" or "Has she been to the Forest of Arden?" The Forest of Arden did not simply become a place but became a process, an idea. We suddenly saw the possibility of exploring the forest from a very subjective point of view— from the point of view of refugees suffering hardship, hopefully preparing for their return, and from the point of view of lovers. We tried to examine adolescence, a period that may seem rather a long time ago! Shakespeare was one of the great poets of adolescence, but not just of falling in love, but falling in love to the point of madness: "Love is merely a madness; and, I tell you, deserves as well a dark house and a whip as madmen do." Rosalind is in love deep as "the Bay of Portugal"—dangerous waters that kill people and sailors as they cross the Bay of Biscay. This is not a benign jolly romp of a place, this is adolescent country. This is country where we have terrifying dreams, where we believe that if the girl or boy doesn't love us, we will die. This is the world of the sonnets where love is a consuming dangerous passion, where Cupid is no pleasant little boy but is a nasty little bugger with an arrow who hits at random. With our Forest of Arden we saw the need to be able to transmute our world. We had to find a stage solution to that. We also started seeing disguise in the play in a slightly different context, not just as a convention to enable certain people to meet who maybe otherwise wouldn't meet, but as a release. I'm sure Freud would say it was a release of libido. Parents will know that if they put their kiddies in stage makeup or fancy dress, they are unstoppable, they become dangerous fellows. The mask is a release, and indeed the entire oeuvre of Italian drama is based, it would appear, on that one single idea. In masks we can say words that we shall never say again, do actions that we shall not do again.

I should like to mention here a pattern that we found through our work in Stratford relating to chaos, those wild ceremonies that lead toward marriage in the case of *As You Like It,* those rituals of chaos that turn to harmony, and Shakespeare's use of disguise, because of course they are related. Look at another play, *The Comedy of Errors.* There the mask, the disguise convention, is the fact that there are twins. They are in disguise without knowing it. Therefore people meet who shouldn't meet. But also in *The Comedy of Errors* they go into another forest. It is a jungle of the cities, however, a place where paranoias can build up, where Angelo the gold-smith suddenly becomes a sorcerer. We know, of course, that he's not, but again in the subjective man we see the possibility of new aspects in the play as soon as we permit that chaos, that paranoia, that darker side. *Henry V* is similar there, I think, because when the king and his troops leave Harfleur, they enter a long night. They enter a chaotic world where, as death seems to approach, the future is totally uncertain. Henry V goes into disguise, and it becomes a release for him. He learns things and achieves in that marvelous nighttime soliloquy the poise, the presence of mind, the humility, and the grace to conquer chaos. So I do not believe the play is political in the sense that it is finally antiwar, but it is quintessentially Shakespearean in the sense that the pattern of chaos is overcome and disguise is a means leading to harmony.

This is obviously true in *A Midsummer Night's Dream,* as Peter Brook revealed to us in a sensational fashion. In *King Lear,* which was in a way the root of much of my exploration, we see this very strongly on the heath. There is this fantastic quartet of a mad king, a fool who is anonymous, the Duke of Kent in disguise, and the eldest son of the Duke of Gloucester, also in disguise as a madman and a beggar—an extraordinary quartet, a crazy gang, that dances as the world falls apart around them. *King Lear* is a curious play in the sense that I don't believe it does arrive at a state of grace. When we did it, we felt that it related very much to the elements, so we started with earth and water and fire and we civilized them by putting boards down and building walls and furnishing the walls and building rooms on the earth. Then after the abdication, when we moved into the storm, we started destroying our world and the set became a very active, almost dangerous place and we finally got to the section of the wars at the end. I believe an awful stillness sets into the play when there is no reply at all from the heavens. Perhaps that only happened in my production because we killed the fool—well, Shakespeare killed the fool in fact, dumped him anyway. Because if the experience of Shakespeare is about wholeness, then the absence of a fool makes that impossible. I'll never forget something Edward Bond said to me once. He said that Shakespeare's greatest act of cowardice was not to have the fool in the last scene of *King Lear.* That may sound foolish, but I don't think it is, in the sense that it would be an awful blow if the fool was there, but the critical ear is possible, the folly is possible, and the contradiction is possible, though it's not at the end of *King Lear,* which is why it is his bleakest and most harrowing piece to work on and to see.

We come back to that essential issue about which books have been written, humanity and its relationship to nature, because it is through a discussion of that that we come to ideas of Shakespearean design and theatrical architecture, which are not only an aesthetic issue but also a political one. If you visit Epidaurus and sit in the theater there, and your friends are down in the middle and shout "hello" up at you, which most people in this room have probably done, you have human figures in the open air. Behind them you see nature, you see greenery, you see rivers, hopefully you see a little bit of sea, you see the sky, you see the elements. You are in one world. When you go to the Elizabethan theater of course, you're still in the open air and indeed you're still in one room. Scenery as we know it has not been introduced. Shakespeare did not have trees in the Forest of Arden. You have a public theater in which all elements of society, we are led to believe, attended. Then perspective was invented.

Perspective is a very interesting political issue because when you move on to the later playhouses the theory is, of course, that there is one perfect place to sit and there are many, many imperfect places to sit. If you're the king, you sit in the one place. If you are a nobleman, you sit in a reasonable place, and if you are a peasant, you probably don't even sit there at all. You may stand and may be even excluded. So theater design and what goes on stage, the consequent scenery that came along with perspective, what was happening on the stage and what was happening in society, the decisions about who was occupying these spaces called theaters, were going hand in hand. Then you come to the Victorian Age in which there was just an orgy of scenery. And now we get to the 1980s, and it always strikes me as very curious that we are still building theaters which are perspective theaters with one good seat and everything going down, although we're trying to vary that a little with types of amphitheater.

But within this short, partisan history of theater design lies the problem and the answer to "Well, this is the Forest of Arden," because we found when working on *As You Like It* that the *As You Like Its* that we'd all seen and loved as children were Victorian ones. They were events that took place in two rooms, with the actors in one room and the public in another room. Our search is to find the scenic region that Shakespeare had in his theater. The answer is not to go back to Globe playhouses. I think that's a non-sense—though it's of academic interest—because the world has moved on. Where do the gods come from in our theaters? Do they fly them in? Do they walk down that aisle from amongst the people? Where do people stand in relationship to nature and to the gods? How do we resolve that, you see? We have different options.

I worked in the round very successfully when I did a production of the *Duchess of Malfi* in a superb theater, the Royal Exchange Theatre in Manchester, which came the nearest for me to creating a public space for a Jacobean play. There could be no scenery but you could create dynamics with the audience, and from this one knew where the gods come from. The gods in 1986 come down that aisle—they have to, curiously enough, they have to come from amongst the people. We tried a promenade in *The Winter's Tale* whereby like a film you could have long shots and suddenly take a scene right up there, so that everyone had to turn and look at it. That immediately gave you a sensuous relationship to the scene at the back totally different to the sensuous relationship you would have to a scene in this hall. The people became the scenery, so it was very strong and exciting.

I won't tell you what we did with *As You Like It* but the more I look at

Shakespeare, the more I actually understand that profound instinct in people that brings them all over the world to Berlin and brings actors to do the plays, to slave on them, because it's bloody difficult stuff. It's because he is a truly public playwright, by which I mean not only is he accessible but his plays are political in the sense that they reveal models for change. At the end of *Measure for Measure* the last scene takes place outside the city wall. Are we ready to walk back into that city? Have we solved the second world of the play, of government? Have we solved that question of government? Are we ready, are we fit to go back in? We've gone through nightmares of fears and agonies and near rapes and, yes, we are fit to go back in.

Shakespeare is political in that sense, he's public in that sense. He's public in that he demands of actors skills and emotions that are almost beyond them. We have to grow into Shakespeare. We can't make him what we want him to be. We can't say, "Well, actually, sod the lions, I'm going to have a nice cosy little Forest of Arden just like the one down from my cottage in the Cotswolds." That's not what he has written. We have to grow into him—we make mistakes doing it, of course. The very execution of a line of Shakespeare in a large theater requires not only a commitment, not only a skill, not only a breadth of emotion, but almost a moral commitment to serving up the play. It's a huge task but it seems to me that we always have to start with what he is and not hold him down to what we are. I'll break off there. I suppose what is quite clear and I hope is quite right is that I have come to no conclusions because my business is not coming to conclusions. My business is putting people on in public places and telling stories, and I have just shared with you some of the problems and contradictions that we have in Stratford involved in that business.

Appendix A
Complete List of Lectures and Papers from the Program of the Congress

Images of Shakespeare
1 to 6 April 1986 (Berlin West)
The International Shakespeare Association

Plenary Session: "Artists' Images of Shakespeare," Samuel Schoenbaum

Plenary Session: "Shakespeare in Performance I," John Barton, Royal Shakespeare Company

Shakespeare and the Visual Arts
Chairman: Stephen Greenblatt
  "Shakespeare and the *Paragone:* a Reading of *Timon of Athens,*" John Dixon Hunt
  "Undercurrents in Victorian Illustrations of Shakespeare," Barbara Melchiori

Changing Images of Shakespearean Characters
Chairman: Kenneth Muir
  "Another Part of the Castle: Some Victorian Hamlets," Russell Jackson
  "*Romeo and Juliet:* Changing Images of Its Protagonists," Jill Levenson
  "'Your Sense Pursues Not Mine': Isabella and Angelo, Lucio and the Duke," Herbert Weil, Jr.

Iconographical Approaches to Shakespeare
Chairman: Karl Josef Höltgen
  "Shakespeare's Horses: *Venus and Adonis,*" John Doebler
  "Ovidian Shakespeare: Wit and the Iconography of the Passions," Judith Dundas
  "The Visual Dimension of Shakespeare's Plays," J.-M. Maguin

Changing Plays in Changing Places
Chairman: Eldred Jones
  "A Chinese Image of Shakespeare," Qui Ke'an
  "'Bless thee! Thou Art Translated!': Shakespeare in Japan," Tetsuo Kishi
  "An Indian Response to Shakespeare," S. Viswanathan

Shakespeare's Metaphors
  Chairman: Jean Fuzier
    "Degrees of Metaphor: *King Lear*," Giorgio Melchiori
    "The Syntax of Metaphor in *Cymbeline*," Ann Thompson and John O. Thompson
    "Taking Tropes Seriously: Language and Violence in Shakespeare's *Rape of Lucrece*," Katharine E. Maus

Shakespeare in Germany
  Chairman: Ulrich Suerbaum
    "Recent Shakespeare Production in the GDR," Maik Hamburger
    "Changing Modes in *Hamlet* Production: Rediscovering Shakespeare after the Iconoclasts," Wilhelm Hortmann
    "German Shakespeare Translation: The State of the Art," Peter Wenzel

Images of Shakespeare I
  Chairman: Kristian Smidt
    " 'There Is a World Elsewhere': William Shakespeare, Businessman," Ernst Honigmann
    "New Shakespeare 'Signature': Image or Autograph," W. Nicholas Knight
    "The Unstable Image of Shakespeare's Text," Stanley Wells

Images of Shakespeare II
  Chairman: Sukanta Chaudhuri
    "Images of Shakespeare's Plays: Contemporary Set Designs," Jay Halio
    "The Secret of Shakespeare's Power in Germany," Lawrence F. McNamee
    "Five Women Eleven Ways: Changing Images of Shakespearean Characters in the Earliest Texts," Steven Urkowitz

Plenary Session: "Dance Images of Shakespeare's Characters," Selma Jeanne Cohen

Plenary Session: " 'Well, This Is the Forest of Arden,' " Adrian Noble

Theater Workshop
  "Shakespeare in Performance II," John Barton

Shakespeare Im Unterricht
  Chairman: Michael Bludau
    "Teaching Shakespeare," Ingeborg Boltz, Norbert Trimm

Shakespeare Translation
  Chairwoman: Yoshiko Kawachi

Appendix B
Seminars and Their Chairpersons

1. Images of the Tragic (J. Leeds Barroll, Marga Munkelt)
2. Shakespeare's Perfectibility (William Green, Alexander Anikst)
3. Stage Images in Shakespeare (David Bevington, Dieter Mehl)
4. New Approaches to Shakespearean Comedy (William C. Carroll, Kurt Tetzeli von Rosador)
5. Images of *King Lear* (David Hoeniger, Zdenek Stribrny)
6. Subversion, Recuperation, Rehearsal: The Ideological Function of the Shakespearean Text (Jean E. Howard, Marion O'Connor)
7. Images of Gender and Power in Shakespeare and Renaissance Culture (Carol Neely, Lisa Jardine)
8. Current Images of Shakespeare's Texts (Michael Warren, Hans Gabler)

Index